SUPPLEMENT IV, Part 2
Susan Howe to Gore Vidal
and
Cumulative Index

AMERICAN WRITERS
A Collection of Literary Biographies

A. WALTON LITZ
Editor in Chief

MOLLY WEIGEL
Assistant Editor

SUPPLEMENT IV, Part 2
Susan Howe to Gore Vidal

and
Cumulative Index
to Volume 1–4 and
Supplements I, II, III, and IV

Charles Scribner's Sons
Macmillan Library Reference USA
Simon & Schuster Macmillan
New York

Simon & Schuster and Prentice Hall International
London Mexico City New Delhi Singapore Sydney Toronto

Copyright © 1996 by Charles Scribner's Sons

Charles Scribner's Sons
An Imprint of Simon & Schuster Macmillan
1633 Broadway
New York, New York 10019

1   3   5   7   9   11   13   15   17   19   20   18   16   14   12   10   8   6   4   2

Library of Congress Cataloging-in-Publication Data

American writers: a collection of literary biographies.

Suppl. 4 edited by A. Walton Litz and Molly Weigel.
The 4-vol. main set consists of 97 of the pamphlets originally published as the
University of Minnesota pamphlets on American writers; some have been rev. and
updated. The supplements cover writers not included in the original series.
Includes bibliographies.
Contents: v. 1. Henry Adams to T. S. Eliot — v. 2. Ralph Waldo Emerson to
Carson McCullers — [etc.] — Supplement[s] — [etc.] — 4, pt. 1. Maya Angelou to
Linda Hogan. 4, pt. 2. Susan Howe to Gore Vidal.
1. American Literature — History and criticism.   2. American literature — Bio-
bibliography.   3. Authors, American — Biography.   I. Unger, Leonard, ed. II. Baechler,
Lea. III. Litz, A. Walton. IV. Weigel, Molly. V. University of Minnesota. Pamphlets on
American writers.

PS129.A55   810′.9   73-1759

ISBN 0-684-19785-5 (Set)
ISBN 0-684-19786-3 (Part 1)
ISBN 0-684-19787-1 (Part 2)

The paper in this publication meets the requirements of ANSI/NISO Z39.48-1992 (Permanence of Paper).

List of Subjects

Part 2

SUPPLEMENT IV, Part 2
Susan Howe to Gore Vidal
and
Cumulative Index

Susan Howe

1937–

SUSAN HOWE, A former visual artist who began writing poetry in the early 1970s, when she was in her late thirties, has achieved prominence as a poet whose radical experiments with language are deeply engaged with the historical and material world. An autodidact who never received a traditional liberal arts education, Howe generates poems out of her encounters with documents, usually literary, theoretical, or historical texts. For her, the practice of scholarship and the practice of poetry are inseparable: both rely on a combination of loving, disciplined attention and a receptiveness to the workings of serendipity. Implicit in this attitude is a desire to relinquish an overt authorial control over a transparent language medium and to allow the forces of language to create their own relations and configurations through the poet. Poetry, or any use of language, says Howe in the long poem *Defenestration of Prague,* is "a play of force and play // of forces": it exists as a dialectic between an imposed ordering and an anarchic play that escapes such control.

Elsewhere, Howe expresses this dialectic through the figure of capture. In poetic essays such as "The Captivity and Restoration of Mrs. Mary Rowlandson," and long sequences such as "Thorow" and *Articulation of Sound Forms in Time,* all from the 1980s, Howe uses capture as an extended metaphor for the process of reading and writing. In her Mary Rowlandson essay, she depicts Rowlandson as a captive of Indians who quotes from Scripture and Puritan doctrine to reassert a familiar, stable identity in the midst of a new, alien context. Rowlandson is thus attempting to recapture herself and the Indians within what she already knows. But, according to Howe, this or any identity may be captured and recaptured endlessly; any act of interpretation or writing is susceptible to proximities and associations beyond the author's control.

In an interview in *The Difficulties,* with Tom Beckett, Howe describes the receptivity to language she cultivates when she writes:

> I think that a poet is like an ethnographer. You open your mind and textual space to many voices, to an interplay and contradiction and complexity of voices. These voices are marks and sounds and they form a polyphony that forms lines and often abolishes lines. This is not to deny that quotations are staged by the quoter.

Howe works with these "marks and sounds" in a variety of ways. She may collage actual words or phrases from other texts into a poem, verbatim or with alterations. Or Howe's free-association from one text may lead her to fragments of other texts. Research is an integral part of Howe's poetic process, and is inscribed in her work through references to those who work "behind the scenes'' with texts: editors, anonymous helpers, transcribers, typographers.

Marjorie Perloff said of Howe that ''[her] subject, broadly speaking, is the impingement of historical or biographical narrative on lyric consciousness.'' The passage quoted above from the *Difficulties* interview describes Howe's view of history, or of any narrative: rather than a logically ordered sequence emanating from a single source or voice, it is a polyphony of voices continually surfacing into each other as they construct their own versions of events. In this view, narrative is full of interpretations and silences from those who, by force or by choice, remain outside, undocumented. By working with the multiplicity and the partialness of narrative, Howe hopes to open a space within it where these missing voices, or the silence that marks them, can have a positive presence. She says in the introduction to *The Europe of Trusts: Selected Poems,* ''I write to break out into perfect primeval Consent. I wish I could tenderly lift from the dark side of history, voices that are anonymous, slighted—inarticulate.''

Howe employs a variety of practices to put these voices from the ''dark side of history'' into the foreground. Her preferred form, the long serial poem, lends itself to the combination of continuity and disjunctiveness that she cultivates. A serial poem is a long poem composed of a number of shorter poems, which are often grouped into sections; these shorter poems may be read both independently and as part of a larger whole. The breaks between the individual shorter poems offer opportunities to connect the poems or to rest in the silence and discontinuity between them. In an essay in *Sagetrieb,* Paul Kenneth Naylor discusses Howe's use of paratactic logic. Parataxis is the placing of phrases or clauses side by side without the connectives that would coordinate them or subordinate one to another. Howe moves paratactically between sections of a long poem and between the unpunctuated, irregularly spaced phrases that comprise each short poem within a section. As Naylor notes, ''Paratactic discourse is not ordered hierarchically.'' Thus it offers a corrective to more traditional narrative, which structures a chaos of facts into apparent coherence through selection and subordination. Paratactic construction necessarily invites the reader to take an active role in the process of composition, but it also invites questions about what the role ought to be: Should readers supply the missing connectives as they desire, or are other interpretive methods possible? Might readers respect the silences between discontinuous phrases? Are there ways of making nonlinear connections among the poem's elements?

The answer to all these questions is probably yes. As befits Howe's nonauthoritarian stance, her writing encourages a variety of different, even contradictory, reading methods. In the brief second sequence of her long serial poem ''Thorow'' (1987), an engagement with Thoreau, early American history, and the effects of contemporary mass culture, Howe offers one picture of what reading—and writing—are:

Fence blown down in a winter storm

darkened by outstripped possession
Field stretching out of the world

this book is as old as the people

There are traces of blood in a fairy tale

Howe's background as a visual artist is evident here, as in much of her poetry, which works with the physical page and the physical presence of words. She writes in an essay published in ''L=A=N=G=U=A=G=E Lines'': ''First I was a painter, so for me, words shimmer. Each one has an aura. Lines are laid on the field of a page, so many washes of watercolor.'' This ''field of a page'' and the ''field stretching out of the world'' from the poem refer to the American poet Charles Olson's ''field composition.'' In Olson's conception of poetry, content and form are in a state of dynamic interaction. They are not predetermined, but act on each other during the writing process. This process creates the poem's structure, including its use of the physical page. Howe, who owes much to Olson, adds to his concept of poetic field an idea of boundary, of working with the page's limits, as a painter works with the extent of a canvas. In the poem above, there are two notions of what constitutes a field. One is the ground that is contained within a fence—that which someone has fenced off in order to possess it. The second field in the poem is larger, stretching out of this known, bounded world into a world that is dark, unknown, and mysterious. The winter storm, a chaotic force stronger than the fence, opens the space between these two kinds of fields. Books and language are also a kind of field, which can be conceived of either as fenced off from the larger material world or as participating in it: "There are traces of blood in a fairy tale."

Howe works with the physical book in a variety of ways. She actively engages the standard book format in poems appearing on facing pages, nearly identical but each upside down in relation to the other. In some poems, lines of poetry appear at different angles, creating a number of possible positions for reading. Other techniques refer to the various stages of the poem's production: gaps and brackets suggest lacunae in a manuscript page and an editor's attempts to interpret or codify them; dropped letters and overlapping lines recall the pitfalls of manual typesetting. On another level of physicality, Howe uses many archaic words, and works with the idea of etymology. In each of these cases, felicitous accident or coincidence creates meaning. The physical presence of a hole in a page, a skewed line, or an extra "e" at the end of a word expresses something, whether what that is can be easily put into words or not. Howe's "etymology" is the creation of a connection between

unrelated words on the basis of a similarity in sound or appearance. At the opening of "Thorow," the word "fort" is connected with the unrelated "fortnight" (a contraction of "fourteen night"). "So many thread," Howe concludes. At its greatest extent, language is a wilderness of myriad traces that participates in the larger material world. The surest way to navigate—or read—this world is to remain open to its "play of forces" in all the many forms it takes.

Howe's experimentalism has been praised by feminist critics who recognize her attempts to write in a new way while acknowledging her links with a primarily male, authoritarian tradition. Rachel Blau DuPlessis writes in *Sulfur* of Howe's "struggle to assemble and maintain a self-questioning (who? how?) cultural position: anti-authoritarian, yet authoritatively provoked by one's female identity." Those critics, such as Linda Reinfeld, who align Howe with the Language poetry movement focus on her use of language not as a transparent medium but as a series of "structures and codes . . . through which both word and world come into meaning." Grouping Howe with Language poets Charles Bernstein and Michael Palmer, Reinfeld discusses how "these writers' sense of displacement, of splitting away from the language they know they must rely on, is complicated by a need to come to terms with the unavoidable complexities of current literary theory and ideological critique. For them there is no simple sense of image, voice, or self." But Howe's work does not fall easily into a single camp. A quality that many critics have remarked on is her serious sense of play. John Taggart writes, "What *is* new and valuable in Susan Howe's poetry is the direct declaration of play as the center of the poem and her ability to concentrate all of its means and intensities into the poem's ongoing composition. Her poetry gives pleasure in its play and produces meaning of human significance."

*   *   *

Howe's complex family background and childhood experiences of wartime helped her to form a sense of self contingent on history and on texts. In the introduction to *The Europe of Trusts: Selected Poems,* Howe wrote of her origins:

> I was born in Boston Massachusetts on June 10th, 1937, to an Irish mother and an American father. My mother had come to Boston on a short visit two years earlier. My father had never been to Europe. She is a wit and he was a scholar. They met at a dinner party when her earring dropped in his soup.

These distinct personalities, Howe's Irish playwright and actress mother, Mary Manning Howe, and American law-professor father, Mark DeWolfe Howe, exerted a powerful force on her artistic and intellectual development, career expectations, and sense of the English language. Howe grew up in Cambridge, Massachusetts, except between the ages of one and five, when her family lived in Buffalo, New York (where Howe now teaches at the State University of New York). Her early years were indelibly marked by the events of World War II. During the war, her father served in North Africa, Italy, and France, setting up military governments in the wake of the allied invasions. He gave up his post as dean of the Law School at the University of Buffalo, and Howe moved to Cambridge with her mother and infant sister, Fanny. At the same time, they were cut off from her mother's family in Ireland between 1940 and 1945.

Howe was steeped in the Harvard academic milieu from an early age. During the war, Mary Howe taught drama at Radcliffe College, and later became involved with the Brattle and the Poets theaters. Howe told Janet Ruth Falon, "I am sure she [her mother] was constantly scandalizing the Harvard community. Women were to be seen and not heard in those days in Cambridge. My mother loves to be heard." After the war, Mark Howe returned to take up a position as professor of law at Harvard. F. O. Matthiessen and Perry Miller, pioneers in American Studies, were close friends of her parents. Howe was fascinated by her father's law school office, which was "a wild disorder of books." She said in the Falon interview, "At home he was fussy about order, but in his office books had taken over. You would look in and just see books, books, books, books, and then you would see my thin little father in the middle." She remembers him working long, tiring hours on his biography of Oliver Wendell Holmes Jr. and then relaxing with "some old Mather or Sewell diary."

Howe developed a special feeling about books. In her father's study at home, all the American books were on one side, and all the Irish books on the other. She described it thus to Falon: "I remember that the Irish books represented freedom and magic. The others represented authority and reality. I used to spend hours in there. My parents were out a lot and the books stood in for them. They seemed warm." Many years later, Howe wrote a paean to eccentric, devotional, obsessive scholarship in the essay "Submarginalia," in *The Birth-mark: Unsettling the Wilderness in American Literary History* (1993), creating a fellowship of men and women of letters through their shared identity as "library-cormorants," Coleridge's term for those who are *"deep* in all out of the way books."

As a child, Howe wanted to be an actress. Her mother strongly encouraged this desire, and Howe had parts in many productions at the theaters where her mother acted and directed. She apprenticed at various theaters as a teenager, and then, instead of going to college, went to Ireland to apprentice at the Gate Theatre in Dublin. After an unsuccessful year in New York, Howe decided on a career change. She enrolled at the Boston Museum School of Fine Arts, where she graduated in 1961 with a first prize in painting. For ten years she worked as a visual artist, while words came to have an increasingly important role in her work until finally she abandoned visual art and began writing poetry. After graduating, Howe spent a year in London with her husband, Harvey Quaytman, and their baby daughter, Rebecca, and then returned to Cambridge to teach art at a girl's school. In 1964 Howe moved to New York. Influenced by minimalist and pop art, and excited by the New York art community's willingness to experiment and cross genre boundaries, Howe often included words in her paintings or collaged in parts of other paintings (which is "another form of quotation," she remarked in an interview with Lynn Keller in *Contemporary Literature*). In 1965 she married David von Schlegell, a sculptor who constructed sculptures out of aluminum and wood. Inspired by von Schlegell, Howe began to make artists' books, placing a photograph or watercolor on a page with a list of names under it. Charles Olson's use of the poetic page as the field on which history, memory, and self are mapped helped her to realize that listing words was not enough. Howe's work with "environments," rooms in which the walls were covered with collages, also became dominated by words instead of images. She explains in the Keller interview, "I had surrounded myself with words that were really composed lines when a friend, the poet Ted Greenwald, came by to look at what I was doing and said to me: 'Actually you have a book on the wall. Why don't you just put it in a book?' " Howe began to write poetry by following the example of an artist friend, Marcia Hafif, who was filling sketchbooks with pencil strokes that were not words but gestures. Howe describes how she worked with the entirely blank page of the sketchbook:

> As the pages are blank and the cover blank . . . there is no up or down, backwards or forwards. You impose a direction by beginning. But where Marcia was using gestural marks, I used words. . . . I moved into writing *physically* because this was

concerned with gesture, the mark of the hand and the pen or pencil, the connection between eye and hand.

In 1972, Howe moved with von Schlegell, her daughter, Rebecca, and her son with von Schlegell, Mark, to Guilford, Connecticut, on the Long Island Sound, which was still her home in 1995. Her first book of poems, *Hinge Picture,* was published in 1974 by Telephone Books, a small press run by the poet Maureen Owen. *Hinge Picture,* like many of Howe's books, is a single long poem composed of a series of shorter poems, many of them untitled, which function both autonomously and in relation to the whole. The first epigraph to the volume, from Marcel Duchamp's *Notes for the Green Box,* helps to clarify the title, which is a central figure for Howe: "Perhaps make a HINGE PICTURE. (folding yardstick, book . . . .) develop the PRINCIPLE OF THE HINGE in the displacements 1st in the plane 2nd in space." Duchamp's *Green Box* is a series of notes written on odd scraps of paper to accompany the *Large Glass, or The Bride Stripped Bare by Her Bachelors, Even,* his painting on a giant sheet of glass. The quotation is an appropriate starting point for a painter turning to the practice of words, since the *Green Box* is a verbal work that challenges the exclusively visual nature of the painting it claims to explicate: it acts as supplement to the *Large Glass* but also forms an essential part of the work, or even assumes dominance. Howe's transition from painting to writing itself figures as a kind of hinge that enables her to pivot between seemingly discrete positions.

In *Hinge Picture,* as in much of her work, doors, borders, and boundaries become agents both of separation and of linkage. Peter Quartermain remarks on this feature of Howe's work: "Her language returns to such cusps again and again, for they mark extremities, turning points, limits, shifts, the nameless edge of mystery where transformations occur and where edge becomes center.'' Many figures of thresholds occur in *Hinge Picture:* birth, the military crossing of mountain passes, the Children of Israel crossing Egypt, trapdoors, mirrors.

A late sequence in the poem demonstrates Howe's intention of working with the idea of a barrier as a kind of medium that filters perception of what lies beyond it:

GLASS SHOT
a motion picture or television
shot in which part of the scene
is made through a glass plate
having other parts of the scene
painted on its surface.

This might refer not only to Duchamp's *Large Glass* but also to language, a primary barrier and link to reality. In *Hinge Picture,* Howe uses the physical aspect of language as a poetic medium. She arranges lines of poetry into variously shaped boxes that emphasize the contrast between black type and white background. One such box uses the line itself as a kind of movable hinge that can be read either horizontally or vertically. Wide, irregular spaces between words create a cascading black-and-white pattern within the box, and a disjunction between words or phrases allows readers to read across or down, as they choose.

Like *Hinge Picture,* Howe's next two books of poetry, *The Western Borders* (1976) and *Secret History of the Dividing Line* (1978), explore border territories through a series of fragments that form a loose, discontinuous narrative. Like *Hinge Picture,* these two books are single long poems composed of a series of shorter poems. *The Western Borders* begins in the Old World, in the Ireland of James Joyce and Howe's mother (''. . . where standing stone and stacks / of skulls where pavements have been / worn and won back through my mother's / childhood . . .''), and moves west to the New World. The allusive, playful opening passage demonstrates the kind of challenge that Howe's work poses to readers:

IRELAND

sandycove
keel

a snicker hugged this face that lay in sand
cliffs are cruel yes cruel rock and rook of
cloud past all   and Ireland a place circled
round by the sea   and Ibex a creature with
horns like a goat   and Ibis a bird that in
Egypt I've read was worshipped while living
and honored when dead   galloped across the
laugh of it all   for a light sand floor am
told to go down   while hills hem dawn into
                    SONG

The name ''sandycove'' evokes the ''Proteus'' episode of Joyce's *Ulysses,* in which Stephen Dedalus wanders musing on Sandymount Strand. The *Ulysses* episode is informed by a strong, if deeply mercurial, individual consciousness, but in Howe's poem it is less clear who is speaking. Like Samuel Beckett, Howe asks, ''What matter who's speaking?'' The passage opens with a potential consciousness, but one that appears incapacitated: ''this face that lay in sand'' recalls one of Beckett's immobilized or paralyzed narrators. Rather than a person lying face down in sand, this is merely a disembodied *face* lying in sand. It is not necessarily the face who is speaking—or, indeed, any single consciousness. Bits of song (''Ibis a bird that in / Egypt I've read was worshipped while living / and honored when dead'') and lore that might have come from a child's encyclopedia float up, as they do in Stephen Dedalus' mind, but the organizational principle here seems to be different. Arbitrary phonemic differences between similar-sounding words—rock and rook; Ireland, ibex, and ibis, which Marjorie Perloff calls ''mythic/historical configurations of 'sound forms' ''—create connections that structure the passage. The ''SONG'' at the end of the passage might be that of language to itself.

How, then, is one to read this poem? Howe retains enough fragmentary narrative elements to enable readers to construct their own ''explanations'' of the passage. "Cliffs are cruel,'' for example, might indicate that the face jumped or fell off the cliffs and landed in the sand. This possible reading is reinforced by ''for a light sand floor am / told to go down.'' The cliff might be another border, between conscious control or intention, and that which eludes one's control (the process of falling, or connections in meaning produced by arbitrary connections in sound). At the same time, any such explanation seems provisional. It is not arrived at easily, but must be strained for, making readers aware of their own activity and participation, as well as their own desire for order. These explanations constitute a kind of play, or free association, with the given elements of the poem.

In *The Western Borders,* this encounter of reader with text has an analogue in the encounter of settler with wilderness. This poem suggests that there is always a new western border. The edge of each precarious settlement in the New World constitutes a border between civilization and wilderness, between the known and the unknown, between structure and chaos. War parties went out beyond the border, but "they found no treasure and wandered perpetually / from place to place / As if fury could explain away the unexplored interior." Howe's next book, *Secret History of the Dividing Line* (1978), which takes place entirely in the New World, concerns itself with the problems of coming to know this unknown, chaotic place by ordering it and drawing lines across it. The title alludes to a New World historical text: William Byrd's *History of the Dividing Line betwixt Virginia and North Carolina* (1841) chronicles the 1728 surveying expedition jointly mounted by the two states to settle their disputed border, in which Byrd participated as commissioner of Virginia. In this dispute, each state drew its own line, and the territory between the two lines became a region of uncertain jurisdiction.

Howe often begins a book of poetry with a situation or concept from another text. In these early works, the association between this concept and the ensuing work is very loose and flexible, almost disjunctive, as if Howe's poem were a jazz piece or abstract painting on which a concrete verbal title had been placed. This association creates another dividing line, in this case between Byrd's text and Howe's, that we are invited to cross.

Howe brings yet another kind of dividing line into play in the poem. The cover illustration of the volume is taken from Jean Dubreuil's *The Practice of Perspective* (1765). The title bisects the page horizontally. Above and below are diagrams of rows of trees that demonstrate the technique of perspective, in which the vanishing point is located along a horizontal line that divides the space of the drawing into two unequal sections. One of the short poems replicates this demonstration of perspective. A horizontal line bisects a mostly blank page; above this line, the word ''MORNING'' appears centered in capital letters, and below the line is the phrase ''SHEET OF WATER AT THE EDGE OF WOODS.'' The word ''MORNING,'' like the sun, rises above the horizon and also serves as a vanishing point, receding into the distance while the lower half of the page becomes a large expanse of water that reflects the light of the sun. The words ''SHEET OF WATER AT THE EDGE OF WOODS'' reflect the sun in the water. The phrase ''*sheet* of water,'' like a sheet of paper, emphasizes the collapse of visual and verbal images.

A vanishing point is where receding parallel lines seem to meet; it is also the point where they disappear. This meeting of the lines is a visual convention: the world is larger than any single individual's visual field, and in actuality the lines continue beyond that field. This visual convention partakes of the larger convention of a unified self. In the second section of *Secret History of the Dividing Line,* ''THE LAST FIRST PEOPLE,'' Howe explores how the convention of linear perspective relates to cultural practices.

We sailed north
it was March
White sands
and fragrant woods
the permanence
of endless distance.

When next I looked he was gone.
      Frame of our Universe
            Our intellectual wilderness
   no longer boundless
                  west
when next I looked he was gone.

The beginning of this passage resembles an entry from Columbus' journal. A new world can be an empty paradise of white sands and fragrant woods as long as it is seen as an extension of what the explorer already knows. If the parallel lines meet at the vanishing point, then the frame, or the limitations, of one's known visual or cultural field becomes invisible. It then seems as if the ''endless distance'' is included in one's field—in other words, that one's field encompasses everything. But the careful explorer discovers that this field of endless distance, this ''wilderness,'' is ''no longer boundless''—that in fact things appear and disappear as they shift in and out of the frame. At this point in the poem, the lines also shift left and right, slipping the frame, the left margin established by the first few lines, while later in the poem, fragments of words appear as if their missing letters were on the wrong side of the frame. Thus Howe supplements Charles Olson's poetic field by focusing on the boundaries of any field and on the mystery of what lies beyond.

With her three works of the early 1980s, Howe began to receive significant critical attention. *The Liberties* (1980), *Pythagorean Silence* (1982), and *Defenestration of Prague* (1983), all published by small presses, exhibit a greater integration of the starting concept with the poetic narrative, an increased focus on the sound quality of words, and a new sureness of linguistic play. During this period Howe was often associated with the Language poetry movement. Her poems and essays appeared in the two main Language anthologies, Bruce Andrews and Charles Bernstein's *The Language Book* (1984) and Ron Silliman's *In the American Tree* (1986). With these three works Howe also found a form that, with variations, she is still using: each book is a single poem with a tripartite structure composed of a tentative, exploratory first section; a long, discursive middle section, typically in couplets; and an experimental, typographically diverse third section. Each section, in turn, is composed of a number of smaller, usually single-page, poems. Howe's introduction to *The Europe of Trusts* (1990), which collects these three poems, signals what they have in common: ''I write to break out into perfect primeval Consent. I wish I could tenderly lift from the dark side of history, voices that are anonymous, slighted—inarticulate.'' With this, Howe announces her writing as a project of recuperation, at the same time acknowledging that these ''voices''—women, Native Americans, religious minorities, and other repressed figures—may not speak in any conventional way, and that her own activity of recuperation must respect their silence. In *Sulfur,* Rachel Blau DuPlessis writes that ''Howe bases her poetics on the evocation or proposition of 'silence' . . . as a trope for an anti-authoritarian practice.'' As she points out, this is a feminist position, but one that includes all marginalized figures, unknown, unwritten, or effaced, from ''the dark side of history'' or from beyond the vanishing point.

The Liberties begins with a prose section, ''Fragments of a Liquidation,'' that explains the romantic relationship between Stella (Esther Johnson) and Jonathan Swift: Stella (Swift's allegorical name for Johnson) grew up on the estate of Sir William Temple, where Swift was secretary, and later moved to Ireland to live near

Swift at his urging, thus placing herself in a position that her society construed as morally questionable. Howe portrays the "liquidation" of Stella's life—how her parentage was uncertain, her real name virtually unremembered, her reputation ambiguous, her letters and poems lost—and this portrait itself is by nature fragmentary, since a liquidation does not leave a coherent picture of its own process.

At the same time, creating a new unified self may not be the solution to Stella's obliteration. As Howe says in "Formation of a Separatist, I," this self is not a whole but a faulty construction:

>   We are
>   discovered
>
> not solid
>
>   the floor
>
>   based
>
> on misunderstanding.

Howe brings another figure to stand beside Stella and enter into dialogue with her: Cordelia, who, when asked what she has to say to demonstrate that she loves her father more than her two sisters do, answers, "Nothing." The loyal daughter, rather than parroting back to the father an image of himself, and thus perpetuating the patriarchal system that victimizes them both, points to the partialness of language and of individual self. Howe's use of graphic space becomes increasingly focused in these works of the early 1980s, participating in her recognition of this silence outside a partial self:

>   I can re
>
> trac
>
> my steps
>
> Iwho
>
> crawl
>
> between thwarts

> Do not come down the ladder
>
> ifor I
>
> haveaten
>
> it a
>
> way

Howe lays out the poem as a kind of ladder of language whose "thwarts" are the lines that the "I" (or "eye") crawls between into empty space. The "I" might be Stella, Cordelia, or Susan Howe, women or others who have moved in the interstices of language, history, and documented reality. These empty spaces might be more hospitable than the lines, which might "thwart" attempts to climb. And these spaces also have a power, menacing the solidity of language and self. The line "ifor I" might be read "eye for eye": if a group is marginalized, relegated to the area of empty space, it is only fitting that it pull the solid, visible reality into itself so that it, too, becomes nothing. But the line might also be read "i for I"—inviting the substitution of an unassuming lowercase identity for a commanding uppercase one—or "if or I"—equating the self with a conditional presence. The sinister command at the end of the poem also holds an edge of triumph. It demonstrates how space not only devours but also opens possibility: the line break in the middle of the word "away" suggests that "eating it away" may open a way.

Play with the given elements of language loosens the hold of the self, offering liberty from it, and this includes the poet herself. In the third section of the poem Howe presents a series of riddles whose answers are the letters of her own name. Tina Darragh wrote of this section, "Literally, [Howe] is spelling out her reason for writing—experimentation with the pattern of words handed down to her equals freedom." Howe's conclusion to *The Liberties* supports Darragh's reading:

Enter FOOL
(Sleeps.)
Here set at liberty

Tear pages from a calendar
scatter them into sunshine and snow

Perhaps the most explicitly autobiographical of Howe's long poems, *Pythagorean Silence* also continues to question the nature of the "I" that speaks about its own life experiences, and the nature of that "I"'s relation to the larger scale of history. The opening section of the poem, "Pearl Harbor," is headed by a place and a date: "Buffalo / 12.7.41." On this, the day Pearl Harbor was bombed, the four-year-old Susan Howe and her father visited the zoo in Buffalo, New York. The "Buffalo" of the heading is not only the specific place of Howe's early childhood but also an animal that represents the obliteration of a way of life, and of a number of life-forms and ecosystems, by early European Americans greedy for the available space. It is also an animal in captivity, an inhabitant of the zoo. This first section begins with a brief dialogue between a "HE" and a "SHE," who might be Howe's parents but who also serve as mythic, satirical embodiments of traditional gender roles:

HE
(Comes through the hall door.)
The research of scholars, lawyers, investigators,
        judges
Demands!
SHE
(With her arms around his neck
whispers.)
Herod had all the little children murdered!

The male voice—rational and on the side of the law—and the female voice—emotional and focused on concrete reality—might be arguing about whether war is necessary and justifiable. However, these are not individuals, but shadows, as Howe writes in the final poem of section 1:

Shadows are seated at the kitchen table
Clock

and shadow of a Clock

A black cloud hangs over the landscape
War

some war—

Howe qualifies and displaces nouns here, threatening their solid existence ("Clock // and shadow of a Clock . . . War // some war—"). The "shadow of a Clock" might be history, the accumulated mass of tradition. Present events and individual identities cannot exist apart from this mass but must participate in it. An imminent war is in part created by the stories told about past wars. In a sense it then loses its particularity and becomes "some war," any war, to be repeated endlessly. Individual men and women, although perhaps unaware of it, are captive to traditional gender roles. Belief in a separate self that can take independent action serves to reinforce this tradition by denying it.

History in its largest sense means story, and *Pythagorean Silence* is full of traditional stories that people call on to construct themselves, especially biblical stories and fairy tales. Howe breaks into and alters these stories to show how tenuous their construction is. Thus section 2, "pythagorean silence," opens with a man (Howe's father?) setting off on a journey to the forests of (wartime?) Germany. "He plodded away through drifts of i / ce / away into inapprehensible peace." The "i" is not solid and personal—rather, it has drifted over time to form the ground (or ice) we walk on. In the next poem of section 2, Howe describes the repeated movement by which this ground composed of the "i" or self has formed:

age of earth and us all chattering

a sentence   or character
suddenly

steps out to seek for truth— —fails
falls

into a stream of ink   Sequence
trails off

must go on

waving fables and faces   War
doings of the war

manoeuvering between points

This character, or fairy-tale hero, inevitably fails in his quest for truth, and his failure to reach his goal interrupts the sequence of the story, which needs a goal in order to keep moving forward. Howe equates this character, or personal identity, with a sentence, a linguistic proposition. When they fail, both fall into "a stream of ink," a chaos of language, history, or reality that obliterates sequence, order, and intention. Because they cannot accept this state of chaos, sentences and characters repeat this sequence endlessly. War, for Howe, is a "manoeuvering between points," "between // any two points   which is / what we want (issues at stake) // bearings and so // holes in a cloud   are minutes passing." We use points—geographical or ideological ("issues at stake")—to get our bearings. Fighting wars is thus one way human beings have of making themselves comfortable in space and time. But these bearings, points, or issues, are just "holes in a cloud."

This poem concludes with a passage of fragmentary lyricism:

which is

which
view   odds of images swept rag-tag

silver and grey
epitomes

seconds   forgeries engender
(are blue)   or blacker

flocks of words flying together   tense

as an order

cast off to crows

This is a kind of lyric poetry that deflates traditional lyric attributes—unity, single voice, a deep connection to nature—without rejecting lyric form. Rather, the lyric receives an infusion through the use of play, punning, and shifts in diction. This collection of "odds of images" (or odds and ends) has a kind of remnant beauty that a reader may read in pieces, finding meaning locally instead of globally. Holey (or holy?) clouds drift apart into "silver and grey / epitomes," which are "seconds," or mechanical reproductions that are not of first quality. It may not matter that these images, these words, are not originals; perhaps, Howe suggests, it is time to rethink our definitions of originality and personal voice. The "flocks of words" fly "tense / as an order," like a military formation setting off to battle, but they "cast off to crows." This tense linguistic formation may be unfastened like a boat, unhooked like a stitch from a knitting needle, to become part of the world beyond language—and a rather raucous, disorderly part, at that. Similarly, late in the second section, the tight formation of the historical character Susan Howe is released to disperse into the air: "Outside at the back of the sky // biography blows away."

Defenestration of Prague (1983) continues Howe's engagement with history, this time taking a more remote historical event as its starting point. The title refers to the violent acts committed against the imperial governors in Prague in 1618. According to the story, they were thrown out of the palace windows by Bohemian Protestants whose religious rights had been violated by Emperor Matthias. A window, like a religion, is a frame or border. It is safe to be inside a window looking out, but not to be thrown out of one. Howe expresses the uncertainty and trepidation of someone who knows that there are Others who exist outside of her—his?—frame of reference, whether these are Protestants, Catholics, Native Americans, or members of the opposite sex:

> Who are they
> (others between the trees)
>
> falling into lines of human
>
> habitation
> Tread softly my misgiving heart
>
> To chart all

Yet a significant portion of *Defenestration* seems to take place outside the window, in a linguistic wilderness populated by cultural elements. Here is a portion of the fifth poem in "Tuning the Sky," the first section:

>   the Lark   (soft-rushing
>   lopen
>   and neighed
>   hinter-time
>   death-chill waking
>   e n d l e s s PROTEANL i n k a g e s

In *The Difficulties,* Stephen-Paul Martin explained how to read this kind of Howe poem:

> in Howe's poem the sense is *in* the words themselves, in the musical and visual patterns of energy they create, and in the virtual space that exists between text and reader. The poem is not a static object offered up for consumption; it is a network of possibilities to be realized by the reader. . . . *Defenestration of Prague* is a metamorphic ("Protean") field, changing with each new "linkage"; it is also series of "inkages," verbal inscriptions that contain a sedimental record of various "ink ages," or periods of writing.

After *Defenestration,* which Howe considers an "Irish" poem (and *The Liberties* would also fall in that category), Howe turned to a series of "American" works that explore—sometimes painfully—the issue of authorial and readerly control. As is evident in her first three books of

poetry, the early European settling of America at the expense of its indigenous inhabitants provides Howe with an especially fruitful paradigm for looking at the use of force in the act of interpretation. She sees this use of force as inevitable—hence her figure of capture—but has difficulty reconciling herself to it, wishing for a kind of writing or reading that could be purely receptive.

My Emily Dickinson, a book-length reading of Dickinson that hovers between criticism and prose poetry, is Howe's first extended work of literary scholarship. It works at the boundaries of the authoritative voice of conventional scholarship, questioning the provenance and nature of that authority. In the introduction to the volume, Howe describes her critical method by comparing her relation to Dickinson with Thoreau's relation to the Concord River: "There came a day at the end of the summer or the beginning of autumn, when he resolved to launch a boat from shore and let the river carry him. Emily Dickinson is my emblematical Concord River." In other words, Howe wishes not to pronounce on the earlier poet but to enter the flow that comprises her. For Howe, this flow incorporates a variety of forces, including American Calvinism as embodied in early texts by Mary Rowlandson, Jonathan Edwards, and Cotton Mather; nineteenth-century British literature from the Brontës to Elizabeth Barrett and Robert Browning, as well as the earlier British tradition of Shakespeare and Milton; the involvement of Thomas Wentworth Higginson in the radical abolitionist movement; and Dickinson's possible reasons for choosing not to publish. Howe's kind of criticism is intensely personal and subjective at the same time that it explodes the idea of a discrete person or subject. Howe's act of attention to Dickinson both creates Dickinson and creates Howe.

Devoting the bulk of the book to a reading of a single poem, "My Life had stood—a Loaded Gun—" Howe delivers an extended meditation on the nature of control, the use of force, and the interplay and exchangeability of submission and dominance. She connects these issues to the nature of gender relations in Dickinson's time as well as our own, the pressures of life under the doctrine of Manifest Destiny, and the challenges of Dickinson's poetic technique to a notion of authorial determination of meaning. Howe acknowledges that this is a feminist enterprise, asking, "How do I, choosing messages from the code of others in order to participate in the universal theme of Language, pull SHE from all the myriad symbols and sightings of HE." Yet she also wishes to question a kind of unreflective feminism that prescribes certain behavior for women writers: "Orders suggest hierarchy and category. Categories and hierarchies suggest property. My voice formed from my life belongs to no one else. What I put into words is no longer my possession. Possibility has opened."

Howe continues to be active in Dickinson scholarship, working closely with Dickinson's manuscripts and the questions about literary production that they raise. Another article on Dickinson, "These Flames and Generosities of the Heart: Emily Dickinson and the Illogic of Sumptuary Values," first published in *Sulfur* in 1991, is collected in *The Birth-mark: Unsettling the Wilderness in American Literary History.* Howe is one of several critics in the early 1990s to focus on the intentional indeterminacy of Dickinson's manuscripts. She argues that the unorthodox line breaks in Dickinson's manuscripts are not arbitrary but "represent an athematic compositional intention," and that the lists of alternate words that appear at the bottom of many Dickinson poems form an integral part of the poems, enacting Dickinson's refusal of closure. Howe's reading of Dickinson reflects her own concern with writing's physicality.

While writing *My Emily Dickinson*, Howe discovered Mary Rowlandson, author of the first captivity narrative, who became an essential bridge to Howe's next books of poetry. In "The Captivity and Restoration of Mrs. Mary Rowlandson" (in *Temblor,* 1985), Howe develops the figure of capture that describes the way she had already been writing. In the *Talisman* interview with Edward Foster, Howe describes the typical three-part structure of many of her works: "I start in a place with fragments, lines and marks, stops and gaps, and then I have more ordered sections, and then things break up again." This structure, or formal expression of a process, also applies to history:

> . . . the outsidedness—these sounds, these pieces of words—comes into the chaos of life, and then you try to order them and to explain something, and the explanation breaks free of itself. I think a lot of my work is about breaking free: starting free and being captured and breaking free again and being captured again.

Howe's next two long poems focus on a forced or voluntary move into wilderness and a subsequent return from wilderness into civilization. In this supposed "wilderness" live other people—Indians—for whom it is not a wilderness. In *Articulation of Sound Forms in Time* and "Thorow" (originally published in 1987 and later collected in *Singularities* [1990]), this progression and encounter with Others refers to writing and to any process of interpreting or contacting the world.

Articulation of Sound Forms in Time begins with a prose section, "The Falls Fight," which tells the story of the Reverend Hope Atherton, who accompanied troops to the Falls Fight above Deerfield, Massachusetts, during King Philip's War in 1676. During a chaotic rout, Atherton became separated from the troops and was lost in the wilderness for several days. When he returned, his congregation doubted his sanity, especially when he claimed that he had attempted to surrender to a band of Indians, who had run away from him. Howe suggests that Hope Atherton's feminine name is emblematic of his liminal experience. Atherton—white, male, and in the service of God and England—verges by virtue of his name on being a female Other, and by virtue of association with the wilderness and its "wild" inhabitants, the Indians, on being crazy or "beside himself" (having become a marginal self, an Other who exists outside the self). At the same time, Atherton is also an Other to those that he sees as Other. This first section concludes with an "EXTRACT from a LETTER (dated June 8, 1781) of Stephen Williams to President Styles," which recounts Atherton's story and presents one participant in the Falls Fight who claims that Indians told him that they ran from Atherton when he approached them, "thinking it was the Englishman's God." The poem thus opens with a demonstration of how easily a figure at the center can become Other, since in actuality there are always a multitude of centers constantly decentering each other. As Rachel Blau DuPlessis wrote in *Sulfur,* "Following from Howe's study of the margins as marginal (in *The Liberties*), *Articulation of Sound Forms in Time* offers a vision of the center as marginal, marginalized, prone to a hopeless—yet potentially saving—breakup of its most cherished paradigms." This vision also corresponds to Howe's understanding of history as a chaos of multiple perspectives presented as a single, coherent sequence.

Section 2, "Hope Atherton's Wanderings," explores the breakdown of this historical and personal "center." Atherton speaks of his wilderness ordeal in compressed, cryptic, almost telegraphic poems into which fragments from local histories of Hatfield and Hadley, Massachusetts, have been collaged. The movement of the section is paratactic; individual words stand in isolation, as if they are trying to connect with each other, but failing. In this wilderness of language, in which individual words become "sound forms in time," indicators of time and place surface, but they, too, remain isolated, unable to order or orient. As the section progresses, the provisional consciousness seems to fall apart almost completely in a series of poems in which individual words are separated by wide spaces or run together with no spaces, in what Marjorie Perloff calls "a kind of aphasia" where words have no apparent relationship to each other at all. These poems each have the rough form of a box, and the first "box" poem ends, "Epithets young in a box told as you fly." The reader, like Pandora, approaches the poem, only to see its contents disperse in all directions. But hope—or Hope—remains, an ambiguous figure. In the final poem of section 2, Hope Atherton returns to preach a sermon to his dubious flock:

> Loving Friends and Kindred:—
>
> When I look back
>
> So short in charity and good works
>
> We are a small remnant
>
> Of signal escapes wonderful in themselves
>
> We march from our camp a little
>
> and come home.

While there is a relief for the reader in this return into the known world of connected language, there is also a lingering doubt: What is this hope about? Is it something to place trust in, or not?

> We must not worry
>
> how few we are and fall from each other
>
> More than language can express
>
> Hope for the artist in America & etc
>
> This is my birthday
>
> These are the old home trees

Howe ends the section on an ambiguous note. Sentimentality may be a subversive force, an excess of feeling that spills over boundaries or limits to become "more than language can express," or it may be a conventionalized version of emotion whose inarticulateness expresses insubstantiality ("Hope for the artist in America & etc").

The third and final section of the poem is eccentrically discursive and theoretical, representing an alternative kind of return from the wilderness into order. Its title, "Taking the Forest," again represents an ambivalence toward the authority of critical discourse: Is "taking the forest" what we really want to do? Can we help it? A counterstrain emerges in the section, a feminine presence that counters "logical determination of position." Instead of "knocking sense into" Atherton or whoever might be in need of it, this is a "complexity kissing sense into empty . . .": the object of this potential violence diverted into a caress has disappeared. Here there is no position to determine; it is replaced by song: "Threadbare evergreen season / Mother and maiden // singing into the draft." "Draft" here refers both to cold air coming through a hole in a structure and to a conscription into military service that also produces a kind of hole in the social fabric. "Sound forms" flow in this air current or social gap, as those left at home during war allow something to emerge from thin absence or opening in space and time.

"Thorow" constitutes another encounter with a linguistic, material, and perceptual wilderness, this time figured more as an exploration than as a battle. Howe's recurring figure in the poem is a scout who follows tracks in the landscape. She works closely with Thoreau's journals, in which he records his own encounters with the wilderness, careful observations of natural phenomena, and trackings of animals. Howe herself tracks Thoreau, and invites readers to follow her tracks by uncovering her research and readings. The poem begins with a prose description of Howe's stay on Lake George in the Adirondacks in the winter and spring of 1987. The present town of Lake George is a tourist trap, "a fake fort where a real one once stood . . . and a four-star Ramada Inn built over an ancient Indian burial ground."

Howe is wary of a kind of navigation of unknown territory that seeks simply to possess or co-opt it: "Pathfinding believers in God and grammar spelled the lake into *place.*" In section 1, Howe presents fragmented explorer's diary entries, some bits of which are drawn from Thoreau's journals. These reach toward an alternative way of knowing the wilderness:

Eating nothing but hominey

Scribbling the ineffable

See only the tracks of rabbit

A mouse-nest of grass

Howe, Thoreau, rabbit, and mouse are all "scribbling the ineffable"; there is a continuum between the rabbit's tracks, the jottings of Thoreau, and Howe's incorporation of Thoreau's jottings into a passage whose phrases hang together as much on the basis of sound as of sense. At the same time, Howe wonders if the enterprise of writing can avoid being part of a forceful appropriation of this "ineffable." This passage from section 2 might describe her own associative method as well as an explorer's greed for possessing new territory and controlling its indigenous peoples:

Thaw has washed away snow
covering the old ice

the Lake a dull crust

Force made desire wander
Jumping from one subject

to another
Besieged and besieged

in a chain of Cause
The eternal First Cause

I stretch out my arms
to the author

Even the associative method—which starts with fragments of text and allows ideas to take shape from them ("jumping from one subject // to an other'') rather than imposing ideas from outside —may be driven by force. At the end of section 2, the poet–scout destroys her compass:

> I pick my compass to pieces
>
> Dark here in the driftings
> in the spaces of drifting
>
> Complicity battling redemption

Like the boy in William Faulkner's "The Bear," who leaves his compass at the edge of the forest in order to face the bear alone, Howe may now attain knowledge of the wilderness by meeting it on equal terms. For Howe, this wilderness includes Lake George, the page, and the mind. The "driftings" that she allows to determine her movement include this struggle between complicity and redemption, which might refer, among other things, to her inevitable use of force. The knowledge of her complicity with force and her desire to be redeemed from it struggle in her mind. If she cannot free herself from using force, she may at least free herself from attempting to control this battle.

The two opening poems of section 3, which are inverted mirror images of each other, dispense with ordinary horizontal lines of poetry that all face the same direction. Sequences of lines and isolated words appear upside down in relation to each other, drifting into each other at odd angles. The sequences have to do with battles with the Indians ("Gone to have a Treaty // with the French at Oswego // & singing their war song") and exploration ("Places to walk out to" heads a list of words that seem to have progressively less and less connection to the heading). But the desire to explore is tempered by fear. As Peter Quartermain has remarked, there is a tension in Howe "between her impassioned attraction to, and sheer terror of, the wilderness." At the top of one of these poems appear the words "Gabion / Parapet": a safe (?) place from which the self may watch the battle—between different

systems of representation, or between the mind's desire to relinquish force and its understanding that it cannot. Ironically, as these works, which first appeared in small presses or magazines, began to be published by more mainstream publishing houses, Howe faced new restrictions on the number and size of pages, and had to fight for her freedom to represent the wilderness in graphic space.

Howe's later works include a collection of poetic essays, *The Birth-mark: Unsettling the Wilderness in American Literary History* (1993); a collection of four long poems, *The Nonconformist's Memorial* (1993); and a long essay on the documentary filmmaker Chris Marker, "Sorting Facts; or, Nineteen Ways of Looking at Marker," in *Beyond Document: The Art of Nonfiction Film* (1995). *The Birth-mark* includes the essay on Dickinson's manuscripts and a new, expanded version of "The Captivity and Restoration of Mrs. Mary Rowlandson," the *Talisman* interview with Edward Foster, three new essays, and an introduction. The essays in the collection explore the nature of writing through an examination of all the forces that combine to produce and control published texts, from the Puritan persecution of antinomian preacher Anne Hutchinson, to editorial interventions like the normalization of Emily Dickinson's line and punctuation or the obsessive footnoting of Cotton Mather's *Magnalia Christi Americana,* to anonymous acts of love for texts—preserving or transcribing manuscripts, underlining favorite passages, searching dusty library basements. Any text, or any self, Howe suggests, is a nexus of forces in continual flux. At this nexus Howe poses questions about reading and writing:

> you are straying, seeking, scattering. Was it you or is it me? Where is the stumbling block? Thoughts delivered by love are predestined to distortion by words. If experience forges conception, can quick particularities of calligraphic expression

ever be converted to type? Are words children? What is the exchange value? Where does spirit go? Double yourself stammer stammer. Is there any way to proof it? Who or what survives the work?

The poems in *The Nonconformist's Memorial* work with the same issues. In particular, "A Bibliography of the King's Book or, Eikon Basilike" and "Melville's Marginalia" both engage closely with books about other books. *A Bibliography of the King's Book; or, Eikon Basilike,* by Edward Almack, offers physical descriptions and publication history of all editions of *The Eikon Basilike,* a collection of meditations and justifications said to be written by Charles I and published on the day of his execution, suppressed repeatedly during the Commonwealth and lauded during the Restoration. The collection is spurious, and its true provenance is unknown—but its printers were at first imprisoned, and during the Restoration a bishop advanced his career by claiming authorship. Howe explains that Edward Almack's book came into her hands when her "son found it at one of the sales Sterling Memorial Library sometimes holds to get rid of useless books." The poem intersperses physical descriptions of the *Eikon* with a narrative of the king's execution. Lines cross each other like censor's marks or jail bars; Howe meditates on the essential mystery of authorship and selfhood and the constant and varied attempts to regulate it:

> Finding the way full of People
> Who had placed themselves upon the Theatre
> To behold the Tragedy
> He desired he might have *Room*
> Speech came from his mouth
> Historiography of open fields
>
> Mend the Printers faults
> The place name and field name
> as thou doest them espy
> Centuries of compulsion and forced holding
> For the Author lies in Gaol
>
> and knows not why

"Melville's Marginalia" begins from a book of the same title, originally a doctoral dissertation by Wilson Walker Cowen, that collects and transcribes "every page from every known volume of Herman Melville's library that Melville had marked or annotated." The first part of Howe's poem explores this palimpsest of engagements with texts; the second part works more loosely with *Melville's Marginalia.* Howe explains in the first part that for each poem she chose a word or phrase at random from Cowen's book and then wrote by free association. She adds, "Poetry is thought transference. Free association isn't free." Melville's writing in the margins of others' writing is also her own. This practice is an exchange that is also an endless displacement of margin to center, to margin to center, to margin:

> Melville the source hunter
>
> hawking corollaries for coal
>
> foraging for fuel in copses
>
> What a semi-barbarous ballad
>
> Saw that the saw sawed thought
>
> Skipping oblivion for forfeit
>
> Wide universe no matter what
>
> that their thought may go out
>
> the margin's mile of welcome

Howe has achieved a level of comfort here with the issue of authorial control that allows her to play with grace and humor, to write a "semi-barbarous ballad" or a fusing of forceful interpretation with nonsense song. Here the act of interpreting is figured as a kind of foraging, a looking for fuel in the works of others, or in the material world, with which to continue to exist. This is energy that readers transform so "that their thought may go out" in its turn. Howe divides *The Nonconformist's Memorial* into two sections, "Turning" and "Conversion," ironically recalling T. S. Eliot's "Ash Wednesday," and in this poem she responds to the conclusion of Eliot's early poem "Preludes": "Wipe your hand across your mouth, and laugh; / The worlds revolve like ancient women / Gathering fuel in vacant lots." While Eliot's laugh is a painful dismissal of the redemptive potential in the fragments of human suffering thrown up by modern industrial life, Howe's is liberating, an acknowledgment that all our activity is marginal. The margin has expanded, a "wide universe no matter what" that smiles to welcome us as fellow members.

Howe's 1995 essay "Sorting Facts; or, Nineteen Ways of Looking at Marker," is at once a reading of Marker's films; an analysis of how documentary film, or poetry, or memory, responds to the painful, irretrievable loss of that which it tries to capture; and an elegy for her husband, David von Schlegell, who died October 1992 after suffering a stroke. In nineteen sections, Howe connects individuals dealing with personal loss to societies dealing with war trauma to documentary filmmakers dealing with the impossibility of transferring "reality" to film. She poignantly weaves discussions of Marker's films *La Jetée* and *Sans Soleil*, which imagine a third world war and attempt to come to terms with World War II, with Russian filmmakers after the Revolution attempting to approach the Real; her own childhood memories of watching newsreels of the war before the double feature at the University Theater in Cambridge; letters David von Schlegell wrote home to his parents as a fighter pilot during the war; and her inability since von Schlegell's death to watch a home movie of him shot by his first wife's uncle long before Howe met him. In the process she explores the essential mystery of reality and our attempts to reach it through memory, writing, and film. "All people captured on film are ghosts," Howe writes. "They appear and do not appear . . . Words are the symbols of spirits. The deer and the dear run away." Yet the process of recording is necessary: "In the name of reason I need to record something because I am a survivor in this ocean."

Selected Bibliography

WORKS OF SUSAN HOWE

POETRY

Hinge Picture. Cherry Valley, N.Y.: Telephone Books, 1974.

The Western Borders. Willits, Calif.: Tuumba Press, 1976.

The Secret History of the Dividing Line. New York: Telephone Books, 1978.

Cabbage Gardens. Chicago: Fathom Press, 1979.

Pythagorean Silence. New York: Montemora Foundation, 1982.

Defenestration of Prague. New York: Kulchur Foundation, 1983.

Articulation of Sound Forms in Time. Windsor, Vt.: Awede Press, 1987.

A Bibliography of the King's Book; or, Eikon Basilike. Providence, R.I.: Paradigm Press, 1989.

The Captive Morphology. Santa Fe, N.M.: Weasel Sleeves Press, 1990.

The Europe of Trusts: Selected Poems. Los Angeles: Sun & Moon Press, 1990.

Singularities. Hanover, N.H.: University Press of New England for Wesleyan University Press, 1990.

The Nonconformist's Memorial. New York: New Directions, 1993.

PROSE

My Emily Dickinson. Berkeley, Calif.: North Atlantic Books, 1985.

The Birth-mark: Unsettling the Wilderness in American Literary History. Hanover, N.H.: University Press of New England for Wesleyan University Press, 1993.

UNCOLLECTED POETRY

"Heliopathy." *Temblor,* 4:42–54 (1986).

"Federalist 10." *Abacus,* 30 (1987).

UNCOLLECTED PROSE

"The End of Art." *Archives of American Art Journal,* 14, no. 4:2–7 (1974).

Untitled review of Rae Armantrout's *Extremities.* *L=A=N=G=U=A=G=E,* no. 7:14–16 (March 1979).

"Howe on Owen." *L=A=N=G=U=A=G=E,* no. 13:28–30 (December 1980).

"What Constitutes a Language Environment." *The Difficulties,* 1:29–30 (1980).

"Light in the Darkness: John Taggart's Poetry." *Hambone,* 2:135–138 (Spring 1982).

"Women and Their Effect in the Distance." *Ironwood,* no. 28:58–91 (1986).

"Where Should the Commander Be." *Writing,* 19:13–19 (November 1987).

Untitled brief essay in "L=A=N=G=U=A=G=E Lines." Edited by Charles Bernstein and Bruce Andrews. In *The Line in Postmodern Poetry.* Edited by Robert Frank and Henry Sayre. Urbana: University of Illinois Press, 1988. Pp. 209–210.

"Since a Dialogue We Are." *Acts* 10:166–173 (1989). On Charles Olson.

"Sorting Facts; or, Nineteen Ways of Looking at Marker." In *Beyond Document: The Art of Nonfiction Film.* Edited by Charles Warren. Middletown, Conn.: Wesleyan University Press, 1995.

BIBLIOGRAPHY

"Susan Howe: Contributions toward a Bibliography." *Talisman,* 4:119–122 (Spring 1990).

BIOGRAPHICAL AND CRITICAL STUDIES

Armantrout, Rae. "On 'Pythagorean Silence.'" *Poetics Journal,* no. 2:64–65 (September 1982).

Bachman, Merle Lyn. "Reading Susan Howe: Notes toward a 'Review.'" *Talisman,* 12:103–106 (Spring 1994).

Beckett, Tom, ed. Susan Howe issue. *The Difficulties,* 3, no. 2 (1989). Includes, in addition to the Beckett and Falon interviews listed above, Stephen Ratcliffe, "Idea's Mirror" (43–45); Janet Rodney, "Language and Susan" (46–51); Maureen Owen, "Susan Howe's Poetry" (57–58); Joel Lewis, "Grappling Bigman: The Secret History of the Dividing Line" (59–62); Stephen-Paul Martin, "Endless Protean Linkages" (63–66); Bruce Andrews, "Suture—& Absence of the Social" (67–70); Peter Quartermain, "And the Without: An Interpretive Essay on Susan Howe" (71–83); Charles Bernstein, "'Passed by Examination': Paragraphs for Susan Howe" (84–88); Bruce Campbell, "'Ring of Bodies' / 'Sphere of Sound': An Essay on Susan Howe's *Articulation of Sound Forms in Time*" (89–96); Linda Reinfeld, "On Henry David (Susan Howe) 'Thorow'" (97–104); Dennis Barone, "Re-vision/In Time: Our Susan Howe" (105–116).

Bromidge, David. "Susan Howe." In *Magill's Critical Survey of Poetry. Supplement.* Edited by Frank Magill. Pasadena, Calif.: Salem Press, 1987. Pp. 193–199.

Burke, Carolyn. "Getting Spliced: Modernism and Sexual Difference." *American Quarterly,* 39:98–121 (Spring 1987).

Butterick, George F. "Endless Protean Linkage." *Hambone,* no. 3:150–151 (Fall 1983).

———. "The Mysterious Vision of Susan Howe." *North Dakota Quarterly,* 55:312–321 (Fall 1987).

Darragh, Tina. "Howe." *L=A=N-G=U=A=G=E,* no. 4:68–71 (1982).

DuPlessis, Rachel Blau. "Susan Howe's Poetry." *HOW(ever)* (1984).

———. "Whowe: An Essay on Work by Susan Howe." *Sulfur,* 20:157–165 (Fall 1987).

Foster, Edward, ed. Susan Howe issue. *Talisman,* 4 (Spring 1990). Includes, in addition to the Foster interview and bibliography listed above, David Landrey, "The Spider Self of Emily Dickinson and Susan Howe" (107–109); Geoffrey O'Brien, "Notes While Reading Susan Howe" (110–111); Stephen Ratcliffe, "Writing Ghost Writing" (112–114); Andrew Schelling, "Reading 'Thorow'" (115–118).

Martin, Stephen-Paul. "Susan Howe: The Book of Cordelia." In his *Open Form and the Feminine Imagination: (The Politics of Reading in Twentieth-Century Innovative Writing).* Washington, D.C.: Maisonneuve Press, 1988. Pp. 159–171.

Middleton, Peter. "On Ice: Julia Kristeva, Susan Howe, and Avant Garde Poetics." In *Contemporary Poetry Meets Modern Theory.* Edited by Anthony Easthope and John D. Thompson. Toronto: University of Toronto Press, 1991. Pp. 81–95.

Naylor, Paul Kenneth. "Where Are We Now in Poetry?" *Sagetrieb,* 10:29–44 (Spring–Fall 1991).

Perloff, Marjorie. *Poetic License: Essays on Modernist and Postmodernist Lyric.* Evanston, Ill.: Northwestern University Press, 1990.

Quartermain, Peter. *Disjunctive Poetics: From Gertrude Stein and Louis Zukofsky to Susan Howe.* New York: Cambridge University Press, 1992.

Reinfeld, Linda. *Language Poetry: Writing as Rescue.* Baton Rouge: Louisiana State University Press, 1992.

Taggart, John. *Songs of Degrees: Essays on Contemporary Poetry and Poetics.* Tuscaloosa: University of Alabama Press, 1994.

INTERVIEWS

Beckett, Tom. *"The Difficulties* Interview." *The Difficulties,* 3, no. 2:17–27 (1989).

Falon, Janet Ruth. "Speaking with Susan Howe." *The Difficulties,* 3, no. 2:28–42 (1989).

Foster, Edward. "An Interview with Susan Howe." *Talisman,* 4:14–38 (Spring 1990). Reprinted in *The Birth-mark.* Pp. 155–181.

Keller, Lynn. "An Interview with Susan Howe." *Contemporary Literature,* 36:1–34 (Spring 1995).

—*MOLLY WEIGEL*

Maxine Kumin

1925–

Because of her preference for traditional verse forms and New England settings, Maxine Kumin is frequently compared with Robert Frost. Attempts to label her a "transcendentalist," in the tradition of Thoreau and Emerson, also have been advanced. Although she has never declined the characterization, and has even called the comparison with Frost a "high compliment," there is much in her poetry that must be accounted for by comparing her with her more apparently "confessional" contemporaries—Robert Lowell, Anne Sexton, Sylvia Plath—rather than stressing a simple allegiance to New England predecessors. Alicia Ostriker situates Kumin midway between the contrasting styles of Elizabeth Bishop on the one hand, and Anne Sexton and Sylvia Plath on the other. Like Bishop, Kumin spends much energy on detail. Like Sexton and Plath, however, she writes poetry that frequently appeals and refers to the personal. Likewise, her adherence to traditional literary forms is not simply an attempt to position herself within the traditions of the past. In Kumin's view, this allegiance to form is poetically liberating, allowing her to work with the more personal material of the confessional poets. Asked by Martha Meek if she uses any particular forms for more intimate material, Kumin replied, "I generally choose something complex and difficult. The tougher the form the easier it is for me to handle the poem,

because the form gives permission to be very gut-honest about feelings." Kumin was born into a middle-class world that destined women for home and family life. Against the expectations of her times, she blossomed into a novelist and a Pulitzer Prize–winning poet. As a result of her background, although she often remains within a New England tradition of poetry about nature, she presses against the limitations of that tradition, and introduces into it new themes and perspectives particular to her experience.

For much of her best work, Kumin has exploited the genre of elegy. She told Karla Hammond that she believes "very strongly that poetry is essentially elegiac in its nature, and that all poems are in one sense or another elegies." "Love poems, particularly," she told Hammond, "are elegies, because if we were not informed with a sense of dying we wouldn't be moved to write love poems." Although some of her best poetry takes the loss of family, friends, and the natural world as its subject, Kumin has never been strictly a poet of pessimism. Her work holds to an ironic style, and answers the difficulty and pain of the world with the quiet humor and strength of the born survivor too frequently to be dismissed as a poetry solely about loss. Kumin told Shelley Armitage, "I like to combine grotesqueness and humor. I think they go together. They are very subtle and unexpected, and they keep colliding. That's the saving thing. To be able at least to smile, if not laugh. It's a way of putting up with the world. A way of enduring. Certainly not controlling it, but a way of saving yourself.''

Born Maxine Winokur in the Germantown section of Philadelphia, on June 6, 1925, Kumin was the youngest of the four children of Doll Simon and Peter Winokur, and the only daughter. She hiked and explored the wooded areas around her parents' suburban home. Recollecting these pre-adolescent days in an interview with Jo-Ann Mapson, she remembered them as ''simple and pleasurable.'' At age eleven she spent a summer on a dairy farm, and later worked as a camp counselor. In contrast to this idyllic childhood, Kumin's adolescence was difficult and stormy. She told Mapson, ''I now think looking back on those otherwise gloomy years that the expectation of July–August in the Berkshires of Massachusetts saved my soul.''

After graduating from Radcliffe with an A.B. in 1946, Kumin returned to take an M.A. in history and literature in 1948. She was exposed there to existentialism, and read W. H. Auden, Stephen Spender, Louis MacNeice, and Randall Jarrell. In 1946, she married Victor Kumin, an engineering consultant. Over the next few years they had three children. In retrospect, she would see the time as one of unfocused dissatisfaction. She later described herself and her friend Anne Sexton, as they were when they met in 1957, as ''two shy housewives, a pair of closet poets.'' Poetry became for Kumin an outlet for energy that eluded the confines of the life expected of the postwar American woman—to get a college degree, get married, raise a family. She told Martha Meek, ''I came to poetry as a way of saving myself because I was so wretchedly discontented, and I felt so guilty about being discontented. It just wasn't enough to be a housewife and a mother.''

By 1953 Kumin had begun publishing what she would later call ''comic'' or ''light'' verse in the glossy magazines, and making money at it. ''I made a pact with myself,'' she told Elaine Showalter, ''that if I didn't sell anything by the time this child [her third] was born, I would chuck all my creative discontents. And in about my eighth month I started really landing with little four-liners, there, here and everywhere. *Saturday Evening Post* and *Cosmopolitan,* and so on.'' The avenues for women's poetry, however, were few. In *To Make a Prairie,* she recounts an anecdote that must have been typical of the times: an editor of a national magazine responded to her submission by sending his regrets that he couldn't publish anything of hers for six months or so because the magazine had published a woman poet the previous month.

It was against this background that in 1957 Kumin decided to take a poetry workshop at the Boston Center for Adult Education. This was to be a major turning point in the life and career of the poet. The professor, John Holmes, was a figure in the Boston literary circles of the time, reviewing and writing books of poetry and serving as the president of the New England Poetry Club. He was friends with many of the leading poets of the day and a devoted teacher. When Kumin entered Holmes's class, with what she later would call ''great fear and trembling,'' she began the trajectory that would make her one of the leading poets of the day. The workshop would go on for three years. Holmes's influence was crucial in advancing Kumin's career. He secured her a job teaching composition at Tufts University and helped get her work published. Through the workshop and John Holmes, Kumin met fellow poets and prominent figures in contemporary poetry. Among these were George Starbuck, to whom she would later send manuscripts for comment; the poet and scholar Theodore Weiss; and, most important, Anne Sexton, with whom Kumin rapidly became what she would call after Sexton's death "intimate friends and professional allies." While Sexton would later complain bitterly about John Holmes, Kumin has expressed a high opinion of him. She later said of that group, "We were all writing frantically in response to each other. It was wonderful and terrible all at once. It was a very yeasty and exciting time." John Holmes's best poems, Kumin told Martha Meek, were those he wrote in the company of the workshop. At Sexton's funeral, Kumin chose to recall the days of the workshop, and the eagerness with which the budding poets "prayed that our poems would rise to the top of the pile under Professor Holmes's fingers as he alternately fussed with his pipe and shuffled pages."

At first the friendship between Kumin and Sexton must have seemed unlikely. In later descriptions of their first meetings, Sexton appears as the well-dressed sophisticate, and Kumin as something of the dowdy housewife. In a conversation with both poets recorded by Elaine Showalter in 1974, Sexton recalls Kumin's appearance as "the most frump of the frumps," and Kumin recalls Sexton as "a little flower child . . . the ex-fashion model." Because Kumin had recently lost a friend to suicide, she was initially "put off by Sexton's self-dramatizing references to the mental hospital." Nevertheless, their relationship grew increasingly close and productive. According to Kumin's account of it, their telephone conversations became so frequent that each installed a second phone line in order to speak privately and at leisure.

The strain of being a housewife as well as a poet is very evident in these early years of their relationship. Sexton recounts being on the telephone, at the time of the Holmes workshop, and having to quiet her children so that she could hear Kumin read her poems. Because the children were so small, the poets could not leave them alone; therefore they relied upon the telephone to revise poems together. Kumin describes it in *To Make a Prairie:*

> I confess we sometimes connected with a phone call and kept that line linked for hours at a stretch, interrupting poem-talk to stir the spaghetti sauce, switch the laundry, or try out a new image on the typewriter; we whistled into the receiver for each other when we were ready to resume.

What is perhaps most striking about that passage is the casual integration of the daily routine of the housewife with the work of poetry. Kumin's easy movement between laundry, meal, and typewriter is telling of the pressures that her role as a wife and homemaker imposed. Lacking the framework of the women's movement, both women later described a guilty sense that their close friendship and habit of writing were wrong. They felt the need to keep poetry a secret.

The literary products of Kumin and Sexton's friendship, nevertheless, were immediate and outstanding. A great many of the poems that Sexton was writing in Holmes's workshop appeared in her first book, *To Bedlam and Part Way Back* (1960). Kumin's first book, *Halfway,* appeared in 1961. The reviewers made clear that the idea of a woman poet was still a little odd. The *Saturday Review* called her style "womanly" in its attention to detail, and the *Christian Science Monitor* found it necessary to remind its readers that the term "poetess" had fallen out of use with the Victorians.

Although Kumin has asserted that she has developed much from this first volume, and it has been, perhaps, the least well received of her volumes, much of her later development is prefigured in it. Many of the themes that Kumin would make her own appear in *Halfway:* loss and the fear of loss, cultural identity, religion, and the importance of dreams. An elegy, "One Dead Friend," prefigures many of the poems of mourning that she wrote later in the 1960s and 1970s:

poems mourning the death of her father, brother, and friends. Likewise, in the poem ''Nightmare,'' which begins as if comforting a terrified child, the line ''I hold my heartbeat on my lap and cannot comfort her'' reveals the body to be physically permeable to terror. In treating the response of the body as if it were something separate and detachable, ''Nightmare'' offers a taste of much more developed poems, such as ''Apostrophe to a Dead Friend'' and ''Body and Soul: A Meditation,'' that dwell on the split between body and mind. Poems such as ''Nightmare,'' ''The Journey: For Jane at Thirteen,'' and ''Poem for my Son'' begin the persistent theme of her ''tribal poems,'' which address Kumin's geographical and personal roots, and her sense of their overwhelming importance.

Only her father's disapproval of bathing suits prevented Kumin from becoming an Olympic or professional swimmer. Perhaps because of this early frustration of an ambition, swimming in her poems is frequently a metaphor for poetic achievement. Susan Ludvigson points out that the sestina ''High Dive: A Variant'' uses the metaphor of the diver to explore the poet's persistent challenge: ''to perfect technical skills through diligent study and practice, and then to take chances—to attempt more than one can be sure of accomplishing, no matter how high the price of failure.'' Likewise, her most unconventional experiment with form is the poem ''400-Meter Free Style,'' in which the lines imitate the swimmer's back-and-forth motion. The volume as a whole is strong evidence of Kumin's early mastery of conventional technique rather than of an experimental temperament. She skillfully uses rhyme and half rhyme as well as traditional meters.

Kumin's second book, *The Privilege* (1965), came armed with evidence of her increasing technical facility. This facility, however, is carefully tied to the developing themes and preoccupations of her poetry. These poems often meditate on poetry as a dialogue with the past. There is a new emphasis in *The Privilege* on Kumin's roots and her painful childhood experiences with anti-Semitism. Particularly in the elegies for her father, ''Lately, at Night'' and ''The Pawnbroker,'' the impact of the past on the present is a central concern. In interviews, Kumin has stressed the importance that she attributes to background and heritage. She told Karla Hammond, ''I feel I have a strong sense of tribe and ancestor, an ancestor worship or desire to find out about my roots.'' The attempt is not purely to develop a personal history, but ''the hope that the poem draws on some sort of unconscious, collective, archetypal thing so that myth and experience will cohere.'' She seems to be attempting to develop a relationship to the past from which she can draw support and strength. It is to this sense of heritage that the title seems to refer; the past gives something to the present, or the present takes something from the past.

Poems in *The Privilege* address not only Kumin's religious heritage but also the internal disquiet that it caused her. Her early life was that of a religious outsider. She grew up next to a convent in a predominantly Protestant suburb. Despite being a Jew, Kumin went to the convent school because it was convenient. ''To a child who is looking for absolutes,'' she wrote, ''these two [Christian and Jewish] opposing views of the world are terribly confusing.'' This early need to situate herself in a religious context would become an important theme in Kumin's poetry. The poem ''Mother Rosarine'' praises one of the nuns whom she remembered from childhood. God, however, would gradually become less absolute and identified more often with poetry. Echoing advice a young priest gave her friend Anne Sexton, Kumin told Martha Meek in 1975, ''Words are the only 'holy' for me. Any God that exists for me is in the typewriter keys.'' She seems to mean that it is language, rather than a divine existence, that creates form and order.

In "Sisyphus" a young girl's reaction to anti-Semitism is explored through her relationship, part fear and part awe, to a legless man given to roadside preaching. She accepts her conscription out of a sense of duty to God, and perhaps shame, to wheel the man about town. For her kindness, the man calls her a "perfect Christian child." The end-stopped and rhythmically regular lines of the second-to-last-couplet throw her reaction into stark relief against the rest of the poem, which is enjambed and relaxed:

> One day I said I was a Jew.
> I wished I had. I wanted to.
>
> The basket man is gone; the stone
> I push uphill is all my own.

In the final couplet "gone" and "stone" are a visual, but not an aural, rhyme. The unsure nature of the rhyme emphasizes the unsure nature of the claim that the "going" of the past still holds upon the present. In place of the "gone" basket man, the poet now pushes a "stone" totally "her own." It is as if the "going" has been transformed into the "stone." The impact of the passing of the past is to create a burden in the present, a burden of which the poet is in sole possession. A profound gap separates the world of the dead legless beggar from the world of the grown-up poet, but it is this gap that makes the child's silence about her religion the weight of the event, because it cannot be changed or affected. It remains whole and inaccessible to rectification. The little girl of "Sisyphus" mourns the gap between what she wanted to say and what she could not say. She must live instead with her silence. In later elegies it is made clear that figures from the past remain to haunt the present and insist on a joint possession of the past, but the little girl in "Sisyphus" is left alone, bearing a burden of which she must accept complete possession—"my own."

Another poem, "The Pawnbroker," presents the poet's relationship to the past as a debt that must be fulfilled. In Kumin's "tribal poems," acknowledging a "debt" becomes a means of claiming a cultural heritage. This poem is one of two elegies for Kumin's father in *The Privilege*. This particular one she called "the hardest poem I ever wrote." What is striking about the poem is the insistence that the poet's relationship with the dead father is one of economic exchange. The father is the poet's "creditor" and "appraiser." She writes:

> I was the bearer he paid up on demand
> with one small pearl of selfhood. Portionless,
> I am oystering still to earn it.

The metaphors are, of course, appropriate to the father's occupation. They are used to imagine the poet's relationship with the dead. The poet, calling herself the "bearer," has received "one small pearl of selfhood" for whatever it is that she has pawned. The problem then becomes how to "pay off" the debt, evening the score and assuaging grief. Figured as an economic exchange, the past can be bought off. The poet, then, is "oystering still to earn" back "the pearl of selfhood," something without price. Yet "portionless" indicates that there has been no inheritance from the father, and there is no way to pay off the debt. This is, then, the significance of the metaphor of pawning. The debt that cannot be paid to the banker becomes a debt that the banker comes back to collect; a debt owed to the pawnbroker, however, becomes the permanent loss of the item pawned.

Later in the poem the poet and her brothers drink a bottle of Scotch to alleviate the pain of "easing down the ways" their father has "ruled off the balance sheet." The process of mourning is figured as the process of pawning, in which after thirty days, "giver and lender, no longer in hock to himself. / ruled off the balance sheet." Likewise, the poet concedes her debt and forfeits what was originally pawned to the past. In actual pawning, what is left to the debtor is the ticket, a valueless reminder of what could not be salvaged from debt. As in "Sisyphus," the loss in the past results in an ambiguous figure of loss in the present. In "Sisyphus," it is the stone that symbolizes a failure that cannot be rectified. In "The Pawnbroker," it is the ticket, representing a debt that is forfeited. Owing everything, but unable to pay it, the poet instead calls it even and accepts this exchange. This relationship to the past will change over the course of Kumin's career as she explores the potential and healing power of poetry. Here the "I" is stabilized by the past. Memory does not erode the poet's sense of self but instead reinforces it. These poems view the past as irrecoverable and respond to it with the need to make sense of it, even though they lack access to its truth.

Although Kumin is best known as a poet, she also has produced a substantial body of prose fiction that has received critical acclaim. In addition, alone and with Sexton, she has written many children's books. In interviews, Kumin has stated that she considers herself equally a fiction writer and a poet. They are, however, quite distinct enterprises to her. In contrast to poetry, which is about the unconscious and the symbolic events of dreams, and so "closer to the well-spring," "fiction is more a matter of invention and manipulation. There's much less shaping paradoxically, in being a poet than there is in being a writer of novels." In 1965, the year that *The Privilege* was published, Kumin's first novel, *Through Dooms of Love,* appeared. The story works over much the same ground as the tribal poems. Set in 1939, it is based on the conflict between a Bolshevik daughter and her pawnbroker father. The *New York Times* review of *Through Dooms of Love* praised its "lyric intensity" and the "luminous brilliance" with which Kumin defines her characters.

Kumin's next novel, *The Passions of Uxport* (1968), is a revealing account of her emerging relationship with Anne Sexton. Despite Sexton's strenuous denial that she is represented by the character Sukey, Kumin affirms that the novel is based on the early years of their relationship. Diane Middlebrook claims that Sexton even had an enthusiastic hand in writing whole speeches. The story concerns two suburban housewives: Sukey, who has a death wish, and Hallie, who has a psychosomatic pain in her stomach. While flirting with sentimentality (the novel begins with a mare named Cassandra failing to conceive and ends with her success), the book is most interesting for being about the bond between women. Elaine Showalter comments, "There are very few relationships in books that are like it [Hallie and Sukey's]. Women are generally supposed to destroy each other." Because of this new theme, book reviewers expressed much uncertainty as to what to make of *The Passions of Uxport.* Many of the reviews seem puzzled by the central drama concerning such ordinary characters as housewives, and even offended by the suggestion that the problems of suburbia might be worth noting. In the *New York Times Book Review,* Mary Carter compares the novel to a television drama, dismissing it as "two housewives' neuroses." Carter seems vexed that "the anguish seems so arbitrary, risen not from a universal, but a private source, willful, insulated and resistant." Her response to the novel, while admiring of the style, is a rather prim dislike for the characters, and she closes by sneering that Sukey does not seem to find her children sufficient. The *Yale Review* protests that the psychoanalyst is not handled with sufficient depth and sympathy, and finally describes the problems of the Sexton character as being rooted in the sexual loss of her husband.

Questions of growing up Jewish in a Christian culture return powerfully in Kumin's next volume of poetry, *The Nightmare Factory* (1970).

Kumin seems to have shed any reluctance to embrace this portion of her heritage. The same debt to the past that was present in the previous collection is apparent in her address to another ancestor, but now is gratefully acknowledged: ''Welcome ancestor, Rosenburg, The Tailor, / I choose to be a lifetime in your debt.'' The third section of the book is titled ''Tribal Poems,'' and it focuses on family members. The fourth section is a series of love poems, some of which detail an apparently fictional adulterous love affair. These, however, seem less convincing than her more affirmative love poems. This may reflect Kumin's uneasiness with the conventions of the confessional mode.

Written to exorcise a series of bad dreams about her father, who had just died, ''The Nightmare Factory'' was a way of surviving something ''inchoate and very painful.'' ''I then had this fantasy,'' Kumin told Martha Meek, ''that there is some distant Detroit-of-the-Soul where all bad dreams are created and that out of the warehouse of goods we are assigned certain recurrent nightmares. . . . One must descend into the abyss and dream the nightmare of one's choice and dream it through to the very end.'' Raising the unconscious into the conscious is, therefore, a major concern of the poem: ''I have a lot of reverence for what goes on at the dream level in the unconscious—those symbolic events,'' Kumin told Martha Meek. ''I have a tremendous reverence for raising it up into language, which I think is what it's all about.'' She uses dreams as a way of addressing an unbearable truth. Some things are manageable only through dreams, she seems to imply. But those unmanageable truths are not just personal; they reach back into the general historical experience:

> night after night in
> the bowels of good citizens
> nazis and cossacks ride
> klansmen and judases.

Another poem, ''The Presence,'' is also a meditation on absent things. As ''The Nightmare Factory'' attempts to imagine the unimaginable unconscious, so ''The Presence'' attempts to penetrate the veil of otherness that separates nature from the mind. In its concentration on traces rather than substance, the poem is more reminiscent of ''The Wood-Pile'' by Robert Frost. In that poem the speaker encounters a pile of firewood in a place in the forest that seems to be no place:

> The view was all in lines . . .
> Too much alike to mark a name or place by
> So as to say for certain I was here
> Or somewhere else.

Where the woodpile lies, seems to resist man. No one's footprints appear in the snow around the woodpile; the ''hard snow'' seems to repel prints from the poet's shoes. Nature itself seems to have absorbed that person and his work. It is the work of poetry to recover the lost story. Like the mysterious ''someone'' in Frost's poem, the ''presence'' in Kumin's poem is understood only as a ''something.'' Its reality and importance are insisted on, even though they are evident only from traces left behind—marks left in the snow.

> Something went crabwise
> across the snow this morning.
> Something went hard and slow
> over our hayfield.

Kumin, like Frost, does not accept the otherness and inaccessibility of the ''something'' that has passed out of sight. In the lines that follow, it is the role of the imagination to reconstruct, as a detective does, that ''something's'' identity, what that presence could have been. She considers first absurd yet familiarized anthropomorphic images, a ''raccoon/lugging a knapsack,'' or a ''porcupine/carrying a tennis racket.'' Whatever it was, however, she imagines at last that it must have been linked to the natural process of killing and eating. Her last suggestion is a scene believably out of nature: a red fox dragging its prey back to its lair. The traces, though, are already in the process of becoming renewed:

> those bones are seeds now
> pure as baby teeth
> lined up in the burrow.

The last lines insist that even the devoured carcass, in the very act of its consumption, has become a "seed," a potential to become something new. The transformation of the bones to seeds is not done literally, as one might imagine the merely naturalistic observation might have been. Bones are what is not eaten, what is left behind as the residue of the animal. Rather, the bones are seeds for the imagination, which can build from residue, as the entire scene is built up from mere markings on the snow.

Despite her insistence on the distinct identity of whatever it was that has passed, the poet retains a critical role in nature. The poem does not end with the imagined scene enacted below ground, where it remains out of the reach of the human, but with the reintroduction of the observing "I" into the landscape. The poet, too, drifts over the landscape, relying on mediation from the remains of the animal that went into making her snowshoes:

> I cross on snowshoes
> cunningly woven from
> the skin and sinews of
> something else that went before.

Her passage over the snow, then, is similar to the imagination's reconstitution of the unseen animal, and the chewed-up bones. From something left behind, the remains of something natural, she has gained the power to interact with nature. Again something dead is the means for gaining an insight or passage. Ludvigson sees the poem

as demonstrating the "irresponsible dominance" of man over the natural world. She allies it with "The Vealers" in protesting humanity's misuse of the natural. Perhaps because the poem is in the first person, however, Kumin does not seem to allow so much distance between herself and the subject of the poem. Instead, she seems invested in this as a necessary sacrifice. This attitude is one of profound respect for the otherness of nature, of allowing that nature has an autonomous existence. Kumin is allowed to approach nature only through the traces of what once was. In another poem, "Country House," she imagines the world without humans. The house of the title is a space where things run riot, "the walls break into conversation," "Two clocks tick themselves witless." Unstructured by time, this is a place that is incomprehensible to normal experience. It might, however, be accessible to poetry.

Although these later sections of the book, and particularly the title poem, are decidedly dark, the book is on balance an affirmation. The first part, "Pasture Poems," is much more typical Kumin nature poetry. It contains the first of a series of "Henry Manley" poems that serve as a precursor to the more famous "hermit" poems in her Pulitzer Prize–winning volume, *Up Country*. These poems are not entirely distinct from the poems in the later sections, sharing the theme of pressing against the isolation of the mind. "Hello, Hello Henry" is a poem about communication and the difficulty of communication. While Kumin's older neighbor, "shy as a girl come calling," walks two miles to ask her to telephone him once in a while, the poet misses her own telephone call made to her home in Boston. Neither the telephone nor a face-to-face meeting seems adequate communication. The poem ends by again attempting to talk: "Hello, hello Henry? Is that you?" It is not clear, however, that even the poem is received. We are not sure that Manley has answered. Making that connection is vitally important for Kumin. Henry

Manley is a figure of mortality and aging, but most important, he is one who is alone. As Alicia Ostriker wrote in the *New York Times,* "If she [Kumin] had her way, no loved (or hated) human or animal would die unremembered."

Up Country won the Pulitzer Prize in 1973. The volume takes the New England countryside as its heart, strongly recalling Frost and Thoreau. The poems are not transcendental, however, in that Kumin does not imply that mankind should or can merge with nature. Joyce Carol Oates acknowledges Kumin's debt to her New England predecessors, "though in my opinion Kumin's poetry gives us a sharp-edged, unflinching and occasionally nightmarish subjectivity exasperatingly absent in Thoreau." That subjectivity, embodied in the eight "hermit" poems that begin the volume, is asserted in the face of a life in which "nothing is sure." Oates claims that Kumin's more powerful restatement of the transcendental experience is that it is rooted firmly in experience, "however private or eccentric."

Despite its apparent orientation toward nature poetry, Kumin has acknowledged the impact of Anne Sexton on *Up Country.* Sexton actually named it (as Kumin named Sexton's *Transformations*). Barbara Swan, who illustrated several volumes for Sexton, contributed drawings. Sexton's input was vital in the final wording of the last stanza of "The Hermit Meets the Skunk." Kumin told Diana Hume George:

> When I wrote "The Hermit Meets the Skunk," I probably rewrote that final stanza thirty times, because I couldn't decide on the order of those final things. And so of course I showed them to Annie, and she said immediately, the mother bed, the ripe taste of carrion, the green kiss. That was the order. I just absolutely trusted her instincts in a situation like that.

In an interview after Sexton's death, Kumin acknowledged that Sexton could at times function as a type of poetic "id." She considered that her "directness, openness" and her "ability to confront feelings" were a "natural outcome" of the development of her relationship with Sexton.

The figure of the hermit, Kumin has acknowledged, is a close stand-in for herself. In their interview, Kumin agreed with Meek that the family, the tribe, is the last unit of society that can be "balanced between order and disorder." She denied that the hermit repudiates modern life; rather, he is just a "cop-out." Kumin noted that the writer's profession is by nature solitary. "You lock yourself up to do your job," she told Meek. It is this extreme sense of privacy and isolation that serves as a revision of Thoreau and the idea of the visionary. Ludvigson notes that, confronted with mounting unknowns, Kumin's hermit responds by seeming to go on as he ever has. The poems end with a return to the ordinariness of everyday life in "The Hermit Picks Berries":

> The hermit whistles as he picks.
> Later he will put on his shirt
> and walk to town for some cream.

What is gained from nature is a matter-of-fact acceptance of the close relationship that humanity has with nature.

Other poems are in the form of extended observations of things in nature, as in "Stones," where Kumin surprises us with rocks.

> Eyeless and unsurprised they behave
> in the manner of stones: swallow turnips, heave graves
> rise up openmouthed into walls and from time
> to time imitate oysters or mushrooms.

The priority of description in this poem recalls the importance that things in themselves hold for Kumin. The stones are not seen as doing anything special; it is the power of the poet's imagination in seeing them that is extraordinary. The power of description makes the poem. Nature's surface here is impenetrable to seeing, permeable only to the imagination.

The autonomy of things has been very important for Kumin's poetics. In *House, Bridge, Fountain, Gate* (1975), she catalogs her usual subjects with a detailed accuracy but a refusal to elaborate. The title of the book derives from the importance of naming. Kumin found the title in Louis Simpson's memoirs, *North of Jamaica:* "Poetry is a mixture of thoughts and objects," he wrote, "it is as though things are trying to express themselves through us. It may be, as a poet had said, we are here only to say house, bridge, fountain, gate." She placed this sentence in the book as an epigraph. In her interview with Meek, Kumin stressed the importance of the naming and particularization of things: "I think that the one thing that's been consistently true about my poetry is this determination to get at that authenticity of detail."

In the *New York Times Book Review,* Helen Vendler complained that *House, Bridge, Fountain, Gate* suffers from a "disease of similes." As examples, she gives "naked as almonds," kisses like "polka dots," and a visit "as important as summer." While there may be some truth to this charge, there are also counterexamples of similes that seem especially apt and startlingly fresh: Ludvigson mentions "Grandmother's corset / spread out like a filleted fish." It might be best, however, to remember that simile and metaphor go hand in hand with the project of naming. To produce a simile is to find a new name that surprises the reader by revealing a side of the thing that is ordinarily forgotten or missed. Robert Frost often uses similes in this way. In "The Silken Tent," for instance, he constructs a sonnet by exploring at length the possibilities in a single unlikely simile—comparing a women to a tent. Just as a tent balloons in the breeze as if it were ready to fly, yet remains firmly staked to the earth, so the woman in Frost's poem looks res-olutely heavenward with "sureness of soul," yet is bound to the earth by "silken ties of love and thought." The unlikely simile precisely captures a tension in the woman's personality.

A woman is not usually thought of as being like a tent. Frost's surprising simile invites the reader to look at the familiar with new eyes. Likewise, Kumin's poem "Heaven as Anus" uses the simile in the title to make the reader rethink his or her presuppositions about both "heaven" and "anus." Kumin described this to Karla Hammond as an "anti-war, anti-behavior-modification poem"; she uses the process of renaming to disturb our commonsense notions of good and bad, heaven and earth. After graphically describing the torture of animals in Defense Department tests, Kumin asks,

> And what is this to the godhead,
> these squeals, whines, writhings, unexpected
>   jumps,
> whose children burn alive, booby-trap the dead,
> lop ears and testicles, core and disembowel?

The answer may be that God does not care, and that realization may make possible the shocking simile of the title, a yoking together of the idea of a holy place with the anus. The poem, however, goes further. It insists on raising up the idea of excrement even as it deflates the idea of heaven.

> It all ends at the hole. No words may enter
> the house of excrement. We will meet there
> as the sphincter of the good Lord opens wide
> and He takes us all inside.

Heaven and anus meet in the impossibility of appeal and the limit of knowing. There is no knowledge of what lies ahead, no passing through in the same form. Indeed, even the passage into heaven is equated with a sense of the reversal of the usual bodily functions. In "The Excrement Poem," Kumin writes, "I honor shit for saying: We go on." Body and soul are inseparable here. Sybil Estes writes, "Kumin, unlike Bradstreet or Dickinson, cannot imagine soul or Spirit apart from body or matter. . . . For her, the body gives evidence that Spirit is."

The Retrieval System (1978), Kumin's next volume, is dedicated to her daughters. Alicia Ostriker said that "no poet writes more richly and more subtly of mother-daughter relations." Perhaps this dedication's emphasis on inheritance and renewal was a reaction to the profound impact of a tragedy outside of the family. Anne Sexton committed suicide in October 1974, just before the publication of *House, Bridge, Fountain, Gate.* Since that book was already at the press, it includes no poems that address her suicide. It is not until *The Retrieval System* that Sexton's death is faced at length. The incompleteness of Sexton's goodbye is the subject of "Splitting Wood at Six Above"; Kumin addresses her friend: "See you tomorrow, you said. / You lied." The two friends had met the day before the suicide to review galleys for Sexton's upcoming book. Kumin recalls that Sexton gave no warning of the decision she apparently had made: "when she was ready to kill herself," Kumin recalls, "she kept it a deep dark secret." Sexton's death seems to have precipitated a crisis in Kumin's poetic career as well as her personal life. At a Women's Writer's Conference in 1979, Kumin informed a public audience that she was very concerned that she could not write after Sexton died, that she had lost a vital link to her art. For a writer who had previously written elegies on deaths in the family, Sexton's death touched a deeper nerve, one that rendered the project of elegy difficult. Sexton's death was a challenge to poetry that previous deaths had not been.

Sybil Estess admires "Splitting Wood at Six Above" as one of Kumin's saddest poems about Sexton. She argues that "the underlying thematic question of the poem, however, is what happens to the 'soul' of something after death." Although

Kumin seems to settle with herself that Sexton has safely reached "the other side," the poem focuses on what still bothers her, the "sound of your [Sexton's] going." The poem, it seems, has been sparked by the sound of the ax into the wood, which Kumin associates with the sound of the soul leaving the body:

> It is the sound
> of your going I drive
> into heartwood.

What is disconcerting is the sense that the poet is driving the sound itself into the wood, rather than simply producing it. Although she is responsible for repeating the very sound that torments her, that sound seems dissociated from the actions presumably producing it. Naming of the wood with a body part, repeated again in the next lines, where the split wood lies "face up," identifies Sexton with nature in a particularly gruesome way. Further, metrically, the poem carries the chopping sound associated with Sexton's "going." Estess points out that "the chopping rhythm of the poem suggests the hard, flint-like reality of being split apart"; forty-three lines end with a stressed monosyllable, and many of the disyllabic line endings are spondaic, both syllables stressed equally. Far from being gone, Sexton's spirit is imbued in nature and everything surrounding the poet. Yet Kumin derives no comfort from her friend's presence. It seems, rather, to be threatening.

Kumin's inability to dispel her sense of guilt or anger at Sexton's death might be, in part, linked to her unwillingness to attach an easy explanation to the suicide. In an interview with Diana Hume George, coeditor of Sexton's *Selected Poems,* Kumin declined the invitation to frame Sexton's suicide in political and philosophical terms. Sexton's suicide, Kumin insisted, was not a "protest against mortality," as George suggested, but a reaction to the overwhelming "sense of total hopelessness" that overcame her. While feminism might have offered a valuable support system, Kumin told George, it would not have addressed the critical problem, which was medical: "If she had stayed on Thorazine, in my opinion she would be alive today." Sexton's death, in other words, served no cause, responded to no politics.

In two essays, one printed in the collection *Aging and Gender in Literature,* the other in *Original Essays on the Poetry of Anne Sexton,* Diana Hume George has produced some of the more interesting academic writing on Kumin, focusing most usefully on the elegies for Sexton. According to George, Sexton's death was a turning point in Kumin's career. In *Original Essays,* she argues that "since Sexton's death, Kumin has become Sexton's successor, her inheritor, the voice that speaks both of and for Sexton now that Sexton is silent." The implication is that Kumin, after Sexton's death, developed very Sexton-like qualities in her poetry. The two poets, according to George, are inextricably linked, differentiated only by minor characteristics and the "choice" each made, one to live and one to die. This argument rests on the difference between Kumin's poetry of mourning before and after Sexton's suicide. In *Aging and Gender,* George argues that "although many of these poems [on the deaths of "her uncles, her brother, her animals, her Anne"] were written before Anne Sexton's death, that death seems to have allowed her to do sustained instead of intermittent mourning." She points out that in the elegies Sexton joins Kumin in "every activity of daily life." The conversations between them are always picked up as if they were constantly ongoing. All of Kumin's elegies to Sexton could have been written at the same time; there seems to be no progression of the style or mourning. For George, that "sustained mourning" is what allows Kumin to step into Sexton's shoes. George admits that, of Kumin's work, she vastly prefers the poetry written

after the suicide, which she calls Kumin's "mature period," to that written before.

It is true that after Sexton's death, Kumin's poetry takes a radically different attitude toward the dead. In a 1917 essay, "Mourning and Melancholia," Sigmund Freud distinguishes between mourning, which is the normal healing process of grief, and melancholia, a pathological state of interminable sorrow that defies cure. It has been suggested by Peter Sacks, in *The English Elegy: Studies in the Genre from Spenser to Yeats* (1985), that elegy plays a role in the normal process of mourning. Sacks argues that an elegy, by working through the loss of its object, assists the poet in overcoming sorrow and proceeding with life. Kumin's elegies for Sexton, however, do not seem to follow this model. Instead of providing a healing counterweight to Sexton's death, they appear to be bound to a repetition of the loss. In "Itinerary of an Obsession" Kumin addresses her dead friend, "here you come / leaping out of the coffin again." Instead of the enabling relationship that she had ascribed to the dead animals that made up her snowshoes, and the power of the dead and absent relatives in her tribal poetry, Sexton as a dead friend becomes a persistent shade, refusing to stay safely buried. Another critic, Jahan Ramazani, suggests in *Poetry of Mourning: The Modern Elegy from Hardy to Heaney* (1994) that this type of poem, an elegy of melancholy rather than of mourning, is a distinctly twentieth-century phenomenon.

In its structure, Kumin's next book, *Our Ground Time Here Will Be Brief* (1982), revises her previous view of the past. *Our Ground Time* includes both new poems and a selection of the best poems from her previous six volumes. Unconventionally, the poems are ordered from most recent to earliest. Reading backward seems to demand that the older poems be read in the light of the newer ones. With this odd configuration of the volume, Kumin seems to insist on the priority of the present in understanding the past, rather than the more apparent need to have the past in order to understand the present, which was the theme of ''The Pawnbroker'' and ''Sisyphus.'' Priority is given to the most recent work, as if it were the most relevant. In *The Privilege* and *The Nightmare Factory,* the past enters the present in symbols of its loss. In *The Retrieval System* and *Our Ground Time Here Will Be Brief,* the past enters the present still living, and impossible to escape.

Of the series of stunning elegies for Sexton included in *Our Ground Time,* perhaps the most affecting is ''Apostrophe to a Dead Friend.'' As the subtitle ''(On Being Interviewed by Her Biographer)'' makes clear, this poem comes out of an experience of testimony: the retelling of the friendship between the two poets to Sexton's biographer, Diane Wood Middlebrook. The first lines of the poem divide the voice of the poet from her body and her ''gender'':

> Little by little my gender drifts away
> leaving the bones of this person
> whose shoe size was your size.

Referring to her body as ''this person'' objectifies it. Further, because the speaker refers to her body as if it were a corpse—''bones''—and puts her own shoe size in the past tense, her body seems to become the object mourned. In the last stanza the confusion of time suggests that the dead Sexton is more present than the live body that belongs to the poet's voice.

> Soon I will be sixty.
> How it was with you now
> hardly more vivid than how
> it is without you, I carry
> the sheer weight of the telling
> like a large infant, on one hip.
> I who am remaindered in the conspiracy
> doom, doom on my lips.

Although the syntax is difficult, it seems that the ''How it was'' in the past is more vivid than

the ''how it is'' in the present. The line ''How it was with you now'' has the effect of making ''was'' seem as if it were ''now.'' Confusing the past with the present, the living with the dead, the poet reverses the neat process of inheritance from the dead formed in her earlier poetry. Carried in place of an infant, ''telling'' takes the place of inheritance. But this metaphor does not equate the telling with the infant, as one might expect; the metaphor only describes in what way the telling is carried. Telling, then, is only carried like an infant; it does not have the infant's power of continuing a lineage and producing descendants. In place of reproduction, the poem allows only a continual telling. Unlike her earlier poems, which contemplated a relationship with the past that was productive, in this poem Kumin asserts a relationship to the past that produces nothing but a repetition of the difference between ''how it was'' and ''how it is.'' It produces only a repetition of loss.

Many of the themes that Kumin develops in the elegies to Sexton are echoed throughout these two volumes in poems that otherwise seem to having nothing to do with Sexton's death. In ''Henry Manley, Living Alone, Keeps Time,'' from *The Retrieval System,* Kumin returns to Manley, who has, in the meanwhile, aged and, ''los[ing] words when the light fades,'' stands in danger of losing his grip on language. As Ludvigson notes, in Manley's awkward attempts to remember the words *''window, wristwatch, cup, knife''* we hear a faded echo of the confidence in the power of naming that provided the title for Kumin's *House, Bridge, Fountain, Gate.* Manley's difficulty with language suggests the difficulty that Kumin's poetry has encountered in assimilating loss. Another poem, ''Henry Manley Looks Back,'' in *Our Ground Time Here Will Be Brief,* explores the failure of memory as a compensation for loss. Convalescing in bed with a broken hip, ''Henry loves / his new life as the sage of yesteryear,'' but, face to face with the collapse of his home that results from his absence, Manley can only muse *"You can't look back."* He is no longer able to accept stories about the past as compensation for what is gone.

In "Body and Soul: A Meditation," also in *The Retrieval System,* the soul is disassociated from the body in much the same way as it is in the elegy for Sexton, "Apostrophe to a Dead Friend." Like the division between gender, voice, and body in that elegy, in this poem there is a division between soul, body, and voice. In an optimistic tone, Estess interprets "Body and Soul: A Meditation" to mean that the "soul, or Spirit, both exists and survives the body's destruction." The poem, however, undermines such an optimistic reading. Nowhere apparent in the body, the soul arrives stealthily in a simile:

> Still unlocated, drifting,
> my airmail half-ounce soul
> shows up from time to time
> like those old-fashioned
> doctors who used to cheer
> their patients in girls' boarding schools
> with midnight bedside visits.

While the soul may continue to exist, and while it returns to the body, it does so in the guise of the deeply suspicious figure of the doctor. An "old-fashioned" doctor who is prone to "midnight bedside visits" may be a figure of nostalgia, but he may also be a rapist or child molester. A few lines later the relationship between the soul and the body is explicitly sexualized, when soul and "we [body and voice] touch tongue." In these lines, the power of the soul over the body seems threatening. Their reunion may be joyful, but it is just as likely to be a moment of trauma.

Kumin's next book, *The Long Approach* (1985), takes up where *Our Ground Time Here* left off, with the question of the poet's responsibility to the world. Both titles refer to air travel, but whereas *Our Ground Time* implies the brev-

ity and transitoriness of life, *The Long Approach* refers to a careful, and permanent, setting down. Printed last in the volume, the title poem departs from the rural setting in favor of a highway scene, and then an imagined plane ride. The "long approach," we find out, is the soft landing that a horse needs when it is transported by plane. A horse is loaded facing the tail of the plane so that it can brace its feet during takeoff. At landing, however, the horse is on its own, relying on luck and the pilot's willingness to set down with an easy "long approach." Here, at the very end of the volume, Kumin reveals to us what she has been doing. The poems together provide Kumin with a soft landing from the crisis of Sexton's death and a reentrance into her long-running theme of the plight of nature and humanity in a world that increasingly wishes to deny both.

In structure, this book moves through three sections, from private to public to the farm. The first section is a collection of detailed remembrances and vignettes in family poems addressed, once more, to Kumin's father, mother, and ancestors. At the heart of "The Chain," a pair of braids discovered coiled in a hatbox brings the poet to imagine having her mother's memories. The poem warns us, however, that recovering the past is not simply a personal affair. This is a "nation losing its memory," dedicated to "turning / its battle grounds into parking lots." Other poems in the volume dwell on the risks inherent in remembering. In "Introducing the Fathers," a pair of dead fathers, Kumin's and a friend's, are likened to a pair of hot air balloons: "Macy daddies ready for the big parade." While conversing, they become something like a pair of grotesque dandies, "matching net worths, winning big at blackjack," and "rising toward the Big Crash." "Big Crash" refers, of course, to the Great Depression, but it also implies that there is a point when memory itself becomes dangerous, as an overfilled hot air balloon might explode.

The next section is devoted to public poems, concerned with Kumin's Judaism and the burden of history. In details of a trip to Israel, and musings on politics, Kumin attempts to situate herself in history. Critics have complained that the politics, especially the meditations on the atomic bomb, are predictable. Wendy Lesser, in the *Washington Post Book World,* complains that the "poems on 'issues' . . . founder on their opinion making." Nevertheless, Kumin's efforts to site her distinctive voice inside this historical frame are frequently unique and gripping. History, and the poet's relationship to it, have always been in the background of her poetry—in "The Nightmare Factory," for instance. In this volume, history seems to be the impact of the unpredictable and unimaginable—terrorism, nuclear war, the holocaust—on the individual. For Kumin, the past and public resurface only by colliding sharply with the present and personal. In "In the Absence of Bliss," subtitled "Museum of the Diaspora, Tel Aviv," she writes,

> We walk away from twenty-two
> graphic centuries of kill-the-Jew
> and hail, of all things, a Mercedes
> taxi,

which is all the more surprising for including a couplet. In these lines, the past gains its power by disrupting the way that things are seen in the present. Unless seen in the light of history, a Mercedes taxi is just another car. These poems, however they raise difficult questions, refuse to resort to easy answers. Kumin recognizes that the urge to self-immolation is deep inside the practice of religion, and not limited to the crimes of historical figures. Her attempt to ground speculation on a "higher moral plane" is necessarily a failure, one that ends on the same note as "In the Absence of Bliss" ends: with "No answers. Only questions."

The third section of *The Long Approach* is titled "On the Farm." In the context of the book,

however, these poems come to query the possibility of a simple pastoral retreat out of the world, in the mode of the hermit. The first poem of this last section opens with an apology "for all the snow falling in / this poem so early in the season." It proceeds to weave an elaborate metaphor around the snow, never surrendering the primary reference to the weather but refusing to lose sight of larger issues. This is an "elegiac snow," a "biographical snow," weather that is to be endured. The snow, in cutting off the outside world, may stifle the sounds of the bombs and cries of the previous section, but it does not eliminate them. In "In the Upper Pastures," a title that might imply the promise of a route toward the transcendental, Kumin asks, "Is this a pastoral?" Her answer is that despite the wealth of pastoral detail, the animal skins and smells, there is no cause for comfort: "Each of us whimpers his way through the forest alone." What the poem can do is preserve a small space, not unlike a pasture, "out of the weather." A "small thing," to be sure, yet one that at least provides a minimum of shelter.

Kumin's volumes, *Nurture* (1989) and *Looking for Luck* (1992), return to pastoral scenes similar to those of *Up Country.* This has left her vulnerable to criticisms, such as that of Lisa Zeidner, that "[Kumin] seems so at peace with herself and the world, so downright nice, that it is hard to imagine what tension or turbulence keeps her writing. In *Looking for Luck,* as in past collections, she sets herself the daunting task of documenting ordinary happiness. Whole poems concern not bliss but contentment." This criticism, however, is far from self-evident. One might recall the found poem, "You Are in Bear Country," that opens *The Long Approach.* Kumin breaks into poetic lines with a public service pamphlet warning the camper of the danger from grizzly bears. What appears to be pastoral poetry, she implies, might well reveal itself to be bear country.

Carol Muske argues that the poems in *Nurture* are better seen as an ongoing writing of elegies for nature: "These poems are exhaustive in their sorrow: they are predominantly short, brutal, elegies for the natural world. She recites, in bitter, gripping litanies, the roster of extinct life-forms, along with those about to be extinct, and casts a cynical eye on humankind, the 'unaware' species responsible for the destruction of the living world." Remarking on the terse, understated couplets, Muske says, "The overall effect is one of anguished enumeration—as if the poet stood on the deck of a sinking Noah's ark, counting again each animal we are losing." Nowhere is the disconnection between Kumin's complacent image and the hard-edged elegiac tone of much of her poetry as apparent as in the cover of *Nurture,* a fawn nesting in a grassy bower. Kumin complained at the publisher's decision to market the book in this fashion. She told Jo-Ann Mapson, "They stuck me with that terrible Bambi cover that looks like it ought to be on the front of a feminine hygiene product."

In the title poem of *Nurture,* Kumin issues a challenge to the critical cynicism that accuses her of "an overabundance of maternal genes." The poem goes on to insist on the value of this "fault." Kumin imagines a wild child brought to her home, mute and uncomprehending, for her to care for. This is not, however, merely a case of an overprotective mother. As Muske points out, instead of merely trying to appropriate the wild child and "smother the wild creature with love," Kumin wishes to "find a way to talk to wildness." In *House, Bridge, Fountain, Gate,* Kumin insisted on the importance of naming things. Here the process of naming lies in its ability not merely to bond members of society together but also to insist on a place in the social for what seems to be outside of its protection. The wild child is recovered through language, through the language that

we two, same and not-same,
might have constructed from sign,
scratch, grimace, grunt, vowel:

Laughter our first noun, and our long verb, howl.

Kumin's project of extending language to the speechless extends as well to natural things. In "Sleeping with Animals," the poet insists that we are bound by languages that are available to us merely as a result of being loving creatures. Watching and touching her horse as it sleeps, Kumin writes,

What we say to each other in the cold black
of April, conveyed in a wordless yet perfect
language of touch and tremor, connects
us most surely to the wet cave we all
once burst from gasping, naked or furred,
into our separate species.

We are bound to animals by a sense of common existence that is as sure and palpable as language, should we choose to acknowledge it. Other poems also associate the possession of a voice with the ability to resist extinction. In "Bringing Back the Trumpeter Swan," for example, the cost of bringing back the "klaxon"-voiced trumpeter swan in the nest of the mute swan is the "eggs of the mute." This poem, and others, recall Marianne Moore's "He 'Digesteth Harde Yron,' " in which the ostrich is deemed heroic for his resistance to being made into a symbol. Like Moore's ostrich, Kumin's animals insist on their separate and autonomous existence, and thus the real importance of their deaths.

The prologue of *Looking for Luck* begins with a prayerlike statement of belief in the power of transformation:

I believe in magic. I believe in the rights of
animals to leap out of our skins
as recorded in the Kiowa legend:
Directly there was a boy where the bear had been.

The border between human and animal, the world and poetry, viewed as permeable, is at the heart of this book. It is no coincidence that Kumin chooses as an epigraph a line from Howard Nemerov appealing to a flight of swallows to know that "poems are not / The point. Finding again the world, / That is the point." In this spirit, she gives the title "*Ars Poetica:* A Found Poem" to a monologue in which a trainer gains the trust of a foal. The first part of the title, "*Ars Poetica,*" uses the process of approaching a wild animal as a metaphor for the process by which a poem is realized. Never called a "foal," but only "him," the foal holds the place of the perfectly realized poem. Although in a note at the back of the book Kumin reveals that this is indeed a "found poem," drawn from the words of a horse trainer, the subtitle "found poem" also refers to the horse itself, discovered beautiful and whole in nature. As in *Nurture,* communicating with nature and finding a poem are the same process.

Using nature, however, bears risks. Kumin's poem "Taking the Lambs to Market" acknowledges that the use of nature is destructive, however much our own desires may be gratified. In "The Presence" Kumin willingly paid the price for a privileged view of nature—the body of an animal destroyed to make her snowshoes; in "Taking the Lambs to Market" she insists on acknowledging that this is a necessary hypocrisy. Even Keats, she tells us, after imagining a type of unity with a sparrow, sat down to a dinner of mutton. The "naming" that has played such an important role in her poetry is here used to tell her butcher exactly what cuts of meat she wants. In this poem the butcher stands for one who, "no matter how much we deplore his profession," "deserves our praise." Perhaps he merits praise precisely because, as a "decent man who blurs the line of sight / between our conscience and our appetite," the butcher makes clear to us our own complicity in the destruction of what we admire.

In the epilogue poem to this volume, "The Rendezvous," Kumin returns to the figure of the bear. The first four sentences do not have verbs

or subjects. They are assertions of "how," as if the poem is a paraphrase of another story. We are told first "how" the bear's trail through the forest is; then "how," "according to the legend," a woman confronted by a bear should remove her clothes, as bears are capable of feeling shame and will run away from the sight of a naked woman; "how" the poet herself meets a bear and then removes her clothes. Instead of fleeing, however, the bear reciprocates by removing his fur, "which he casts to the ground / for a rug." Their actions serve to break down the differences between them. The bear begins acting human; the poet, naked, might be viewed as becoming more animal-like. The volume closes by repeating "how":

> How
> can he run away, unfurred?
> How can I, without any clothes?
>
> How we prepare a new legend.

Looking for Luck ends with an affirmation that even if this new story of man and nature intermingled cannot yet be told, and perhaps can never be told, at least the warning against pastoral that appeared in "You Are in Bear Country" has been circumvented. Although the poet admits that she is "wet with fear," she has come to confront nature once more.

Selected Bibliography

WORKS OF MAXINE KUMIN

FICTION

Through Dooms of Love. New York: Harper & Row, 1965.

The Passions of Uxport. New York: Harper & Row, 1968.

The Abduction. New York: Harper & Row, 1971.
The Designated Heir. New York: Viking, 1974.

SHORT STORIES

Why Can't We Live Together like Civilized Human Beings? New York: Viking, 1982.
Women, Animals, and Vegetables: Essays and Stories. New York: Norton, 1994.

ESSAYS

To Make a Prairie: Essays on Poets, Poetry, and Country Living. Ann Arbor: University of Michigan Press, 1979.
In Deep: Country Essays. New York: Viking, 1987.

POETRY

Halfway. New York: Harper & Row, 1961.
The Privilege. New York: Harper & Row, 1965.
The Nightmare Factory. New York: Harper & Row, 1970.
Up Country: Poems of New England. New York: Harper & Row, 1972.
House, Bridge, Fountain, Gate. New York: Viking, 1975.
The Retrieval System. New York: Viking, 1978.
Our Ground Time Here Will Be Brief. New York: Viking, 1982.
Closing the Ring. Bucknell University Fine Editions, Series in Contemporary Poetry. Edited by John Wheatcroft. Lewisburg, Pa.: Press of Appletree Valley/Bucknell University, 1984.
The Long Approach. New York: Viking, 1985.
Nurture. New York: Viking, 1989.
Looking for Luck. New York: Norton, 1992.

CHILDREN'S BOOKS.

Sebastian and the Dragon. New York: Putnam's 1960.
Follow the Fall. New York: Putnam's, 1961.
Spring Things. New York: Putnam's, 1961.
A Summer Story. New York: Putnam's, 1961.
A Winter Friend. New York: Putnam's, 1961.
No One Writes a Letter to the Snail. New York: Putnam's 1962.
Archibald, the Traveling Poodle. New York: Putnam's, 1963.
Eggs of Things. New York: Putnam's, 1963. Written with Anne Sexton.

The Beach before Breakfast. New York: Putnam's, 1964.
More Eggs of Things. New York: Putnam's, 1964. Written with Anne Sexton.
Speedy Digs Downside Up. New York: Putnam's, 1964.
Paul Bunyan. New York: Putnam's, 1966.
Faraway Farm. New York: Norton, 1967.
The Wonderful Babies of 1809 and Other Years. New York: Putnam's, 1968.
When Grandmother Was Young. New York: Putnam's, 1969.
When Mother Was Young. New York: Putnam's, 1970.
Joey and the Birthday Present. New York: McGraw-Hill, 1971. Written with Anne Sexton.
When Great-Grandmother Was Young. New York: Putnam's, 1971.
The Wizard's Tears. New York: McGraw-Hill, 1975. Written with Anne Sexton.
What Color Is Caesar? New York: McGraw-Hill, 1978.
The Microscope. New York: Harper & Row, 1984.

AUDIOCASSETTE

Progress Report. Washington, D.C.: Watershed Tapes, 1977.

BIOGRAPHICAL AND CRITICAL STUDIES

Beaver, Harold. "Refuge in the Library, on the Farm, and in Memories." *New York Times Book Review,* March 2, 1986, pp. 14–15.
Booth, Philip. "Poet, not Poetess." *Christian Science Monitor,* August 9, 1961, p. 9.
———. "Maxine Kumin's Survival." *American Poetry Review,* 7:18–19 (November-December 1978).
Carter, Mary. "Hallie and Sukey's Hangups." *New York Times Book Review,* May 5, 1968, p. 37.
DuPlessis, Rachel Blau. "Individual Writers: Maxine Kumin in Deep." *Journal of Modern Literature,* 15, nos. 2–3:366–367 (1988).
Estess, Sybil P. "Past Halfway: *The Retrieval System,* by Maxine Kumin." *Iowa Review,* 10:99–109 (Fall 1979).
Gearhart, Jean B. "Courage to Survive—Maxine Kumin." *Pembroke Magazine,* no. 20:272–275 (1988).

George, Diana Hume. "Itinerary of an Obsession: Maxine Kumin's Poems to Anne Sexton." In *Original Essays on the Poetry of Anne Sexton.* Edited by Frances Bixler. Conway: University of Central Arkansas Press, 1988. Pp. 243–266.

———. " 'Keeping Our Working Distance': Maxine Kumin's Poetry of Loss and Survival." In *Aging and Gender in Literature: Studies in Creativity.* Edited by Anne M. Wyatt-Brown and Janice Rossen. University Press of Virginia, 1993. Pp. 314–338.

Gordon, David J. "New Books in Review." *Yale Review,* 58:119–121 (Autumn 1968).

Lesser, Wendy. "Poetic Sense and Sensibility." *Washington Post Book World,* February 2, 1986, p. 11.

Ludvigson, Susan. "Maxine Kumin." In *Dictionary of Literary Biography.* Vol. 5, *American Poets since World War II,* pt. 1. Edited by D. J. Greiner. Detroit: Gale Research, 1980. Pp. 416–423.

Middlebrook, Diane Wood. *Anne Sexton: A Biography.* Boston: Houghton Mifflin, 1991.

Miller, David. "Out Far and In Deep." *Sewanee Review,* 96, no. 4:684–687 (1988).

Muske, Carol. "Go Be a King in a Field of Weeds." *New York Times Book Review,* November 5, 1989, pp. 32–33.

Oates, Joyce Carol. "One for Life, One for Death." *New York Times Book Review,* November 19, 1972, pp. 7, 14.

Ostriker, Alicia. "Memory and Attachment." *New York Times Book Review,* August 8, 1982, pp. 10, 22.

Park, Clara Claiborne. "Mature Fruits." *The Nation,* July 24–30, 1982, pp. 89–90.

Raver, Anne. "The Storyteller in the Garden." *New York Times Book Review,* August 28, 1994, p. 12.

Slater, J. Joseph. "All's Well in the Garden of Verse." *Saturday Review,* May 6, 1961, pp. 29–30.

Vendler, Helen. "False Poets and Real Poets." *New York Times Book Review,* September 7, 1975, pp. 6–8, 10.

Vertreace, Martha M. "Secrets Left to Tell: Creativity and Continuity in the Mother/Daughter Dyad." In *Mother Puzzles: Daughters and Mothers in Contemporary American Literature.* Edited by Mickey Pearlman. Westport, Conn.: Greenwood, 1989. Pp. 77–89.

Webster, Harvey Curtis. "Six Poets." *Poetry,* 133, no. 4:227–234 (1979).

Zeidner, Lisa. "Empty Beds, Nests, and Cities." *New York Times Book Review,* March 21, 1993, p. 14.

INTERVIEWS

Armitage, Shelley. "An Interview with Maxine Kumin." *Paintbrush,* 7–8, nos. 13–16:48–57 (1981).

George, Diana Hume. "Kumin on Kumin and Sexton: An Interview." *Poesis,* 6, no. 2:1–18 (1985).

Hammond, Karla. "An Interview with Maxine Kumin." *Western Humanities Review,* 33, no. 1:1–15 (1979).

Mapson, Jo-Ann. "An Interview with Maxine Kumin." *High Plains Literary Review,* 7, no. 2:68–86 (1992).

Meek, Martha George. "An Interview with Maxine Kumin." *Massachusetts Review,* 16, no. 1:317–327 (1975).

Showalter, Elaine, and Carol Smith. "A Nurturing Relationship: A Conversation with Anne Sexton and Maxine Kumin." *Women's Studies,* 4, no. 1:115–135 (1976).

—*STEVEN A. NARDI*

Ross Macdonald

1915–1983

LEW ARCHER WAS born sometime between 1914 and 1920 in a working-class tract of Long Beach, a harbor town in Southern California. He went to grade school in Oakland, California, spent part of his youth stealing cars and brawling with gangs, then reformed with the stern encouragement of a fatherly police officer. He started but did not finish college. This schooling plus an interest in Freud, existentialism, and the arts gave him a subdued air of learnedness. He joined the Long Beach Police Department where he achieved the rank of detective sergeant before being fired for excessive honesty. His religious background came from his Catholic mother and grandmother. His parents were divorced, dead, or both.

In World War II he served as a naval intelligence officer and saw combat off Okinawa. Afterward he became a private detective, operating a seedy, sparsely furnished two-room office in Hollywood on his own—no partner and no secretary. His fee started at fifty dollars a day plus expenses and reached its maximum, one hundred dollars a day, in the 1960s. When offered more, he suspected the client of trying to buy his morals. Most of his cases for the first decade involved marital infidelity or blackmail; eventually he specialized in lethal family epics among the well-to-do. He married an ash blonde named Sue soon after the war, but she divorced him on the

grounds of mental cruelty. Thereafter guilt, loneliness, and the loss of a chance at a normal middle-class life haunted him and motivated his work. Romance for him, including the strenuous sublimation of sexual feeling for the waifs, worldly women, and deranged killers that he met on the job, was fragmentary and ill-advised. This pattern changed when, nearing sixty, he found love with Betty Jo Siddon, a gutsy young reporter who assisted with his last case.

Six feet two inches tall, 190 pounds, with dark hair and blue-gray eyes, Archer resembled Paul Newman. He owned two suits and drove a Ford. A social drinker—Scotch, bourbon, gin, beer, and ale were his choices—he refused alcohol while working and before lunch. He smoked heavily for thirty years, then quit. More a fistman than a gunman, he was tough in his youth but became self-effacing and empathetic as he aged, taking a paternal interest in troubled young people. His professional equipment included a license, phony business cards, an old deputy's badge, and a contact microphone that he rarely used. He did not mull over material evidence like a scientist; his methods were comparable to those of a priest or psychologist. His special talents were eliciting people's stories, following intricate plotlines to the historical roots of contemporary mayhem, and tracing the links among the urban underworld, the suburbs of the nouveau riche, and the desperate side streets of down-beaten respectability. Aside from chess, his avocations took him outdoors: he fished, gambled on horse races, watched birds, and fought for the preservation of the natural environment. A liberal humanist at heart, he made sparing use of his intellect but generous use of his ethics; his passion was mercy but, he said, justice was what most people got.

This is the biography of a fictional nonhero, a private eye who, although called on paperback covers "the hardest of the hard-boiled dicks," outlived and outgrew his genre.

Hard-boiled fiction was a distinctively American type of urban realism, a mass-produced popular literature that originated in debates among intellectuals on the political left in the early decades of the twentieth century. The Left's prevailing view of mass culture was strongly negative: it was seen as a drug that prevented the lower classes from perceiving their oppression and taking action to liberate themselves. A different view gained strength by the mid-1930s, however, the view that popular culture could voice resistance to the status quo and expose the falseness of the myths that supported it. Hard-boiled fiction gained its early vigor from the desires of leftist writers to ally themselves with the struggling economic classes, romanticized as "the people," through a literature that would both gratify their fantasies and indirectly preach to them about the need for social change.

The commercial success of hard-boiled fiction, combined with the impact of world events on leftist political thinking, altered the genre by the 1940s. Authors and publishing houses whose only mission was to make money took up the production of hard-boiled fiction, and conservative ideas proved to fit as well in the genre as did subversive ones. Meanwhile, both fascist and communist totalitarianism rose in Europe, with mass culture serving as an instrument for har-nessing popular sentiment to the goals of the totalitarian regimes. The traditional Marxist idea that a revolutionary working class would bring about a just social order, an idea that contributed to the formation of hard-boiled fiction, lost much of its relevance. Following World War II, rapid advances in technology, big business, education, and the standard of living—driven in large part by the ideological contest between the United States and the Soviet Union that became known as the cold war—together with the civil rights and women's movements, created a society in flux that could not be described in simple terms of class.

Lew Archer was conceived in this postwar world. His creator, Ross Macdonald, was another fiction, a pseudonym concocted by the novelist Kenneth Millar to occupy the shaded area where his ambition to create literary art overlapped with his desire for a popular audience. Millar believed his dual Canadian-American citizenship and his long childhood exile from the United States, the country of his birth, specially qualified him as a cultural critic; to know one's own culture, he said, one must have known another. He and his critics have made much of the influence of his impoverished and disrupted early life on his writings: the first decade of his career is often described as a struggle toward the maturity he needed to transform into fiction what he had experienced in his life. As Millar told it, his was a story of exile and return, an updated version of the ancient Greek tragedy of Oedipus, which Sigmund Freud placed at the center of his theory of how the human psyche is formed and how civilization began. In the myth, Oedipus discovers that a man he killed and the woman he married are his father and mother; his self-knowledge depends on his recognizing the tragic depths of human destiny. In Millar's version, Oedipus is angry with his parents for sending him away from home in an attempt to avoid their doom.

*   *   *

Beyond providing evidence of the personal anguish of one rather private man, the novels of Ross Macdonald highlight a thread of American cultural history. If exile and return shaped Kenneth Millar's life, in more complex ways they shaped the collective lives of Americans during the middle decades of the twentieth century. The Great Depression of the 1930s exiled the many whom it impoverished from the American dream of freedom, progress, and plenty. Just as the economy was recovering, World War II prolonged the exile by focusing the nation's energies on the war effort and radically disrupting private lives. The lost home of American society during these decades was not just an unattainable standard of living; it was also a set of traditional ideals, established in the nineteenth century, about the family and men's and women's roles in it. Men were to be providers and women were to keep the home a pleasant retreat from the competitive public world. The Depression and the war pushed women into the paid workforce while weakening men's earning capacity and separating them from domestic life.

The pursuit of these domestic ideals resumed with new vigor after the war, with the added component that having a family was to be an end in itself, a source of stability and fulfillment for a generation that came of age in the midst of a widespread social disruption. These ideals were reflected and promoted through the burgeoning media of popular culture: film, magazines, romantic fiction, the new medium of television, and popular psychology handbooks, particularly of child-rearing advice. For the middle class, they took form in the suburban home with its modern conveniences and in large bureaucratic organizations where men could climb a lifelong managerial career ladder. There were also new occupations for experts—largely male—trained in intellectual fields, especially in the mental health professions, the field with which Archer's style of investigation is most often identified.

These experts contributed to the shaping of the domestic ideal and, like Archer, came face-to-face with the disparities between reality and ideal. The return from exile in Archer's cases results not in happy reunions but in the necessity of confronting horrors that have been long repressed.

Kenneth Millar, a political liberal who could seethe with rage when speaking of the leading Republicans of his day, appreciated the leftist politics of the foremost hard-boiled authors, Dashiell Hammett and Raymond Chandler, with whom his pseudonym came to form a threesome that defined the scope of the genre. But it was the postwar American family that most interested Millar. Hard-boiled fiction's world of gangsters and hucksters had its models in the Prohibition era and the Depression of the 1920s and 1930s. In Millar's postwar vision, underworld criminals did not dominate social marginality; it ran through the respectable middle-class home, often with its origins in an earlier generation's lust, greed, and desperation. Millar's interest in family dysfunction shows plainly in what he called his revised Oedipal theme, stories of sons separated from their fathers. It also appears strikingly in his female characters—Robert Easton, a fellow writer, claimed in ''A Tribute'' that Millar included more women in more ways than any of his predecessors.

Millar has been charged with misogyny because of his lineup of deranged female killers and fatal beauties who drive men to kill, but hard-boiled is a thoroughly misogynist genre, relying on deeply established negative and positive female stereotypes to symbolize evil and good. Millar began with what he inherited; but his portraits of women, followed over time, read as a kind of affirmative action program, a slow and uncertain struggle toward equality requiring the scrutinizing and dismantling of women's status as objects. A similar struggle engaged society as a whole from the 1950s through the 1970s, when the Ross Macdonald novels were written. Millar explained his abundance of homicidal women characters by saying that a murderer is someone who has been murdered and that society victimizes women, an explanation that sounds nearly feminist.

In *The Moving Target* (1949) Archer says that war, economic pressures, opportunity, bad luck, and the wrong friends cause bad people. People become killers when they find themselves at pressure points where such contingencies intersect. In Millar's vision of postwar American society, it is women who most often find themselves at these pressure points with desperately few options for release. The end point in Millar's succession of female characters is not a killer but Betty Jo Siddon, the love interest in the last Archer novel, *The Blue Hammer* (1976). (The title refers to her pulse.) Surviving a mad artist's attempt to kill her and transform her into art, Betty Jo escapes objectification and proves to be Archer's match as an investigator. At the close of his series, Millar thus brought to life a precursor to the likes of Sarah Paretsky's tough and sociologically savvy V. I. Warshawsky, the feminist sleuths who would flourish in the popular fiction of the coming decades.

The critical reception of Ross Macdonald's novels helps to identify the thread of American cultural history that one can trace in the career of Lew Archer. The popular success of a work of fiction depends on its delivering to an audience desires and values that they already hold; popular art is not so much an expression of its creator's inward life as it is the artist's successful detection of sentiments that a substantial social group shares. Much of the criticism matches Millar's ambitions: he is often described as an author who wrote real novels in a popular genre, novels that appeal to both intellectuals and readers who want only to be entertained. This view has dissenters who see Millar's aims as unavoidably conflicting and the results as marred by preachiness and excessive complexity, factors that give his novels a tone of looking down on the genre in which they were written. Often, too, ardent praise for his work is accompanied by the critic's claim that it is something apart from and better than detective fiction.

Though Millar staunchly defended the idea that popular culture and high art should not be in conflict in a democratic society, the overall reception of the Macdonald novels reflects an ambivalence that educated people commonly share toward popular cultural forms: to avoid them is to be alienated from one's culture, but to embrace them is to degrade one's taste. To embrace and transform them—render them intellectually serious and artistically sophisticated—is to create a hybrid cultural form whose appeal is its internalized search for a middle ground between commercial culture and intellectual tradition, part of educated readers' sense of themselves. Intellectuals' relationship to popular culture can be described as a perpetual state of being exiled and seeking a way to return home.

Writing of how far Lew Archer had departed from his hard-boiled origins by the time of *The Doomsters* (1958), his seventh fictional appearance, Millar noted that Archer was no longer a hunter of criminals but a seeker of understanding, a "representative of man"—a character comparable to Don Quixote or Ivan Karamazov. To capture in fiction something essential about the human condition of their time is a common ambition of serious writers. But if one resists taking the universality of Millar's claim at face value, if one seeks instead the specific social identities that Archer represents, one finds that the eighteen-novel epic of Archer's career is an epic of mid-twentieth-century American white liberalism, of a man whose professional expertise is shaped by a humanistic intellectual heritage, of his working through historical traumas that threatened the foundations of masculine identity.

American detective fiction arises from a tradition of American fiction that represents masculine experience as an individualistic struggle against the influence of a destructive society—a tradition Nina Baym calls "melodramas of beset manhood." James Fenimore Cooper, Nathaniel Hawthorne, Herman Melville, and Mark Twain are the classic nineteenth-century authors in this tradition, and Ernest Hemingway, F. Scott Fitzgerald, and William Faulkner are its modernist masters. In novels within this masculinist tradition, female characters symbolically represent the threat of society; the protagonists must flee both society and women or their ideals and their lives may be destroyed.

The Archer epic begins and partly stays within this tradition, but with differences. The first important female character is Miranda Sampson in *The Moving Target;* she is innocent human raw material representing the potential of the postwar "brave new world"—a figure like Shakespeare's Miranda in *The Tempest.* The ingenues in subsequent Archer novels, however, are killers; Archer detects in the new society the understandable crime of turning against the past, the waste of potential. Allowed to tell the harrowing tales of their victimization, the female killers in the first half of the Archer series elicit increasing sympathy from Archer and the reader, peaking with Mildred Hallman in *The Doomsters.* Women share responsibility for the killings with male professionals, who kill out of their economic subservience combined with their idealizing obsession with women.

The pivotal novel in Millar's career, *The Galton Case* (1959), is less a murder mystery than a romance of identity. The female killers in the later novels are less sympathetic and less interesting than Mildred Hallman. They emerge from a veil of respectability, exposing disorganized sexual histories, usually of World War II vintage, that have muddled identities while entwining the destinies of several families from different social strata. Postwar society in these novels is an aging female desperately concealing sexual secrets and dooming her children with overprotection.

The male killers in the later novels reveal another side of the Archer epic: an intellectual chasing the modernist ideal of a luminous city, a bogus war hero hypocritically preaching a purist masculinity, a compulsively productive artist whose individualism amounts to criminal pathology—none sympathetic. While Archer becomes increasingly aware of his entanglement in the social corruption around him and edges toward its gratifications—sexual love, surrogate parenthood and grandparenthood—the Archer epic tracks down the demons associated with the tradition of masculine individualism and attends at their suicides.

Kenneth Millar was born on December 13, 1915, in Los Gatos, California, the only child of two middle-aged Canadians who had recently moved to the San Francisco Bay Area from the Northwest Territories. John Macdonald Millar, then editor of a local newspaper, announced his son's birth by publishing a poem celebrating the child's mixed northern European ancestry and the American myth of a "melting pot"—an immigrants' democracy embracing all its cultural roots. Kenneth's mother, Anne Moyer Millar, a nurse, descended from Pennsylvania Dutch Mennonites; his father, who restlessly moved from one occupation to another, was of Scots descent. When Kenneth was three the family moved to Vancouver, where John Millar piloted harbor boats; soon afterward, he abandoned his wife and child, leaving them so destitute that as a toddler Kenneth sometimes begged on the street. Unable to support herself and her son because of her poor health, Ann Millar took him to Ontario, where they survived on the charity of relatives. When Kenneth was six, his mother took him as far as the gates of an orphanage while he pleaded not to be left there. She relented, and Kenneth went to live with an uncle and aunt, Rob and Beth Millar, in Wiarton, Ontario, a small town on the shores of Georgian Bay.

Rob Millar ran the local movie theater and on Saturdays took Kenneth to see the serials; the one Millar most often mentioned was *Plunder,* starring stuntwoman Pearl White. Each episode was an exercise in suspense, beginning with the resolution of the previous week's cliff-hanger and ending with new terror as the heroine fled from one peril to another defending her innocence. After Kenneth had spent two stable years with his uncle and aunt, Beth Millar died. John Millar's sister Margaret, a businesswoman in Manitoba, paid for two years of Kenneth's education at Saint John's, a boarding school in Winnipeg. The 1929 stock market crash impoverished Kenneth's benefactor and ended his "semimilitary" education. He went to live with his mother's sister Laura in Medicine Hat, Alberta, for a year, then to Kitchener, Ontario, to live with his mother and grandmother. "My own life, as I moved from home to home and relative to relative," Millar wrote in his introduction to *Kenneth Millar / Ross Macdonald: A Checklist* (1971), "seemed as episodic and unpredictable as a movie serial." By the age of sixteen, he had lived, he calculated, in fifty rooms, compelled by his family's circumstances to play a "deadly game" of upward social climbing and downward slides.

Kenneth saw his father, who continued to drift around western Canada, infrequently during these years. Despite the anguish of his childhood, Millar expressed anger toward his father only indirectly in his fiction. In the later Lew Archer novels, he took up the theme of separated fathers and sons so frequently that some reviewers wearied of it. He recalled as the happiest day of his life a day when his father let him help steer the harbor boat in Vancouver. Yet, in later childhood, he refused an opportunity to join his father, choosing instead to go to boarding school—a decision that he later wrote about with remorse. Invalided and rendered speechless by strokes, John Millar ended his wandering in a government hospital in Ontario when Kenneth was in his teens. In *Self-Portrait: Ceaselessly into the Past* (1981), Millar recalls the last time he saw his father, and seems intent on claiming him as the source of his own literary calling: "He wrote me a few lines in a book on his knee. I wish I could tell you what he wrote to me that day. His writing was so shaky that I couldn't make out the words. But I could see that it was written in rhymed couplets."

The literary enthusiasms that formed his career as Ross Macdonald began early in Millar's life. At the age of eleven, he read Charles Dickens' novel of childhood poverty, *Oliver Twist,* with such fervor that his mother feared for his health. In boarding school he wrote Western stories and a narrative poem about the Scottish romantic hero Bonnie Prince Charlie, searching (he later wrote) for a literary tradition as a westerner and a descendent of Scots. At twelve he read Edgar Allan Poe's tales of mystery and imagination; at thirteen, he consumed stories about Falcon Swift the Monocled Manhunter, a detective in an English boys' magazine—preparation for his later immersion in the mystery fiction of Arthur Conan Doyle, Dorothy Sayers, Dashiell Hammett, and Raymond Chandler.

During his high school years, feeling like an unwanted guest in his puritanical grandmother's home, Millar made the public library his second home. He wrote crime fiction while his fellow debating team member Margaret Sturm wrote Gothic tales. His first published story, which appeared in their high school magazine, the Kitchener-Waterloo Collegiate and Vocational School *Grumbler,* parodied Conan Doyle's Sherlock Holmes stories in the style of the Canadian humorist Stephen Leacock. For both himself and Margaret, Kenneth later speculated, writing in violent, brooding modes was an expression of their anger about being provincial—feeling hopelessly removed from the historical and cultural centers of Great Britain and the United States. Millar's mother encouraged this sense of alienation and exile by continually reminding him that he was a Californian by birth and nourishing his ambitions to become worthy of the ''dream of goodness'' that this birthright represented to her.

Millar graduated from Kitchener in 1932, then spent a year working on a farm for his board. His father's death during that year brought Millar a twenty-five-hundred-dollar life insurance payment that enabled him to enroll at the University of Western Ontario. In college he became fascinated with Samuel Taylor Coleridge's unfinished long poem, *Christabel,* and tried to complete it. The poem's innocent young heroine, wandering in the woods outside her father's palace, discovers Geraldine, a damsel in distress, who proceeds to take control of Christabel while manifesting demonic traits. Millar's obsession with Coleridge thus gave him early practice with the Gothic device of female doubles, two women characters who are uncannily alike and yet moral opposites. This practice was useful background for Millar's entry into the hard-boiled genre, which relies heavily on morally polarized representations of women.

Millar's mother died suddenly in 1935. Recovering from the loss, he took a year off from college and bicycled around Europe, where he witnessed nazism on the rise. Margaret Sturm, with whom Millar had never spoken in high school, reentered his life during his last year of college—he found her reading classical Greek in a public library—and they married the day after his college graduation in June 1938. Millar then took graduate courses at the University of Toronto for a year and, from 1939 to 1941, taught English and history at his and Margaret's alma mater. The impetus to begin writing professionally came in the spring of 1939, when Margaret was pregnant and Kenneth was facing a summer

without an income. He won a typewriter on a radio quiz show and used it to write stories, verse, and humorous sketches, which he sold for one cent a word to *Saturday Night,* a Toronto political and literary publication. Within a few weeks he had earned over a hundred dollars, enough to pay the hospital bills for the birth of their daughter Linda Jane.

Margaret Millar prepared the way for her husband to turn his talents to writing mysteries by doing so herself. In bed with a heart ailment in September 1940, Margaret wrote her first mystery novel, *The Invisible Worm;* she sent it to a large New York publisher and quickly received notification of its acceptance. Margaret's success enabled Kenneth to quit teaching and begin graduate study with a fellowship at the University of Michigan in the fall of 1941. The poet W. H. Auden was a visiting professor that semester. A mystery buff, Auden liked Margaret's work and encouraged both Millars to regard the writing of popular fiction as a legitimate calling. Millar credited Auden with directing his career plans away from scholarship and toward creative writing. Inspired by Margaret's success and instructed by her skill, Kenneth wrote his first novel, *The Dark Tunnel,* during a month of late nights in a nearly empty academic building in Ann Arbor, Michigan.

Millar published four novels before he began shuffling pseudonyms and honing a part of himself into Lew Archer, private detective. Critics generally regard these novels as Millar's apprenticeship in the hard-boiled genre. The character of an observer-listener who crosses social boundaries—the ''all-purpose man,'' as Millar described his detective—begins to take form in these novels. They also show the beginnings of what would become one of Millar's special stamps on detective fiction: as in classical Greek tragedy, the destinies of family members are psychologically interconnected, and the crises that engulf them have their roots deep in the past.

The Dark Tunnel takes place on a university campus much like the one in Ann Arbor and makes use of Millar's experiences in Nazi Germany as the backdrop for a spy thriller. Professor Bob Branch, the narrator-protagonist, could be a young prototype for Archer. Traces of Branch's self-conscious erudition, which lures the sophisticated reader into sharing his sense of superiority to those around him, linger in Archer. The mystery in which Branch becomes embroiled takes the form of a locked-room murder, an artifice of the aristocratic, puzzle-solving style of mystery fiction that Millar later repudiated. The theme of the female double makes its appearance in this first novel, with Branch's lost love Ruth Esch, as the Christabel, and her cross-dressing brother, a homosexual Nazi spy, as the Geraldine figure. With this luridly stereotyped villain, Millar embodied the paranoia about homosexuality that the U.S. military perpetrated during World War II on the pretext that homosexuals were a threat to national security.

The United States had entered World War II at the end of 1941. In 1943 Millar tried to enlist but failed the physical exam. As the war progressed, standards were relaxed, and he was accepted in the U.S. Naval Reserve in 1944. He was at officer training school in Princeton, New Jersey, when *The Dark Tunnel* was published. He served below deck as a communications officer on the U.S.S. *Shipley Bay,* which saw combat off Okinawa in the spring of 1945. When the war in the Pacific ended that summer, the *Shipley Bay* transported troops back to the States, docking at San Diego and San Francisco. Millar began his second spy novel, interrupted it for two evenings to write his first hard-boiled detective story, then finished the novel, all at sea.

The story, "Find the Woman," won a four-hundred-dollar prize in the Queen's Awards for 1946, an annual contest held by *Ellery Queen's Mystery Magazine,* the premier forum for crime fiction. It anticipates the Lew Archer series in featuring a private eye as the narrator. This detective, originally named Rogers, was eventually turned into Archer for a collection of Millar's stories called *The Name Is Archer* (1955). The novel, *Trouble Follows Me* (1946), is narrated by Sam Drake, a navy journalist who follows the trail of a subversive group from Hawaii to Detroit to San Diego. Millar's aim of creating an "all-purpose man" shows in Drake's self-description: "I'm an intellectual among roughnecks and a roughneck among intellectuals." More restrained in his humanist posturing than Branch was, Drake serves Millar as a vehicle for tracking racial issues, and particularly white anxieties about racial differences, that surfaced in American society in response to the war against the Japanese and to African Americans' postwar demands for social justice at home.

In 1945, Margaret Millar took the train from Toronto to San Diego to visit her husband while his ship was docked. Headed back to Toronto, she saw the seaside town of Santa Barbara through the window, got off the train, and bought a small house. Except for brief periods elsewhere, the Millars lived in Santa Barbara for the rest of their lives; as Santa Teresa it is the scene of many of Archer's cases. Serving for two years as an officer in the United States military partially mitigated Millar's sense that he did not belong in his native country. On his discharge from the service in March 1946, he returned to the state where he was born: the exile of his childhood was physically, if not psychologically, at an end.

During the remaining months of 1946, Millar wrote *Blue City* (1947) and *The Three Roads* (1948) in what he described as an "angry rapture." Both novels, set just after the war, address the theme of exile and partial return that Millar transposed from his life into his fiction, but they are moral opposites that contrast also in their visions of gender. In *Blue City* a discharged soldier, John Weather, returns to his midwestern home to find that the city has been taken over by gangsters and his father, the political boss, has been murdered. Weather solves the murder, cleans up the city, and steps into his father's position of power. Millar considered this his first important book and some later critics, looking back over his career, thought it the best of his early novels, but reviewers at the time found it a mix of adolescent moralizing and hypermasculinity. And, when one reads these novels knowing that an extraordinary series of female killers will follow, *The Three Roads* seems the more telling of the pair.

In *The Three Roads,* the discharged soldier, Bret Taylor, is amnesiac and helpless; the limited-omniscient narrative centers at first on his fiancée, Paula West. As the story of a woman in love with a mysterious man, the novel opens like a popular romance written for female readers. When Bret recovers enough to become active, the plot turns to his quest to solve the mysteries of his past. Like *Blue City, The Three Roads* thus explores a veteran's anxieties about civilian life, but while Millar made Weather a heroic righter of wrongs in the postwar domestic world, he invested Bret Taylor with a deeply buried guilt—partially deflected onto Bret's promiscuous mother, his fiancée Paula, and the unfaithful wife he killed during the war—for the corruption and violence at home. Did these female characters narrowly escape being drawn as killers? Who was to blame for the returning soldier's alienation from peacetime society—the women who stayed at home, or the men who took part in the violent enterprise of defending the idea of home?

The following year, Millar made his first attempt to write an autobiographical novel, but the effort to confront his childhood bogged him down in "sloppy feelings and groping prose," causing him to doubt whether he should continue his career as an author. He said of this time that he was in trouble and the invention of Lew Archer got him out; Kenneth Millar, troubled young man, was Archer's original and sustaining client.

In print, Kenneth Millar explained that he devised a pseudonym in order to avoid entangling his career with that of Margaret, who had published nine novels by this time and was better known than her husband. His correspondence with his agent and his publisher, however, tells a more complicated story, involving his and their doubts about the merits of the genre of which he was to become a recognized master. Dodd, Mead published his first two novels but rejected *Blue City;* Alfred A. Knopf, the leading publisher of hardcover mysteries, accepted it and *The Three Roads* but initially rejected the first Lew Archer novel, *The Moving Target,* and cautioned Millar to avoid detective fiction if he wanted his writing to be taken seriously. Millar then proposed that the novel carry a pseudonym—he used his father's first and middle names, John Macdonald—and Knopf agreed to publish *The Moving Target* with revisions. Far from recognizing that he had begun his lifework, Millar expressed relief that his own name would not be on the book and doubt that he would try crime fiction again. The pseudonym needed altering when John D. MacDonald, whose crime stories had appeared widely in magazines and whose first full-length novel came out in 1950, objected to being confused with Archer's creator. Millar picked the name "Ross" for its Scots association, and the next five Archer novels were attributed to John Ross Macdonald. The publishers disclosed the author's real identity on the dust jacket of *Find a Victim* (1954); thereafter, the pseudonym was trimmed to Ross Macdonald.

In later years, Millar became an articulate theorist of popular suspense genres. (The prolific and best-selling horror fiction author Stephen King has named him as an influence.) Crime and detective fiction, according to Millar, was a leading form of the novel for his generation. He pointed out that since the time of classical Greece, writers have examined the problems in their society through the crime of murder. Murder serves symbolic purposes, he said in a 1981 interview with Jane S. Bakerman: it is an extreme metaphor for judgments that everyone must frequently make, such as "accepting people or banishing them." In a 1973 interview with Sam Grogg Jr., he said that murder stands for and reflects other crimes and is "the objective correlative . . . of spiritual death." Though drawn to the hard-boiled crime genre, Millar's stance toward it was critical; he described his own writing as an offshoot of hard-boiled that attempted to reach beyond its source.

The hard-boiled novel gave form to fears and desires that threatened to undermine the optimism through which official public forces sought to promote social cohesion during difficult times. Its tough-guy protagonists, romantic idealists turned cynics, were often but not always detectives, men of brutal honesty who gave and took a lot of battering as they explored the underside of modern American life. To act was the only chance to counter a pervasive moral vacuousness, but it invited doom—there were no happy endings. Women served as barometers of the moral chaos in this intensely masculine world, objects that absorbed attributes of the protagonist's conflicts. They were either victims or killers, either threatened ideals or threatening demons, and the business of the plot was often to disclose which. Being concerned with how one knows the realities behind the official line, hard-boiled was a flexible vehicle for representing the relationship between male intellectuals—the authors and the heroes they invented—and the larger culture. The stance of both was one of alienation from the world around them mixed with a longing to redeem it.

The categories "literature" and "popular fiction" collapse in the genealogy of hard-boiled, which counts Mark Twain and Gertrude Stein among its precursors and Ernest Hemingway, William Faulkner, and F. Scott Fitzgerald (whose *The Great Gatsby* Millar read annually) among its early practitioners. Its recognized founder was Dashiell Hammett, its first full-blown manifestation Hammett's novel *Red Harvest,* published just as the prosperity of the 1920s collapsed into the Depression of the 1930s. A clear-sighted, grimly witty tone suited the genre during the bitter years of the Depression, but this tone changed in the 1940s. In 1939 the paperback industry began publishing hard-boiled fiction, turning it into a twenty-five-cent commodity with lurid cover art. Increased demand opened the hard-boiled market to a group of new writers, to whom the publishers assigned the task of imitating formulas that had proven commercially successful. At the same time, as the war and news of the horrors of European fascism spread, the tone of hard-boiled fiction took on a new aura of terror and powerlessness; reality had become more horrible than fantasy.

The popular demand for hard-boiled fiction did not end with the war. Like film noir, its counterpart in the movies, the hard-boiled novel thrived through the late 1950s. Hard-boiled still had work to do in the American culture, posing grim countermyths to the myths of prosperity and familial bliss through which Americans sought to bind the enduring wounds of the Depression and the war, and registering the challenges of new social movements, such as the rebellious youth culture, the growing visibility of racial minorities, and the women's liberation movement. Offshoots of the hard-boiled school persist today but, at its most characteristic, it was nourished by the series of traumas that the historical crises of the 1930s and 1940s inflicted on the popular imagination. As Millar explains in Matthew Bruccoli's *Ross Macdonald,* writing hard-boiled was for him "a substitute for a postwar nervous breakdown," a way of coping with an "enormous erosion of sensibility'' and ''enormous changes in the quality of a civilization.''

The hard-boiled genre was at its peak or, as Millar came to see it, in decline when he entered the field. It offered him an established market and a set of conventions with which to begin. His ambitions, however, reached beyond the conventions, which he believed popular authors, particularly Mickey Spillane, had already destroyed by reducing it to clichéd violence. He saw Hammett's works as part of an ongoing dynamic interchange between high and popular culture through which popular commercial genres provide art with fresh, realistic materials and art instructs popular culture about craft. He regarded the new style of popular detective fiction as fundamentally democratic.

The traditional detective story, as practiced by Edgar Allan Poe and his British heirs, including Arthur Conan Doyle and Agatha Christie, involved puzzles that a brilliant rational thinker could solve, thus reassuring the reader that, for all its horrors, the world made sense. Millar observed that this kind of fiction reflected and reinforced a stratified society; the detective was an aristocrat of the mind, a defender of the existing social order. Hard-boiled, in contrast, stylistically defined by an American vernacular language that Millar believed leveled social differences, reflected a society undergoing constant change as it struggled toward equality. Millar regarded Hammett and Chandler as continuing the ''masculine and egalitarian'' traditions of the American frontier in the disjointed modern urban wilderness. The new detective was a direct descendant of James Fenimore Cooper's hero of the nineteenth-century frontier, Natty Bumppo, the pathfinder. The sin of the aristocratic detective was pride, thinking himself superior to those around him; the hard-boiled character's sin was slothful acceptance of the vices associated with democracy.

Millar had in common with Hammett and Chandler the terrain of Southern California, which Millar regarded as the polar opposite of the structured society represented in traditional detective fiction—a place where people, money, and values were in constant flux, where the past seemed forgettable and wealth the key to mastery over the future. After the war, ''it seemed that a brave new world was being born here, on the last frontier,'' Millar wrote in his introduction to *Kenneth Millar / Ross Macdonald: A Checklist.* Into this world Millar inserted Lew Archer, ''a socially mobile man who knows all the levels of Southern California life and takes a peculiar wry pleasure in exploring its secret passages.'' Like other hard-boiled detectives, Archer was a truth-seeker who had few possessions and no personal life. However, he was slower to violence, more introspective, and less dissipated than most hard-boiled heroes. Millar insisted in *Self-Portrait* that Archer was not the protagonist but the moral and psychological center of his novels: ''He is less a doer than a questioner, a consciousness in which the meanings of other lives emerge.''

A fictional detective serves as a protective shield between his creator and material that is too hot to handle, Millar said; and, in his case, the shield was doubly thick, with the fictional writer Ross Macdonald distancing Millar from the fictional private investigator. This double mask reflects Millar's sense that the genre strictly limited what a serious writer could do—Ross Macdonald was only part of Millar. It also distanced him from his detective, who was, as Millar said, another self. A writer creates a detective as an idealized version of himself, Millar wrote—the person he would be if he were a man of action instead of a ''solitary fantasist.'' Archer is even closer to his creator than this comment suggests. An eliciter of others' stories rather than a hero, Archer assumes the responsibilities of the novelist, mediating for his audience and piecing sense together amid the complexities of his creator's imagination.

Critics have noted that the earliest Archer novels show the extensive influence of Raymond Chandler. Lew Archer resembles Chandler's private detective, Philip Marlowe, in being a wisecracking modern knight battling for morality, but from the start Millar worked at making Archer less romantic than Marlowe and heightening the social realism of Archer's milieu. While Chandler's subject was conflict between good and evil, Millar's was human error and exploitation. The flaw in Chandler's works, according to Millar, was that he made Marlowe the redeeming feature of his stories, when redemption should take place in the overall structure of the work. In *The Moving Target* Archer tells Miranda Sampson, the daughter of the missing oilman whom he has been hired to find, that he inherited his job from a younger, more idealistic self who believed the world was made up of good people and bad people—someone matching Millar's description of Philip Marlowe. Besides complicating the moral vision that he inherited, Millar also changed the venue of action from the usual hardboiled locale, the urban underworld of professional gangsters, to the prosperous suburbs. Archer's search for Ralph Sampson takes him through the seamy underside of Los Angeles, but the motives for murder lie in the struggle over the possession of property and authority, legitimate activities of the middle and upper classes, corrupted by greed muddled with sexual desire.

Chandler was less than receptive to the work of his new disciple. On reading *The Moving Target,* Chandler wrote scathingly about it to mystery reviewer James Sandoe—not the only such letter he wrote. He perceived Millar's dual ambition of writing a work that would be both literary and popular but thought the result was marred by the author's pretentious egotism and, as quoted in Bruccoli's *Ross Macdonald,* "lack of some kind of natural animal emotion." Chandler pointed out sophisticated words in the novel's figurative language and charged that the author used similes to call attention to himself.

Millar, for his part, thought that Chandler overused similes and that his style was too vulgar—it would quickly become dated.

Contentiousness over style is of some importance to the hard-boiled genre, since its authors tried to imitate the colorful richness of colloquial American speech—an effort that Millar believed was the defining feature of the genre. The disparity in how this speech is reproduced by Chandler and Millar, both of whom heard it as partial outsiders (Chandler was educated in England), calls attention to its artificiality; the hard-boiled style was a generalization and extension of the colloquial language of specific regions and social groups. Millar tried to purify hard-boiled style, writing with one ear to common language and one to the Oxford English Dictionary and classic literature, and he aimed to invest figures of speech with symbolic depth. Describing Cabrillo Canyon, where *The Moving Target* begins, for example, Millar paints a picture of illusion, wealth, and waste: "The light-blue haze in the lower canyon was like a thin smoke from slowly burning money." In his later novels, as he distanced himself from the hard-boiled genre, Millar stripped much of the figurative language from his prose; readers who relish the early novels' style miss it in the later works.

The Millars returned to Ann Arbor, Michigan, in 1948 and Kenneth received his Ph.D. in February 1952. His dissertation on Coleridge's critical theory and its relationship to the tradition of psychological thought won the highest praise from the English faculty at the University of Michigan. While working on his dissertation, he continued trying unsuccessfully to write an autobiographical novel and published two more Archer books, *The Drowning Pool* (1950) and *The Way Some People Die* (1951). Rather than seeking full-time employment as an academic, Millar returned to Santa Barbara, taught part-time at the city college for two years, settled into the local literary and political life, and continued to develop his revision of hard-boiled fiction.

*   *   *

As Millar worked through Chandler's influence in the first seven Archer novels, he embedded his struggle to break the limits of hard-boiled conventions in his characters and plots. In *The Moving Target* Archer drowns a thug named Puddler, ''a savage accidentally dropped in the steel-and-concrete jungle, a trained beast of burden, a fighting machine.'' A naturalistic, subhuman figure who operates by reflex, Puddler is the hard-boiled villain taken to an extreme; through Archer's uncharacteristically lethal act, Millar began to kill off the genre and submerge it beneath the surface of his fiction. Elizabeth Benning in *The Ivory Grin* (1952) is another hard-boiled stereotype, a ''mystery blonde,'' the femme fatale character who brings evil to those who desire her. In Archer's office toward the end of the novel, her fatal beauty disintegrates, exposing the harrowing story of her life: ''Her past was coming out on her face like latent handwriting.'' There are stories behind the surfaces of the hard-boiled icons that explain why they function as they do.

Projecting a compassionate narrator who recognizes his own complicity in the corruption around him; moving the end point of the detective's search from the world of professional crime to the growing suburban communities; locating the origins of individuals' criminality deep in their familial past: these were central aspects of the Archer epic that Millar began to establish in the early novels. Most distinctively, Millar began to devise intricate narrative structures, doubling plots with subplots, illuminating the ties among the plot threads through reversals in Archer's understanding, and unfolding endings in a rhythm of revelations that reverberate with tragedy. Discussing the Ross Macdonald novels in the context of the hard-boiled movement as a whole, Geoffrey O'Brien wrote that their plots ''have a baroque splendor unprecedented in the genre.''

Raymond Chandler's realism is centered in the scene, while the plot that holds the scenes together can be clichéd and unbelievable; it is a kind of storytelling suited to sensory immediacy and instinctual action but not to moral complexity. Chandler believed it impossible both to construct elegant narratives and at the same time to write realistically about contemporary people and places, but this, according to O'Brien, is what Millar achieved at his best. To Millar, the overall structure of a novel is the essential means of its realism. Plots, he said, are composed of interactions among individuals, social levels, and temporal tiers; they must be complex enough to reflect the complexity of contemporary life. Mystery fiction lays on its authors the special task of embedding a linear logic of cause and effect in the structure, but such a structure is unsatisfying unless balanced by the nonlinear logic of imagination—the dreamlike transformation of fears and desires. Archer solves cases not through rational induction but through flashes of insight into people's motivation or through someone's finally releasing, under the pressure of Archer's search, the last missing piece of the story.

Millar wrote in *A Checklist* that in the first three Archer novels, he tried ''to develop both imagery and structure in the direction of psychological and symbolic meaning.'' Archer himself is the vehicle for this development in *The Moving Target:* ''a psychological and moral detective'' who explored people's lives rather than ''terrain and clues,'' as Millar told Sam Grogg Jr. Millar did not consider the second Archer novel, *The Drowning Pool,* an advance over *The Moving Target,* but with *The Way Some People Die* and *The Ivory Grin* he tightened and elaborated his plotting technique. With these two novels Millar seems to retreat from the psychological intensity of family relationships found in *The Drowning Pool* back into the standard hard-boiled criminal world, but he takes advantage of the retreat to delve into the workings of the conventions. Archer says of Galatea Lawrence, the killer in *The Way Some People Die,* ''It's sort of sad. . . . All that energy and ingenuity wasted.'' In *The Ivory Grin,* he tells Dr. Samuel Benning, ''It's the human idea you've been butchering and boiling down and trying to burn away. . . . You can't stand the human idea.'' Through Archer, Millar leveled charges of wasted effort and dehumanization against the hard-boiled genre.

Millar took a break from Archer with his next novel, *Meet Me at the Morgue* (1953); the narrator is a probation officer, Howard Cross. Using a first-person narrator other than a private eye gave Millar the opportunity to assess aspects of the developing Archer epic from a different viewpoint. In complicating Archer's moral universe, Millar had heightened Archer's awareness of how his own desires and questions were linked to the chains of causality that triggered violence. Cross remarks of an Archer-like detective that he is a ''hungry barracuda wearing a bowtie,'' soiled by the moral filth that he investigates. Millar also allows Cross to fall happily in love and thus to escape the convention of preserving the hero's masculine independence by keeping him out of lasting relationships. Archer's isolation, however, unlike that of other hard-boiled detectives, is explained as a failure—the grounds for his divorce, mental cruelty, associate him with the violence that he tracks and judges. Living the lives of whole social groupings—not merely individuals—through voyeuristic empathy, Archer seems to long for kinship, lethal as it repeatedly proves to be. In *Find a Victim* (1954), such a desire drives him deep into the private anguish of three families.

Millar had written *The Ivory Grin* in reaction to the excessive physical violence that characterized the hard-boiled school, which he believed ''tended to kill it off with literate readers.'' Yet before publishing his books, Knopf had them read by the paperback house that reprinted them, which judged their marketability based on their conforming to generic formulas. Thus in seeking a ''literate'' audience, Millar still had to satisfy the popular market's expectations. Knopf re-

quired revisions of *Find a Victim.* Outlining his plans to decrease the novel's wordiness and bring sex and violence closer to the surface, Millar admitted that the first version represented an overreaction to Mickey Spillane, whose paperbacks epitomized the formulaic violence that Millar despised. Although the final version of *Find a Victim* powerfully dramatizes a psychosexual family tragedy, the early chapters are so packed with tough sensationalism that they read like a parody of Spillane.

With *The Barbarous Coast* (1956) and *The Doomsters* (1958), Millar magnified and then eliminated the structural interplay between the hard-boiled criminal world and his emerging theme of family relationships. *The Barbarous Coast,* which he called his ''largest book so far, in both social range and moral complexity,'' amplifies the obsessions of postwar society through Hollywood and its outgrowth of the 1950s, the Las Vegas gambling industry: the film business' illusions of material plenty create victims for a new brand of semilegitimate organized crime. In *The Doomsters* there is no crime world. Criminality is fully internalized in the psychology of sex, money, and kinship, taking the classical tragic form of destiny. ''I have decided to relinquish my amateur status!'' Millar exulted to his agent, announcing that he was now tracing ''concentric rings'' around his masters, Hammett and Chandler.

The Millars moved north to Menlo Park, near Kenneth's birthplace, in 1956; Millar wrote in *Self-Portrait* that this was a time of ''seismic disturbances'' when his Canadian youth ''rose like a corpse from the bottom of the sea.'' Though he did not mention her in published accounts of this time, their daughter Linda, then seventeen, was the catalyst. Charged with vehicular homicide, she was placed on eight years of probation and required to undergo psychiatric treatment. Millar, too, entered psychotherapy. These events had immediate and long-range consequences for Millar's career. The legal and medical expenses meant that he had to keep producing, and therapy helped Millar at last to convert his life into fiction, thus transforming his writing. He wrote *The Doomsters* while in therapy and *The Galton Case* after moving back to Santa Barbara in 1958.

Trying again to work with the material of his childhood, Millar framed his revision of the story of Oedipus for *The Galton Case* and produced two drafts whose narrator was an imaginary Canadian ''boy imposter'' who, like Millar, had ''committed the sin of poverty.'' The novel did not take shape until Millar brought another version of himself, Lew Archer, back to take charge of the quest for the boy's identity. In the preface to a reprint of *The Galton Case* in *Archer at Large* (1970), he described the psychological work of the novel as bridging the split between rich and poor in the world of his early experience as well as that between the abstract dualisms of worthy and less worthy substances—idea and matter, spirit and flesh. The novel also concluded Millar's sense of exile: it ''stated and made good the right to my inheritance as an American citizen and writer.'' This was, to Millar and later critics, his breakthrough novel, yet no one seemed to notice at the time.

To date, none of Millar's novels had sold well, although a handful of reviewers praised them. Anthony Boucher, who wrote brief mystery reviews for the *New York Times Book Review,* was particularly enthusiastic, consistently describing Millar's books as among the best in the field. *Find a Victim* was lauded in *Time* magazine, where Millar was named the successor to Hammett and Chandler. After *The Galton Case,* Knopf urged Millar to give up writing series mysteries; they were not attracting as much attention as they should. In response Millar wrote his last non-Archer novel, *The Ferguson Affair* (1960), which was more commercially successful than any of his previous books. Critics writing about Millar's career as a whole, however, have re-

served their highest praise for the seven Archer novels that followed between 1961 and 1969, even though some of their plots and characters blur together.

Having broken through to the material of his life with *The Galton Case,* Millar continued to refine it in the subsequent novels: all of them concern problems of identity or paternity, and in all cases, Archer must delve a generation into the past. Geoffrey O'Brien singles out *The Zebra-Striped Hearse* (1962), *The Chill* (1964), *The Far Side of the Dollar* (1965), and *The Goodbye Look* (1969) as examples of Millar's exceptional skill in creating ''sure and beautiful'' architectural structures. Millar's fiction met with gradually increasing critical attention, readership, and recognition from his peers in the 1960s. He received a Silver Dagger Award for *The Chill* and a Gold Dagger for *The Far Side of the Dollar* from the British Crime Writers' Association; the Mystery Writers of America nominated *The Wycherly Woman* and *The Zebra-Striped Hearse* for Edgar Allan Poe Awards (neither won) and elected Millar president in 1965. Still, in the early 1960s, with Margaret producing books about as frequently as her husband, the Millars' combined annual income was about fifteen thousand dollars, equivalent to that of a schoolteacher.

The reception of the Ross Macdonald novels, together with the Millars' financial status, changed dramatically in the last half of the 1960s. In 1966 *The Moving Target* was produced as the film *Harper* with a cast of well-known Hollywood stars headed by Paul Newman. (Archer's name was changed to Lew Harper because, after starring in several successful films whose titles began with *H,* Newman believed that *H* was his lucky letter.) The film attracted attention to the Archer series, which Bantam began to reprint in paperback. On Millar's suggestion, Knopf republished three early novels that had sold poorly, *The Moving Target, The Way Some People Die,* and *The Barbarous Coast,* in a single hardbound volume titled *Archer in Hollywood* (1967). Then, with *The Goodbye Look,* Millar finally had a best-seller—but he may never have achieved this measure of popularity without the conspiring of two editors at Knopf, Ashbel Green and Robert Gottlieb. Over lunch, Green and Gottlieb persuaded John Leonard, the editor of the *New York Times Book Review,* that the forthcoming Macdonald novel should get a full-length review, not just a notice on the mystery fiction page. William Goldman, the screenwriter who had written the script for *Harper,* wrote the review, and it was published on the front page of the *Book Review* with the headline ''The finest series of detective novels ever written by an American.'' Goldman declared that *The Goodbye Look* had ''nothing remotely to do with hard-boiled.'' In an accompanying interview, Leonard announced that with *The Galton Case,* Ross Macdonald had become a ''major American novelist.''

The attention escalated with the publication of *The Underground Man* (1971). Again Millar made the front page of the *New York Times Book Review,* this time in a rave review by a respected literary author, Eudora Welty. Millar's face graced the cover of *Newsweek* for March 22, 1971. The cover story insisted that Macdonald's novels had surpassed popular fiction. Increased attention also meant increased negative attention, particularly from reviewers who regarded the new critical acclaim as inflated: Ross Macdonald's novels were escapism, not art; the novels pontificated; they had become predictable, these critics complained. Still, the wave of high sales persisted through *Sleeping Beauty,* published in 1973. Millar was in demand for interviews, and academic writers began to give his work serious attention. There were new editions of the Archer novels, and Millar edited a collection of short fiction titled *Great Stories of Suspense* for Knopf in 1974. There were also more media productions: Peter Graves played Archer in a television movie of *The Underground Man* in 1974, Brian Keith played him in a short-lived TV series called *Archer,* and Paul Newman reprised the role in a

movie of *The Drowning Pool* in 1975. The University of Michigan, the Mystery Writers of America, the Popular Culture Association, and the *Los Angeles Times* all recognized Millar's lifetime achievement with awards between 1972 and 1982.

From their scraping years when both Millars passed winters writing bundled up in jackets in a small unheated house to the days when they would return from Hollywood or New York to an expensive home in an elite neighborhood, Santa Barbara was the geographic center of the Millars' life. Besides being a nouveau riche community whose criminal courts provided Millar with material for Archer's cases, Santa Barbara was a university town and artists' and writers' haven. The Millars immersed themselves in the literary community; among those with whom Kenneth exchanged ideas and writing were the scholars Hugh Kenner and Marshall McLuhan, the poet Donald Davie, and the novelist Robert Easton. Political conservatism dominated the town and, during the late 1960s, the escalating war in Indochina further polarized local conservatives and those liberal intellectuals who, like the Millars, opposed the United States' role in the war.

Yet Santa Barbarans shared a commitment to preserving the town's fragile harmony with the natural surroundings, protected since World War II by the banning of smoky industry and severe restrictions on development. Half of Santa Barbara County was mountainous national forest—a wilderness where the endangered California condor and other species found refuge. An active member of the Audubon Society and the Sierra Club, Millar fought for the preservation of this environment and joined the public protest when, in January 1969, one of Union Oil's offshore oil wells polluted twelve hundred square miles of ocean, killing thousands of seabirds. He wrote articles on environmental issues for *Sports Illustrated* and, in *The Underground Man* and *Sleeping Beauty,* set stories of people's abuse of one another within frameworks of ecological crime.

The decade of increasing recognition was also a decade of personal tragedies for the Millars. In 1970 Linda died of a stroke at age 31, leaving a husband and a young son, after whom Millar modeled little Ronny Broadhurst in *The Underground Man.* Kenneth's mental clarity deteriorated during the late 1970s and in 1981 he was diagnosed with Alzheimer's. Though the disease gradually robbed him of the use of language, Margaret reported to an interviewer that he would spend hours lovingly handling his books. Margaret, who was losing her eyesight, shielded Kenneth from the public. Millar wrote at the time he was working on *The Blue Hammer* that he intended to write an autobiography, but he never did. By way of filling this void, in 1981 Ralph B. Sipper collected essays by Millar that refer to his life for a Santa Barbara press in *Self-Portrait: Ceaselessly into the Past.* The subtitle comes from the closing passage of the novel that Millar reread addictively, *The Great Gatsby*—the story of a young imposter, of, as Millar described it, "American ideals ruined by American greed." Millar died on July 11, 1983, at sixty-seven years of age.

Selected Bibliography

WORKS OF ROSS MACDONALD (KENNETH MILLAR)

NOVELS
The Dark Tunnel. New York: Dodd, Mead, 1944.
Trouble Follows Me. New York: Dodd, Mead, 1946.
Blue City. New York: Knopf, 1947.
The Three Roads. New York: Knopf, 1948.

Under the pseudonym John Macdonald
The Moving Target. New York: Knopf, 1949.

Under the pseudonym John Ross Macdonald
The Drowning Pool. New York: Knopf, 1950.
The Way Some People Die. New York: Knopf, 1951.
The Ivory Grin. New York: Knopf, 1952.

Meet Me at the Morgue. New York: Knopf, 1953.
Find a Victim. New York: Knopf, 1954.

Under the pseudonym Ross Macdonald
The Barbarous Coast. New York: Knopf, 1956.
The Doomsters. New York: Knopf, 1958.
The Galton Case. New York: Knopf, 1959.
The Ferguson Affair. New York: Knopf, 1960.
The Wycherly Woman. New York: Knopf, 1961.
The Zebra-Striped Hearse. New York: Knopf, 1962.
The Chill. New York: Knopf, 1964.
The Far Side of the Dollar. New York: Knopf, 1965.
Black Money. New York: Knopf, 1966.
The Instant Enemy. New York: Knopf, 1968.
The Goodbye Look. New York: Knopf, 1969.
The Underground Man. New York: Knopf, 1971.
Sleeping Beauty. New York: Knopf, 1973.
The Blue Hammer. New York: Knopf, 1976.

COLLECTED NOVELS
Archer in Hollywood (*The Moving Target, The Way Some People Die, The Barbarous Coast*). New York: Knopf, 1967.
Archer at Large (*The Galton Case, The Chill, Black Money*). New York: Knopf, 1970.
Archer in Jeopardy (*The Doomsters, The Zebra-Striped Hearse, The Instant Enemy*). New York: Knopf, 1979.

SHORT STORIES
"Find the Woman." *Ellery Queen's Mystery Magazine,* 7:102–119 (June 1946). Reprinted in *The Queen's Awards, 1946.* Edited by Ellery Queen. Boston: Little, Brown, 1946.
"The Bearded Lady." *American Magazine,* 146:152–166 (October 1948). Reprinted as "Murder Is a Public Matter." *Ellery Queen's Mystery Magazine,* 34:21–38, 60–74, 95–104 (October 1959).
"Shock Treatment." *Manhunt,* 1:71–80 (January 1953).
"The Imaginary Blonde." *Manhunt,* 1:1–27 (February 1953). Reprinted as "Gone Girl" in *The Name is Archer.*
"The Guilty Ones." *Manhunt,* 1:1–21 (May 1953). Reprinted as "The Sinister Habit" in *The Name is Archer.*
"The Beat-Up Sister." *Manhunt,* 1:110–140 (October 1953). Reprinted as "The Suicide" in *The Name Is Archer.*
"Guilt-Edged Blonde." *Manhunt,* 2:1–12 (January 1954).

"Wild Goose Chase." *Ellery Queen's Mystery Magazine*, 24:123–141 (July 1954). Reprinted in *Ellery Queen's Awards: Ninth Series*. Edited by Ellery Queen. Boston: Little, Brown, 1954.

"Midnight Blue." *Ed McBain's Mystery Magazine*, 1:2–24 (October 1960). Reprinted in *Best Detective Stories of the Year*. Edited by Brett Halliday. New York: Dutton, 1962.

"The Sleeping Dog." *Argosy*, 360:42–43, 90–95 (April 1965). Reprinted in *Best Detective Stories of the Year*. Edited by Anthony Boucher. New York: Dutton, 1966.

COLLECTED SHORT STORIES

The Name Is Archer ("Find the Woman," "Gone Girl," "The Bearded Lady," "The Suicide," "Guilt-Edged Blonde," "The Sinister Habit," "Wild Goose Chase"). New York: Bantam, 1955.

Lew Archer, Private Investigator. Includes the stories from *The Name Is Archer*, with the addition of "Midnight Blue" and "The Sleeping Dog." New York: Mysterious Press, 1977.

ESSAYS

"A Death Road for the Condor." *Sports Illustrated*, April 6, 1964, pp. 86–89.

"Homage to Dashiell Hammett." *Mystery Writers' Annual* (1964). Pp. 8, 24.

"Life with the Blob." *Sports Illustrated*, April 21, 1969, pp. 50–52, 57–60.

"Santa Barbarans Cite an 11th Commandment: 'Thou Shalt Not Abuse the Earth.' " With Robert Easton. *New York Times Magazine*, October 12, 1969, pp. 32–33, 142–149, 151, 156.

"The Writer as Detective Hero." *Show*, 5:34–36 (January 1965). Reprinted in *Essays Classic & Contemporary*. Edited by R. W. Lid. Philadelphia: Lippincott, 1967.

COLLECTED ESSAYS

A Collection of Reviews. Northridge, Calif.: Lord John Press, 1979.

Self-Portrait: Ceaselessly into the Past. Edited by Ralph B. Sipper. Santa Barbara, Calif.: Capra, 1981. A collection of autobiographical essays.

On Crime Writing. Santa Barbara, Calif.: Capra, 1973.

BIBLIOGRAPHIES

Bruccoli, Matthew J. *Kenneth Millar / Ross Macdonald: A Checklist*. Detroit: Gale, 1971.

Bruccoli, Matthew J. *Ross Macdonald / Kenneth Millar: A Descriptive Bibliography*. Pittsburgh: University of Pittsburgh Press, 1983.

MANUSCRIPT PAPERS

Kenneth Millar's papers and manuscripts are at the University of California at Irvine.

BIOGRAPHICAL AND CRITICAL STUDIES

BIOGRAPHY

Bruccoli, Matthew J. *Ross Macdonald*. San Diego: Harcourt Brace Jovanovich, 1984.

CRITICISM AND REVIEWS

Easton, Robert. "A Tribute." In *Dictionary of Literary Biography Yearbook: 1983*. Edited by Mary Bruccoli and Jean W. Ross. Detroit, Mich.: Gale Research, 1984.

Goldman, William. Review of *The Goodbye Look*. *New York Times Book Review*, June 1, 1969, pp. 1–2.

Mahan, Jeffrey Howard. *A Long Way from Solving That One: Psycho/Social and Ethical Implications of Ross Macdonald's Lew Archer Tales*. New York: University Press of America, 1990.

O'Brien, Geoffrey. *Hardboiled America: The Lurid Years of Paperbacks*. New York: Van Nostrand Reinhold, 1981.

Schopen, Bernard A. *Ross Macdonald*. Boston: Twayne, 1990.

Symons, Julian. *Mortal Consequences: A History—from the Detective Story to the Crime Novel*. New York: Harper and Row, 1972.

Weinkauf, Mary S. *Hard-Boiled Heretic: The Lew Archer Novels of Ross Macdonald*. San Bernardino, Calif.: Brownstone Books, 1994.

Welty, Eudora. Review of *The Underground Man*. *New York Times Book Review*, February 14, 1971, pp. 1, 28–30.

White, Jean. "Going for the Freudian Vein." Review of *Sleeping Beauty*. *Washington Post Book World*, May 20, 1973, p. 12.

Wolfe, Peter. *Dreamers Who Live Their Dreams: The World of Ross Macdonald's Novels.* Bowling Green, Ohio: Bowling Green University Popular Press, 1976.

INTERVIEWS

Adler, Dick. "Will the Real Ross Macdonald Please Keep Writing?" *Los Angeles Times West,* December 10, 1967, pp. 79–86.
Bakerman, Jane S. "A Slightly Stylized Conversation with Ross Macdonald." *Writer's Yearbook,* 52:86, 88–89, 111 (1981).

Grogg, Sam, Jr. "Ross Macdonald: At the Edge." *Journal of Popular Culture,* 7:213–222 (Summer 1973).
Jones, Robert F. "A New Raymond Chandler?" *Los Angeles Magazine,* 5:58–59 (March 1963).
Leonard, John. "Ross Macdonald, His Lew Archer, and Other Secret Selves." *New York Times Book Review,* June 1, 1969, pp. 2, 19.
Sokolov, Raymond A. "The Art of Murder." *Newsweek,* March 22, 1971, pp. 101–104, 106, 108.

—*JANET GRAY*

N. Scott Momaday

1934–

PERHAPS NO ONE has spoken more about what it means to be an American Indian writer today than has N. Scott Momaday. Accessible and forthright about discussing his poetry, prose, fiction, and art, Momaday has given dozens of interviews and lectures during the years since his first novel, *House Made of Dawn*, was published in 1968.

Momaday was born Novarro Scott Mammedaty at the Kiowa and Comanche Indian Hospital in Lawton, Oklahoma, on February 27, 1934. The Kiowa Indian Census roll says that he is seven-eighths degree Indian blood. His mother, Natachee Scott, who is one-eighth Cherokee, and his father, Alfred Morris Mammedaty, a full-blood Kiowa, were teachers who were well educated. Alfred Momaday (he changed the family name from Mammedaty to Momaday) was educated at Bacone College in Oklahoma, the University of New Mexico, and the University of California; Natachee Scott was educated at Haskell Institute, Crescent Girls College, and the University of New Mexico. As a young woman, Natachee Scott explored and identified with her Indian background so strongly that later she influenced her son to fully recognize and develop his sense of his tribal roots.

In 1936, the Momadays moved to the Navajo reservation at Shiprock, New Mexico, but also lived for a time in Arizona on the San Carlos Apache reservation. It was during those years, 1936–1943, that the young Momaday learned about the Navajo. In his autobiography, *The Names*, published in 1976, Momaday describes his early life with the Navajo: "Just at the time I was learning to talk, I heard the Navajo language spoken all around me. And just as I was coming alive to the wide world, the vast and beautiful landscape of *Dine bikeyah* [the Navajo reservation] *was* my world, all of it that I could perceive." In 1946 the family moved to Jemez Pueblo, New Mexico, when both parents secured jobs as teachers—Alfred Momaday was hired as the principal too—at the Jemez Day School.

It was at Jemez that Momaday says that he learned to dream, to listen to old Kiowa songs, and to watch his artist father paint. Remarking upon those years in *The Names*, Momaday says: "In that span and in that place were invested many days of my life, and many of the very best." As outsiders, the Momadays did not participate in the rituals of the Jemez people, but Momaday learned much about tribal life at their pueblo, which up until World War II was protected from the encroachment of the modern world by its relative isolation. Momaday absorbed the Jemez culture. The striking and haunting descriptions of landscapes in *House Made of Dawn*, which is partially set at Jemez, show that even in adolescence Momaday was detailing in his memory the beauty of the canyons, mesas, and mountain areas, and the rich native heritage of Walotowa, the "village of the bear." As he describes the landscape in a passage in *The Names*,

Nothing there of the earth could be taken for granted; you felt that Creation was going on in your sight. You see things in the high air that you do not see farther down in the lowlands. In the plains you can see farther than you have ever seen, and that is to gain a great freedom. But in the high country all objects bear upon you, and you touch hard upon the earth. The air of the mountains is itself an element in which vision is made acute; eagles bear me out. From my home of Jemez I could see the huge, billowing clouds above the Valle Grande, how, even motionless, they drew close upon me and merged with my life.

Momaday spent his childhood summers with his father's people at Rainy Mountain. It was the southern Plains, sacred Kiowa country, that stirred his imagination and inspired him to seek and affirm his Kiowa heritage. This search for his tribal roots took Momaday much of his lifetime; it was a physical and imaginative journey particularly appropriate to a Kiowa, for the Kiowa Indians explain their very being as a journey, which they call the "coming out." The creation story of the Kiowa tells us that the Kiowa people came into the world through a hollow log and then migrated from the mountains of Montana through the Black Hills and Wyoming and out onto the southern Plains in the late eighteenth century. That is why the Kiowa call themselves the "coming out people," the *Kwuda*. This journey is also the journey of Tai-me, the sacred Sun Dance fetish of the Kiowa; all Kiowa can make Tai-me's journey through their ancestral memory. Momaday has traced that route and has recognized and developed imaginatively his ancestral oral traditions, traditions that infuse his written work and his visual art.

After graduating from the University of New Mexico in 1958 with a degree in political science, Momaday accepted a teaching position at Dulce, on the Jicarilla Apache reservation in New Mexico. He applied for and won the Wallace Stegner Creative Writing Scholarship at Stanford, subsequently earning his master's degree in creative writing in 1960 and his doctorate in English literature by 1963. His revised Ph.D. dissertation, *The Complete Poems of Frederick Goddard Tuckerman*, was published in 1965. At Stanford he met and studied with Yvor Winters, who became his mentor and friend. Winters encouraged Momaday to develop his voice especially because Momaday was a writer of American Indian descent writing about tribal people. Winters praised the remarkable quality of Momaday's style, saying, "N. Scott Momaday can hardly drop a short phrase which does not haunt one."

Momaday spent his academic career at the University of California at Santa Barbara and at Berkeley, and at Stanford, Princeton, and Columbia. In 1996, he was Regents Professor and Professor of English at the University of Arizona. He has traveled worldwide and has taught in Russia. His work is recognized and read throughout the world and has been translated into more than five languages. Momaday won the Pulitzer Prize in 1969 for *House Made of Dawn*, the Academy of American Poets Prize in 1962 for his poem "The Bear," and Italy's highest award for literature, the *Premio Letterario Internazionale Mondello,* in 1979. His Indian background provides energy and power for his work; his continued participation in the rituals, ceremonies, and culture of his native heritage fosters his creative imagination. Momaday has been a member since 1969 of the Kiowa Gourd Dance Society (*Taimpe*), a traditional soldier society, and he dances annually with his tribal people.

No matter how critics approach Momaday's work, they generally agree that he is an American Indian writer deeply involved with the native relationship to the land and with the native oral tradition with its exceptional reverence for language. These two relationships constitute and to a great extent define Indian identity. Momaday has said that we are what we imagine ourselves to be and that this imaginative act must be put into words. What we dream ourselves to be, and what we say about ourselves, becomes our identity. The sources of Indian identity are the land—what Momaday calls in his 1976 essay "Native American Attitudes to the Environment" a "reciprocal appropriation"—and language, particularly the oral tradition. In perhaps his most famous essay, "The Man Made of Words," published originally in 1970 in *Indian Voices*, Momaday speaks about the relationship between language and identity: "in a certain sense we are all made of words . . . our most essential being consists in language. It is the element in which we think and dream and act, in which we live our daily lives. There is no way in which we can exist apart from the morality of a verbal dimension." Indian identity, still deeply involved as it is in oral tradition, is centered in language: an "Indian is an idea which a given man has of himself. And it is a moral idea, for it accounts for the way in which he reacts to other men and to the world in general. And that idea, in order to be realized completely, has to be expressed." Momaday comes back to this idea again and again from different angles, creating in his work a rich texture of perspectives.

Momaday's poem, "Carriers of the Dream Wheel," published first in 1976 in his book *The Gourd Dancer*, is an invocation of the larger narrative that constitutes the body of his work:

This is the Wheel of Dreams
Which is carried on their voices,
By means of which their voices turn
And center upon being.
It encircles the First World,
This powerful wheel.
They shape their songs upon the wheel

And spin the names of the earth and sky,
The aboriginal names.
They are old men, or men
Who are old in their voices,
And they carry the wheel among the camps,
Saying: Come, come,
Let us tell the old stories,
Let us sing the sacred songs.

The wheel in this poem represents all the themes in Momaday's work: the power of language and song; the vitality of community; the importance of dreams and the imagination; how names encompass the essence of being; the Indian relationship with the land; and the joy that those who preserve the oral tradition take in repeating images and stories.

Momaday drew on his developing sense of his Kiowa heritage as well as his life experiences on the Navajo and Jemez Pueblo reservations for his first novel, *House Made of Dawn*. Like a number of novels written by other American Indians, *House Made of Dawn* tells the story of a young Indian, his loss of identification with his tribal roots, and his tortured return to understanding himself, his place in the world, and his native heritage. Most critics of *House Made of Dawn* focus on the theme of finding and healing the self in a modern environment—or rather, two environments: one defined by tribal tradition; the other created by a culture and a set of circumstances the Indian finds nearly incomprehensible. Abel, a Jemez Pueblo Indian, is alienated from his tribe and his Indian heritage partially by white culture and its effects on the reservation, alcoholism, and violence. Abel's mother is Jemez and Abel's father is perhaps Navajo or perhaps from another tribe; this uncertainty estranges him from the Jemez from the start. Abel's mother and brother Vidal both die young from alcoholism. Abel's grandfather—a mission sacristan and a traditional Jemez medicine man, a "longhair"—raises him, urging that he take up the traditional ways of the tribe to ensure continuance of the rituals and ceremonies so important to the life of the community.

Although Abel participates in tribal rituals, he cannot draw meaning from them. Saddened, even disgusted, rather than enriched or transformed by the experiences, he remains isolated emotionally from the tribal heritage his grandfather Francisco tries to pass on to him as a member of the next generation. Unlike his grandfather, who draws great significance from his first bear hunt, when he became almost one in spirit with the bear he stalked and killed—reenacting what he considers an ''ancient and inviolable . . . bond''—Abel is shamed by the animals' loss of life and unable to find meaning in it.

Drafted for combat in World War II, Abel leaves Jemez. In a brief but incisive scene that captures the painful consequences of cultural conflict, he returns home from duty to Francisco reeling drunk. Although Abel attempts to rejoin tribal life, he remains profoundly alienated from it, which affects even his relationship with his closest kin. He cannot speak with his grandfather:

> he could not say the things he wanted; he had tried to pray, to sing, to enter into the old rhythm of the tongue, but he was no longer attuned to it. . . . Had he been able to say it, anything of his own language—even the commonplace formula of greeting . . . would once again have shown him whole to himself; but he was dumb. Not dumb—silence was the older and better part of custom still—but *inarticulate.*

He is muted by the confusion, the chaos of war. In a 1959 poem, ''Los Alamos,'' Momaday gives a grim picture of war as something that overwhelms and destroys the natural world:

> Machinery is scattered over the earth like hurled coins.
> I have heard the angry monotone

> Retching into troughs the pins of war
> When I walked in the wood to hear rain

In *House Made of Dawn* Momaday depicts people who cannot reach across the racial gulf and unite against adversity that affects them equally. The men whom Abel fights beside try to deprive him of his Indian humanity; they treat him as if he were crazy and refer to him stereotypically as ''chief.''

At the feast of Santiago, Abel becomes obsessed with an albino Indian; convinced of the albino's inherent evil, Abel stabs and disembowels him. Many critics interpret this grisly and mysterious scene symbolically seeing it as Abel's confrontation with the larger cultural conflict about color between traditional native and Western culture. Others contend conversely that the albino represents pagan tradition that conflicts with Abel's Christian mission upbringing, producing in him an explosive psychic disharmony. Still others focus on the albino himself as a symbol of white oppression, to Abel's mind a witch who threatens the village. Abel's trial—with which Momaday frames an indictment of the American legal system—dramatizes the power that language has to construct cultural identity and ''reality.'' Abel himself recognizes the ironic discrepancy between their language and himself; thinking about the men who bring him to trial he realizes: ''Word by word by word these men were disposing of him in language, *their* language, and they were making a bad job of it. They were strangely uneasy, full of hesitation, reluctance. He wanted to help them. He could understand, however imperfectly, what they were doing to him, but he could not understand what they were doing to each other.''

Abel becomes inarticulate because he is alienated from his tribal roots; the legal system is inherently inarticulate because it cannot express, much less control through language, Jemez Pueblo belief. While the white justice system condemns and sentences Abel for murder, the Jemez, although they would not condone violence against a tribal member, would recognize that Abel had done what he felt compelled to do. For Abel, it is simple: "a man kills such an enemy if he can." In *The Names*, Momaday recalls being at Jemez as a young man, doing his homework, and suddenly understanding the depth of the Jemez fear of witches: "There, at that window one night, I saw a group of old men on the moonlit road, running in ceremonial garb after witches. It is a vision that I shall carry in my mind as long as I live." "The Well," a short story Momaday published in 1963, portrays in sympathetic yet complex terms an old woman, Muñoz, believed to be a witch by the Jicarilla people at Stone Lake; the story indicates Momaday's early interest in these enigmatic and extraordinarily influential people called witches.

In *House Made of Dawn*, Momaday's belief in the primacy of language, especially as it functions in the oral tradition and the power language has to destroy or heal the self, is expressed through two men of words: the Kiowa peyote priest of the Sun, Tosamah, and Ben Benally, Abel's Navajo friend who sings over Abel the Navajo Night Chant, a ritual healing song. Relocated to Los Angeles after his release from prison, Abel goes with Benally to the Native American Church and hears Tosamah's sermon on the Christian Word from the Gospel according to John. Tosamah, Momaday says, is a mouthpiece for his own views on language. Tosamah is a master manipulator of words and his sermon on the Logos demonstrates that language is primary and that it creates human perception. For native people, words in the oral tradition mediate between the people and the world. Tosamah also focuses Indian mythic perception, vision, and healing through ceremony, including the ritual use of peyote.

Readers of the all-night ceremony passage see the mystical experience as a matter of healing through vision. Tosamah brings together Navajo and Kiowa beliefs. Benally's Navajo Night Chant cures mental and physical disharmony, restoring the psychic and bodily balance necessary for individual and tribal wholeness. This ancient chant is central to the novel in general: it begins, "House made of dawn, / House made of evening light," lines from which the title and structure of the novel are drawn. The chant connects the language and the land, for the Navajo chantways are oral journeys toward balance through a cultural landscape. Benally chants over Abel after he suffers a near fatal beating in Los Angeles by a vicious and prejudiced Chicano cop. Purifying and healing, the mythic oral ceremony begins the way for Abel to reconnect with his tribal heritage. He eventually returns to Jemez and slowly, even through Francisco's death, reestablishes his racial understanding of tribal ritual and draws deep meaning from his native belief. At the close of the novel, set in the early hours of dawn, Abel takes his place as a sacred tribal runner, making a new beginning in his life.

When *House Made of Dawn* was published in 1968, few expected that the following year it would earn the Pulitzer Prize for fiction. It was the first time that an American Indian writer had been given the prestigious award and the publishing world was astonished—"stunned" in the words of one critic. Early reviews of *House Made of Dawn* were mixed. Some critics gave unqualified praise for its lyricism; others, unfamiliar with American Indian spirituality, cosmic perception, and oral tradition, found it unstructured, confusing, and obscure. By the early 1980s, however, *House Made of Dawn* had earned considerable scholarly attention and respect. In the twenty-five years after the novel was published critics became more familiar with Momaday's aesthetic and its connection to oral tradition and native spiritual patterns; by the 1990s scholars regarded Momaday's work as exemplary of the way an American Indian writer might create. The publication of *House Made of Dawn* began what is known as the Native American Renaissance: it opened the way for gifted writers of American Indian descent to be published, read, and appreciated by scholars and the general reading public.

Much of the power of *House Made of Dawn* comes from Momaday's skill in portraying the New Mexico landscape and wildlife. His imagery often displays the eternal and inevitable violence that is part of its profound beauty; in one passage, for example, he writes:

> It is said that hawks, when they have nothing to fear in the open land, dance upon the warm carnage of their kills. In the highest heat of the day, rattlesnakes lie outstretched upon the dunes, as if the sun had wound them out and lain upon them like a line of fire, or, knowing of some vibrant presence on the air, they writhe away in the agony of time. And of their own accord they go at sundown into the earth, hopelessly, as if to some unimaginable reckoning in the underworld.

In *House Made of Dawn* Momaday shows that landscape, the Pueblo people, and their rituals are inseparable. Francisco, the old longhair, thinks simultaneously of landscape, song, and the drum, which are permanently imprinted in his mind:

> He could hear the distant sound of the drums and the deep, welling voice of the singers. He tried not to think of the dance, but it was there, going on in his brain. He could see the dancers perfectly in the mind's eye, could see even how they bowed and turned, where they were in relation to the walls and the doors and the slope of the earth. He had an old and infallible sense of what they were doing and had to do.

In "The Morality of Indian Hating," an essay he published in 1964, Momaday speaks of the strength of the cultural spirit, tribal sense or memory, and its connection to the power of language: "None who has heard the deep droning concert of the singers and the insistent vibration of the drums can have mistaken the old, sacred respect for sound and silence which makes the magic of words and literatures."

In his speech accepting the 1976 National Book Award (for his 1975 novel, *J R*), William Gaddis said that "a writer should be read and not heard, let alone seen . . . there seems so often today to be a tendency to . . . turn the creative artist into a performing one." It is quite the opposite for Momaday. In his essay "The Man Made of Words" he says that writing is "recorded speech. In order to consider seriously the meaning of language and of literature, we must consider first the meaning of the oral tradition . . . that process by which the myths, legends, tales, and lore of a people are formulated, communicated, and preserved in language by word of mouth, as opposed to writing." Momaday is concerned about the fact that people generally give precedence to writing over speaking and tend to relegate the oral tradition of the Indians to the realm of "fairy tales," quaint relics of vanishing or assimilating cultures. He argues instead that oral storytelling is a rich tradition of knowledge, profound in its simplicity and clarity of language. Performance, he points out, "sends a voice." The vocal performance, because what is said is the "imaginative act" of expressing the self, sends out to the world the essential identity of the Indian storyteller. Voice quality, intonation, gestures, pauses, sound, and phrase repetition— all these characteristics of the oral tradition also create meaning for the listener. Critics have noticed Momaday's careful attention to reproducing these oral qualities—especially resonance and symmetry, what Charles L. Woodard in *Ancestral Voice* (1989) calls the "incantatory quality"—in his writing. In the prefatory note to an anthology of contemporary native poetry, *Carriers of the Dream Wheel* (1975), Momaday says that "words, as they are carried on from one generation to another solely by means of the human voice, are sacred. Nothing is so potent . . . original . . . originative . . . so close to beauty."

In one of his most memorable and often-quoted passages in "The Man Made of Words,"

Momaday evokes three major themes in his work at once: cultural landscape, angle of vision, and the qualities of the oral tradition. He writes, ''Once in his life a man ought to concentrate his mind upon the remembered earth. . . . He ought to give himself up to a particular landscape in his experience, to look at it from as many angles as he can, to wonder about it, to dwell upon it. He ought to imagine that he touches it with his hands at every season and listens to the sounds that are made upon it.'' Momaday's specific portrayals of the landscapes at Jemez and Rainy Mountain reflect this sort of ''concentration,'' this perception of many ''angles,'' many times, and hearing many sounds from all sides. The passage from ''The Man Made of Words'' also suggests Momaday's overarching creative strategy: to employ recurring images, characters, events, and also to return and double back in circles, constricting and widening circles of meaning and imagination. Momaday explains in *Ancestral Voice* that this is the way his imagination works; he likes to build upon a story: ''I carry it on from book to book. There's a continuum. . . . [My] exploration of my story is an ongoing process.'' For the reader, there is the pleasure of remembrance, the feeling of the familiar in coming upon an image, a character, or an event met before, and another perhaps broader recognition and understanding found in this familiarity, one which is almost inexpressible. In his poem, ''Angle of Geese,'' the title poem of his 1974 collection, Momaday represents the idea of a symmetry beyond words, a perception recognized, and an angle of vision in the image of birds, and he asks the key question for himself as a poet: ''How shall we adorn / Recognition with our speech?'' In other words, how do we speak, how do we write, of our complex human experience of the world that comes from multilayered associations, perceptions from many vantage points?

In 1967, Momaday privately printed one hundred copies of *The Journey of Tai-me*, the ''archetype,'' as he says, of *The Way to Rainy Mountain*. In 1969, he published what became the well-known version, with beautiful drawings by his father, Al Momaday. In *Ancestral Voice*, which is a book-length interview, Momaday speaks about the genesis of *The Way to Rainy Mountain*, about the Kiowa stories that make it up, and speaks, as he does in many articles and interviews, about racial memory: ''Every writer is forced to rely, at some point, on the imagination. . . . I can take credit for setting down those Kiowa stories in English, in *The Way to Rainy Mountain*, but I didn't invent them. The imagination that informs those stories is really not mine, though it exists, I think, in my blood. It's an ancestral imagination.'' Momaday believes that Kiowa history, the creation story of the Kiowa, and the other stories that make up Kiowa oral tradition are all part of his racial memory— what he represents in *House Made of Dawn* as Francisco's ancient Jemez ''infallible sense''—a primordial and genetic imprint of tribal narrative in the Kiowa mind.

This concept of the imagination is first expressed in the prologue to *The Way to Rainy Mountain*, where Momaday asserts that the combination of racial memory and language constitutes Kiowa tribal identity: ''In one sense . . . the way to Rainy Mountain is preeminently the history of an idea, man's idea of himself, and it has old and essential being in language. . . . It is a whole journey . . . made with the whole memory, that experience of the mind which is legendary as well as historical, personal as well as cultural.'' For this reason, *The Way to Rainy Mountain* may be considered autobiographical; it is Momaday's journey of imagination and self-discovery.

Although not entirely necessary to a reader's appreciation of this text, an explanation of its structure, a subject that has attracted much scholarly attention, can be helpful for a first-time reader. *The Way to Rainy Mountain* is arranged in three main parts entitled ''The Setting Out,'' ''The Going On,'' and ''The Closing In.'' A poem, "Headwaters," precedes the rest of the text, followed by a prologue and an introduction. An epilogue followed by a poem, "Rainy Mountain Cemetery," closes the text. Within the three main parts are twenty-four consecutively numbered sections, each with three parts of its own. (There are also illustrative and thematic groupings of four, the number four being sacred in Indian spirituality.) Alan R. Velie describes the three principal, thematically linked parts in his book *Four American Indian Literary Masters* (1982) as a Kiowa "legend or story, a historical anecdote or observation, and a personal reminiscence." In "The Man Made of Words," Momaday identifies the parts with the mythical, the historical, and the immediate. Together, the three parts make up the Kiowa racial memory.

In the introduction, Momaday tells of Aho, his grandmother, who lived at Rainy Mountain all her life and was born when "the Kiowas were living the last great moment of their history." At one time, "in alliance with the Comanches, [the Kiowa] had ruled the whole of the southern Plains." Momaday calls the Kiowa the "centaurs of the Plains" here, using an image that he often evokes to recall the grand horse culture the Kiowa developed and to express an essential aspect of the Kiowa inheritance that he as well as some of his characters are conscious of. The actual and imaginative memory of Aho is a thread that runs through *The Way to Rainy Mountain* and a significant portion of Momaday's other autobiography, *The Names*. Aho is one of the last generation of Kiowa who lived in an exclusively oral culture. The final moment of *The Way to Rainy Mountain* takes place at her burial site; in this passage Momaday brings together the themes of racial memory and cultural landscape: "There, where it ought to be, at the end of a long and legendary way, was my grandmother's grave. Here and there on the dark stones were ancestral names. Looking back once, I saw the mountain and came away." Aho lived until Momaday was

an adult. She told him one of his two favorite Kiowa legends, one that Momaday includes in the introduction, the story of Rock-tree Boy, Tsoai-talee. Tsoai-talee is one of Momaday's Indian names, given to him when he was a baby at the site of the legend, Devil's Tower in Wyoming, by his Kiowa great-grandfather, Pohd-lohk. As the legend goes,

> Eight children were there at play, seven sisters and their brother. Suddenly the boy was struck dumb; he trembled and began to run upon his hands and feet. His fingers became claws, and his body was covered with fur. Directly there was a bear where the boy had been. The sisters were terrified; they ran, and the bear after them. They came to the stump of a great tree, and the tree spoke to them. It bade them climb upon it, and as they did so it began to rise into the air. The bear came to kill them, but they were just beyond its reach. It reared against the tree and scored the bark all around with its claws. The seven sisters were borne into the sky, and they became the stars of the Big Dipper.

This legend holds special significance for Momaday because the bear is his creative power, transforming him into energy, spirit, vitality: he explains in *Ancestral Voice*, "I am a bear. I do have this capacity to become a bear. The bear sometimes takes me over and I am transformed. . . . My name proceeds from that story [of Tsoai-talee]. I have being in that story somehow, and I am curious to know as much as I can about it."

Critics have remarked on the bear stories in *House Made of Dawn*, where the bear is paradoxically both enemy and healer. In her 1990 book *Landmarks of Healing*, Susan Scarberry-García argues that the themes of the bear stories include "fleeing from evil, accumulation of spiritual power, and transformation." She quotes a letter to the scholar Matthias Schubnell in which Momaday speaks of his years at Jemez as an outsider, asking: "How did I survive that? How did I come through that experience with my tongue in one piece? It was of course medicine. The bear was watching close by. The bear is always there.'' In his poem "The Bear," which appears in *Angle of Geese*, the bear is omnipresent: "Seen, he does not come, / move, but seems forever there." The bear guards Momaday's power to create through language. For many tribal people of the Plains, the bear holds a special and paradoxical place. To the Oglala Lakota, the bear has powers to know what is under the earth, the knowledge of the roots and herbs used for healing. Although fierce and menacing, the bear is considered to have kinship with humans, also, as Joseph Epes Brown points out in *Animals of the Soul: Sacred Animals of the Oglala Sioux* (1992). Brown quotes Bear with White Paws as saying that "the Bear has a soul like ours, and his soul talks to mine and tells me what to do."

Momaday's other favorite Kiowa legend is about the arrowmaker:

If an arrow is well made, it will have tooth marks upon it. That is how you know. The Kiowas made fine arrows and straightened them in their teeth. Then they drew them to the bow to see if they were straight. Once there was a man and his wife. They were alone at night in their tipi. By the light of the fire the man was making arrows. After a while he caught sight of something. There was a small opening in the tipi where two hides were sewn together. Someone was there on the outside, looking in. The man went on with his work, but he said to his wife: "Someone is standing outside. Do not be afraid. Let us talk easily, as of ordinary things." He took up an arrow and straightened it in his teeth; then, as it was right for him to do, he drew it to the bow and took aim, first in this direction and then in that. And all the while he was talking, as if to his wife. But this is how he spoke: "I know that you are there on the outside, for I can feel your eyes upon me. If you are a Kiowa, you will understand what I am saying, and you will speak your name." But there was no answer, and the man went on in the same way, pointing the arrow all around. At last his aim fell upon the place where his enemy stood, and he let go of the string. The arrow went straight to the enemy's heart.

This story more than any other demonstrates Momaday's preoccupation with language and the oral tradition. As he explains this legend in "The Man Made of Words," the arrowmaker *is* the man of words, and he saves himself through language. He has "consummate being in language," and the arrowmaker realizes this himself when he says that the person outside, if he is Kiowa, will understand his words and speak his Kiowa name aloud. The story concerns not only the arrowmaker and language but all literature: "The point of the story lies, not so much in what the arrowmaker does, but in what he says—and indeed that he says it. . . . he speaks, and in so doing he places his very life in the balance. . . . here . . . language becomes most conscious of itself; we are close to the origin and object of literature."

Like his grandmother Aho, Momaday's grandfather Mammedaty, son of the chief Lone Wolf, figures prominently in Momaday's work although he died before Momaday was born. Mammedaty appears in the 1976 collection of poems named after him, *The Gourd Dancer*. In the title poem, Mammedaty dances, dressed as he is in a photograph included in *The Names*; he "takes the inward, mincing steps / That conjure old processions and returns." Then, someone "spoke his name, Mammedaty, in which his essence was and is. It was a serious matter that his name should be spoken there in the circle, among the many people, and he was thoughtful, full of wonder, and aware of himself and of his name." He is given a beautiful horse, and "all of this was for Mammedaty, in his honor, as even now it is in the telling, and will be, as long as there are those who imagine him in his name." Like the arrowmaker, Mammedaty in this passage has his "consummate being in language."

A peyote man, Mammedaty had visions and "powerful medicine." In section 21 of *The Way to Rainy Mountain*, the mythical passage captures the image of Mammedaty alone on the southern Plains early in the morning, hearing only the song of the meadowlarks. Suddenly, he hears a whistle. He sees the head of a small boy over the grass. He looks again carefully, but "there was no one; there was nothing there. He looked for a long time, but there was nothing there." The accompanying historical anecdote describes the only photograph extant of Mammedaty, the one reproduced in *The Names*. The personal passage, third in the sequence, reminisces about Mammedaty's power, explaining that it was confirmed in the Kiowa imagination when Mammedaty witnessed a mole "*bl[o]w . . . earth out of its mouth*" at the entrance to its burrow, signifying "that Mammedaty had got possession of a powerful medicine." The mole in Plains belief holds extraordinary meaning because it is an animal, like the bear, that transcends the margins above and below the earth; it is closely associated with the power of the Lakota leader Crazy Horse.

The image of the child over the grass and Mammedaty's gaining possession of powerful medicine are not just events of the past to Momaday. The imaginative journey to Rainy Mountain to find his tribal heritage culminates in the personal reminiscences that Momaday calls "immediate." In *The Names* Momaday says of Mammedaty: "he came to be imagined posthumously in the going on of the blood, having invested the shadow of his presence in an object or a word, in his name above all. He enters into my dreams; he persists in his name." The stories of the past become part of the present and part of Momaday's creative imagination. The child, for example, reappears *as* powerful medicine in Momaday's novel from 1989, *The Ancient Child.*

In telling of the remarkable figure Ko-sahn, a one-hundred-year-old Kiowa woman, Momaday brings alive both tribal history and the power of language and naming. Ko-sahn, older than Aho but her friend, is one of the few remaining Kiowa at that time who witnessed the last Sun Dance in 1887 before this ceremony was prohibited by the

government, before most of the buffalo were slaughtered, before the tribe was diminished and herded to Fort Sill. Momaday says in *The Way to Rainy Mountain* that the grand time of the "centaurs of the Plains" was short but through Ko-sahn he is able to recover it: "it is within the reach of memory still, though tenuously now, and moreover it is even defined in a remarkably rich and living verbal tradition which demands to be preserved for its own sake. The living memory and the verbal tradition which transcends it were brought together for me once and for all in the person of Ko-sahn." Ko-sahn appears in the epilogue to *The Names*, in the final section of Momaday's imaginary journey back to Kiowa country. He finds her among his ancestors and she speaks his Indian name. Ko-sahn, Momaday writes, seemed to "know of everything that happened to [the Kiowa], to the coming-out people, from the beginning. She was very old, and I loved the age in her; it was a thing hard to come by, great and noble in itself. . . . In the evenings we told stories, the old people and I."

In "An American Land Ethic," an essay that appears in *Ecotactics: The Sierra Club Handbook for Environment Activists* (1970), Momaday discusses Ko-sahn's imprinted memory of Kiowa history:

> in the racial memory, Ko-sahn had seen the falling stars [the 1833 meteor shower that marks the start of Kiowa tribal history]. For her there was no distinction between the individual and the racial experience, even as there was none between the mythical and the historical. Both were realized for her in the one memory, and that was of the land. This landscape, in which she had lived for a hundred years, was the common denominator of everything that she knew and would ever know.

Ko-sahn's name itself, just the saying of her name, invokes tribal history.

In "The Man Made of Words," Momaday recounts the difficulties of writing *The Way to*

Rainy Mountain. Unable to grasp in any immediate way the meaning of what he had written, his eyes fell upon Ko-sahn's name: "And all at once everything seemed suddenly to refer to that name. The name seemed to humanize the whole complexity of language. All at once, absolutely, I had the sense of the magic of words and of names. Ko-sahn, I said, and I said again KO-SAHN." Then, he recalls, Ko-sahn appeared to him, saying, "You imagine that I am here in this room. . . . That is worth something. You see, I have existence, whole being, in your imagination. It is but one kind of being, to be sure, but it is perhaps the best of all kinds. . . . Then she turned slowly around, nodding once, and receded into the language I had made."

Through thinking of Ko-sahn, Momaday is able to journey in his racial memory back to the headwaters of the Yellowstone River in western Montana, where he recaptures the moment of the emergence of his tribe. He explains in *The Names,* "There were meadows full of wildflowers. . . . And in one of these, in a pool of low light, [I] touched the fallen tree, the hollow log there in the thin crust of ice"; thus he knows he has journeyed back to the creation of Kiowa history. He explains in *Ancestral Voice* that names are of great significance for him: "Naming is very complicated, and a sacred business. . . . When you name something, you confer being upon it at the same time. . . . Language is essentially a process of naming. . . . If there is one unimaginable tragedy, it is to be without a name, because then your existence is entirely suspect. You may not exist at all without a name."

Momaday carries his belief that naming *is* existence into the novel *The Ancient Child. The Ancient Child* tells the story of Locke Setman, called Set, an artist of some reputation who finds in middle age that his work is personally unsatisfying since it panders to public taste. Although he is comfortably situated in San Francisco, with a talented agent, a growing international reputation, and a beautiful lover, Lola Bourne, Set no longer creates as he once did. With sarcasm, he says that he paints "in vain, in order to relieve the terrible boredom of God." He wishes "to see and to paint with excitement, with a child's excitement," a longing that moves him to withdraw slowly from the demand for his work and "endeavor" instead "to save his soul." Momaday explains this idea of art in an essay he published in 1974, "I Am Alive": "[The Indian child] sees with both his physical eye and the eye of his mind; he sees what is really there to be seen, including the effect of his own observation upon the scene. It is the kind of vision that is developed in poets and painters and photographers, often over a span of many years."

Half Kiowa, Set is orphaned by the time he is seven years old, then adopted by a retired scholar, Bent Sandridge, who is, except for scattered memories, the only father Set has ever known: "all that he had of his forebears was a sediment in his memory, the memory of words his [Indian] father had spoken long ago." The novel opens not with Set, but with an account of the death of Billy the Kid (William Bonney), perhaps the American Southwest's most legendary young outlaw, and with a depiction of a fantasy relationship between Billy and the novel's other main character, Grey, a young Navajo-Kiowa medicine woman and visionary. In many ways, Grey reflects Momaday himself, especially in her fascination with the legend of William Bonney. Momaday considers himself an authority on Billy the Kid, calling him a reflection of the Wild West, as important to the Western imagination as the Oglala Lakota Crazy Horse. Grey's imaginary relationship with Billy permeates the novel, culminating in her writing poems and stories about him (these appear again in the collection Momaday published in 1992, *In the Presence of the Sun*) and ending only when she accepts her power as a medicine woman. As one who writes about

Billy the Kid, she gains insight into the "marriage of history and myth" that is the American West: "she saw more deeply than most into that side of Billy that was kind and gentle, that part of him that secured his legend beyond time. It is, she knew, the admixture of the violent and the benign that seems so central to the American experience and so powerful in the American imagination."

Set's crippling psychic illness begins after he returns to Oklahoma, responding to a mysterious telegram about the impending death of Grey's great-grandmother Kope'mah. As an elder like Aho and Ko-sahn, Kope'mah connects Grey to the time of Kiowa grand history, when Set-angya (Sitting Bear) and others lived as great warrior chiefs. Set's journey and the experience of meeting Grey awaken his Indian consciousness, the missing piece of himself that causes his pain. Like many half-breeds or Indians estranged from their cultural identity, Set had "an incomplete idea of himself." The passing of a medicine bundle from Kope'mah to Set begins his struggle, which is nearly to the death, to accept and to learn to live in harmony with his animal spirit, the bear. Once the medicine bundle is in his possession, the bear comes forth: "Set reels and turns inside himself. He applies color to his brain with a knife. Smoke permeates the medicine bundle; a low heat emanates from it. Dancers touch their feet to the earth. A deranged boy glares from the shadows. An ancient woman inhabits the body of a girl. Death displaces the silver, scintillant fish. The bear comes forth." This highly suggestive and metaphoric brief chapter, typical of the novel's spiritual center, begins the process of Set's transformation that dominates the rest of the novel.

The Ancient Child alludes to many more myths than the one of Billy the Kid; Edward B. St. John notes in his review that the novel is a web of "what Levi-Strauss calls mythemes, tiny facets of meaning that inexorably draw the reader in." Undeniably, these mythemes draw the reader in;

moreover, they create the network of connections that not only gives the novel thematic shape but also links it to Momaday's other fiction and poetry. The mytheme of the buffalo is a good example. Kope'mah, in her last hours with Grey at her side, enters into a state of consciousness described as "strangely lucent" in which "she became for the last time her own being . . . as on the day she was born, a hundred years ago." As a child, holding her father's hand, she has a vision of buffalo on the "peneplain" of the Washita River:

> [The buffalo] seemed to her very noble and meticulous and, indeed, sacred, as they moved in slowest motion through a mist of colored rain. . . . The herd seemed a great, black, bushy vegetation on the earth, moving like sediment in water, slow as the shadow of the summer cloud. But that night her father told her, to her astonishment, that the herd was already a day's ride to the west.

A Kiowa folktale told by Old Lady Horse (included in Peter Nabokov's *Native American Testimony*) tells a similar story, about a young woman who got up very early and saw the end of the buffalo. As she looks across Medicine Creek through the early morning mist, "she saw the last buffalo herd appear like a spirit dream. Straight to Mount Scott the leader of the herd walked. . . . Inside Mount Scott the world was green and fresh, as it had been when she was a small girl. . . . Into this world of beauty the buffalo walked, never to be seen again."

Besides being crucial to the survival of the Plains Indians, the buffalo took on mythic significance; it became a once-and-future creature. In contemporary American Indian art the buffalo often appears magically radiant and steaming, emerging from talismanic shields and clouds. In Momaday's prose poem from 1974, "The Colors of Night," which appears in the collection *In the Presence of the Sun*, a man kills a buffalo for no reason. The pointless death of the "great, old, noble beast" grieves and shames the people: Momaday writes, "in the west they could see the hump and spine of the huge beast which lay dying along the edge of the world. They could see its bright blood run into the sky, where it dried, darkening, and was at last flecked with flakes of light." For contemporary Plains tribes, the rebirth of the White Buffalo Calf is immanent and imminent. The successful buffalo hunt is regarded as the highest achievement in predatory skill; its reenactment, a Plains cultural dream still vivid, filling men and women with intense nostalgic yearning, in literature if not also in actuality.

The mytheme of the ancient child is inextricably linked with the figure of the bear from Momaday's favorite legend of Tsoai. This legend frames *The Ancient Child*: it is recounted in the prologue and then reenacted by Set at the end (in the section called "Shadows") when Set goes on his vision quest. In *Rainy Mountain* the appearance of a boy to Mammedaty, which is one of the four powerful events in his life, is first in racial memory in the story told to the Kiowa by the Piegan band of the Blackfeet and told to Set by his Kiowa father. A child comes into the Piegan camp, seemingly from nowhere, joins the Piegan band with little fear, but does not speak their language. Without a name and without language, the puzzle of the Piegan is, "How can we believe in the child?" (As Momaday says, to be without a name is the greatest tragedy, intolerable.) After the child has disappeared, the Piegan decide it must have been a bear. This tale appears in *Ancient Child* in the chapter called "This matter of having no name is perhaps the center of the story." When Set makes his first journey to Kiowa country, he suddenly sees a boy in the arbor at a distance, just as Mammedaty did on the Plains. The appearance of this mysterious child lingers in Set's mind, recurring after his adoptive father has died and his illness has already begun; Set's final, healing journey is to find this manifestation of the ancient child.

Set and Grey return to Navajo country, Lukachukai, where Set slowly comes to terms with his Indian heritage and the spiritual identity inherent in his name, Set; comes to understand the meaning of ancestral memory; and comes to know the appropriate way to live his life. (Momaday discusses this matter of "appropriateness," which includes at its heart a respect for one's native heritage, in "Native American Attitudes to the Environment.") The deepest part of himself, Set realizes, is that which comes from Set-angya (the warrior chief), history, and myth, and from Tsoai-talee, the ancient child who became the bear. The novel closes with Set's vision quest. In the presence of Tsoai, the rock tree, Set sees "the image of a great bear, rearing against Tsoai. It was the vision he had sought."

In the Presence of the Sun is a remarkable collection of stories, poems, and drawings spanning thirty years of Momaday's creative life, 1961–1991. The volume is divided into four sections. The poems in the section titled "Selected Poems" have all previously appeared in either *Angle of Geese* or *The Gourd Dancer*, with the exception of one poem, "Sun Dance Shield." This poem is both a personal song about Plains identity and an introduction to the preface of section 3, called "In the Presence of the Sun: A Gathering of Shields." This is the poem:

Mine is a dangerous shield;
there is anger in it,
there is boasting in it.

Mine is a beautiful shield;
there is yellow pollen in it,
there is red earth in it.

Mine is a sacred shield;
there is vision in it,
there is remembrance in it.

Mine is a powerful shield;
there is medicine in it,
there is a sun dance in it.

My life is in this shield,
my life is in this shield.

The shield contains all things of individual and sacred importance: all life is contained on the shield. The description of the Plains shield and its significance begins with a brief story of the shield of the Hunkpapa Lakota, Sitting Bull, and goes on to a description of a shield's construction, ending with the powerful statement: "first and above all the shield is medicine."

In addition to being a work of art, "highly evolved in terms of proportion, design, symmetry, color and imagination," the Plains shield has a nearly inexpressible relationship to its bearer: "the Plains warrior *is* his shield. It is his personal flag, the realization of his vision and his name, the object of his holiest quest, the tangible expression of his deepest being. . . . the shield is its own story." As Momaday introduces the sixteen drawings of shields that follow (significantly, sixteen is a multiple of the native sacred number four) and introduces the stories that are paired with the drawings, he situates both drawings and stories in a world of language and identifies them as "meditations that make a round of life." The small, feathered shield that ends the preface is a lovely and unusual combination of line drawing and calligraphy, an emblem of the close connection Momaday sees between the two mediums.

The sixteen shields are line drawings; the stories that accompany them reveal the essence of each shield and tell of the owners or the histories of the shields. While the drawings and the stories are best appreciated when seen side by side, a description of one pair will show the way they work. The fourth shield, called "Bote-talee's Shield," depicts a spider's web. The story that goes with it tells of Bote-talee's discovery of Spider Woman, who is for many tribes the bringer of wisdom, creativity, and beauty. The Cherokee believe that Spider Woman brought intelligence and the light of human understanding of history to their people. Here, Momaday uses this ancient belief to infuse the shield with spiritual power:

Bote-talee found the Spider Woman. In the early morning he went swimming. When he reached the bank he looked directly up into the sun. There, just before his eyes, was a spider's web. It was a luminous, glistening shield. Bote-talee looked at it for a long time. It was so beautiful that he wanted to cry. He wondered if it were strong as well as beautiful. He flung water upon it, heavy water, again and again, but it remained whole and glistened all the more. Then a sun spider entered upon the web. "Spider Woman," Bote-talee said, "Will you give me this perfect shield?" "Bote-talee," said Spider Woman, "This is your shield."

The prose poems about Billy the Kid, which form the second section of the book, are introduced by a brief biography of Billy—brief because so little is known about him. The record of his birth, his death, and the number of men he killed exists. He met a Sister Blandina Segale, a nun from the Sisters of Charity, twice in his life, and he attended his mother's wedding. With the final line of his biography of Billy the Kid, Momaday again reminds us that identity is to a great extent imaginary; we are what we imagine and what is imagined about us. About the twenty-one stories and poems that follow, Momaday says: "All else of what follows is imagined; nonetheless, it is so." And the poem "Wide Empty Landscape with a Death in the Foreground" suggests that Billy never really dies:

Now that he is dead he bears
Upon the vision
Merely, without resistance.
Death displaces him
No more than life displaced him;
He was always here.

More myth than a figure of history, Billy the Kid exemplifies all that Momaday believes about the American imagination. Rather than offering a "romantic treatment" of the murderous Billy the Kid (as Ed Marston claimed Momaday did in his review of *The Ancient Child*), Momaday illustrates in these poems *how* the myth of the American West was made and remade; indeed, as a Marxist critic would probably say, in these poems Momaday shows how all ideology works.

The final section of *In the Presence of the Sun* contains twenty-seven new poems, many written during the time Momaday spent as a teacher at Moscow State University in 1974. Momaday describes his time there as one of "creative explosion," during which he wrote new poems about the Southwest, his family and ancestors, and one about the 1890 massacre at Wounded Knee. "The Great Fillmore Street Buffalo Drive" is a poignant poem that is connected to the section in *The Way to Rainy Mountain* where Momaday recounts how he and his father were chased by a buffalo cow and also to the mytheme of the buffalo in *The Ancient Child*. In this poem, past and present, history and myth merge. The man on horseback on San Francisco's Pacific Heights drives the buffalo herd into the sea, "their wild grace gone . . . blood blisters at their teeth." At the same time he feels the loss he creates, loss of the great herd forced from the last reaches of the continent into the ocean by westward expansion, and he dreams back the mythic buffalo landscape:

One bull, animal representation of the sun,
he dreams back from the brink
to the green refuge of his hunter's heart.
It grazes near a canyon wall,
along a ribbon of light, among redbud trees,
eventually into shadow.

Beginning in the 1980s Momaday developed a fine reputation as a visual artist. He told Laura Coltelli in a 1985 interview published in her book *Winged Words* (1990) that he sees a very close connection between drawing and writing; to him, they are inseparable. Before "a man could write, he could draw," Momaday observes. "But writing is drawing, and so the image and the word cannot be divided." In *Ancestral Voice*, Woodard devotes thirty-six pages to interviewing Momaday about his art. He began by doing pencil and graphite drawings, then turned to painting in acrylics and watercolors. Al Momaday worked almost exclusively in watercolor, paying special attention to meticulous detail in his paintings on traditional Indian themes. Momaday prefers to work quickly and spontaneously in different media, capturing in rapid strokes the essence of his object. Of his horse's head drawing in *The Gourd Dancer* he says that "the pen did not come off the page until I had finished. . . . I make no attempt to reflect an object in all of its dimensions . . . I attempt to express the essence of the dancer or horse's head or whatever." He sees this technique as critical to achieving a wholeness or integrity of vision that he seeks in his writing as well. His artwork includes a series of paintings of dolls and fetishes, one of which, *Rainy Mountain Christmas Doll*, painted in 1986, is reprinted in *Ancestral Voice*. Kiowa visual tradition does not focus on landscapes, but Momaday is very interested in portraits and has done several of Set-angya, the historic Kiowa leader. While Momaday's art has been exhibited across the United States and in Europe, it also appears in his books; there are sixty of his illustrations in *In the Presence of the Sun*. Readers of this book are able to experience immediately the integration of Momaday's writing and drawing.

It is nearly impossible to express the range and depth of Momaday's impact on American literature, especially American Indian literature. While criticism on his work will continue, it perhaps will never capture just what he has accomplished. For native people, the accomplishment constitutes a story of cultural spirit and the sacred power of language. In describing himself and his work, Momaday says that he writes with the assumption that he is telling a story and that a reader will listen. I have listened to him as a scholar, but also and more closely as an American Indian, and I think that would please him.

Selected Bibliography

WORKS OF N. SCOTT MOMADAY

POETRY AND FICTION

"Los Alamos." *New Mexico Quarterly,* 29, no. 3:306 (Autumn 1979).

"Eve My Mother." *Sequoia,* 5, no. 1:37 (1959).

"The Well." *Ramparts,* 2, no. 1:49–52 (May 1963).

The Journey of Tai-me. Santa Barbara: Privately printed, 1967.

House Made of Dawn. New York: Harper & Row, 1968.

The Way to Rainy Mountain. Albuquerque: University of New Mexico Press, 1969.

"The Bear and the Colt." In *American Indian Authors.* Edited by Natachee Scott Momaday. Boston: Houghton Mifflin, 1972. Pp. 119–124.

Angle of Geese and Other Poems. Boston: David R. Godine, 1974.

"The Pear-Shaped Legend: A Figment of the American Imagination." *Stanford Magazine,* 3, no. 1:46–48 (Spring–Summer 1975).

"Praise So Dear." *Imprint of the Stanford Library Associates,* 1, no. 2:5–9 (1975).

"To the Singing, to the Drum." *Natural History,* 84, no. 2:41–44 (1975).

"But Then and There the Sun Bore Down." In *Carriers of the Dream Wheel: Contemporary Native American Poetry.* Edited by Duane Niatum. New York: Harper & Row, 1975. P. 105.

The Gourd Dancer. New York: Harper & Row, 1976.

"Kiowa Legends from *The Journey of Tai-Me.*" *Sun Tracks: An American Indian Literary Magazine,* 3, no. 1:6–9 (Fall 1976).

"There, Outside, the Long Light of August. . . ." *Museum of the American Indian Newsletter,* 3, no. 2 (1978).

"Tsoai and the Shield Maker." *Four Winds,* 1, no. 3:38–43 (1980).

The Ancient Child: A Novel. New York: Doubleday, 1989.

In the Presence of the Sun: Stories and Poems, 1961–1991. New York: St. Martin's Press, 1992.

Circle of Wonder: A Native American Christmas Story. Santa Fe: Clear Light, 1994.

NONFICTION

"The Morality of Indian Hating." *Ramparts,* 3, no. 1:29–40 (1964).

The Complete Poems of Frederick Goddard Tuckerman. Edited by N. Scott Momaday. New York: Oxford University Press, 1965.

"An American Land Ethic." In *Ecotactics: The Sierra Club Handbook for Environment Activists.* Edited by John G. Mitchell and Constance L. Stallings. New York: Trident, 1970. Pp. 97–105.

"A Vision beyond Time and Place." *Life,* July 1971, p. 67.

Colorado: Summer, Fall, Winter, Spring. New York: Rand McNally, 1973.

"I Am Alive." In *The World of the American Indian.* Washington, D.C.: National Geographic Society, 1974. Pp. 11–26.

"A First American Views His Land." *National Geographic Magazine,* 105, no. 1:13–18 (1976).

The Names: A Memoir. New York: Harper and Row, 1976; Tucson: University of Arizona Press, 1976.

"Native American Attitudes to the Environment." In *Seeing with a Native Eye: Essays on Native American Religion.* Edited by Walter Holden Capps. New York: Harper & Row, 1976. Pp. 79–85.

"Oral Tradition and the American Indian." In *Contemporary Native American Address.* Edited by John R. Maestas. Provo, Utah: Brigham Young University, 1976. Pp. 294–306.

"The Man Made of Words." In *The Remembered Earth: An Anthology of Contemporary Native American Literature.* Edited by Geary Hobson. Albuquerque: University of New Mexico Press, 1981. Pp. 162–176.

"Confronting Columbus Again." In *Native American Testimony: An Anthology of Indian and White Relations: First Encounter to Dispossession.* Edited by Peter Nabokov. New York: Harper and Row, 1978. Pp. 436–439.

BIOGRAPHICAL AND CRITICAL STUDIES

Ballinger, Franchot. "The Responsible Center: Man and Nature in Pueblo and Navajo Ritual Songs and Prayers." *American Quarterly,* 30:90–107 (1978).

Barry, Nora Baker. "The Bear's Son Folk Tale in *When the Legends Die* and *House Made of Dawn.*" *Western American Literature,* 12:275–287 (1978).

Billingsley, R. G. "*House Made of Dawn:* Momaday's Treatise on the Word." *Southwestern American Literature,* 5:81–87 (1975).

Blaeser, Kimberly. "*The Way to Rainy Mountain*: Momaday's Work in Motion." In *Narrative Chance: Postmodern Discourse on Native American Indian Literatures.* Edited by Gerald Vizenor. Albuquerque: University of New Mexico Press, 1989; Norman: University of Oklahoma Press, 1993. Pp. 39–54.

Brown, Joseph Epes. *Animals of the Soul: Sacred Animals of the Oglala Sioux.* Rockport, Mass.: Element, 1992.

Davis, Jack L. "The Whorf Hypothesis and Native American Literature." *South Dakota Review,* 14, no. 2:69–72 (Summer 1976).

Dunn, Dorothy. *American Indian Painting of the Southwest and Plains Area.* Albuquerque: University of New Mexico Press, 1968.

Dutton, Bertha P. *Indians of the American Southwest.* Englewood Cliffs, N.J.: Prentice-Hall, 1977.

Evers, Lawrence J. "Words and Place: A Reading of *House Made of Dawn.*" *Western American Literature,* 11:297–320 (February 1977).

Finnegan, Ruth. *Oral Poetry: Its Nature, Significance, and Social Context.* Bloomington: Indiana University Press, 1992.

Garrett, Roland. "The Notion of Language in Some Kiowa Folk Tales." *Indian Historian,* 5, no. 2:32–37, 40 (1972).

Gunn Allen, Paula. "N. Scott Momaday and James Welch: Transition and Transcendence." In her *The Sacred Hoop: Recovering the Feminine in American Indian Traditions.* Boston: Beacon Press, 1992. Pp. 86–94.

Kerr, Baine. "The Novel as Sacred Text: N. Scott Momaday's Myth-Making Ethic." *Southwest Review,* 63, no. 2:172–179 (Spring 1978).

Kluckhohn, Clyde, and Dorothea Leighton. *The Navaho.* 1946; Repr. New York: Doubleday, 1962.

Lincoln, Kenneth. "Word Senders: Black Elk and N. Scott Momaday." In *Native American Renaissance.* Berkeley and Los Angeles: University of California Press, 1983. Pp. 82–121.

———. "Tai-me to Rainy Mountain: The Makings of American Indian Literature." *American Indian Quarterly,* 10, no. 2:101–117 (Spring 1986).

Littlebird, Larry. "American Indian Image on Film: The Southwest." Paper on the film *House Made of Dawn,* presented at the University of New Mexico, Albuquerque, February 1982.

McAllister, Mick. "The Topology of Remembrance in *The Way to Rainy Mountain.*" *Denver Quarterly,* 12, no. 4:19–31 (1978).

Marriott, Alice. *Saynday's People: The Kiowa Indians and the Stories They Told.* Lincoln: University of Nebraska Press, 1963.

Marston, Ed. Review of *The Ancient Child. New York Times Book Review,* December 31, 1989, p. 14.

Mayhall, Mildred P. *The Kiowas.* 2d ed. Norman: University of Oklahoma Press, 1971.

Meredith, Howard. "N. Scott Momaday: A Man Made of Words." *World Literature Today,* 64, no. 3:405–407 (Summer 1990).

Mooney, James. *Calendar History of the Kiowa Indians.* Washington, D.C., 1898; Washington, D.C.: Smithsonian Institution, 1979.

Nicholas, Charles A. "*The Way to Rainy Mountain*: N. Scott Momaday's Hard Journey Back." *South Dakota Review,* 13, no. 4:149–158 (1975–1976).

Nye, Wilbur Sturtevant. *Bad Medicine and Good: Tales of the Kiowas.* Norman: University of Oklahoma Press, 1962.

Ortiz, Alfonso, ed. *New Perspectives on the Pueblos.* Albuquerque: University of New Mexico Press, 1972.

Prampolini, Gaetano. "*The Ancient Child*: A Conversation with N. Scott Momaday." *Native American Literatures: Forum,* 2–3:77–100 (1990–1991).

Roemer, Kenneth M., ed. *Approaches to Teaching Momaday's "The Way to Rainy Mountain."* New York: Modern Language Association, 1988.

Ruoff, A. LaVonne Brown. "Oral Literatures." In her *American Indian Literatures: An Introduction, Bibliographic Review, and Selected Bibliography.* New York: Modern Language Association, 1990. Pp. 5–52.

St. John, Edward B. Review of *The Ancient Child. Library Journal,* 114:165 (August 1989).

Scarberry-García, Susan. *Landmarks of Healing: A Study of* House Made of Dawn. Albuquerque: University of New Mexico Press, 1990.

Schneider, Jack W. "The New Indian: Alienation and the Rise of the Indian Novel." *South Dakota Review,* 17, no. 4:67–76 (1979).

Schubnell, Matthias. *N. Scott Momaday: The Cultural and Literary Background.* Norman: University of Oklahoma Press, 1985.

Strelke, Barbara. "N. Scott Momaday: Racial Memory and Individual Imagination." In *Interpretations: A Gathering of Indian Memories, Symbolic*

Contexts, and Literary Criticism. Edited by Abraham Chapman. New York: Meridian-NAL, 1975. Pp. 348–357.

Swann, Brian, ed. *Smoothing the Ground: Essays on Native American Oral Literature.* Berkeley and Los Angeles: University of California Press, 1983.

Swann, Brian, and Arnold Krupat, eds. *Recovering the Word: Essays on Native American Literature.* Berkeley and Los Angeles: University of California Press, 1987.

Taylor, Paul Beekman. "Repetition as Cure in Native American Story: Silko's *Ceremony* and Momaday's *The Ancient Child.*" In *Repetition.* Edited by Andreas Fischer. Tübingen, Germany: Narr, 1994. Pp. 221–242.

Trimble, Martha Scott. "N. Scott Momaday." In *Fifty Western Writers: A Bio-bibliographical Sourcebook.* Edited by Fred Erisman and Richard W. Etulain. Westport, Conn.: Greenwood, 1982. Pp. 313–324.

Velie, Alan R. *Four American Indian Literary Masters: N. Scott Momaday, James Welch, Leslie Marmon Silko, and Gerald Vizenor.* Norman: University of Oklahoma Press, 1982.

Watkins, Floyd C. *In Time and Place: Some Origins of American Fiction.* Athens: University of Georgia Press, 1977.

Witherspoon, Gary. *Language and Art in the Navajo Universe.* Ann Arbor: University of Michigan Press, 1977.

INTERVIEWS

Abbott, Lee. "An Interview with N. Scott Momaday." *Puerto Del Sol*, 12, no. 2:21–38 (1973).

Bataille, Gretchen M. "An Interview with N. Scott Momaday—April 16, 1977." *Iowa English Bulletin*, 29, no. 1:28–32 (1979).

———. "Interview with N. Scott Momaday—April 11, 1979." *Newsletter of the Association for the Study of American Indian Literature*, n.s., 4, no. 1:1–3 (1980).

Bruchac, Joseph. "The Magic of Words: An Interview with N. Scott Momaday." In *Survival This Way: Interviews with American Indian Poets.* Edited by Joseph Bruchac. Tucson: University of Arizona Press, 1987. Pp. 173–191.

———. "N. Scott Momaday." *American Poetry Review*, 13, no. 4:13–18 (July–August 1984).

Coltelli, Laura. "N. Scott Momaday." In *Winged Words: American Indian Writers Speak.* Lincoln: University of Nebraska Press, 1990. Pp. 89–100.

Evers, Lawrence J. "A Conversation with N. Scott Momaday." *Sun Tracks: An American Indian Literary Magazine*, 2, no. 2:18–21 (1976).

Owens, Louis. "N. Scott Momaday." In *This Is about Vision: Interviews with Southwestern Writers.* Edited by William Balassi, John F. Crawford, Annie O. Eysturoy. Albuquerque: University of New Mexico Press, 1990. Pp. 59–69.

"Shouting at the Machine: An Interview with N. Scott Momaday." *Persona: The University of Arizona Undergraduate Magazine of Literature and Art*, 24–44 (Spring 1984).

Woodard, Charles L. *Ancestral Voice: Conversations with N. Scott Momaday.* Lincoln: University of Nebraska Press, 1989.

AUDIO AND VIDEO RECORDINGS

Remember My Horse. Cambridge, Mass.: Credo Records, 1976.

N. Scott Momaday. Columbia, Mo.: American Audio Prose Library, 1983. Interview and reading by N. Scott Momaday.

Winds of Change: A Matter of Promises. Hosted by N. Scott Momaday. Beverly Hills: Pacific Arts Video Publishing, 1990.

Our Vanishing Forests. Narrated by N. Scott Momaday. Bethesda, Md.: Public Interest Video Network, 1992.

—SALLY L. JOYCE

Simon J. Ortiz
1941–

POET, SHORT STORY WRITER, editor, and teacher, Simon Ortiz draws deeply on his roots as an Acoma Pueblo Indian and on the movements for equal rights and social justice that inspired many writers who began to publish in the 1960s. His work, though largely written in English, models itself on the Keresan oral tradition of storytelling, song, and everyday conversational rhythms. Ortiz often chooses for his subjects the old-time stories of creation, heroes, and tricksters with all their mishaps and triumphs. But he also writes about the more recent history of the Acoma people and other Native Americans on reservations and in cities and about the contemporary political, environmental, health, and labor conditions that touch them. Keenly aware of other cultures and of class issues, Ortiz reaches out in his work to all people who are disempowered:

> . . . the language of our struggle
> just sounds and reads like an Indian,
> Okie, Cajun, Black, Mexican hero story—

he writes in the poem "What I Mean," which appears in his book *Fight Back: For the Sake of the People, for the Sake of the Land,* a brilliant pastiche of essay and poetry published in 1980.

In his writing, Ortiz seeks to make connections between his particular experience as an Acoma Pueblo man living in the last half of the twentieth century and universal experience. Compassion, laughter, hope, and the courage to fight back against oppression—these are the traditional Pueblo values Ortiz embraces in his work, values that have enabled his people to survive. In an interview with Laura Coltelli that was published in her book *Winged Words: American Indian Writers Speak* (1990), Ortiz says of his writing, "It's hopeful and optimistic in the sense that struggle is always hopeful and optimistic." His is no easy optimism. Ortiz is well acquainted with loss and despair, both in his personal life and in the history of the Acoma people, who were brutalized by the Spanish in colonial times; subsequently encroached upon by railroad and mining interests; subjected, too, to two centuries of genocidal government policies aimed at annihilating American Indian identity. But as Ortiz has remarked in many contexts, cynicism is a cowardly response and a very un-pueblo one. If Ortiz' writing has a dominant theme, it is the ongoing quest of ordinary people "to live in a good way"; he traces that quest in traditional stories, recorded history, and his own observations of contemporary life.

Ortiz says in *A Good Journey,* his second book of poems, published in 1977, "*The source of these narratives is my home.*" Home for Ortiz is primarily Acoma Pueblo in New Mexico. The

Spanish who entered what is now the southwestern United States in the sixteenth century encountered many groups of sedentary people living in stone or adobe houses clustered around a central plaza. Such places reminded the newcomers of the little Spanish towns they had left behind, so they classified all the native town-dwellers together as *Indios de los Pueblos.* In fact, the Pueblo Indians of New Mexico and Arizona are a heterogeneous people who today are recognized by the federal government as nineteen separate tribes. Though they share many cultural characteristics, Pueblo peoples have different systems of reckoning kinship and inheritance, and they speak dialects of four distinct languages. Keres is the language spoken at Zia, Santa Ana, San Felipe, Santo Domingo, Cochiti, Laguna, and Acoma Pueblos. Keres-speaking people tend to settle on heights overlooking river valleys. They are matrilineal; they consider houses, in particular, to be the property of women.

Ortiz' Acoma, identified on tourists' postcards as "Sky City," is a village atop a 350-foot-high bone-colored mesa that is seventy miles southwest of Albuquerque, New Mexico. Aacqu, the name for Acoma in Keresan, is often said to mean "white rock," but Ortiz agrees with Acoma elders that *aacqu* actually means "which is prepared." After the people emerged from the lower worlds, they migrated slowly about on the earth-surface until they came at last to Aacqu, the place the gods prepared for them to dwell. According to archeologists, the great rock has been home to the Acoma people since at least the thirteenth century, making it, together with the Hopi village of Oraibi, one of the two oldest continuously inhabited sites in the United States. Acoma elders date their presence at Aacqu still further back, to time immemorial. In *Fight Back: For the Sake of the People, For the Sake of the Land,* Ortiz imagines those ancestors who found their way to Acoma from earlier homes at Mesa Verde or Chaco Canyon and muses on what the wanderers must have experienced back in that dawn of their becoming *Aacqumeh hanoh,* "the Acoma people":

> The valley of Aacqu is a beautiful and peaceful place. It must have been wealthy with grass growing in the dark fertile soil nourished by the nearby volcanic mountain slopes and a number of perennial springs gushing forth. It must have been cool and restful in the shade of the tall mesa which would be their eventual home. Their journey had been long and difficult from the northwest through vast experience, trials, and crises. Kaashkatruti, that's where we lived before, the people say in their oral tradition, pointing northwestward.

Home for Ortiz is not just Acoma, the ancient town on the rock citadel, but also Acomita and McCarty's, the two outlying Acoman villages on the flatland below the mesa, where most Acoma people keep house and live their everyday lives. Always, Acoma people grew their crops of corn, squash, and beans on the valley floor, and as the danger of military invasion decreased, more people chose to live near the farmlands. Ortiz himself was raised at McCarty's in a stone house whose two original rooms were built by his grandfather, though like most Acomas the family maintains a house on top of the rock for feast days and other ceremonial occasions.

McCarty's is named in English for an Irishman who pumped water for the boilers of the Atchison, Topeka, and Santa Fe locomotives. Acomas call it Deetzeyamah, the "North Door," because, as Ortiz explains in *Fight Back,* "Looking northward from Aacqu and the tall rock monolith on which the mother pueblo sits, there is an opening, like a gateway, between two mesas." Home encompasses as well the blue-forested volcanic woman-mountain rising on the northern horizon. She is called Kaweshtima, "Snow Peaked," at Acoma and Tseh-pi-nah, "Woman Veiled in Clouds," at neighboring Laguna Pueblo. On English speakers' maps of this heavily Native American and Hispanic region,

Kaweshtima shows up as Mount Taylor, ungendered but named in honor of Zachary Taylor, hero of the Black Hawk War, the campaigns against the Seminole, and the Battle of Buena Vista, who served briefly as the twelfth president of the United States. Place names—the differences between the naming practices of the native people and the names on maps—are significant; Keresan names honor a place itself, celebrating its qualities or recalling some event that happened there, rather than glorifying a single human being. As Ortiz remarks in *Fight Back,* ''Those Aacqumeh names do not appear anywhere except in the people's hearts and souls and history and oral tradition, and in their love.'' Place, language, and worldview are inseparable, and thus home for Ortiz is also the Keres language, his first language, and the Keresan oral tradition of song and story, his first texts.

Around Ortiz' Acoma, the land, the roads, and the buildings shaped of rock and earth speak of all the history recounted in old-time tales and in more recent written annals, including ones written by Simon Ortiz. Nearly every feature, every landform around Acoma and Laguna is storied. There lie the black swirling lava beds that congealed from the blood of the monster the hero twins slew back at the beginning of time: see the poem that begins, ''I sat for a long time,'' in *Fight Back.* There rises the rock pinnacle whence Coyote fell to her death; here her desiccated corpse lay until Skeleton Fixer came along and put the dry bones back together. A restored Coyote trotted off, once again an emblem of sheer survival: ''*And there is always one more story,*'' in *A Good Journey.* There on the east side of the adobe wall that encloses the Acoma cemetery a hole has been carefully carved out for the children sent into Mexican servitude in 1599 by the Spanish invading army under Don Juan de Oñate; when at last they find their way home, their spirits will enter the village through that opening. Ortiz tells that story in two places: ''The Story of How a Wall Stands'' in *Going for the Rain,* a book of poems he published in 1976, and ''Always the Stories'' in *Coyote Was Here,* a collection of essays edited by Bo Schöler and published in 1984. That dirt road is where back in 1952 the Felipe brothers lured the sadistic state policeman off the road so they could kill him; some say that when they did him in they used the ritual way for dispatching a witch. Ortiz recounts this incident in ''The Killing of a State Cop,'' a story that appears in an anthology from 1974, *The Man to Send Rain Clouds,* edited by Kenneth Rosen. As Ortiz says, ''There is always one more story.''

Given the overwhelming presence of the land and the stories that have grown up around it, perhaps it is not so surprising that Acoma and Laguna pueblos, with a combined population of fewer than ten thousand people, have produced so many Native American writers since the late 1960s. Not only Simon Ortiz but Paula Gunn Allen, Carollee Sanchez, Lee Francis, Leslie Marmon Silko, Larry and Harold Littlebird, and Aaron Carrall come from these pueblos; poets Joy Harjo (Creek), Luci Tapahonso (Navajo), and Bill Oandasan (Yuki) all spent time at Acoma or Laguna among their in-laws. As a nurturer of writers, the land around Acoma and Laguna is comparable to turn-of-the-century Dublin.

Simon Joseph Ortiz was born in Albuquerque on May 27, 1941, the fourth child and first son among eight brothers and sisters. Ortiz' mother, Mamie Toribio Ortiz, a lively, intelligent woman who cared deeply about her family's well-being, was a potter like previous generations of women in her family, painting beautiful red and black polychrome designs on the white slip of her pots and jars with hand-ground pigments and a yucca brush. Ortiz writes of her in a 1977 poem in *Sun Tracks,* ''My Mother and My Sisters'':

She paints with movements whose origin
has only to do with years of knowing

just the right consistency of paint
the tensile vibrancy of the yucca stem
and the design that things are supposed to have.

Ortiz' father, Joe Ortiz, was known for his singing and storytelling, for his woodcarvings of dancers, and for his skill as a stonemason. In "Song / Poetry and Language—Expression and Perception," a wonderful little essay that first appeared in 1977 in the *Sun Tracks* series published by the University of Arizona and was subsequently published as a chapbook by Navajo Community College Press, Ortiz pays moving tribute to his father:

> His movements are very deliberate. He holds the Buffalo Dancer in the piece of cottonwood poised on the edge of his knee, and he traces—almost caresses—the motion of the dancer's crook of the right elbow, the way it is held just below midchest, and flicks a cut with the razor-edged carving knife. And he does it again. He knows exactly how it is at that point in a Buffalo Dance Song, the motion of elbow, arm, body, and mind.

Ortiz is grateful that as a child he got to help his father carry sandstone and mix adobe mortar as they added rooms to their house at McCarty's, for in that way he came early to an understanding of craft that he would later apply to writing. In "The Language We Know"—published in 1987 in *I Tell You Now,* a collection of autobiographical essays by Native Americans, edited by Brian Swann and Arnold Krupat—Ortiz explains that stonework

> takes time, persistence, patience, and the belief that the walls that come to stand will do so for a long, long time. . . . I like to think that by helping to mix mud and carry stone for my father and other elders I managed to bring that influence into my consciousness as a writer.

Walls made of stone and adobe, characteristic of pueblo architecture, have remained a crucial image for this Pueblo writer.

Acoma lies twenty-five miles from Grants, the nearest sizable Anglo town. In the Acoma of the 1940s it was still possible to raise a child almost entirely within a Keresan world, at least until he or she started school. This was Ortiz' experience. Unlike most contemporary Native American writers, Ortiz is full-blooded, and his first language was his native tongue, though it took him a while to begin to use it. Though he recalls always loving speech and stories, family legend has it that Ortiz was a late talker who did not speak until he was almost four. The silence ended when his grandfather took a large brass skeleton key and inserted it between the child's lips and turned it, unlocking language. As Ortiz grew older, his father noticed how he would quietly eavesdrop on adults sitting around the kitchen table swapping traditional stories, family anecdotes, and gossip, and he nicknamed his son Simon "the reporter."

Since his father was a cacique (religious leader) of the Antelope clan, and he was also surrounded by members of his and his mother's Eagle Clan, Ortiz grew up immersed in the Keres language and Acoma culture. Though Ortiz can trace between his and his parents' lifetimes a gradual weakening of the traditional social structure, the clan system remains strong at Acoma. One of Ortiz' most self-defining memories goes back to the night he and one of his sisters were taken by his grandfather to an all-night ceremony of initiation. The twelve-year-old Simon struggled to stay awake during the songs and prayers and the ritual recitation of the story of Acoma (from creation to the present), a story the youngsters needed to know because they were entering the age of maturity and responsibility. As he walked home at dawn holding his grandfather's and his sister's hands, Ortiz felt himself transformed. He writes about this experience in "Always the Stories":

> I remember there was a moon in the south western sky. Hearing a mockingbird speaking

from the rocks near my grandmother's house at Aacqu, I remember trembling with the new knowledge which had been shared to me [sic]. . . . When we got home, we found apples and oranges strung on yucca cord hanging on the doorknob, and later we could eat salt again with our meals. That occasion is more than memory to me. . . . The tribal memory remembered specific practices and a philosophy to insure continuity, but . . . there had to be active participation in order to state the belief that life was important.

Ortiz has believed ever since that as an Acoma person and as a writer he must be an active affirmer of his beliefs.

Ortiz emphasizes the profound distinction that struck him early in life between Acoma and *howchaatya dhuuh*, "the world beyond." Both of Ortiz' parents received some schooling as boarding students at Saint Catherine's Indian School in Santa Fe and were more exposed to Euro-American culture than many of their contemporaries at Acoma. Both saw the necessity for their own children to be educated. "It was implied that education was necessary for employment and to live a bountiful, better life," Ortiz recalls in the introduction to *Woven Stone,* published in 1992, which reprints three of his previous books. But the Ortizes were also well aware that the educational system was designed to erode Indian identity, and they urged their children to use their education to preserve their heritage rather than to leave it behind:

Often and again, I heard elders repeat, 'Go to school, stay in school, and get educated so you can help our people.' Later when I learned the language to think and talk about colonialism I knew the Aacqumeh hanoh were in resistance against the more destructive elements of American education and policy.

Ortiz' first exposure to the world beyond Acoma was relatively gentle, for he was able to attend the Bureau of Indian Affairs (BIA) day school at McCarty's instead of being yanked off to a boarding school. When he began, the only English he knew was the ABCs and the phrase his older sisters had taught him: "Good Morning, Miss Oleman." As at most BIA and mission schools, the children were punished by a sharp crack on the knuckles if they were caught speaking their native language. Looking back, Ortiz expresses surprise that he has so many pleasant memories of his early schooling, for "the reality of it then," he writes in *Woven Stone,* "was harsher than my recollections." But he was a precocious child already in love with language and story, and he quickly became fluent and literate in English. Like many bright children, he read omnivorously and indiscriminately—the ubiquitous Dick and Jane readers, children's classics, comic books, *My Weekly Reader,* the *Reader's Digest,* and pulp romance and western magazines. Those texts, many of which spoke of a world of pale people with green lawns, picket fences, small families, and fathers in suits, began to prepare him for further adventures in *howchaatya dhuuh.*

Though the Ortiz family did subsistence farming, their main income came from Mr. Ortiz' work as a laborer and welder for the Santa Fe Railroad. Simon was in the fifth grade when his father's job brought the family for a year to Skull Valley, Arizona, where they lived in shabby company housing built for the Santa Fe Railroad section crews and their families who were mostly Hispanics and Native Americans. At the one-room Skull Valley schoolhouse, where the Ortiz children were the only Indian students, Ortiz experienced for the first time the feeling of being a minority. He perceived that it was not only race that set him apart from his schoolmates but poverty as well. Perhaps it was partly class that allied Ortiz with his first white friend, a boy who was the only other fifth grader, the son of an itinerant ranch hand; the two boys would play "cowboys and Indians,'' unself-consciously taking turns at the roles. At Skull Valley, Ortiz earned his first typewriter as a premium for selling ointment door-to-door, and here his first poem, a Mother's Day tribute to Mamie Ortiz, was published in the school newspaper.

The Skull Valley teacher urged the children to read, and Ortiz discovered Sherlock Holmes, *Robinson Crusoe, Huckleberry Finn,* and other children's classics in the three-shelf school library. Above all, the year seems to have taught him that he could indeed live among white people, though they were very different from him:

> As a people, I distrusted them less, although I was still wary of something that drove them willfully, aggressively, powerfully, and arrogantly. In that first time of living outside of Acoma, I didn't know it was that same drive that had settled its domain and rule over Native American lands and enforced an educational policy disguised as civilization.

After sixth grade back at the McCarty's Day School, Ortiz became a boarding student, first at Saint Catherine's Indian School in Santa Fe, the school his parents had attended, then briefly at the BIA's Albuquerque Indian School. He finished his secondary education at Grants High School. Few Native American students in the area chose to go to public school at Grants, but Ortiz was successful and popular there, winning academic and athletic plums ranging from Honor Boy to Boy's State to co-captain of the football team. Ortiz has vivid memories of a school banquet in his honor where he was astonished and disturbed to hear his proud mother, who usually talked only Keres at home, take great care to speak exclusively in English. He wanted her to feel at ease; she wanted not to disgrace him.

During these adolescent years, Ortiz began to try his hand at writing. He reports that nothing in his juvenilia marked him as Native American. His models were the non-Indian authors he was reading—Hamlin Garland, Edgar Lee Masters, Carl Sandburg, Sherwood Anderson, William Saroyan, William Faulkner, John Steinbeck, Carson McCullers, J. D. Salinger, and especially Ernest Hemingway. His early sketches and stories, he says, were usually about poor working people, but the characters were not situated ethnically or culturally. Toward his last years of high school he came across the Beats and responded strongly to the Buddhism he found in Allen Ginsberg and Gary Snyder, which seemed to him to bear many affinities to Acoma philosophy and spirituality. The Beat writers first gave him, he says, an idea that he could write out of his Acoma experience.

Ortiz' career is not simple to trace after high school, largely because of the alcoholism he has fought since his late teens. He himself acknowledges in ''Always the Stories,'' ''Alcohol has taken a terrific and painful toll on me personally, and I've struggled for recovery for years.'' There have been for him many teaching jobs and projects begun and abandoned, many attempts at recovery, many places of residence, many relationships. The remarkable thing is that Ortiz has produced work of such high quality as a writer and as a spokesman for Native American issues. As an editor of two anthologies—the 1981 volume *A Ceremony of Brotherhood,* coedited with Rudolfo A. Anaya, and the 1983 book *Earth Power Coming,* a fine collection of short fiction by American Indian writers—he has been, like Maurice Kenny, Gerald Vizenor, Paula Gunn Allen, Geary Hobson, and Joe Bruchac, one of the people instrumental in decolonizing American Indian literature by putting it in the hands of American Indian editors and publishers.

Ortiz did not make a serious try at college in the first few years after his graduation. Instead, like many young men in the area, in 1960 he went to work for the Kerr-McGee Corporation in the uranium mines at nearby Ambrosia Lake, then prospering on account of the cold war. Ortiz mostly worked aboveground, loading and crushing yellowcake ore. The company did little or nothing to protect its laborers from the dangers of handling radioactive material. Twenty years later, Ortiz would chronicle his experience of working at low pay under hazardous conditions in *Fight Back: For the Sake of the People, for the Sake of the Land.*

After a brief stint at Fort Lewis College in Durango, Colorado, during the year 1961–1962, when he discovered that his stated ambition to be a chemist did not match his real talents, Ortiz joined the U.S. Army and served from 1962 to 1965, rising to the rank of sergeant. During basic training in Louisiana, the young private had his first encounter with undisguised racism when he and a Chicano buddy hitchhiked to Lake Charles on a weekend pass. As Ortiz relates in the preface to *Woven Stories,* a concerned African American sergeant picked them up and swiftly educated the naive Southwesterners, warning them, "Dark people get killed around here." Ortiz had long admired from afar Dr. Martin Luther King and the civil rights movement, without quite understanding that he himself might be intimately connected to that struggle. Later during his time in the army, at a bus station where he was expected to use the "Colored Only" facilities, Ortiz was swept by memories of the lesser but very real discrimination he had felt as a child in Skull Valley. His first sustained attempt at a series of connected texts, epistolary (unpublished) poems he called "Dear America," grew from that experience.

From 1966 to 1968 Ortiz was enrolled at the University of New Mexico, and during the year 1968–1969 he was a Fellow in the International Writing Program at the University of Iowa. His first exposure in a nationally known periodical came that same year with the publication of four poems in John R. Milton's extraordinary special issue of the *South Dakota Review* (volume 7, number 2), devoted exclusively to writing by Native Americans. (Milton titled his introduction "American Indians Speak for Themselves.")

The journal also featured work by James Welch, Ronald Rodgers, and Janet Campbell (Hale), among others. Readers of that issue who were accustomed to thinking of American Indian poetry only in terms of literary "translations" or "renderings" of traditional material by anthropologists, folklorists, and writers like Oliver La Farge, Mary Austin, and Henry Wadsworth Longfellow would be quite comfortable with a poem like Ortiz' "Smoking My Prayers": such readers would recognize the ritual subject matter of the poem, its simplicity, and its technique of incremental repetition.

now that i have lighted my smoke
i am motioning to the east
i am walking in thought that direction
i am listening for your voices.

But those same readers would be jolted by Ortiz' fresh and edged colloquial voice in "Ten O'Clock News":

berstein disc jockey
telling about indians
on ten o'clock news
o they have been screwed
i know everybody's talking
about indians yesterday.

(A much-revised version of this poem appears in *A Good Journey.*) With great economy, the speaker wearily suggests the pro-Indian rap of a white liberal disc jockey. Like all modish people in the late 1960s, this disc jockey claims to "know" and feel bad about what Indians have experienced. He strings together pious words "about indians yesterday / murdering conquest the buffalo," but he seems to have no idea that Indians today are among his listeners. Many of them, in fact, have come to rely upon the ten o'clock news rather than "ghost dance dreams" for vital information. The disc jockey deplores "railroad hustling progress," the genocidal policies of Manifest Destiny that advocated the slaughter of buffalo in order to starve out those Plains tribes who made crossing the continent a perilous enterprise. Of course the man on the radio is right: Indians *have* been "screwed." But his awareness of Native America stops at about 1888. He does not know about people like Ortiz' own family, for whom in this century the railroad rather than the buffalo has been the main source of food, clothing, and shelter—an ironic truth but a truth nevertheless.

In the second half of the poem, Ortiz suggests that even though the Ghost Dancers' dreams in the 1880s of undoing the European invasion through sheer spiritual power have not yet come true, perhaps in a fresh spate of inspired dreaming the Indian listeners out there in radioland will receive a new prophetic revelation: the media has no idea what contemporary Native Americans are really thinking. Ah, but then again, Indians themselves may not know what is in their hearts, because

> . . . they believe in trains
> and what berstein tells them
> on ten o'clock news

That is, if they listen less to their dreams or their own leaders and more to what romantics say about them, they will be cut off from themselves. In the end, the poem turns upon itself, not in the form of a sacred hoop but rather in a perverse and disquieting circle.

There are many things a reader with stereotyped ideas about American Indian poetry would not be prepared for in "Ten O'Clock News," such as Ortiz' sophisticated use of line breaks. The poem invites us to examine each line as a unit of meaning at the same time we are reading for larger grammatical structures. A line like "i know everybody's talking" is part of the larger thought "i know everybody's talking about Indians," but it also suggests that what every white liberal is saying about civil rights and American

history is "I know"; most people of color have encountered the type of white sympathizer who professes to know more about Indian oppression and to feel it more keenly than the oppressed Native Americans themselves. Another surprise for the unwary is the sinister humor of this poem. Wit and teasing are in fact integral to much everyday American Indian discourse, but non-Indian people have often seemed to prefer to think of Indians as stoic, unsmiling "wooden-Indian" stereotypes like Hank Williams' Kawligea rather than sly tricksters or outrageous clowns.

In 1969, the year of the special issue of the *South Dakota Review,* the Kiowa author Scott Momaday's *House Made of Dawn* won the Pulitzer Prize and the lawyer-educator Vine Deloria, Jr., came out with *Custer Died for Your Sins,* his lively exegesis of American history from the Sioux point of view. In 1970, Dee Brown published his popular history of the Plains wars, *Bury My Heart at Wounded Knee.* Antiwar and civil rights organizations, including the American Indian Movement, founded in July 1968, were much in the news, and in November 1969 Native American demonstrators began their one-and-a-half-year occupation of Alcatraz. Native Americans were themselves beginning to establish small presses and journals. A fresh wave of interest in writings by and about American Indians had begun.

Ortiz, working by the early seventies at jobs as a public relations specialist at Rough Rock Demonstration School in Arizona and as a community organizer and newsletter editor for the National Indian Youth Council, found himself engaged by many issues. He was one of the first to print stories about such subjects as the devastation wrought by Peabody Coal's strip mining on Navajo land at Black Mesa in Arizona. His writing was greatly energized by the events going on around him. He explains in "Always the Stories," "It was a dynamic time; the Red Power movement . . . dramatically expressed itself by the seizure of Alcatraz Island, AIM activism. . . . it was tremendously encouraging to be who you were. . . . I had no concept of myself as a Native American writer in earlier years. But now I was a writer and poet who was Native American from Acoma Pueblo.'' Ortiz began to be widely anthologized in a number of texts like Brother Benet Tvedten's *An American Indian Anthology* (1971), Shirley Hill Witt and Stan Steiner's *The Way* (1972), and Duane Niatum's *Carriers of the Dream Wheel* (1975). Kenneth Rosen's anthology of American Indian short fiction, *The Man to Send Rain Clouds* (1974), called special attention to Ortiz' short stories; out of the nineteen texts that Rosen included, five are by Ortiz, seven by Leslie Marmon Silko, and one by Larry Littlebird and his Circle Film collective, which gives this whole landmark collection a decidedly Acoma/Laguna Pueblo focus.

With his success at the end of the sixties and early seventies, Ortiz became determined to move beyond anthologies and journals to a book of his own. His first unwieldy manuscript of four hundred pages was, at editors' suggestions, cut down, divided in two, and revised; the results were two books that followed one another in rapid succession, *Going for the Rain,* brought out in 1976 by the Native American Publishing Program at Harper & Row, and *A Good Journey,* published by Turtle Island Press in 1977. Together, these books established Ortiz as a major voice in American poetry.

Going for the Rain takes for its dominant metaphor the journey. The four carefully arranged sections of the book are named for the stages of a successful journey in search of renewal: ''The Preparation,'' ''Leaving,'' ''Returning,'' and ''The Rain Falls.'' Many kinds of journeys are alluded to here. On the grandest scale there is the ultimate and all-encompassing Keresan journey, the great and evolutionary journey of all created beings, beginning with their difficult ascent up through three lower worlds into this surface world of light; continuing with their migrations here and there and their adventures as they seek for Aacqu, the place readied for them; and their ongoing attempts, once they have found their home, to do right by it. This last includes fulfilling their ritual obligations to ''go for the rain'': in Keresan culture, certain people are given the responsibility of traveling to various shrines to ask the gods for rain.

The first section of *Going for the Rain,* ''The Preparation,'' fittingly enough opens with an account called ''The Creation, According to Coyote,'' in which the narrator of the poem listens to Coyote give a delightful and moving rapid-montage excursion through all Acoma history:

And later on, they came to light
after many exciting and colorful
and tragic things of adventure;
and this is the life, all these, all these.

Acoma history is good to think back upon as preparation for any of the various journeys undertaken in the poems that follow. The important thing is that the old stories are real, and true in the most important ways, for they teach us that through all vicissitudes, all stages of their complex history, Acoma people have continued, not just as grim survivors but as people with a keen capacity for wonder who are thankful for multiple forms of abundance. Though Coyote is often a tall-tale teller and a b.s. artist, as Ortiz' narrator concedes, he is also the quintessential survivor; the narrator is right to believe Coyote when he tells his age-old tale of the ''Great Journey'' toward a better life. Ortiz likes to play with the version of this journey that anthropologists tell, too, the Bering Strait land bridge theory, which posits the idea that people from Asia gradually migrated to the Americas. In ''The Poet'' Ortiz evokes a genetic memory of a cave scene where

A woman was moaning,
and later she was laughing,
not very far from a glacier's edge.

But whether the Acoma people emerged from below or traveled a perilous, island-hopping passage over icy waters, both stories—as Ortiz tells them—testify to the people's courage and endurance.

It is important to note that Ortiz, like most Native American authors, does not write only as an individual, a private soul chronicling his idiosyncratic thoughts and emotions, but as a member of a community, a particular tribal people. And the image of the journey has special, complex meanings for Keresans and other Pueblo peoples. In Keresan culture, for example, all human beings (not just the rain priests) are understood to be intimately connected with rain. Moreover, rain is not sought only for the sake of the crops. Rather, it is thought to make up part of the essence of every human being. In Keres thought, animating, moisture-laden wind enters people's bodies at birth and circulates through them in the form of their breath for as long as they live. When death comes, this spirit-breath is exhaled and journeys toward the dwelling place of the dead ancestors. The newly dead are often entreated to send back rain because ancestor spirits, the *shiwana* (whose ranks the dead now join), can take the shape of rain clouds and return in that form to visit the pueblo: a prayer for rain is a prayer for such a visit from the dead. When fat, dark thunderclouds mass on the summer horizon, or when snow veils the slopes of Kaweshtima, it is the old ones making a return journey, bringing the blessing of lifegiving moisture back to their people, taking part in a cycle of love and care and renewal that extends beyond death. The image of a person who is at once both an individual and a member of a people venturing along the road toward death and beyond haunts this book and much of Ortiz' other writing.

On the simplest level, the title *Going for the Rain* alludes to ordinary journeys from one physical place to another. As Ortiz pointed out to Joseph Bruchac, the editor of *Survival This Way: Interviews with American Indian Poets,* a collection published in 1987, Native Americans, though deeply connected to their own homelands, have always been great travelers, whether they were following migratory buffalo herds across the plains, venturing to the Pacific to gather coral and abalone, trading for live parrots in Mexico, or just plain visiting back and forth with one another. Some of Ortiz' poems concern his own hikes and camping trips in the Southwest natural world he observes so acutely. For example, there is ''A Snowy Mountain Song,'' in which he describes Kaweshtima, Snow-Peaked, in winter:

a white scarf
tied to her head
the lines on her face
are strong.

Other poems deal with Ortiz' more epic quests across the country as writer, activist, and scholar, such as the trip he made in 1970 across the deep South and through the Northeast in order to reaffirm his conviction that, rather than being a race on the margin of extinction, ''Indians are everywhere.'' Much of the pleasure this book gives comes from poems that relate what happened during Ortiz' chance encounters, including conversations with other Americans in bars, in buses, in national parks. Many of the people in the poems are American Indians who persist in still being here, despite the opinions of folks like the park ranger in ''Travels in the South'' who solemnly assures Ortiz that ''this place is noted for the Indians / that don't live here anymore.''

Another important autobiographical journey that figures in *Going for the Rain* concerns children. The manuscript of this book was taking shape around the time in July 1973 when a daughter was born to Ortiz and the Creek poet

Joy Harjo. The book is suffused with references to the journey of the child from conception through interuterine growth, birth, and the stages of infancy; it also tells the concomitant story of the father's journey into parenthood. (Significantly, Ortiz and Harjo named their daughter Rainy Dawn.) Many poems in *Going for the Rain,* like "My Children, and a Prayer for Us," urge continuity and awareness on Rainy and on her elder stepbrother Raho Nez, two Acoma people newly embarked on the journey of life. But not all the journeys represented in *Going for the Rain,* or not all legs of them, are so affirmative. Especially in the two middle sections of the book, there are many poems about the anomie, despair, and loss that are associated with the alcoholism of both the speaker and the people whom he observes. And yet, the book is always canted toward survival. In "The Poems I Have Lost," one of the grimmer poems in the collection, a poem about missed connections, lost poems and relationships, and alcoholic confusion, "fragments" of memory are presented as enough, though just barely enough, to keep the speaker in touch with his identity and his life.

What saves the speaker, what calls him home, is often something that another person might find inconsequential and of no value. But Ortiz' culture has taught him to infer the larger whole from the visible shard of it. Another poem, "Fragment," finds the down-and-out speaker on his way "to city court / to be judged again." In the midst of his apprehension, he picks up a small stone and slips it in his pocket as a talisman. Fingering it, he suddenly realizes that this is no idle good luck charm, but "a fragment / of the earth center / and I know that it is / my redemption."

This small stone, which seems so humble and yet possesses so much connective power, comes to mind again when Ortiz, in a poem in the final section of the book, which largely celebrates homecoming and renewal, writes about the walls

of the Acoma graveyard that his stonemason father helps to maintain; the poem is called "A Story of How a Wall Stands." The wall appears precarious, with its stones apparently loosely set into the outer layer of mortar, but as his father patiently explains, "That's just the part you see." Then he demonstrates for his son the intricacy of the inner construction of the wall by interlacing his hands:

> . . . Underneath
> what looks like loose stone,
> there is stone woven together.

Crafted with infinite care, the wall which seems so fragile is certain to last "for a long, long time." The true nature of the wall cannot be inferred from just studying one aspect of it; its strength cannot be gauged from one stone, or several, or even all the stones one can see. The wall is a carefully knit construction of many stones, most of them not immediately visible, though they are there. The wall must be understood as a whole. Those artisans who know most about such walls can describe the whole to the rest of us. This poem is not only about the skill that goes into a pueblo-built wall. It is about all sorts of artisanship and art, including the making of poetry, and the responsibility to create with care. As Kenneth Lincoln remarks in the "Now Day Indi'ns" chapter of his critical study *Native American Renaissance* (1983):

> As the father shaped wood and layered stone, so the son fits words. . . . [Ortiz] then learns from his father the tradition of "weaving stone"—not piece work individually, no more than words exist separately, but a tapestry of stones, a pattern that connects. It is a mortaring, too, of son to father, inner to outer being, stone to spirit, concrete particle to abstract design.

The poem is also, by extension, about Ortiz' Acoma culture and, ultimately, perhaps, about the most astonishing of creators and creations, the gods and the universe itself.

In the essay "Song / Poetry and Language—Expression and Perception," written in 1977, shortly after both *Going for the Rain* and *A Good Journey* appeared, Ortiz makes an explicit connection between his father's worldview and a holistic view of language and poetry. Here, Ortiz gives us several wonderful vignettes of his father; we see Mr. Ortiz at work in his woodcarving shop, making ritual preparations to go deer hunting, shaping prayer sticks, and affectionately recalling the way a beloved Pueblo elder whom he knew in the old days used to sing and dance. In between these beautifully realized moments, Ortiz weaves thoughts on his own poetics. In each vignette, the father instructs the son in some subtle but important knowledge, but when the linguistically trained son explicitly asks for instruction, the father cannot help him because the question the son asks makes no sense to him:

> When my father has said a word,—in speech or in song—and I ask him, 'What does that word break down to? I mean breaking it down to the syllables of sound or phrases of sound, what do each of these parts mean?' And he has looked at me with exasperated—slightly pained—expression on his face, wondering what I mean. And he tells me, "It doesn't break down to anything."

This impasse is very like the one Navajo poet Luci Tapahonso describes in her poem "All I Want," when the speaker, hoping to make bread like her Acoma mother-in-law's, asks, "How many cups of flour?" and the woman replies:

> Ah yaa ah, she says
> tossing flour and salt into a large silver bowl
> I don't measure with cups.
> I just know by my hands,
> just a little like this is right, see?
> You young people always ask
> those kinds of questions,
> she says

> thrusting her arms into the dough
> and turning it over and over again.

When the natural cook makes bread, she is thinking of the feel of the dough beneath her hands, not the cupful of flour, or the spoonful of salt, water, leavening. To the stoneworker who knows about walls, the wall is a whole, not an assemblage of individual stones. To a linguist, words "break down," but to the native speaker, speech or song is a spontaneous response to the moment as he perceives it, a whole composed of both perception and expression in response to that moment. The Native American ideal of wholeness and harmony both in art and in living one's life is crucial in Ortiz' work.

The penultimate poem in *Going for the Rain* both qualifies and affirms the sense of wholeness, renewal, and homecoming that marks most of the final section. The title, "For Joy to Leave Upon," clearly signals the end of a relationship or of a stage in that relationship, though the speaker's specific circumstances are never directly mentioned. Instead, the speaker recalls getting out of the army and trying to revive his late grandfather's long-neglected grapevines. His project meets with some success:

> But I left that Summer. Later,
> I came back and saw a few green new shoots,
> and then I left again.
>
> Tonight, there is a waning moon.

The poem suggests that, as the last poem of the book concludes, "It doesn't end." This lack of ending can be positive or negative, good or wistful. Life goes on, so do joy and pain and loss. Some journeys might be better not undertaken, and yet it is the nature of people to seek for things and to go through phases as the moon does. But if the moon-mother waxes, she wanes again, too: grapevines can be coaxed back. Human tribulation and restless seeking do not end, but neither does the promise of renewal, the possibility of going for the rain.

A Good Journey, carved out of the same original fat manuscript as *Going for the Rain,* understandably pursues many of the same themes. It is a more freewheeling book, both in terms of its overall structure and also in terms of the way individual poems are put together. It also seems at once more joyous and more angry. Exuberance especially marks the opening section, "Telling," where Ortiz experiments with ways to capture in print the experience of being a member of an oral community. *Going for the Rain* and *A Good Journey* both contain many poems in which Ortiz, whose ear for colloquial English is flawless, dramatizes conversations his speaker participates in or overhears. But in "Telling," in a series of long poems, Ortiz takes on the considerable challenge of evoking the storytelling sessions of his Acoma boyhood, attempting to recreate not only the speaking voice of the storyteller but the intimate and complex social arena of the telling. Ortiz does not set the scene of these poems for us at all pictorially, with a kitchen warmed by a woodstove or the like. What he gives us instead in abundance are the voices. We are given more whole passages in Keresan, not all of them translated, than in any of Ortiz' previous poems. Children interrupt excitedly; listeners reflect on the story, or argue with the storyteller about the way *they* heard it; one story naturally suggests another to some member of the audience, who then takes his turn as storyteller. Like the anthropologist Dennis Tedlock, who published his groundbreaking *Finding the Center: Narrative Poetry of the Zuni Indians* in 1972, Ortiz experiments with typography and spacing to try to convey some of the nuances of sound level as well as the pauses and silences at a storytelling session. As Ortiz suggests in the prologue to the poem "And there is always one more story," many voices can be heard besides the voices of those actually present at the telling:

> *My mother was telling this one. It must be an old story but this time she heard a woman telling it at one of those Sunday meetings. The woman was telling about her grandson who was telling the story which was told to him by somebody else. All these voices telling the story, including the voices in the story—yes, it must be an old one.*

Most of the old-time stories being told, retold, discussed, and argued about in this book concern Coyote, the great Southwestern trickster and emblem of Native American survival. As I said in my 1979 essay, "Coyote Ortiz: *Canis latrans latrans* in the Poetry of Simon Ortiz," Ortiz' Coyote, "in his myriad-mindedness, his actions silly and shrewd . . . sets forth the range of human possibility. He is what we are and what we could be."

In the strong, angry poems of the fourth section of *A Good Journey,* entitled "Will Come Forth in Tongues and Fury," Ortiz—as Andrew Wiget asserts in his critical biography, *Simon Ortiz,* published in 1986—"contrasts the effects of 'civilization' as he sees them with the implicit claims made for the benefits of 'progress,' exposing the rhetoric's ability to disguise reality." Ortiz accurately perceives fraud and desecration in many guises. In the poem entitled "A Designated National Park," for example, the speaker visits Montezuma Castle, a cliff house site in Arizona once inhabited by the Anasazi. He is resentful because "I have to buy a permit to get back home," but as he spends time sitting quietly among the dwellings, he feels himself drawing close psychically to the daily rhythms by which his ancestors once lived. Back at the educational exhibits put up by the Park Service, he obeys the instructions on a display case to "PRESS BUTTON. . . . for a glimpse into the lives / of these people who lived here.' " He is horrified when a panel slides back to reveal not the usual diorama of tiny figures at work and play in the fields and plazas but the exhumed body of an Anasazi child, her dignity violated, her afterlife journey cruelly interrupted:

Girl, my daughter, my mother,
softly asleep.
They have unearthed you.

Like *Going for the Rain, A Good Journey* is suffused with Ortiz' concern for children, his own and other people's, and his desire, evident in many poems, to pass on the sort of knowledge children most urgently need to know. In 1977, the same year *A Good Journey* saw print, Ortiz published *The People Shall Continue,* an extraordinary account of Native American history for children. In twenty-three pages Ortiz brings his readers from creation to the present day; one of the best things about the book is the way Ortiz gives children a sense of the great diversity of American Indian cultures. He suggests the beauty and integrity of Native American lifeways without romanticizing the times before the coming of the Europeans, and he is straightforward about the devastation and loss that occurred as a result of European incursion. He concludes hopefully by describing Native Americans making common cause with others of all races who have been oppressed and offering to share with them Native American stories about survival and maintaining balance:

We must take great care with each other.
We must share our concern with each other.
Nothing is separate from us.
We are all one body of people.
We must struggle to share our human lives with
    each other.
We must fight against those forces
which will take our humanity from us.
We must ensure that life continues.

Ortiz' book remains the single best overview of American Indian history written for children.

The majority of Americans and Europeans were aware of the 1992 quincentennial of Columbus' landfall, but most significant anniversaries in American Indian history pass unnoticed by the general population. August 1980 marked the three hundredth year since the Pueblo Revolt, when pueblo-dwelling people and some Apache groups across what is now New Mexico banded together under the direction of a leader from San Juan Pueblo named Popé and secretly conspired to force the Spanish from the land. Runners carried knotted cords from community to community, with the number of knots encoding the information that on August 11th all the Native American towns would simultaneously revolt. Even though word of the plan leaked out shortly before the chosen time, the Pueblo people successfully drove the Spanish into an exile that lasted for twelve years. The 1692 reconquest under Vargas was inevitable, but the Pueblos have always been proud that they mounted what Jemez Pueblo historian Joe S. Sando has called —in his "The Pueblo Revolt," in *Handbook of North American Indians* (1979)—"perhaps the most successful revolt by natives of the New World."

Fight Back—For the Sake of the People, for the Sake of the Land (1980) was published in commemoration of that August three centuries before when the people successfully did fight back. (Ironically, the same year *Fight Back* was published, Ortiz was invited by the Carter administration to the White House Salute to American Poetry and Poets.) *Fight Back* is the most overtly political of all Ortiz' books. As Willard Gingerich remarks in his 1984 essay, "Simon Ortiz," "[Ortiz] knows the spiritual geography and the secret histories of power, struggle, exploitation, deceit, promise, and survival which cycles of conquest . . . have taught the peoples of this region."

Fight Back is a rich mix of poems, personal narrative, history, and essay, and it is marked as much by the respect and affection Ortiz feels for ordinary working people as by his clear-sighted anger at corporate America. The book is hard-hitting because it focuses on one small area of the country—Grants, New Mexico, and the cluster of communities surrounding it—and clearly traces the history of racism, landgrabbing, and exploitation practiced first by the invading Spanish conquistadores and missionaries and continued into the twentieth century by lumber, railroad, and mining companies. Acoma elders in Ortiz' youth could recall when their valley floor was threaded by any number of springs and the lush native grasses grew high enough to brush the belly of a horse; in *Fight Back* Ortiz carefully sets out the reasons why the water table was lowered so drastically, the native vegetation devastated, the people forced out of farming and raising livestock and into jobs that make them dependent on the military-industrial complex for their very lives. Though Ortiz concentrates on his own homeland, he extends what he observes to other parts of the country. In one poem, ''That's the Place Indians Talk About,'' he describes a conversation with a Paiute elder who recalls the days before Coso Hot Springs, a sacred healing site, was fenced in by the navy.

The book is not simply directed toward venting indignant anger; ultimately it seeks to offer solutions, creative ways to fight back:

> If the survival and quality of the life of Indian peoples is not assured, then no one else's life is, because those same economic, social, and political forces which destroy them will surely destroy others. It is not only a matter of preserving and protecting Indian lands as some kind of natural wilderness or cultural parks; rather it is a matter of how those lands can be productive in terms which are Indian people's to make, instead of Indian people being forced to serve a U.S. national interest which has never adequately served them. Those lands can be productive to serve humanity, just like the oral tradition of the Aacqumeh hanoh says, and

the people can be productive and serve the land so that it is not wasted and destroyed.

In *Fight Back,* ''the people'' means all people. One of the outstanding sections of this book is the long narrative poem ''To Change in a Good Way,'' which Ortiz previously published in several other contexts, sometimes as a poem, sometimes as a prose narrative. This piece tells the story of the friendship shared by two couples, Bill and Ida, who are Okies living in a Milan trailer park, and Pete and Mary, Laguna Pueblo people. The two men carpool to work at their hazardous jobs in Kerr-McGee's uranium mines; the friendship between the couples grows as Pete and Mary bring manure to enrich Ida's tiny vegetable garden and Ida babysits for their children. Bill and Ida themselves are childless, and they dote on and worry about Bill's handsome, cocky kid brother Slick, who is serving in Vietnam. When Slick is killed stepping on an American mine, Pete and Mary bring Bill and Ida oven bread for their sad journey back home for the funeral. Pete and Mary bring nourishment of another sort as well: a perfect ear of corn, to remind Bill and Ida that life continues, and a medicine bundle of prayer sticks enclosed in a corn husk, which Bill is to put

> . . . someplace important
> that you think might be good, maybe
> to change life in a good way,
> that you think Slick
> would be helping us with.

On the drive home, after a family gathering where Bill and Ida have listened to patriotic family members compare Slick to the brave people who fought Indians in the olden days—and so made the world a safer place—Bill suddenly understands what it is that he must do with the bundle from Pete and Mary. Carrying it deep into a mine, he lays the bundle down beneath the doubtful roof ''the damn company / don't put enough timbers and bolts in.'' As Pete has instructed him, he begins to address the spirit of his dead brother, awkwardly at first but with increasing urgency:

> .   .   .   I got this here
> Indian thing, feathers and sticks,
> and at home, at home we got the corn
> by your picture, and Pete and Mary said
> to do this because it's important
> even if we're Okies
> and not Indians who do this.
> It's for your travel they said
> and to help us with our life here
> from where you are at now and they said
> to maybe change things in a good way
> for a good life and God knows us Okies
> always wanted that though we maybe
> have been wrong sometimes.
> Pete said he didn't know
> exactly the right thing
> but somehow I believe he's more righter
> than we've ever been, and now I'm trying too.

In these gentle, understated lines, love spans the distances separating the Native American from the Anglo-American, the living from the dead, as Ortiz envisions them working together ''to maybe change things in a good way.''

Though Ortiz' next volume of poetry, *From Sand Creek: Rising in This Heart Which Is Our America,* did not appear until 1981, it grew out of Ortiz' experiences during the period 1974–1975 when he was a patient being treated for alcoholism at Fort Lyon Veteran's Administration Hospital in Colorado. On walks around the hospital grounds adjoining the Arkansas River, he was delighted by the vastness of the high plains, a landscape, he recalls in ''Always the Stories,'' that he found ''all encompassing, welcoming, accepting and loving.'' But at one point he suddenly realized that in 1864 Fort Lyon was ''the U.S. military garrison from which seven hundred soldiers marched against the Cheyenne and Arapaho at Sand Creek thirty miles to the east.'' The Cheyennes' leader, Black Kettle, was earnestly

seeking peace, and at the advice of the military commandant at Fort Lyon his people had purposely made camp only thirty miles from the garrison. The Reverend J. M. Chivington, a colonel in the Colorado volunteers, was not interested in making fine distinctions between Indians who were avowedly peaceable and those who were not; he ordered his troops to fall upon the unsuspecting encampment and kill all the Indians they could—including children, for ''nits make lice,'' he observed. The troops obeyed, even though Black Kettle ran up a white flag beside the American flag President Lincoln had recently presented to him. Over three hundred Cheyenne and Arapaho people were slaughtered at Sand Creek, the majority women and children.

Ortiz says that when he began to compose *From Sand Creek* in 1979 he was haunted by ''a vast symphonic music'' he could not identify. The book, a deep reflection on the Vietnam era and the American penchant for violence, represents the patient/poet asking questions simultaneously about what has put him in the hospital and what has brought America to its present condition; the double set of questions, it is implied, may have similar answers. The book is set up in such a way as to invite the reader to relate each pair of facing pages. On the left side, Ortiz makes observations in terse prose about Sand Creek, the present-day military, the hospital, and the American power structure; the poems appear on the right side, elaborating, illustrating, connecting seemingly discrete events, like My Lai and Sand Creek, to one another. Ortiz said that in this book he wished to write poems that would unequivocally be seen as poems, not stories. The poetry of *From Sand Creek* is sparer and involves less narrative and sometimes, as befits a work about war and a mental hospital, is more surreal than Ortiz' earlier writing. In one poem that may be about Sand Creek, My Lai, or any massacre in between, Ortiz images a sheer abundance of carnage:

Spurting
    sparkling
splashing, bubbling, steady
hot arcing streams.
      Red
and bright and vivid
unto the grassed plains.
        Steaming.
So bright and amazing.
They were awed.

One of the most moving aspects of *From Sand Creek* is Ortiz' depiction of his fellow patients, white, Hispanic, and Indian, many of them Vietnam veterans to whose stories the book continually alludes. The illnesses of Billy, the Oklahoma Boy, Nez, the Apache Kid, are intertwined with references to modern massacres like My Lai they have borne witness to; even if they have been participants in such horror, Ortiz suggests they, too, are victims.

Fightin', Ortiz' second collection of short stories, appeared in 1983, bringing together some but by no means all of the fiction Ortiz previously published in Rosen's *The Man to Send Rain Clouds* and in *Howbah Indians,* his first slim book of stories, which was published in 1978. While Ortiz is known primarily as a poet, at its best his fiction is just as compelling as his poetry. It often blends a grim realism with a lyrical prose, as for example in ''Woman Singing,'' a story about Navajo migrant farm workers in the potato fields far from home. Clyde, the main character, overhears a married woman in the next shack singing a Navajo song that evokes for him images of his Arizona childhood: sheep camps, mutton stew, piñon smoke, and dogs crowding around the hogan door. During the course of a boozy Saturday night, Clyde watches passively as his boorish boss manipulates the singing woman into sleeping with him. Half-drunk, an angry and depressed Clyde—who had been so moved by the woman's song earlier—now decides

the woman singing was something a long time ago and would not happen any more. If it did, he would not believe it. He would not listen. Finally, he moved away from the door and began to search . . . for a bottle. But there was no bottle of anything except the kerosene and for a moment he thought of drinking kerosene. It was a silly thought, and so he laughed.

In the end, Clyde heads back to Arizona, convinced once again of the reality of the Navajo song, despite the fallibility of the singer, and determined to find his place within what that music represents.

After and Before the Lightning, the collection of poems Ortiz published in 1994, constitutes a real departure for Ortiz. The poems grew out of his experience during the year 1985–1986 when he was teaching at the Indian-run Sinte Gleska College on the Rosebud Lakota Sioux reservation in South Dakota. The title of the book refers to a common Sioux definition of the prairie winter, when thunderstorms are in abeyance; the book is about surviving winter, not only in the literal sense from the perspective of a southwestern pueblo person unaccustomed to the bitter South Dakota blue northers. It is also about surviving what fellow American Indian writer James Welch calls ''winter in the blood''; that is, the violent American history that weighs especially heavily upon one in Sioux country, plus the personal despair over aging, failure, various things one has left undone. Ortiz does not entirely abandon his characteristic narrative bent here; the book clearly takes us from November to the spring equinox and tells us plenty that happens in between. But this is a far more meditative and philosophical text than anything Ortiz wrote previously; he himself remarks in the preface, ''When the poems came about and I wrote them, I felt like I was putting together a map of where I was in the cosmos.'' It is almost as if the relatively abstract landscape of snow-blanketed prairie and big sky, so unlike his own richly colored homescape of mesas and mountains, turns Ortiz to thinking about space, time, and the nature of existence. The natural images that dominate here are celestial ones: sun, moon, sky, stars, planets, galaxies. What preserves the poet through this season of physical and spiritual shutting-down are the memories of old-time Acoma stories about survival and keeping-on, the warmth of friends, and, above all, a commitment to maintain a kind of focused awareness from day to freezing day, a determination to face what is there to be seen, however blood- and bone-chilling the prospect.

Ortiz' work is attracting new interest, thanks to the fact that the University of Arizona issued a handsome reprint of three books—*Going for the Rain, A Good Journey,* and *Fight Back*—in the single volume called *Woven Stone* (1992). (The title of this volume refers, of course, to Ortiz' long-standing fascination with Pueblo stonework as an image for enduring artistic creation of all sorts.) Living and writing in Tucson, Arizona, Ortiz continues to work toward finishing a long-term project, a book on the Big Mountain land dispute, plus a planned collection of his fiction. As often as possible, he returns to Aacqu, where he served terms as tribal historian and lieutenant governor in the late eighties. As always, he writes for his children, Raho Nez, Rainy Dawn, and Sara Marie, and now for grandchildren as well. Like Coyote, Ortiz is a survivor. And like the wall around the Acoma churchyard, his work still stands, holds firm, endures.

Selected Bibliography

WORKS OF SIMON J. ORTIZ

POETRY

Naked in the Wind. Pembroke, N.C.: Quetzal-Vihio Press, 1971.

Going for the Rain. New York: Harper & Row, 1976.
A Good Journey. Berkeley, Calif.: Turtle Island Press, 1977; Tucson: University of Arizona Press, 1984.
A Poem Is a Journey. Bourbonnais, Ill.: Pteranadon Press, 1981.
From Sand Creek: Rising in This Heart Which Is Our America. New York: Thunder's Mouth Press, 1981.
After and Before the Lightning. Tucson: University of Arizona Press, 1994.

FICTION

Howbah Indians. Tucson: Blue Moon Press, 1978.
Fightin': New and Collected Stories. Chicago: Thunder's Mouth Press, 1983.

NONFICTION

"The Killing of a State Cop." In *The Man to Send Rain Clouds.* Edited by Kenneth Rosen. New York: Viking Press, 1974. Pp. 101–108.
Song/Poetry and Language—Expression and Perception. Tsaile, Arizona: Navajo Community College Press, 1978.
Fight Back: For the Sake of the People, For the Sake of the Land. Albuquerque: Institute for Native American Development, 1980.
"Towards a National Indian Literature: Cultural Authenticity in Nationalism." *MELUS,* 8, no. 2:7–12 (Summer 1981).
"Always the Stories: A Brief History and Thoughts on My Writing." In *Coyote Was Here: Essays on Contemporary Native American Literary and Political Mobilization.* Edited by Bo Schöler. Aarhus, Denmark: SEKLOS, 1984. Pp. 57–69.
"The Creative Process." *Wicazo SA Review,* 1, no. 1:45–49 (Spring 1985).
"The Language We Know." In *I Tell You Now: Autobiographical Essays by Native American Writers.* Edited by Brian Swann and Arnold Krupat. Lincoln: University of Nebraska Press, 1987. Pp. 185–194.

BOOKS FOR YOUNG READERS

The People Shall Continue. Illustrated by Sharol Graves. San Francisco: Children's Press, 1977. Revised edition, 1988.
Blue and Red. Acoma, N.M.: Acoma Partners in Basics, 1982.
The Importance of Childhood. Acoma, N.M.: Acoma Partners in Basics, 1982.

BOOKS EDITED

A Ceremony of Brotherhood. Coedited by Rudolfo A. Anaya. Albuquerque: Academia Publications, 1981.

Earth Power Coming. Tsaile, Arizona: Navajo Community College Press, 1983.

COLLECTED WORKS

Woven Stone. Tucson: University of Arizona Press, 1992.

BIBLIOGRAPHY

Ruoff, LaVonne Brown. "Simon Ortiz: A.S.A.I.L. Bibliography 7." *Studies in American Indian Literature,* 8, nos. 3–4:57–58. (Summer–Fall 1984).

CRITICAL STUDIES

Cole, Diana. *New York Times Book Review,* April 29, 1984, 323.

Evers, Lawrence J. "The Killing of a New Mexican State Trooper: Ways of Telling a Historical Event." *Wicazo SA Review,* 1, no. 1:17–25 (Spring 1985).

Gingerich, Willard. "The Old Voices of Acoma: Simon Ortiz's Mythic Indigenism." *Southwest Review,* 64:18–30 (1979).

———. "Simon Ortiz." *Fiction International,* 15, no. 1:208–212 (1984).

Gleason, Judith. "Reclaiming the Valley of the Shadows." *Parnassus: Poetry in Review,* 12 no. 1:21–71 (Fall–Winter 1984).

Hoilman, Dennis. "The Ethnic Imagination: A Case History." *Canadian Journal of Native Studies,* 5, no. 2:167–175 (1985).

Jaffe, Harold. "Speaking Memory." *Nation,* April 3, 1982, pp. 406–408.

Lincoln, Kenneth. *Native American Renaissance.* Berkeley and Los Angeles: University of California Press, 1983.

Oandasan, William. "Simon Ortiz: The Poet and His Landscape." *Studies in American Indian Literature,* 11:26–37 (1987).

Silko, Leslie Marmon. "Language and Literature from a Pueblo Indian Perspective." In *English Literature: Opening Up the Canon.* Edited by Leslie A. Fiedler and Houston A. Baker. Baltimore: Johns Hopkins University Press, 1981. Pp. 54–72.

Smith, Patricia Clark. "Coyote Ortiz: *Canis latrans latrans* in the Poetry of Simon Ortiz." In Paula Gunn Allen, ed., *Studies in American Indian Literature: Critical Essays and Course Designs.* New York: Modern Language Association, 1983. Pp. 192–210.

Warner, Nicholas O. "Images of Drinking and 'Woman Singing,' *Ceremony,* and *House Made of Dawn.*" *Journal of the Society for the Study of the Multi-Ethnic Literature of the United States,* 11, no. 4:15–30 (Winter 1984).

Wiget, Andrew. *Simon Ortiz.* Boise: Boise State University Press, 1986.

INTERVIEWS

Bruchac, Joseph. "The Story Never Ends: An Interview with Simon Ortiz." In his *Survival This Way: Interviews with American Indian Poets.* Tucson: Arizona University Press, 1987. Pp. 211–229.

Coltelli, Laura. *Winged Words: American Indian Writers Speak.* Lincoln: University of Nebraska Press, 1990.

Manley, Kathleen, and Paul W. Rea. "An Interview with Simon Ortiz." *Journal of the Southwest,* 31, no. 3:362–377 (Autumn 1989).

—PATRICIA CLARK SMITH

Ayn Rand

1905–1982

*F*EW TWENTIETH-CENTURY American writers have provoked as much controversy as the novelist and philosopher Ayn Rand. Author of *The Fountainhead* and *Atlas Shrugged*, and of numerous other works of fiction, drama, and nonfiction, Rand conceived a philosophic system founded on "the concept of man as a heroic being, with his own happiness as the moral purpose of his life, with productive achievement as his noblest activity, and reason as his only absolute," as she put it in *Atlas Shrugged*. She offered distinctive insights on the source and nature of knowledge, art, ethics, and politics. She eschewed contemporary alternatives in each of these areas of human concern, and forged an original philosophy that she called Objectivism.

In the realm of politics, for example, Rand was a self-proclaimed "radical for capitalism." She vehemently opposed the regulatory and welfare state advocated by the liberal and socialist Left. But as an avowed atheist, she rejected the religious views of traditional conservatives, and was unwavering in her support of civil liberties and abortion rights.

Rand viewed modern liberalism and conservativism as false alternatives whose apparent opposition obscures a shared ignorance of integrated human nature. She argued that liberals typically seek to control material production, even while they defend intellectual freedom.

They sanction the state's eradication of economic liberties to promote what Rand regarded as spurious notions of social justice. By contrast, the conservatives want the state to regulate peoples' mores. Though they frequently defend economic freedom, they seek to control the individual's moral life by appeals to faith and tradition.

According to Rand, liberals and conservatives grant freedom only to those activities that they regard as unimportant, and they seek to govern those areas that they believe to be central to human life. Ultimately, Rand argued in *Philosophy: Who Needs It*, each is authoritarian, using the coercive powers of the state to stifle individual autonomy and a free society: "Both camps hold the same premise—*the mind–body dichotomy*—but choose opposite sides of this lethal fallacy. . . . Neither camp holds freedom as a value. The conservatives want to rule man's consciousness; the liberals, his body."

The prevalence of this liberal–conservative polarity in American politics was, for Rand, a symptom of the nation's intellectual bankruptcy. She argued that no genuine political renaissance could be achieved in the absence of a full philosophic revolution. Rand saw herself as the intellectual source of such a transformation. She affirmed to Alvin Toffler in a 1964 *Playboy* interview that she was "challenging the cultural tradition of two-and-a-half-thousand years."

Rand's philosophy, exhaustive in its scope, rejected the "mind–body dichotomy" in all of its manifestations. This age-old doctrine presupposed an irreconcilable antagonism between human consciousness and the material world, between ideas and reality, theory and practice, logic and experience, reason and emotion, morality and practicality. In Rand's view, an enriched conception of the integrated human being required an understanding of the essential interdependence of mind and body.

Born Alissa Zinovievna Rosenbaum in St. Petersburg, Russia, on February 2, 1905, Rand spent her first years in a country ravaged by civil war and famine, revolution and repression. Her experiences strongly influenced her personal and intellectual evolution.

In her early years, Rand became quite proficient at both mathematics and logic. One of her teachers even encouraged her to pursue mathematics as a career. But Rand was not interested in the purely abstract; she was absorbed by the relationship between abstract ideas and human experience. Later, this concern was manifested in her conviction that philosophic ideas were the primary causal factor in historical development. She wrote in *Capitalism:* "There is only one power that determines the course of history, just as it determines the course of every individual life: the power of man's rational faculty—*the power of ideas*. If you know a man's convictions, you can predict his actions. If you understand the dominant philosophy of a society, you can predict its course."

Having lived through the revolutionary period in Russia, Rand could attest to the power of ideas in shaping history. Russian culture was a battleground of mystic and collectivist philosophies, of religious idealists and Bolshevik materialists. In her view, these opposing cultural forces were fundamentally alike in their hostility to reason and to the individual. She observed that both religion and communism sought to maintain their cultural dominance through coercion, because both advocated that individuals suspend their own rational judgment in deference to an allegedly superior power. Whereas religious advocates yearned for a theocracy, communists replaced the concept of God with the notion of an omnipotent state. Despite their espoused secular materialism, they were "neo-mystics" in their glorification of the collective.

Given this almost apocalyptic struggle between religion and communism, Rand later viewed them as the embodiments, respectively, of faith and force, two sides of the same fraudulent coin. In her typically provocative style, she later argued (in *Philosophy: Who Needs It*) that mysticism, the acceptance of claims without sensory evidence or proof, "will always lead to the rule of brutality," just as the initiation of political force in collectivism will always violate the rational autonomy of individuals.

In her early teens, Rand was exhilarated by the revolt against the tsar, for she hoped that Russian society would move in the direction of republican ideals. Her father, Zinovy Rosenbaum, a chemist and pharmacist, tried to shelter his children from the approaching revolution by avoiding any overt political discussions. But Rand, the eldest of three children, soon realized that she and her father shared an opposition to communism and a belief in individualism. Her relationship with her mother, Anna Rosenbaum, was more strained, although it was her mother who first introduced her to some of the classics of foreign literature. The works of Victor Hugo, Edmond Rostand, and Henryk Sienkiewicz (author of *Quo Vadis?*) inspired her passion for the heroic.

When the civil war intensified, the Rosenbaum family sought refuge in the Crimea, where Rand completed her high school studies. Once the civil war ended and the Bolsheviks emerged victorious, the family returned to Petrograd (formerly

St. Petersburg), where Rand entered the university in the fall of 1921. Pursuing a three-year course in the college of social science, she enrolled in the department of social pedagogy, which included the historical and philosophic disciplines. At the university, she studied Schiller, Shakespeare, Dostoyevsky, and Nietzsche. Rand was most impressed with Dostoyevsky's literary method, and she later credited him as one of her most important literary influences. Her novels, like those of Dostoyevsky, focus on conflicting fundamental principles as embodied in various characters.

Rand's early interest in the work of Nietzsche also left its mark. Reading *Thus Spake Zarathustra* and *Beyond Good and Evil,* she was inspired by Nietzsche's poetic celebration of the ''noble soul'' and by his ceaseless attacks on the ''slave morality'' of altruism. In such works as *The Birth of Tragedy,* however, she recognized that Nietzsche's ''individualism'' was ''subjectivist,'' expressive of a ''Dionysian'' emotionalism and not of an ''objective,'' rational egoism.

Among Rand's teachers, the distinguished philosopher N. O. Lossky may have been an important formative influence. He is the only professor whose tutelage she ever acknowledged. Rand may well have absorbed from Lossky and her other Russian teachers a dialectical method of analysis, in which philosophic and social problems are viewed as interrelated elements within a larger context.

Having decided at a very young age to pursue a writing career, Rand chose history as her major field of study because she believed that a knowledge of the past was essential to a writer. As the new regime's propaganda infiltrated the social science curriculum, Rand had to fulfill various ''Soviet'' requirements. She consequently became adept at examining her own fundamental premises and those of others, in an effort to define complex philosophic issues by grasping their essential principles. ''No matter what you are

taught,'' she later admonished, ''listen to it critically, whether you agree or not. And if you disagree, formulate your reasons.''

As graduation day approached, Rand witnessed the notorious university purges, designed to make room for more ''proletarian'' students. Nonproletarian, or ''bourgeois,'' pupils were expelled, and many of them were exiled to Siberian labor camps. Because the period of study for the fulfillment of degree requirements had been shortened, however, Rand managed to escape the purge. She graduated in the summer of 1924.

In the days following her graduation, Rand worked at the Peter and Paul Fortress as a museum guide, and later enrolled in the State Institute for Cinema Arts. A collection of essays written by Rand, *Hollywood: American Movie-City,* was published without the author's permission in St. Petersburg in 1926, after she emigrated to the United States.

In 1917, Zinovy Rosenbaum's chemist shop had been nationalized by the Bolsheviks. In the early 1920s, however, the New Economic Policy was instituted to encourage private ownership and exchange. Zinovy attempted to open a new chemist shop in cooperation with other former pharmacy owners. Within a year, however, this shop was expropriated by the Bolsheviks. The family faced state terror, starvation, and disease. Rand believed that communism was strangling any possibility of a humane and moral society, and she soon began the arduous process of securing a passport to leave Russia. Hoping that the Soviets would allow her to visit relatives in Chicago, she planned never to return to a country dominated by arbitrary force, one-party rule, and censorship. She obtained a passport in the fall of 1925, and set out for America by way of Latvia, Berlin, and Paris, arriving in New York in mid-February 1926. She never again saw her parents, who died during the Nazi bombardment of Leningrad (St. Petersburg).

In America, Alissa Rosenbaum assumed the

name Ayn Rand. By midsummer, she left Chicago for Hollywood, where she eventually worked in the studio of Cecil B. DeMille. On the set of DeMille's *King of Kings,* she met a young actor named Frank O'Connor, whom she married on April 15, 1929. They remained together until his death fifty years later.

In the late 1920s, after DeMille's studio closed, Rand struggled financially, working as a waitress, a file clerk, and various other temporary positions. Having become an American citizen in 1931, she was deeply disappointed by the leftist politics that predominated among intellectuals in her adopted country. During the ''Red Decade'' of the 1930s, many American writers and intellectuals were attracted by the collectivist experiments of the Soviet Union. Rand thought it imperative to combat their views.

In her early literary efforts, Rand sought to understand and criticize the cultural forces that had dictated her Russian past, focusing on what she regarded as the close affinity between religion and communism. In 1931–1932 she wrote ''Red Pawn,'' an original movie scenario and screenplay, which was first published years later, in *The Early Ayn Rand* (1984). According to the Objectivist philosopher Leonard Peikoff, this work was the first published expression of Rand's belief that communism is, in effect, a secular equivalent of religion.

The nature of communism and the totalitarian state is explored in greater depth in Rand's first novel, *We the Living,* originally titled *Air Tight: A Novel of Red Russia.* Written between 1930 and 1933, the book was, Rand later said, ''as near to an autobiography'' as she would ever write. Although the heroine of the novel, Kira Argounova, differs from Rand in the details of her life, her convictions and values are essentially the same.

Like the author, Kira is a student enrolled at the University of Petrograd in the early 1920s.

Unlike the author, she becomes embroiled in a romantic triangle with the two men who love her. Early in the novel, Kira falls passionately in love with Leo Kovalensky, an aristocrat. When he develops tuberculosis, she becomes the mistress of Andrei Taganov, an influential and idealistic Communist revolutionary, so that she can obtain food and medical care for Leo. After he has recovered, Leo emerges from the sanitarium as a cynical, self-destructive alcoholic and unprincipled opportunist. Once Kira's deceit is exposed, the novel comes to a tragic climax. Ultimately, Kira loses Leo. And Andrei, disillusioned by the corruption of the regime he had fought so hard to establish, commits suicide. With nothing left for her in Russia, Kira tries to escape but is shot by the border patrol. In her final moments, Kira realizes that ''life, undefeated, existed and could exist,'' but certainly not in the airtight conditions of totalitarian oppression. Rand suggests that it is not Kira's dishonesty that has made this tragedy inevitable; it is the system that crushes ''the living'' by sabotaging the possibility for honesty in human relationships.

We the Living was the first of Rand's works to be transposed to the screen. During World War II, Italian filmmakers produced an unauthorized but remarkably faithful cinematic version starring Alida Valli as Kira, Rossano Brazzi as Leo, and Fosco Giachetti as Andrei. The film, directed by Goffredo Allessandrini, was over four and half hours long and was released in two parts: *Noi vivi* and *Addio Kira.* Though it was enormously popular and won the Volpe Cup at the Venice Film Festival in 1942, it was suppressed by fascist authorities who may have objected to its antiauthoritarian implications. In 1988, the film was rereleased in a reedited, condensed version with English subtitles.

The publishing history of the novel is also significant. In 1936, Macmillan had issued *We the Living* in a limited edition of three thousand copies, which soon went out of print. In 1959, when

Rand's popularity prompted a reissue, she made a number of revisions, claiming that the original version reflected "the transitional state of mind thinking no longer in Russian, but not yet fully in English." Although Rand characterized her revisions as merely "grammatical" or "editorial line-changes," some interpreters have questioned her assessment. For instance, Ronald Merrill claims that Rand's editing was substantive as well. He argues that, in the revised edition, she expurgated passages that would have placed her closer to a "Nietzschean" worldview that sanctioned the sacrifice of the weak for the sake of the strong.

Whether or not Merrill's appraisal is accurate, Rand clearly viewed her fiction as part of a broader philosophic endeavor. In the few excerpts from her private journals that have been published, she dissected the ideas of other thinkers such as Albert Jay Nock, H. L. Mencken, Peter Kropotkin, and José Ortega y Gasset. Rand aimed to develop an enriched concept of individual freedom. She later declared that the goal of her fiction was *"the projection of an ideal man."* She argued in *The Romantic Manifesto* that this goal was "an end in itself—to which any didactic, intellectual or philosophical values contained . . . are only the means." But in Rand's view, the "ideal man," fully autonomous and self-directed, could not be understood apart from "the conditions which make him possible and which his existence requires."

The literary and the philosophic in Rand's work cannot be isolated. "In a certain sense," she wrote in *For the New Intellectual,* "every novelist is a philosopher, because one cannot present a picture of human existence without a philosophical framework; the novelist's only choice is whether that framework is present in his story explicitly or implicitly, whether he is aware of it or not, whether he holds his philosophical convictions consciously or subconsciously."

While Rand's fundamental philosophic convictions are readily apparent throughout her fiction, their implications are explored in greater detail with each successive work. One might say that she provided an ever more explicit articulation of her views as she moved from the political themes of *We the Living* to the ethical, epistemological, and metaphysical themes of *The Fountainhead* and *Atlas Shrugged.* In *The Fountainhead,* Rand presented the first principles of a new egoism.

The Fountainhead details the struggles of Howard Roark, a brilliantly creative architect who rejects conventional styles in a display of his artistic individuality. A man of integrity, Roark is expelled from architecture school for his unwillingness to conform to the traditional standards of the profession.

Rand contrasts Roark with Peter Keating, his former classmate, who had depended on Roark for help with many of his school projects. In his professional life, Keating achieves apparent success by manipulating people and constantly replicating conventional architecture. Engaged in a "second-hand" life, Keating is without any clearly defined notion of "self."

Other important characters in *The Fountainhead* include Dominique Francon, Gail Wynand, and Ellsworth Toohey. Dominique is in love with Roark, the only man of integrity she has ever met, but she is convinced that a life of principle is impossible in a world ruled by mediocrity. Fearing that Roark will be destroyed by that world, she struggles against him to spare him the ultimate destruction.

Wynand, perhaps the most tragic of Rand's fictional characters, is a powerful newspaper magnate who panders to, and believes that he can manipulate, public opinion. Previously convinced that there is no integrity in this world, Wynand is irresistibly drawn to Roark, who perseveres in the face of every obstacle and who seems to embody the true nobility that has eluded

Wynand's grasp. Roark is attracted to Wynand, the self-made man, who despite his cynicism, was able to emerge from Hell's Kitchen, a rough neighborhood on the West Side of Manhattan, to create his own enterprise.

Ellsworth Toohey—the architectural critic for Wynand's newspaper, *The Banner*—practices a full-fledged collectivism that opposes Roark's individualism. Through his lectures and columns, he incites public condemnation of Roark for his "selfish" displays of stylistic originality.

In the climax of the novel, Peter Keating seeks to secure a profitable architectural contract for a public housing project. Knowing that he does not possess the expertise to complete plans for the project, Keating once again turns to Roark. Roark knows that he will never have the opportunity to implement some of his daringly cost-effective designs for public housing. He agrees to allow his plans to be submitted in Keating's name, on the condition that they not be altered in any way. When the project is significantly altered during construction, the outraged Roark dynamites it, and is subsequently put on trial.

Wynand is convinced that he will be able to wage a successful public relations campaign in support of Roark. To his surprise, he discovers that he is unable to effect such a change in popular perceptions. He acknowledges to himself: "You were a ruler of men. You held a leash. A leash is only a rope with a noose at both ends." He realizes that he has attained wealth and power by pandering to the masses; he is their slave, not their master.

In his own defense, Roark clearly enunciates the basic principles of ethical egoism. Standing before a jury of his peers, he defends his right to destroy his creation because it had been altered without permission. Decrying a world that "is perishing from an orgy of self-sacrificing," Roark champions independence and the rational individual. In the end, he is vindicated.

The Fountainhead was Rand's first commer-cially successful novel. Despite mixed reviews, some critics, like Lorine Pruette, praised the book. Writing for the *New York Times Book Review,* Pruette observed that "Rand is a writer of great power. She has a subtle and ingenious mind and the capacity of writing brilliantly, beautifully, bitterly." She compared the novel to such classics as Thomas Mann's *The Magic Mountain* and Henrik Ibsen's *The Master Builder.* It was "the only novel of ideas written by an American woman" that she could recall.

The Fountainhead typifies Rand's literary method. Rand viewed her characters as representations of specific human attributes emphasized "more sharply and consistently than in average human beings." She was "interested in philosophical principles only as they affect[ed] the actual existence of men; and in men, only as they reflect[ed] philosophical principles." Her characters are motivated by essential ideas that are at the very core of their identity. Rand omits the accidental and contingent elements in the lives of her characters; she is concerned only with their primary motivations.

In *The Fountainhead,* Rand sought to identify the underlying principles that motivate people who live secondhand lives. In fact, this phrase served as her original working title for the novel before she decided to emphasize the primacy of the ego as the "fountainhead" of human progress. "Second-handers" are people who lack a clear self-concept. They seek social approval for all their beliefs and actions. Other people dictate their convictions and their very idea of truth. Based on this understanding of the second-handers' psychology, Rand explored its diverse incarnations in such characters as Peter Keating, Ellsworth Toohey, and Gail Wynand.

In contrast to these "second-handers," Rand created her first fully developed "ideal man" in the person of Howard Roark. In her early notes for *The Fountainhead,* written primarily in the late 1930s, Rand characterized Roark as the "noble soul par excellence,'' the ''self-sufficient, self-confident, the end of ends, the reason unto himself, the joy of living personified.'' Despite Roark's struggle, he is ''at complete peace with himself.''

Rand's novel develops as an organic unity. At all times, she is concerned with ''the composition and its meaning as a whole.'' The essential principles guiding the characters are brought into dynamic conflict, leading to a triumphant resolution for Roark and for the ideals that Rand celebrates. The novel illustrates Rand's commitment to the organic integration of theme, characterization, and plot. These elements, in Rand's view, are interrelated ''attributes, not separable parts,'' constituents of an ''indivisible'' literary totality. The attributes, she writes in *The Romantic Manifesto,* ''unite into so integrated a sum that no starting point can be discerned.'' Thus, she stated in a letter to Gerald Loeb, ''A STORY IS AN END IN ITSELF. . . . It is written as a man is born—an organic whole, dictated only by its own laws and its own necessity.'' Stephen Cox argues (in *The Fountainhead: A Fiftieth Anniversary Celebration*) that this ''startling intensity of integration'' is central to Rand's literary craft, exhibiting

the idea, associated with Aristotle, that all the parts of a literary work should be rationally adjusted to its central rhetorical intention; the idea, current in the Romantic movement and perhaps best expressed by Coleridge, that all the parts of a literary work should be shaped into an organic whole by the unifying force of the individual imagination; and the working assumption, current among skilled literary craftsmen in many ages, that the materials employed in a literary work must be selected in accordance with their likely effect on the work as a whole.

Thus, for Cox, novels such as *The Fountainhead* exhibit a ''romantic individualism'' that ''is like DNA; it's present in every cell, and it controls every cell.'' This ''romantic individualism'' can also be found in *Anthem,* a novelette written in 1937, published in England in 1938, but not issued in America until 1946.

Anthem is a futuristic story depicting the inevitably primitive conditions brought about by a fully collectivist society. Rand's fictional dystopia has obliterated industry and knowledge. It has replaced personal names with generic code words and numbers. The society is so imbued with the collectivist spirit that it no longer uses the word ''I.'' The rediscovery of this word by Rand's protagonist, Equality 7-2521, is a paean to the sanctity of the individual:

I am. I think. I will. . . . What must I say besides? These are the words. This is the answer. . . . This, my body and spirit, this is the end of the quest. I wished to know the meaning of things. I am the meaning. I wished to find a warrant for being. I need no warrant for being, and no word of sanction upon my being. I am the warrant and the sanction.

By the end of the story, Equality 7-2521 flees with the woman he loves to forge a new culture of individualism. Not without irony, he renames himself Prometheus—a tribute to the renegade of Greek legend. Similar allusions to mythology occur in Rand's magnum opus, *Atlas Shrugged,* in which she likens her fictional utopia to Atlantis, and describes her hero, John Galt, as ''Prometheus who changed his mind. After centuries of being torn by vultures in payment for having brought to men the fire of the gods, he broke his chains and he withdrew his fire—until the day when men withdraw their vultures.'' This reality led Howard Roark to observe similarly in *The Fountainhead* that the first man who ''discovered how to make fire . . . was probably burned at the stake he had taught his brothers to light.'' The question of why the innovators, the ''men of the mind,'' have allowed themselves to be sacrificed on the altar of the ''public good'' became one of Rand's chief theoretical preoccupations.

*   *   *

Throughout the 1940s, Rand worked on various film-related projects. Among those movie scripts written for Hal Wallis Productions, but not produced, were "The Crying Sisters" and "The House of Mist." She also wrote two successful screen adaptations for Paramount: *You Came Along,* which starred Robert Cummings and Lizabeth Scott, and *Love Letters,* a film starring Jennifer Jones and Joseph Cotten. Whereas *You Came Along* was a collaborative product, *Love Letters* was Rand's first exclusive film adaptation. Derived from the novel *The Love Letters,* written by Chris Massie, the film exhibits Rand's characteristic sense of life. It centers on Victoria, a woman who falls in love with an English soldier named Roger, who had corresponded with her during the war. She eventually learns that Roger's love letters were actually ghost-written by Alan Quinton, an English officer. She had yearned for a man like Alan, who looked at life "not as a burden or a punishment, but as a dream of beauty which we can make real." Alan sees Victoria as a "pinup girl of the spirit," and through a series of plot twists and tragedies, the two are ultimately united. They recognize that happiness cannot be obtained by stealing another person's soul, and that lies never work, "no matter what our motives."

Rand's final film adaptation was of her own novel, *The Fountainhead.* Directed by King Vidor for Warner Brothers, the movie starred Gary Cooper as Howard Roark, Patricia Neal as Dominique Francon, and Raymond Massey as Gail Wynand. Released in 1949 to mostly negative reviews, the film is noteworthy for what Stephen Cox has described as a "non-naturalistic technique," a kind of "mythic expressionism." Rand's intricate philosophical novel is transformed on screen into "a series of mythic scenes," in Cox's view, that are sometimes "rather awkward" but not without ambition. Ultimately, Rand's formidable presence on the movie set was such that she achieved, according to Cox (in *The Films of Ayn Rand*) "more influence on production than any other Hollywood writer has ever acquired."

Rand's relationship to the film industry eventually led her to compose "Screen Guide for Americans" for the Motion Picture Alliance for the Preservation of American Ideals, to alert moviegoers to Communist propaganda in the cinema. So strident was Rand's opposition to communism that in 1947 she agreed to appear as a "friendly witness" before the House Un-American Activities Committee, an event about which she later expressed grave misgivings on several counts.

During this period, Rand also published the first of many nonfiction essays: "The Only Path to Tomorrow." She hoped that this *Reader's Digest* article might serve as the credo of a broad Old Right political movement. She had met several leading conservatives and libertarians of the day, including Albert Jay Nock, Rose Wilder Lane, Isabel Paterson, Henry Hazlitt, and Ludwig von Mises (the father of the contemporary Austrian school of economics and the teacher of the Nobel laureate Friedrich A. von Hayek). Perhaps because these individuals were intellectually so diverse, the proposed union never materialized. Indeed, Rand was deeply disappointed at the cynicism, subjectivism, and mysticism that, she thought, characterized many intellectuals on the Right.

"The Only Path to Tomorrow" postulated an age-old clash between "Active Man" and "Passive Man," between the individualist and the second-hander. "Active Man" seeks independence, whereas "Passive Man" is a "parasite," rich or poor, who survives by feeding off the productive achievements of the innovators.

The issue Rand analyzed in "The Only Path to Tomorrow," the exploitation of the genuine creators of wealth by parasitical "looters," is fully dramatized in *Atlas Shrugged.* Rand began to outline this novel as early as 1943, but its main plot device is foreshadowed in *The Fountainhead,* in which the hero, Howard Roark, asks: ''What would happen to the world without those who do, think, work, produce?'' Rand knew the answer, and to explore its social ramifications fully, she imagined a world in which the men and women ''of the mind,'' the creative ''prime movers,'' go on strike against the parasites. Originally titled *The Strike,* the book is ''a picture of the whole,'' in Rand's words. Unlike *The Fountainhead,* which explored ''the nature . . . of the creator and the second-hander'' and their personal interaction, *Atlas Shrugged* highlights the social relations between two classes of people: authentic moneymakers and manipulative money appropriators. It was an ambitious undertaking that led Rand to explore the interconnections between factors as disparate as economics, sex, epistemology, education, art, metaphysics, psychology, and ethics.

Despite its broad scope and its large number of characters, the novel's intricate plot centers on Dagny Taggart and Hank Rearden, two brilliant enterpreneurs who struggle to keep their businesses afloat in an economy strangled by excessive government regulations. Unknown to Dagny and Hank, the society's disintegration is being hastened by a conspiracy of the most creative minds in the fields of commerce, industry, science, and philosophy. These conspirators refuse to sanction their own victimization by aiding and abetting the statist ''looters.'' Led by John Galt, the novel's elusive chief protagonist, they escape to the mountains of Colorado, where they establish their own free society, which Rand ironically characterized as a ''utopia of greed.'' Galt's personal motto becomes the guiding principle of the utopia: ''I swear by my life and my love of it that I will never live for the sake of another man, nor ask another man to live for mine.''

Rand introduces other admirable characters, chief among them Francisco d'Anconia, owner of the once fabulous d'Anconia copper mines in Argentina, who becomes a playboy rather than produce for the benefit of state expropriators; and Ragnar Danneskjöld, a philosopher-turned-pirate, who steals from the looters by raiding and sinking foreign-aid freighters, then returns the booty to the producers. The novel's assorted villains, such as Floyd Ferris, Wesley Mouch, and James Taggart, are united by their desire for the unearned, and by what Rand later characterized as a *''hatred of the good for being the good.''*

The novel's pivotal character, John Galt, is the spokesperson for Rand's philosophy. Engineer, scientist, and philosopher, Galt is Rand's ''ideal man'' incarnate, a perfect integration of mind and body—the thinker who is also a man of action. As the leader of the strike, for example, he develops technology to control the airwaves. As a desperate nation waits urgently for Mr. Thompson, the head of state, to deliver a speech on the world crisis, it is Galt's voice that comes to them instead. Galt explains the erroneous philosophic premises underlying the country's disintegration. The speech is a lengthy distillation of Rand's philosophy. At its conclusion, Galt asks those producers who have not yet joined the strike to withdraw from the statist social order. When the world is completely paralyzed by the strike, Galt and his followers agree to return to establish a new society founded on a morality of rational self-interest.

Atlas Shrugged incorporates elements of science fiction and fantasy, symbolism and realism. As a complex tome, it inspired the most passionate responses from both fans and critics. John Chamberlain, writing for the *New York Herald Tribune,* commended the book as a ''vibrant and powerful novel of ideas,'' a ''philosophical detective story'' in the tradition of Dostoyevsky's *Crime and Punishment.* But most reviewers exhibited an intense hostility to Rand's novel and its long philosophic monologues. Critics on the Left abhorred her preoccupation with capitalism, and conservatives were offended by her atheism.

Granville Hicks observed, in the *New York Times Book Review,* "that the book is written out of hate," a mean-spirited polemic against politicians, bureaucrats, and the incompetent. Whittaker Chambers, writing for *National Review,* characterized the novel as "remarkably silly" and "preposterous." Tracing ominous parallels between Rand and Marx, Chambers bemoaned the ideal "Randian man" who "is made the center of a godless world." Despite this frosty critical reception, *Atlas Shrugged,* like *The Fountainhead,* eventually became a long-term best-seller.

During the 1950s, Rand formed a friendship with two young UCLA students who greatly respected her work: Nathaniel Blumenthal and Barbara Weidman, who later married and assumed the surname Branden. The Brandens constituted the core of a growing circle of admirers, ironically dubbed "The Collective," that included the economic consultant Alan Greenspan, the future chairman of the Federal Reserve Board, and the philosopher Leonard Peikoff, Rand's appointed legal and intellectual heir.

In 1958, in New York City, Nathaniel Branden established the Nathaniel Branden Lectures, later incorporated as the Nathaniel Branden Institute (N.B.I.). N.B.I. was dedicated to the systematic presentation of Rand's philosophy. In subsequent years, N.B.I. disseminated Objectivist ideas through live lectures and audiotaped courses. Rand appeared on numerous college campuses across the country, including Columbia, Princeton, Harvard, Yale, and New York University. She wrote articles for national newspapers and magazines, and was interviewed on radio and television by such hosts as Johnny Carson, Phil Donahue, Merv Griffin, Edwin Newman, and Mike Wallace. No longer merely a best-selling novelist, Rand quickly became a popular philosopher.

*   *   *

In her first published nonfiction work, *For the New Intellectual* (1961), Rand wrote an introductory polemic on the history of Western philosophy. That history, she explained, has been a clash between the rational secularism of Aristotelian thought and the mystic dualism of Plato. The majority of Western philosophers have perpetuated the Platonic mind–body dichotomy, and have sought to resolve the tension by emphasizing one realm over the other. Those who accentuate matter (the body, the physical) over mind, who regard brute force as the primary means of social control, Rand called the Attilas. Those who accentuate mind (the spirit) over matter, who rely on faith as the only source of knowledge, are the Witch Doctors, in Rand's view. The Attilas and the Witch Doctors, however, depend upon each other for their existence. The Attilas need the Witch Doctors in order to legitimate their conquests; the Witch Doctors need the Attilas to secure power. Both are fundamentally opposed to human reason and creative production.

Rand argued that Aristotle's secular orientation challenged the mind–body dichotomy at its core. Aristotle considered the senses to be reliable sources of knowledge, and human reason to be a valid, efficacious instrument for understanding reality. Moreover, he recognized that consciousness depends on sensory experience; there can be no fundamental antagonism between mind and body.

Despite the rational influence of Aristotle's philosophy on early Greco-Roman culture, Rand argued, resurgent statism and mysticism plunged the world into the Dark Ages. Only with Thomas Aquinas' rediscovery of Aristotle did the Renaissance, the Enlightenment, and the industrial revolution become possible. In Rand's view, the establishment of the United States as a constitutional republic dedicated to the protection of individual rights was the ultimate political outgrowth of this predominantly secular, Aristotelian trend.

But no culture could survive the effect of sustained philosophic deterioration. In Rand's opinion, the demise of Enlightenment culture was, however unwittingly, accelerated by one of its leading thinkers: Immanuel Kant. Rand held that Kant's philosophy had the consequence of undercutting the efficacy of the human mind. She asserted that Kant's assault on human consciousness was bequeathed, with disastrous results, to all his modern successors. In opposition to the Platonic and Kantian worldviews, Rand regarded her own philosophy as the fulfillment of the Aristotelian legacy. The bulk of *For the New Intellectual* consists of philosophic passages culled from the body of Rand's fiction, illustrating various principles of Objectivism.

The book was not well received by most critics. Some commentators, however, like Joel Rosenbloom in *The New Republic,* recognized Rand's approach as unlike any on the intellectual Right. Though Rosenbloom characterized the book as "pretentious nonsense," he observed that Rand's "irreligious, or even anti-religious . . . position" alienated her from American conservatives who might otherwise be attracted to some of her principles.

Rand and her followers continued to explore these principles in greater depth in a series of publications they founded: *The Objectivist Newsletter* (1962–1965), *The Objectivist* (1966–1971), and *The Ayn Rand Letter* (1971–1976). Key essays from these periodicals were later reprinted in nonfiction anthologies: *The Virtue of Selfishness: A New Concept of Egoism* (1964), *Capitalism: The Unknown Ideal* (1967), *The New Left: The Anti-Industrial Revolution* (1971), *The Romantic Manifesto: A Philosophy of Literature* (1971), *Introduction to Objectivist Epistemology* (1979), and such posthumously published works as *Philosophy: Who Needs It* (1982) and *The Voice of Reason: Essays in Objectivist Thought* (1989).

Throughout the 1960s, even as the sales of Rand's books and the circulation of Objectivist periodicals increased, the public excitement over her ideas seemed to incite ridicule among academics and intellectuals. Although on October 2, 1963, Lewis and Clark College in Portland, Oregon, awarded Rand the honorary Doctor of Humane Letters (L.H.D.), many intellectuals dismissed her ideas as reactionary propaganda or pop philosophy, and viewed her success as the result of hero worship among fanatical followers. For example, philosopher Sidney Hook, in his review of *For the New Intellectual,* objected to its "extravagant absurdity," asserting that it was written "in the style of a prophetess of a cult." And when psychologist Albert Ellis asked, *Is Objectivism a Religion?,* he concluded that Rand and her followers were indeed "unscientific, inhumane, and . . . devoutly religious" in their "extremist" approach to human affairs.

The critics' skepticism was further fueled in 1968, when Rand broke off her personal and professional relationship with the Brandens. This schism only lent further credence to the charge that the movement was based not on a serious commitment to ideas but on a "cult of personality" that gave rise to authoritarian purges. Years later, the Brandens acknowledged with regret that they had inadvertently played a role in encouraging such cultlike behavior. It became clear, however, that the split was primarily of a personal nature, linked to the disintegration of an extramarital affair between Ayn Rand and Nathaniel Branden that had begun in the 1950s.

After her break with the Brandens and the concomitant dissolution of N.B.I., Rand continued to write and to lecture. Though she produced no other works of fiction, she published a "final, definitive version" of her play *Night of January 16th* (formerly titled *Penthouse Legend*), which had had a mild Broadway success in 1935. Foremost, Rand remained a maverick commentator on current events. She characterized George Wallace and his American Independent Party as a "fascist" political incarnation, and she opposed John F. Kennedy's New Frontier and Lyndon B. Johnson's Great Society for similar reasons. Despite her own opposition to the military draft and the Vietnam war, Rand considered Senator George McGovern, the 1972 antiwar Democratic presidential candidate, to be a left-wing statist at heart. She thought that Watergate was the inevitable by-product of a corrupt mixed economy, and she viewed Richard Nixon as an unprincipled pragmatist. She rejected the Supreme Court's censorship decisions on obscenity and pornography, and in an essay that appeared in the posthumously published *Voice of Reason* she warned that Ronald Reagan's connection to the "Moral Majority" portended an "unconstitutional union of religion and politics."

In November 1981, Rand delivered her final public address, "The Sanction of the Victims" (published posthumously in *The Voice of Reason*), at a New Orleans conference sponsored by the National Committee for Monetary Reform. The talk harked back to a theme she explored in *Atlas Shrugged*. Rand died on March 6, 1982, and was buried in Valhalla, New York, next to her husband, who had died four years earlier.

In the years since Rand's death, Objectivism has been gradually emerging as a full-fledged philosophic school. Discussions of her philosophy regularly appear in college textbooks and scholarly journals in philosophy, politics, economics, and sociology. Her ideas are being explored by scholars under the auspices of such organizations as the Ayn Rand Institute, the Institute for Objectivist Studies, and the Ayn Rand Society, an affiliate of the American Philosophical Association. Philosophers influenced by Objectivism include Douglas Den Uyl, Allan Gotthelf, John Hospers, David Kelley, Tibor Machan, Douglas Rasmussen, and George Walsh, as well

as a new generation of graduate students in philosophy and related disciplines. And Nathaniel Branden, regarded by many as the "father of the self-esteem movement," continues to extend Objectivist theoretical concepts into the realm of psychology.

Moreover, Rand's ideas have had a significant impact on American political culture. Her thought was a major inspiration to the founders of the Libertarian Party. That her name has become synonymous with individualism and free-market capitalism is evidenced by the frequent references to her in popular books, movies, radio, and television.

In her work, Rand presented Objectivism as an integrated system with implications for every major branch of philosophy. In metaphysics (the study of the nature of existence), Rand argued in favor of an "objective reality." In epistemology (the study of the nature and means of knowledge), she accepted the validity of sensory perception and the efficacy of human reason. In aesthetics (the study of the nature and function of art), she examined the conceptual basis of art and its role in human life. In ethics (the study of the nature and proper principles of morality), she advocated "rational self-interest." And in politics (the study of the principles guiding a proper social system), she favored individualism and laissez-faire capitalism.

Rand's system is founded on the principles of philosophic realism. She believed that an objective reality exists, that it is what it is, independent of what human beings think or feel about it. But "existence" is not merely an abstract category. To exist is to be something specific; everything that exists has a definite nature. Consciousness is the means of grasping the identity of the elements that exist.

In her *Introduction to Objectivist Epistemology* (1979), Rand developed her view of consciousness, and presented her theory of concept formation and definition. She regarded consciousness as an active faculty, involving three interactive levels: the sensational, the perceptual, and the conceptual. Because the mind cannot retain isolated sensations in memory, Rand argued, the foundation of human knowledge is sensory perception. She maintained that the "form," or way, in which we perceive objects is a product of the means by which we perceive. This important aspect of her theory, stated briefly in "Excerpts from the Epistemology Workshops," an appendix to the expanded second edition of *Introduction* (1990), is developed more thoroughly by David Kelley in *The Evidence of the Senses* (1986). It is one of a number of original tenets of Objectivism that Rand never fully explored in print, and that can be found only in her taped lectures or in courses given by her associates. Rand's estate has begun to publish some of this material, and Leonard Peikoff, the executor of the estate, has announced his intention to release all of it in time.

Clearly, Rand exalted the role of consciousness and reason in human life. In her view, reason is a "faculty that perceives, identifies and integrates the material provided by [the] senses." It is not just a logical capacity but one that has application to practical living. Moreover, it is distinctive to the human, conceptual level of consciousness. Rand emphasizes that thinking is a volitional activity, and that our ability to focus, to move to a higher degree of awareness—which she expressed epigrammatically as the choice "to think or not to think"—is the prime cause in cognition. Since each of us has the capacity to evade thought, this fundamental choice lies at the base of all human rationality and morality.

Most basic is Rand's conviction that human knowledge is valid, that concepts constitute an objective relation between consciousness and existence. They are neither "intrinsic" (that is, existent in reality apart from consciousness) nor "subjective" inventions (that is, purely of the mind, having no relation to the external world).

The task of epistemology is to elucidate the "rules of cognition," rules deriving from the nature of both existence and consciousness.

Rand maintains that for human beings, the mind is the "basic tool of survival." But the mind is not an exclusively analytical faculty. It includes subconscious, emotional components as well as conscious, reasoning ones. It is also interdependent with the body.

While Rand stressed the role of reason, she rejected the belief that there was an inherent antagonism between reason and emotion. She acknowledged the importance of emotion to a fully integrated existence. She viewed emotions as responses emanating from a subconscious estimate "of that which furthers man's values or threatens them, that which is *for* him or *against* him." She argued that "emotions are not tools of cognition," that is, they cannot, in themselves, guarantee the validity of one's subconscious evaluations.

Central to Rand's understanding of emotion was her conviction that the subconscious mind was a mechanism for the spontaneous integration of experience and the automatization of knowledge. This developed conception was primarily an outgrowth of Rand's essays on the nature and function of art.

Torres and Kamhi (1996) point out that Rand's aesthetics has been largely neglected even by Objectivist philosophers, who have tended to focus on other aspects of her thought. The main principles of her aesthetics can be found in a series of essays that were published as the first four chapters of *The Romantic Manifesto.* The book is much more than *A Philosophy of Literature,* as its subtitle suggests. It offers a substantial contribution to the philosophy of art. Rand's aesthetics is primarily an exploration of the nature of art and its role in human life.

According to Rand, "the source of art lies in the fact that man's cognitive faculty is *concep-*

tual.'' All art—painting, sculpture, literature, music, and their related performing arts—is the means by which one brings into conscious awareness a view of oneself and of the nature of existence. Rand explained in *Manifesto: "Art brings man's concepts to the perceptual level of his consciousness and allows him to grasp them directly, as if they were percepts.''*

Rand defined art as *"a selective re-creation of reality according to an artist's metaphysical value-judgments.''* ''Metaphysical value-judgments'' are estimates of the world that are relevant to human life. In art, such ''metaphysical value-judgments'' are often held implicitly, or subconsciously, in the form of a ''sense of life''—which Rand characterized as ''an emotional, subconsciously integrated appraisal of man and of existence.'' ''Sense of life'' is crucially important to both artistic creation and aesthetic response. The artist translates a broad abstraction into concrete form, whereas the responder grasps the abstraction through a perception of the concrete form in which it is expressed.

Because art concretized important life values, Rand opposed most contemporary avant-garde art. In her view, modern art was unintelligible, and hence could not serve the function of integrating human experience. Its nonobjective and nonrepresentational forms, Rand claimed, could only *''disintegrate* man's consciousness.''

Torres and Kamhi conclude that despite her polemic tone and her occasionally arbitrary assertions of personal artistic taste, Rand provided a compelling answer to the basic questions of aesthetics: What is art? and What purpose does art serve?

Grasping the integrated function of the conscious and subconscious dimensions of mind in art, and in life, Rand argued that no person could escape from the need to analyze and understand the beliefs underlying thoughts, emotions, actions, and institutions. She emphasized that people face an essential alternative: whether they will be guided by conscious, articulated convictions and values chosen and validated by their minds, or by subconscious, tacit impulses whose basis and consequences remain largely unknown and unanalyzed.

Human beings are not creatures of pure instinct; they are by nature rational and conceptual beings who must choose to think if they wish to maintain their lives. Rand views the relationship between values and facts, morality and practicality, as integrated. According to Rand, the concept of value is implied in the concept of life because values are not possible without life, and the sustenance of genuinely human life is not possible without the rational pursuit of objective values. What human beings are—rational animals—determines what they ought to do. If they choose to live, they must articulate and act on philosophic and moral principles that have practical significance for their survival.

Thus, according to Rand, ethics is *''an objective, metaphysical necessity of man's survival.''* And since the identity of each life form dictates the means of sustenance, human life—that is, ''man's survival qua man''—is the objective standard of moral values. In Rand's view, ''that which is proper to the life of a rational being is the good; that which negates, opposes or destroys it is the evil.''

Several of Rand's interpreters have debated the nature of her standard of value. Some view it as purely ''survivalist,'' whereas others emphasize her assertion that ''human life'' does not mean a ''*momentary* or . . . merely *physical* survival,'' but an enriched, integrated, ''continuous whole.'' Den Uyl and Rasmussen see this latter interpretation as an outgrowth of Rand's essentially Aristotelian view, in which the value of life is expressed through personal flourishing and self-actualization, which Aristotle called *eudaimonia.*

In the essay ''The Objectivist Ethics,'' in *The*

Virtue of Selfishness: A New Concept of Egoism (1964), Rand details the fundamental ethical principles of Objectivism:

> *Value* is that which one acts to gain and/or keep—*virtue* is the act by which one gains and/or keeps it. The three cardinal values of the Objectivist ethics—the three values which, together, are the means to and the realization of one's ultimate value, one's own life—are: Reason, Purpose, Self-Esteem, with their three corresponding virtues: Rationality, Productiveness, Pride.

For Rand, these values and virtues are different aspects of a single ethical totality. Recognizing the integration of mind and body, she argued that the rational, purposeful, and creative character of human action is manifested in the act of material production. "Production," Rand emphasized in *Capitalism,* "is the application of reason to the problem of survival." And because human survival is not merely physical, people must also act to achieve "the values of character that make [their lives] worth sustaining." Just "as man is a being of self-made wealth, so he is a being of self-made soul." In Rand's usage, the "soul" refers not to a mystic endowment but to human consciousness in all of its complexity.

Rand advocated an ethic of rational, benevolent selfishness. She argued in *The Virtue of Selfishness* that if human life is the standard of value, then each person must be the beneficiary of his or her own moral actions. Echoing John Galt's motto in *Atlas Shrugged,* Rand held in "The Objectivist Ethics" that "man must live for his own sake, neither sacrificing himself to others nor sacrificing others to himself. To live for his own sake means that *the achievement of his own happiness is man's highest moral purpose.*"

Rand's concept of egoism rejects both altruistic self-sacrifice and conventional notions of selfishness. Altruism is not a compassionate morality; its implicit premise is that individuals are not ends in themselves but must serve as means to the welfare of others. Such a prescription for self-abnegation undermines an individual's independence, integrity, and honesty—Rand argued—and leads not to social justice but to a rationale for exploitation.

Rand equally opposed "brute" selfishness, which posits the sacrifice of others to one's own ends. As Ellsworth Toohey asserts in *The Fountainhead:* "Every system of ethics that preached sacrifice grew into a world power and ruled millions of men. . . . The man who speaks to you of sacrifice, speaks of slaves and masters. And intends to be the master."

Rand identified voluntary trade as the only rational, just, and moral principle for all adult human relationships. All forms of human interaction—material exchanges, communication, friendship, and love—ought to be nonexploitative and nonsacrificial. Individuals should act as "independent equals" trading value for value, neither seeking nor granting the unearned.

Rand's political project is the concluding aspect of her systematic philosophy. It aims for the establishment of an ideal society that enables individuals to actualize their unique potentialities. For Rand, individual growth and creativity depend upon appropriate social conditions. Toward that end, she advocated a free society based upon the principle of individual rights. Because individuals must pursue their own rational self-interest in order to sustain their lives, they require a society that protects their ability to do so. Rand opposed the initiation of physical force, because it interferes with an individual's capacity to act on his or her own rational judgment. Individual rights—the rights to life, liberty, property, and the pursuit of happiness—ensure individual freedom in a social context. Rand maintained in *The Virtue of Selfishness:*

> The right to life is the source of all rights—and the right to property is their only implementation. Without property rights, no other rights are possible. Since man has to sustain his life by his own

effort, the man who has no right to the product of his effort has no means to sustain his life. The man who produces while others dispose of his product, is a slave.

In the collection of essays titled *Capitalism: The Unknown Ideal,* Rand developed her view that capitalism is *"a social system based on the recognition of individual rights."* She referred to capitalism as an "unknown ideal" because she believed that it has never existed in pure form and that it has always been undercut by various degrees of government intervention.

Walter Goodman, writing for *Book Week,* dismissed this "ideal" conception of capitalism as an apologia for the rich. In Goodman's view, the call for "laissez-faire" suggested that Objectivism was "in the service of the better classes." Rand denied such charges categorically. She argued that not the free market but government intervention was the fundamental cause of socioeconomic injustice and instability, including militarism, racism, social fragmentation, monopolies, business cycles, inflation, and unemployment. Under such a system, only the state can dispense privileges that benefit some groups at the expense of others. Rand recognized in *The Voice of Reason* that historically, "The attempts to obtain special economic privileges from the government were begun by businessmen . . . who shared the intellectuals' view of the state as an instrument of 'positive' power, serving the 'public good,' and who invoked it to claim that the public good demanded canals or railroads or subsidies or protective tariffs." She held that only pure capitalism could end such injustice.

Under pure capitalism, Rand envisioned a voluntarily financed government strictly limited in its functions to protecting individual rights through a police force, an all-volunteer army, and courts of law. Carefully delineated private property rights would ensure that people kept the product of their efforts while being held accountable for any interference with the rights of others.

Rand rejected any emphasis on economic liberties at the expense of intellectual, political, or spiritual ones. In *For the New Intellectual* she embraced an enriched conception of a free society: "*Intellectual* freedom cannot exist without *political* freedom; political freedom cannot exist without *economic* freedom; *a free mind and a free market are corollaries.*"

According to Rand, the emergence of capitalism was the logical culmination of a secular Aristotelian worldview. She emphasized that whereas the industrial revolution irrefutably demonstrated the practical efficacy of reason, the emergent capitalist system was hampered from its earliest moments, not only by a predatory state but also by an altruist culture that implicitly condoned human sacrifice. The fundamental "inner contradiction" of America, Rand maintained, has been the attempt to synthesize the pursuit of individual happiness with an altruist moral code. Capitalism cannot survive on such a cultural base, she argued; it requires a fully rational, secular ethos untainted by religious mysticism or altruism.

Statism, by contrast, requires a culture directed toward the "obliteration of man's rational faculty." It depends upon a docile, hopeless, and stagnant citizenry. Since "thinking men cannot be ruled," and "ambitious men do not stagnate," statism must institutionalize the antirational. Under statism, irrationality pervades all of human life, including culture and politics. Each sphere reflects and perpetuates a war on reason, freedom, and individualism. Even the educational system militates against the integration of knowledge, because it fosters "anti-conceptual" methods of learning and the fragmentation of the curriculum.

Because reason and freedom are interdependent, a cultural war against reason inevitably undermines freedom. Therefore, it was inevitable that the United States would degenerate into neofascism, in which force replaced trade "as the basic element and ultimate arbiter in all human relationships." Rand explained in a passage that appears in the posthumously published *Ayn Rand*

Column that the "real warfare" of the neofascist "mixed" economy is not between classes but within them. The genuinely productive individuals within each profession—who create legitimate values—are sacrificed to the appropriators, who achieve their position through political pull. Such a mixed economy benefits "the worst type of predatory rich, the rich-by-force, the rich-by-political-privilege." It fosters "parasitism, favoritism, corruption, and greed for the unearned."

Rand asserted that as long as government has the capacity to dispense privilege, citizens will form pressure groups in self-defense. Such pressure groups transcend purely economic interests. Indeed, in Rand's view, state intervention splinters the society in countless ways—along material, racial, ethnic, sexual, generational, and other lines. It thereby generates a collectivist mentality as "every group becomes both the slave and the enslaver of every other group."

Rand refused to accept the present circumstances as unalterable. All human institutions, she argued in *Philosophy: Who Needs It,* must be critically assessed and "then accepted or rejected and changed when necessary." She envisioned a radically new politics that transcended the limitations of Left and Right. But this project was merely one facet of her distinctive and exhaustive view of human existence. Ultimately, Rand considered Objectivism to be the necessary precondition of a full philosophic and cultural renaissance.

Selected Bibliography

WORKS OF AYN RAND

FICTION

We the Living. New York: Macmillan, 1936. 2d ed. New York: New American Library, 1959.

The Fountainhead. Indianapolis: Bobbs-Merrill, 1943. 50th anniversary ed. New York: Bobbs-Merrill, 1993.

Anthem. Los Angeles: Pamphleteers, Inc., 1946. 50th anniversary ed. New York: Dutton, 1995.

Atlas Shrugged. New York: Random House, 1957. 35th anniversary ed. New York: Dutton, 1992.

The Early Ayn Rand: A Selection from Her Unpublished Fiction. Edited by Leonard Peikoff. New York: New American Library, 1984.

NONFICTION

For the New Intellectual: The Philosophy of Ayn Rand. New York: New American Library, 1961.

The Virtue of Selfishness: A New Concept of Egoism. New York: New American Library, 1964.

Capitalism: The Unknown Ideal. New York: New American Library, 1967.

The New Left: The Anti-Industrial Revolution. 2d rev. ed. New York: New American Library, 1975.

The Romantic Manifesto: A Philosophy of Literature. 2d rev. ed. New York: New American Library, 1975.

Philosophy: Who Needs It. New York: Bobbs-Merrill, 1982.

The Voice of Reason: Essays in Objectivist Thought. Edited by Leonard Peikoff. New York: New American Library, 1982.

Introduction to Objectivist Epistemology. Enl. 2d ed. Edited by Harry Binswanger and Leonard Peikoff. New York: New American Library, 1990.

The Ayn Rand Column. Oceanside, Calif.: Second Renaissance Books, 1991.

DRAMA

Night of January 16th. New York: World, 1968.

ARTICLES

"The Only Path to Tomorrow." *Reader's Digest,* January 1944, pp. 88–90.

"Screen Guide for Americans." *Plain Talk,* November 1947, pp. 37–42.

CORRESPONDENCE

Letters of Ayn Rand. Edited by Michael S. Berliner. New York: Penguin Dutton, 1995.

MANUSCRIPT PAPERS

Rand's manuscripts and personal papers are in the Library of Congress.

PERIODICALS EDITED BY RAND

The Ayn Rand Letter. Vols. 1–4. 1971–1976. Palo Alto, Calif.: Palo Alto Book Service, 1979. Now published by Second Renaissance Books, New Milford, Conn.

The Objectivist. Edited by Rand and Nathaniel Branden (January 1966–April 1968), then by Rand (May 1968–September 1971). Vols. 5–10. Palo Alto, Calif.: Palo Alto Book Service, 1982. Now published by Second Renaissance Books, New Milford, Conn.

The Objectivist Newsletter. Edited by Rand and Nathaniel Branden. Vols. 1–4. 1962–1965. Palo Alto, Calif.: Palo Alto Book Service, 1982.

RAND-INFLUENCED PUBLICATIONS

Aristos: The Journal of Esthetics. Vols 1–8. Edited by Louis Torres (July 1982–September 1991) and by Louis Torres and Michelle Marder Kamhi (since January 1992).

Binswanger, Harry. *The Biological Basis of Teleological Concepts.* Los Angeles: Ayn Rand Institute, 1990.

Branden, Nathaniel. *The Psychology of Self-Esteem: A New Concept of Man's Psychological Nature.* Los Angeles: Nash, 1969.

———. *The Six Pillars of Self-Esteem.* New York: Bantam, 1994.

The Intellectual Activist. Vols. 1–9. Edited by Peter Schwartz (October 1979–September 1991), Linda Rearden (November 1991–May 1994), and Robert W. Stubblefield (since July 1994).

Kelley, David. *The Evidence of the Senses: A Realist Theory of Perception.* Baton Rouge: Louisiana State University Press, 1986.

———. *Truth and Toleration.* Verbank, N.Y.: Institute for Objectivist Studies, 1990.

The Objectivist Forum. Edited by Harry Binswanger. Vols. 1–8. 1980–1987.

Peikoff, Leonard. *The Ominous Parallels: The End of Freedom in America.* New York: Stein and Day, 1982.

———. *Objectivism: The Philosophy of Ayn Rand.* New York: Dutton, 1991.

BIBLIOGRAPHIES AND REFERENCE GUIDES

Binswanger, Harry, ed. *The Ayn Rand Lexicon: Objectivism from A to Z.* New York: New American Library, 1986.

Gladstein, Mimi Reisel. *The Ayn Rand Companion.* Westport, Conn.: Greenwood Press, 1984.

Perinn, Vincent L., comp. *Ayn Rand: First Descriptive Bibliography.* Rockville, Md.: Quill & Brush, 1990.

BIOGRAPHICAL AND CRITICAL STUDIES

Baker, James T. *Ayn Rand.* Edited by Warren French. Boston: Twayne, 1987.

Branden, Barbara. *The Passion of Ayn Rand.* Garden City, N.Y.: Doubleday, 1986.

Branden, Nathaniel. *Judgment Day: My Years with Ayn Rand.* Boston: Houghton Mifflin, 1989.

Branden, Nathaniel, and Barbara Branden. *Who Is Ayn Rand?: An Analysis of the Novels of Ayn Rand.* New York: Random House, 1962.

Chamberlain, John. "Ayn Rand's Political Parable and Thundering Melodrama." *New York Herald Tribune,* October 6, 1957, sec. 6, pp. 1ff.

Chambers, Whittaker. "Big Sister Is Watching You." *National Review,* December 28, 1957, pp. 594–596.

Cox, Stephen. "Ayn Rand: Theory versus Creative Life." *Journal of Libertarian Studies,* 8, no. 1:19–29 (Winter 1986).

———. "The Films of Ayn Rand." *Liberty,* 1, no. 1:5–10 (August 1987).

———. "The Literary Achievement of *The Fountainhead.*" In *The Fountainhead: A Fiftieth Anniversary Celebration.* Poughkeepsie, N.Y.: Institute for Objectivist Studies, 1993.

Den Uyl, Douglas, and Douglas B. Rasmussen, eds. *The Philosophic Thought of Ayn Rand.* Urbana: University of Illinois Press, 1984.

Ellis, Albert. *Is Objectivism a Religion?* New York: Lyle Stuart, 1968.

Goodman, Walter. Review of *Capitalism: The Unknown Ideal. Book Week,* November 20, 1966.

Hicks, Granville. "A Parable of Buried Talents." *New York Times Book Review,* October 13, 1957, pp. 4–5.

Hook, Sidney. "Each Man for Himself." *New York Times Book Review,* April 9, 1961, pp. 3, 28.

Merrill, Ronald E. *The Ideas of Ayn Rand.* LaSalle, Ill.: Open Court, 1991.

O'Neill, William. *With Charity toward None: An Analysis of Ayn Rand's Philosophy.* New York: Philosophical Library, 1971.

Pruette, Lorine. "Battle against Evil." *New York Times Book Review,* May 16, 1943, pp. 7, 18.

Robbins, John W. *Answer to Ayn Rand: A Critique of the Philosophy of Objectivism.* Washington, D.C.: Mount Vernon, 1974.

Rosenbloom, Joel. 1961. "The Ends and Means of Ayn Rand." *New Republic,* April 24, 1961, pp. 28–29.

Sciabarra, Chris Matthew. *Ayn Rand: The Russian Radical.* University Park: Pennsylvania State University Press, 1995.

Smith, George H. *Atheism, Ayn Rand, and Other Heresies.* Buffalo, N.Y.: Prometheus Books, 1991.

Torres, Louis, and Michelle Marder Kamhi. 1996. *What Art Is: Ayn Rand's Philosophy of Art in Critical Perspective.* LaSalle, Ill.: Open Court, 1996.

Vermilye, Jerry. *Great Italian Films.* Secaucus, N.J.: Citadel Press, 1994.

INTERVIEW

"*Playboy* Interview with Ayn Rand: A Candid Conversation with the Fountainhead of 'Objectivism.'" *Playboy,* March 1964, pp. 35–40, 42–43, 64.

—*CHRIS MATTHEW SCIABARRA*

Alberto Álvaro Ríos

1952

ALBERTO RÍOS' WRITINGS convert the day-to-day lives of individuals living on the borderlines created between cultures, languages, genders, and geographies into lyric sites where fate dances hand in hand with political resistance, and magic becomes the origin of common sense. Ríos listens carefully to the varieties of speech produced in everyday situations; he records those different types of speech in his poems and short stories and charges them with rich symbolism, while at the same time making audible their musicality and their rhythm. The prime matter of his poems brings together an array of symbolic discourses derived from a range of interests as diverse as Mexican Catholicism, the family, the cartoons of Walt Disney, and the experiences of Chicano manhood and Chicana womanhood.

In defining the task he wants to perform through his writings Ríos quotes from Pablo Neruda in his 1984 essay, "Chicano / Borderlands Literature and Poetry":

> You see there are in our countries rivers which have no names, trees which nobody knows, and birds which nobody has described. . . . Everything we know is new. Our duty, then, as we understand it, is to express what is unheard of.

Pablo Neruda talks about the vast uncharted geographies and landscapes of Latin America as a whole; Alberto Ríos applies Neruda's notion to specific, clearly demarcated geographical and social margins, to the intimate spaces in the lives of people living in small border towns between Mexico and the United States.

The vision of Ríos' poetry is a microscopic one. It explores not grand open territories that have to be conquered by strength or by language but limited spaces where everyday experiences occur. It amplifies the singular inflections of the languages spoken in those spaces to make them audible to the reader. Ríos' writing springs from those places that have been unrepresented, disguised in the cloth of their ordinariness, unexplored because they seemed to be "very well known." Shaving in the morning, sitting on the same side of the sofa every day for years, going for a walk under a bridge, or feeling a small discomfort while preparing the morning coffee become in Ríos' poetry symptoms of the existence of invisible laws in the universe that operate in the time frames created by a consistent repetition of apparently insignificant actions in the home, in the village, and within the family.

The protagonists of Ríos' stories are marginal to the society in which they live in the same way that shaving is marginal to a day's work. These characters cope with a history imposed on them from the outside. Ríos explains in the prologue to *Pig Cookies,* a book of short stories he published in 1995,

I was born of people who were outside of time and place, people who were displaced and unsure, people reduced ultimately to manners rather than to laws for survival. They found the line inside themselves, the things they would and would not do, in there. Their lives are from before the border fences.

This portrait of Ríos' family also describes the characters who populate his poems and stories. Aware of the unpredictable forces arising from living at the margins of two cultures, his characters express their creativity by articulating small resistances to social marginalization and acculturation in their daily routines. They accept the existence of a magic or mythic dimension to life that rules the way they cultivate their gardens, perform their work, and understand their social interactions. These myths and the magic are as real to them as the politics and economics that trace a frontier line down the center of their lives, their very sense of who they are.

Writing is for Ríos an endeavor to explore the knowledge people derive from the daily encounter between Spanish and Anglo cultures that takes place along the margins of Mexico and the United States. The epistemological quest for what Ríos—in an interview with Lupe Cárdenas and Justo Alarcón in 1990—called "everydayness, ordinariness, the real, the pedestrian" influences not only the topics of his writings but also the forms in which they are cast. His poems and short stories use a colloquial English dotted with Spanish words to show that the instability of living in a world between languages yields not a poverty but a richness of linguistic possibilities. This richness allows the poet and the reader to understand experience better by looking at it from at least two points of view. In his essay "Chicano / Borderlands Literature and Poetry" Ríos makes an analogy between his writing technique and the use of binoculars: "we must use both eyes to see the one thing more clearly." The poetics resulting from this intense "binocular" focus—on the self,

the personal, the familiar—fueled by a need to learn from the overlooked, aims to reveal links between the individual and the universal, between particular personal experience and human experience in general.

The poem "The Friday Morning Trial of Mrs. Solano," included in the book of poetry Ríos published in 1988, *The Lime Orchard Woman,* provides an image that suggests an analogy between it and Alberto Ríos' own creative process. The poem depicts the innocent game of cracking piñatas open as a formative experience for Mr. Solano, the protagonist's husband. By repeating the ritual, the poem indicates, Mr. Solano learned the connection between hitting with his stick and obtaining a reward:

> As the loud boy,
> Piñatas had made him
> Expert at hitting.
> Once he had broken
>   Open the body of a rose,
> Had caught in mid air
> A glass piggy bank.
> He knew it was falling, had looked
> That way one is not allowed
> From under the blindfold.

Like the boy with the piñata, Ríos crafts his poetry by cracking open the secrets contained in everyday objects, words, and practices. His blindfold is the dominant culture; guided by furtive glances out from under it, the poet strives to knock the surprising interior out of the common, everyday wrapping. Once released, the familiar objects that populate Ríos' poetry reveal a wealth made of the pleasures, tragedies, histories, and traditions of the vibrant and dislocated people who live between two cultures. But in his exploration of the singularity of an individual's life and of the languages he or she uses to understand his or her environment Ríos attempts to discover universal truths. He uses individual lives and languages to explore new and uncharted territories for American literature: the human experiences arising from the encounter between the different cultures, social classes, and genders that make up the Chicano community.

In his first four books, published between 1981 and 1988, Ríos plunges into his personal past to explore the apparent contradictions that form his identity. Geographical frontiers played an important role in the Ríos family, starting with Ríos' grandparents. His grandfather, Margarito Ríos, played a very active role in the Mexican Revolution on the side of the revolutionary Álvaro Obregón. In an effort to protect his family from reprisals if his faction were to be defeated, Margarito relocated them at the limits of the Mexican nation: first in the south in Tapachula, Chiapas, and then in the north in Mexican Nogales. Tapachula, where Alberto's father was born in 1928 was a frontier space occupied by an unstable population of refugees trying to survive the Revolution. Later the family moved north of the United States–Mexico border to Nogales, Arizona. Alberto Álvaro Ríos was born there on September 18, 1952. His name inverts the order of his father's, in the same way in which their relationships to the frontiers had been inverted. If for Álvaro Alberto Ríos the frontier was a safe haven away from a war, for Alberto Álvaro the frontier became the sign of an existence at the margins of the North and of the South. The frontier became also a way to understand the double character of his inheritance. His mother, Agnes, was British, born in the town of Warrington, Lancashire.

Because of the physical circumstances of his life, Ríos provides the mythic locus of the frontier with a new, living meaning. Departing from traditional interpretations of the frontier—that is, departing from the connotations of conquest and expansion—Ríos focuses on the ways that the frontier allows the flow of life to cross from one side of the border to the other. In ''West Real,''

an essay about his experience growing up in Arizona that he published in 1992, Ríos explains the connection between the concept of frontier and his sense of personal identity: ''I grew up around my father's family, but I look like my mother—which means I got to see two worlds from the beginning, and could even physically experience the difference growing up where I did: I could put, every day of my life, one foot in Mexico and one foot in the United States, at the same time.''

As a child Ríos negotiated the differences between his father's and his mother's cultures without any problems. Spanish was his first language, the one that he spoke with his Mexican grandparents, and he learned English from his mother. But his first year of schooling marked a turning point; English became his main language, and Spanish became something shameful, loaded with negative connotations. In his essay ''Becoming and Breaking: Poet and Poem,'' published in 1984, Ríos explains, ''When we got to that first grade classroom, my friends and I, we were told: you can't speak Spanish.'' Along with this prohibition came the association of the adjective ''bad'' with anything coming from his Mexican cultural inheritance.

In his interview with Lupe Cárdenas and Justo Alarcón, Ríos declares that he grew up reading and rereading comic books, science fiction, fairy tales, and the *World Book Encyclopedia*. He regarded these books as his means of traveling. His reading also became the source for a number of metaphors in his poetry. Ríos began writing in elementary school; there he composed short stories and poems in the back pages of his notebooks and textbooks. Recalling these early writings in his conversation with Cárdenas and Alarcón, Ríos describes two characteristics that became central to his understanding of the writer's job. These writings were not homework but rather ''things that one commits to the page without being asked or told to do so,'' in loneliness, detached from other people. For Ríos "a great deal of writing is private," as were his earliest stories and poems.

After graduating from Nogales High School in 1970, Ríos entered the University of Arizona at Tucson, where he received a B.A. in English literature and creative writing in 1974. During his last year in high school and his first years as an undergraduate, Ríos relearned Spanish. His awareness of this process of forgetting and remembering a language and a culture became an integral part of Ríos' writing. He explains in "West Real," "In having to pay double and triple attention to language—first to forget, and then to relearn—I began to see earnestly how everything, every object, every idea, had at *least* two names." The idea of multiple perspectives suggested here is present in Ríos' poems from the very beginning; it has undergone transformations and fine-tuning throughout his career.

Convinced that he would not be able to find a job as a writer, Ríos completed a second B.A. in psychology in 1975 while at the same time preparing himself for the law school entry examination. He was accepted at Arizona University Law School and attended classes for a year. During that year Ríos realized that by focusing so much on making himself employable he was separating himself from writing. He quit law school and entered the graduate program in creative writing at Arizona State University. In 1979, he received his M.F.A. and won the Writer's Fellowship in Poetry from the Arizona Commission on the Arts. His years as a graduate student had a great impact on his writing. He became deeply aware of traditional and contemporary theories of writing and came to understand writing as a type of craft with rules, conventions, and formal techniques. His writings began to include the experiences that he had witnessed or participated in as he was growing up as a Chicano. "I want to talk loudly about 'limited audiences' and people named 'Rosete' " he declares in his interview

with Cárdenas and Alarcón, remembering his reaction against his teachers' negative comments about his choice of Hispanic names for his characters.

During the late seventies Ríos started to publish his work in numerous magazines such as *Iowa Review, Prairie Schooner,* and the *North American Review.* He made a commitment to share his knowledge and his work by giving poetry and writing workshops in small communities in Arizona in collaboration with the Arizona Artists-in-Education Program and the Central Arizona College Community Writing Project. These projects allowed Ríos to travel throughout Arizona teaching writing in small places like Florence, in the middle of the state, or the Papago Reservation near Sells. In such settings Ríos did a good deal of the listening that he considers essential for his writing. He also published three chapbooks entitled *Elk Heads on the Wall* in 1979, *Sleeping on Fists* in 1981, and *The Warrington Poems.* His work was selected for an anthology of Chicano poets, *Agua Fresca,* published in 1980.

In 1981, Ríos received the Walt Whitman Award for poems published the following year in his book *Whispering to Fool the Wind,* the first collection of his poems to be distributed nationally. *Whispering to Fool the Wind* retells the coming-of-age story of the young poet during the summer of 1967. Each poem reflects on the presence or absence of a family relative, an experience, or a place as seen through the inquisitive eyes of a child. The opening poem of the collection, "Lost on September Trail, 1967," connects the experience of being lost in a forest to the experience of being surrounded by a world yet to be discovered. The poem places the reader in an unfamiliar geography, a world yet to be named and described, outside of history and language, as if the poet were preparing a fresh canvas for his vision:

Having lost our previous names
Somewhere in the rocks as we ran,
we could not yet describe ourselves.

The collection of poems goes on to name the objects and geographies of Ríos' daily life as if they were fragments of a "new world," a world from which the poet estranges himself while questioning the easy familiarity with which he saw this environment before. A masculine narratorial voice provides unity to all the poems, ordering them into a symbolic journey from childhood to adolescence. The speaker relates sensitive portraits of his ancestors and his present family, utilizing the conventions of autobiographical writing. With each portrait, the relationship between absences and presences appears connected to the experience of growing up and the realization of death as a fatal omen present in all the experiences of life. Repeatedly, the poems connect images of animate and inanimate objects, suggesting that the boundaries between life and death are fluid. A simple handkerchief given as a present to the narrator's grandmother becomes in "Belita" the very portrait of her face, "which fit her now like a wrinkled handkerchief." Eventually this present, given as a symbol of love, develops into the shroud that covers the body of the grandmother after her death.

In the poem "At Kino Viejo, Mexico" we find the opposite conceit; here inanimate objects come alive thanks to the putrefaction resulting from being piled up in the same place for too long:

The potatoes of the corner store sing,
sand crickets and green flies full,
fat almost like night beetles,
the burlap bags of dry onions move,
the loose copper skins jumping.

Sometimes the two sides of this powerful paradox—life engenders death which engenders life—appear condensed in a single line. In "Mi Abuelo," the voice of the narrator's grandfather returns from the dead to present his most intimate secret to his grandson: *"I am a man / who has served ants with the attitude / of a waiter."* The characters do not rebel against their physical suffering or demise; instead they openly surrender to it as if their redemption depended on their having good manners in the face of destiny.

A sense of sinister fluidity between corruption and generation haunts the poetic universe Ríos creates in this book. The protagonist's passage from innocence to experience occurs as he realizes and eventually accepts this paradox, a development that is triggered by the death of his grandmother. But neither the realization nor the acceptance provides any comfort to the poet-child. The last poem, "Sundays Visiting," portrays the narrator and his cousin trying to stick to their old routines in an effort to regain the safety of innocence. The meaning of their little games, however, has changed forever: the two friends are on their own now, nothing supports their bodies, and they have learned to mistrust nature, which they embraced full of enthusiasm at the beginning of the book:

Nothing hung in the air,
There was nowhere to sit
but on our thin heels, nothing
closed us in or locked us out
that we couldn't kick down
like weeds with our small feet,
the words of our new language.

By the end of the summer, the poet has succeeded in creating a new language made by reappropriating cartoon images, family stories, his grandmother's cooking recipes, and religious images. As his images of regeneration after death suggest, the poet extracts life from the discarded objects and people of the world where he lives in order to produce his poetry.

In the early 1980s Ríos became assistant professor of creative writing at Arizona State University, a position that he continued to hold in

1996. Teaching, both in the classroom and through his writing, became a central activity in his life. ''As Chicano writers,'' he declares in ''Chicano/Borderlands Literature and Poetry,'' ''we are teachers now—but without having been students; we had no teachers of what we are.'' Together with beginning his academic activities, Ríos started to expand his writing into the short story genre, and he published the results in a group of journals aimed mainly at a Hispanic audience, such as *Blue Moon News, De Colores,* the *Mendocino Review, New Times, Salt Cedar,* and *Revista Chicana-Riqueña.* In 1984 his stories were collected in *The Iguana Killer,* which won for its author the Western States Book Award in Short Fiction.

The Iguana Killer contains a dozen short stories cast in a prose that is marked by the same economy of expression, attention to the symbolic potential of colloquial language, and awareness of rhythmic patterns as Ríos' poems. The sequence of the stories charts the trip from the South to the North that most of the protagonists take or have taken at some point in their lives. Starting in Villahermosa, a town in the rain forest of southern Mexico, close to the Guatemalan border, each story travels a little farther north, through Mexico City, Guaymas, Mexican Nogales, and finally, crossing the border, into Nogales, Arizona.

The characters live between two worlds, Mexico and the United States, connected through family and culture to both of these territories separated by a border. Those who live in Mexico have grandparents or siblings in the States whom they strive to keep in touch with. Those living in the States have nostalgic memories of a Mexican past, and they (especially the children) live divided between the culture of their parents and that of their surroundings. Traveling from the South to the North displaces the characters not only geographically but also morally; as they travel, they move from innocence to experience.

The focus of the stories also shifts from a conjunctive society, where meanings are shared by the whole community, to a disjunctive one in which the characters are never in full possession of the meaning of their own actions and words. While the world of the Mexican jungle incorporates without difficulty any element external to its tradition (it makes foreign additions into useful tools), in the North the opposite is true. For example, a baseball bat sent from the North to the South as a Christmas present becomes an excellent ''iguana killer'' in the hands of Sapito, the protagonist of the first story. In Villahermosa nobody knows about baseball or about baseball bats but everybody can see the usefulness of a well-crafted stick for hunting iguanas. But nothing of what the displaced characters bring from Mexico seems to have the effect it was intended to: instead, those things traveling from the South to the North cause disagreement (tearing apart the community) and endanger the health of the individual who uses them. For example, the Mexican coffee that Adolfo Pineda asks his wife for in ''The Birthday of Mrs. Pineda,'' the last story in the collection, turns out to be dangerous for his health.

Adolfo drinks the coffee despite his doctor's advice and establishes through it a symbolic connection to the world of his childhood in Mexico. His doctor and the English dictionary want to impose a new meaning on the drink he has known for many years, but Adolfo refuses to accept it. He looks up the meaning of the word ''caffeine,'' but as the narrator explains, what he finds in the dictionary does not match what he has always known.

> He could not find in any dictionary—after the doctor had told him about the word—anything about its being what it was: a power from the muscles of the dead, their backs and forearms, their dreams, and how they still want to do things, a kind of leftover need, yes, *seguro que sí,* the power of intentions never met, such strong intentions, and so

many, that they could not go away. Coffee reminded him that he was alive, and would keep him alive, too, not to make him one of those bodies, not like the doctor had said.

Like the coffee Mr. Pineda drinks, the culture, language, and traditions that the characters bring over the frontier become in the North medically or morally dangerous. But just as Adolfo reinterprets coffee, most of the characters come to understand that the baggage they carry to the North from the South is the element that gives them life and energy. It is something to keep in the midst of the opposition offered by their new environment.

"The Child" is the story that marks the transition between the two worlds. Set on a bus trip from Mexico City to Nogales, Arizona, it recounts the story of two widows from Guaymas who are on their way to attend the funeral of a brother who died in the States. In their eagerness to help a man who travels with his sick son, they discover that the child is actually dead and that his corpse is being used as a container to smuggle opium. This dead child emptied of his inner organs becomes a metaphor for the somber side of going to the North. The people, having left their pasts behind, become disemboweled containers, emptied of their culture and feeling as a means to numb the pain of their arrival into the new world beyond the border.

The stories set on the United States side of the border portray the different ways in which misplaced characters, mostly children, manage to cope with the marginal place they have in their families and in society. Some manage to survive by using their bodies as a shield against a society that does not want to include them. The body, especially the functions related to secretions and excretions of bodily substances, becomes a means of articulating resistances to the social oppression and personal abuses that target the protagonists.

Some of the children become the moral con-

science of their social groups. Johnny Ray, in a story that takes his name as its title, refuses to play "cowboys and Indians" even when it is disguised as a harmless school game. Joey, in "His Own Key," refuses to play sexual games and to trivialize the act of reproduction. He feels that he alone carries the burden of the secret of how babies are made. He thinks that adults are ashamed of talking about it because there is something inherently dirty about the process, and that children are too irresponsible to take the future of humanity seriously. In the midst of this situation, Joey reaches the conclusion that having babies is another of those tasks that are necessary for life but that are unpleasant to carry out. He concludes, "someone had to know, just as someone had to empty the garbage." At a very early age the characters in these stories need to make hard choices and come up with creative solutions to the difficult problems of growing up while learning about the frontiers they cross along the way. Their smallest actions are portrayed as heroic feats and given the attention reserved in traditional literature for the mythic deeds of national heroes.

From one story to the next, the characters grow more and more certain of themselves and their views of the world, and so does the narrator. He ceases to speak in mythical tones, as he does in the stories set in Mexico, and sounds instead like a real person. In some stories the narrator employs the idiosyncratic language of high school students; in others he uses the charged language of an adult. In the last three stories the adult narrator harks back with melancholy to the moment when he received the hardest lessons of his life. The narrator seems to need first to borrow the languages and stories of other people in order to become able to articulate the significance of his own past. In "The Secret Lion" and "Eyes like They Say the Devil Has," the narrator turns his attention to his own biography; he condenses and reevaluates the previous lessons of the book by showing how they hold true in his own experience.

In "The Secret Lion" the protagonist's need for adventure and discovery pushes him and his friend Sergio to find a heaven in the hills surrounding their house. Eventually they find a green spot with a "Coke holder" in the middle and make it into their secret playground, their personal oasis in the Arizona desert. Their safe haven turns out to be the green of a golf course, and the "Coke holder" the hole two players are aiming at with their ball. The characters' return home from this "colonized" land represents their expulsion from the innocence of childhood. The second story written in an autobiographical style, "Eyes like They Say the Devil Has," balances the sour taste of the expulsion from paradise with this assurance from a fortune teller: "The future will make you tall." The two ideas—innocence is lost but the future bodes good fortune—summarize the atmosphere of the stories collected in *The Iguana Killer:* all the stories acknowledge loss and yet express hope for a strong future.

Although Ríos' first two books received an extremely positive response in terms of literary awards and book reviews, only two critical articles have been published that analyze these works in any depth: Renato Rosaldo's "Fables of the Fallen Guy"—published in 1991 in *Criticism in the Borderlands,* a collection edited by Hector Calderón and José David Saldívar—and Saldívar's "Towards a Chicano Poetics: The Making of the Chicano Subject, 1969–1982," which was published in the journal *Confluencia* in 1986. Both of the essays agree that Ríos' writing represents the latest stage in the historical development of the Chicano consciousness. Rosaldo analyzes the stories in *The Iguana Killer* and places Ríos in a harmonic relationship with contemporary Chicano authors Sandra Cisneros and Denise Chávez. He points out that all three writers demonstrate how the representation of Chicano culture is veering away from the establishment of any notion of *pureza* (essentialism) but gaining in range and engagement. Saldívar interprets the poem "El Molino Rojo," from the book *Whispering to Fool the Wind,* as one which conceives of the Chicano subject of the 1980s by synthesizing the magical-realist tradition of Latin American literature with the social realism of popular Chicano literature from the 1950s and 1960s.

"El Molino Rojo" focuses on a common scene in a bar where a group of men get together to play pool, drink, and talk. Saldívar contends that the poem elevates the repetitive quality of the scene to the level of ritual and uncovers in it the unwritten laws that regulate the life of the Chicano protagonists, laws which they respect as the basis for their fate:

> They will always come here
> because they have to,
> whose favorite joke is the broken pool table,
> told over and over again,
> dirty like he imagines Robles' pulque
> but he can't do anything to fix it
> even when they ask sometimes without
>   laughing.

"Always" and "over and over" imply that the repetitions the poem describes have no starting point and no foreseeable ending. Reinforcing this sense, "have to" and "can't" suggest an immutability that transcends the individual will. The atmosphere created through these words transcends the laws of life and death. The characters stay around the "Molino Rojo" not of their own free will but because of a tradition that is so powerful it keeps them there even after their death.

In Saldívar's analysis, the poem illustrates the way in which Ríos' work participates in the elaboration of a Chicano poetics. Saldívar identifies three stages in the development of this poetics and of the Chicano subject it represents. In the first stage the writer is preoccupied with form, with the theme of social resistance, and with the realist style of which the poems of José Montoya are the best example. In the second stage he or she presents the Chicano-Chicana subject in fragments and thus resists the conventional interpretations of that subject. An example of this strategy is the work of Bernice Zamora, a poet who expresses revolutionary ideas by showing the inability of any stereotype to capture her identity. Ríos, according to Saldívar, exemplifies the last stage of the Chicano poetics and represents a synthesis of the two previous stages. According to Saldívar, Ríos' writing describes and exemplifies the subject position of contemporary Chicanos since "it expresses a longing for closure and resorts to the marvelous to represent it."

Ríos himself takes up the issue of his role in the creation of a Chicano literature in his article "Chicano/Borderlands Literature and Poetry." There he traces three waves of Chicano writing since the 1960s, but unlike Saldívar, he does not treat these waves as mutually exclusive stages of a historical development. Rather, he sees them as modes of writing and experiencing the Chicano identity that are bound to multiply into an even greater variety in the future. He cites as an example of the first wave of poetry the creations of Omar Salinas and calls them poems of the *vato loco:* "the crazy man out on his own fending off the world and doing the best he can." A second type of poems he calls the poems of the *vato:* "These are poems of stronger allegiances, to craft, to readers, to the art of poetry." The work of Lorna Dee Cervantes and Gary Soto belongs in this group. Ríos finally describes his own poetry as typical of the third wave of Chicano writing: both connected to and exceeding the previous two categories. He calls the poems of this phase "narrative poem-stories." In his own words, "These poems synthesize the other two forms, the *vato loco,* the *vato,* the *loco,* and adds

a story, puts them into a greater context. This is the kind of writing that I do, telling stories. These include lies and truths, meat and myth."

In 1985 Ríos published *Five Indiscretions.* This, his second book of poems traces a genealogy of the seemingly capricious or irrational behavior of human beings by exploring how this behavior develops as a result of the experiences each person goes through in the secrecy of his or her most intimate moments. The book is made up of four parts: the first part explores feminine subjectivity; the second, masculine subjectivity; the third, the coming together of both genders; and the final section portrays the individual as a member of a family. The four parts are organized in terms of the different aspects of human life; the individual poems are ordered according to a reverse chronology. After the first poem, which focuses on a mature woman in the present time, Ríos introduces poems that refer to the past and center on ever-younger women and men. In the last poems the poet explores the connections between the remote past and his present by looking at his ancestors through the objects that they left behind.

The somber vision of death and life continually feeding on each other that one finds in *Whispering to Fool the Wind* becomes in Ríos' third book a powerful source of resistance to the social and natural forces that oppress the protagonists of these poems, a frame within which they develop their politics as a means of personal survival. In the poem that opens the collection, "Taking Away the Name of a Nephew," Susí discovers a picture of the corpse of her disappeared nephew in the newspaper. Instead of accepting the idea that her nephew is dead, Susí reasons with the logic of the death-begets-life paradox:

In that body the three soldiers were fooled, tricked
A good hundred strings of wool put over their eyes:

They did not take away the boy.
They took away his set of hands and his spine
Which in weeks would look like railroad tracks
Along the side of any young mountain.
One of the disappeared looks like this
The newspaper said. She had seen
The photograph which looked like all
Newspaper photographs,
Had thought it does not say *looked* like this,
But *looks* like this, still; had thought
What is being said here is that he did not die.
It was not death that took him.

Susí constructs a logic of presence that defies the abuses of authority that take place in the society in which she lives. She sticks to the literal meaning of the newspaper caption and at the same time refuses to equate the death of the body with the death of the person.

Like Susí, the protagonists in the other poems of this collection use language in a strategic manner. They manipulate the symbolic potential of language, inventing their own metaphors and even developing alternative systems of communication that move away from the spoken or written word. They use their uncharted language to recover from their personal tragedies: their experiences of loss, abuse, infidelity, death, seduction, incestuous desire, and desperation. The poems take the reader to the core of those moments when the characters dare to revisit their tragic experiences and transform these experiences into narratives that make them stronger. In their narratives, the real and the symbolic become so tightly connected to each other that the characters can exchange properties between them at will. Thus Mariquita in "Her Dream Is of the Sea" associates her death wish with the sea, establishing an analogy between her body and the waves, tides, and creatures of the ocean.

The tides are shoulders flexing
or the process of food coming up from the stomach.
One day the sea will do it, she imagines,
a real, green and gray and large upthrowing

of doubloons and penises,
fishheads and pork. She wakes
and in the dimmed light sees her hand,
only her hand, how
cut off in this way of the dark from her arm
it looks like a starfish.

Astute manipulation of tropes like Susí's helps all the characters in *Five Indiscretions* to survive in the midst of the intense instability that is typical of their environment. In a private moment, one character uses a dream to settle an unfinished quarrel with her dead husband; another prays for a lover in the severe atmosphere of a Catholic church; one passes advice to her granddaughter about the similarities between men and scorpions; another sees her husband smile and remembers a time when they were unfaithful to one another. Ríos' poems explore every one of these "survival" techniques, recounting them by means of a narrator-witness who does not pass judgment. The cumulative effect of the poems is to express intense trust in and admiration for the creative ways in which human beings respond to a range of uncertainties.

Language about the body runs through most of these poems; Ríos relishes the way the world may be ingested through the mouth and celebrates the abject products we produce as a result. Sometimes his observations on the body and its excretions serve only as a means to set the stage for a particular story. In "The Birthday of Mrs. Pineda," for example, the emotional obstacles that separate the protagonist from her husband materialize in the form of grime on the floor of a barn: she "had to step over this floor made of sputum from half-shaved, thick men and dying cocks, a floor bloodstained and scuffed into a kind of inexpert, misshapen setting of scab tiles." In other poems the body becomes the site where life and creativity meet death and decay. A body is much more sensitive to time than the people it shelters: "You don't know enough to die," the narrator reproaches the protagonist in "Old Man on the Hospital Porch." In "The Carlos Who Died, and Left Only This," the body becomes literally "a borrowed suit / that was returned." But Ríos' focus on the body has the ulterior goal of reaching the soul, which the narrators of his poems typically describe as unavailable to language. In "The Scent of Unbought Flowers" the speaker explains:

> After all, a man has a soul.
> It is everything he has thought
> and kept unspoken, each thing
> he has felt and for which he could
> find no reasonable name, no sound.

By the final poem in *Five Indiscretions,* the traces and objects left behind by the characters become unerasable indices of who they are even after they have died. The last poem, "I Held His Name," reflects on this idea of life after death through the figure of a deceased husband who remains present to his widow. Serving as the narrator for this piece, the poet takes the reader along on his visit to the widow's house. There he observes the following:

> Everything in the room took care of him,
> she did, the hats did, the dusted pictures of him
> looking at it all without a smile.
> . . . .
> on Thursday nights by myself I had held it
> quick, but carefully, my hands just enough apart.
> Sometimes off the shelf it would fall into my arms.
> Sometimes because I wanted it to, sometimes
> it fell as I hunted other things.

This poem pushes metaphor to its limit. It exchanges qualities between the real and the ideal up to the point where they have exchanged roles. The imaginary element, the head of the dead husband, becomes reified as a decorative memento on a shelf. The hat, on the other hand, loses its materiality, treated by the poet as a pure signifier of the name of the husband that the speaker holds. The widow's livingroom becomes the space where symbols meet with the things they stand for and exchange qualities, each becoming a little bit like the other.

Five Indiscretions focuses on processes of discovery, of learning from the experiences and stories of people, a learning that is not calculated according to a goal that has to be achieved but that is driven by a mixture of desire and chance.

The willful exchange of functions between the real and the imaginary elements of a metaphor becomes an increasingly powerful rhetorical strategy in Ríos' writing. His fourth book, *The Lime Orchard Woman,* published in 1988, revisits many of the topics he introduced in his previous books by examining them through his newly found rhetorical exchanges between the imaginary and the real. Thus the poems in *The Lime Orchard Woman* both expand Ríos' artistic vision and reveal new, sophisticated nuances in that vision. The four sections of this book explore the creative power of failed intentions, of misunderstandings, of death, and of memory. Where Ríos referred to the actual frontier in his previous books, here he evokes a purely imaginary line that separates bodies, genders, the past and the present, reality and its representation— and thus engenders a certain desire.

The men and women protagonists of the first part of the book fail to communicate their love for other people, or their love is not reciprocated. In "The Industry of Hard Kissing," the very first poem, the inability of the lover ever to reach his loved object completely becomes an index of the individual's desire to transcend limitations. Identifying happiness as a cancer and desire as a vocation for life, the poem concludes:

> Again, this small cancer
> Of the happy soul.
> So we kiss harder, or
> Not at all, something
> Saved for the other,
> For the whistles and the cheeses

Of another life,
Another mouth.

Infidelity in *The Lime Orchard Woman* is not the product of anyone's willful decision but the result of fate quietly operating through time. Ríos treats everyday gestures, such as shaving, as signs of the invisible ways in which men are bound to disappear from the lives of their loved ones, gradually abandoning them through the unnoticeable but constant changes brought by each new day. The dividing line of gender appears here as an insurmountable wall that creates an unquenchable desire not so much to possess as to become the other. "Dressing for Dinner" represents this idea with a tangible image:

I imagine a small joy,
A woman, standing
In a shower peeing,
The feel of that.
Other people outside
The small width of the door,
In the living room
Beginning dinner.
. . . .
I can only imagine,
Hold myself close
To my own leg,
Feel the warming go down.
I can only pretend
I am a woman.

Women are characterized in this book as loving, compassionate, and strong when confronting the trials of abuse or infidelity. In "He Will Not Leave a Note," Mariquita understands the fact that her husband will eventually abandon her as a natural consequence of time and change:

Every day he shaved off something of himself.
One day he would be altogether different.
One day she would wake, and look at
The back of a man who was not there.

In "Mason Jars by the Window" another woman finds a way to keep herself and her daughter safe from her abusive husband with glass jars filled with ammonia:

But don't believe it: a happiness exists,
All right, I have seen it for myself,
Touched it, touched the woman
Who with her daughter together keep
Ammonia in Mason jars by the side window.
They will throw it all in his face God
Damn him if he ever comes close again.

Mrs. Solano (in "The Friday Morning Trial of Mrs. Solano") finally faces her abusive husband with a small gun, putting an end to his lifetime confusion of her body with a piñata to be broken.

The poem that gives the title to the collection, "The Lime Orchard Woman," is not only the longest in the book but also the one in which images and messages correspond most closely. The poem tells about the life of María, focusing on the transitions her body undergoes from childhood to womanhood and, eventually, to deterioration:

At 28, she has forgotten what is past.
She sits and watches now her thighs
Flowing out like the broad
Varicosed backs of alligators
She has seen in moving pictures,
Pushed out around the metal
Edges of the lawn chair.

This poem portrays infidelity as a direct consequence of the misunderstandings springing from symbolic communication. María cannot trace the connection between her present and her personal history since "she has forgotten what is past." Instead she identifies with images from movies that only provide her with a negative understanding of her own body. The poet is the only one who can connect María's past to a history of miscommunication. Thus the poem unveils how the changes in María's body are directly related to a misunderstanding between her and her mother. When María's body started to change during puberty her mother explained the changes but left some "obvious" aspects unsaid. About her developing breasts,

> Her mother had told her
> This would come,
> But told her so quickly, so much
> In a hurry and in a small room,
> And with the other things,
> She neglected to say that also
> They would stop growing.

In *The Lime Orchard Woman,* images multiply and spread as if they were contagious. María's varicose veins are compared to alligator skin, and all of a sudden they acquire all the properties of alligators:

> And now the boys cannot
> Come close, dare not
> Dare the alligators
> Which might come after them.

In another poem, "Street, Cloud,"

> The Phoenix pavement sometimes gets
> Away, crawling up to paint
> The buildings and many times the sky
> With itself, the way an unhealthy dog
> Might run its body quickly along the grass.
> The woman, having got herself caught
> In between the cracks of all this, lies gray
> And camouflaged two doors down from the kitchen
> That has never touched a new wife's pastry.

Here, and in other poems in *The Lime Orchard Woman,* the qualities of particular objects spill over onto people, taking them hostage without their realizing it, in the process changing their emotions and their sense of who they are.

Artifacts of popular culture appear in this book to suggest alternative means of communication. *The Lime Orchard Woman* includes a number of elegies for local heroes who follow the social codes and manners of Mexican American culture. But side by side with those poems are others that reflect on the experiences brought into the Mexican American world through films, books, and recordings from other cultures. Thus we learn about the influence of such people as Juan Rulfo, Romy Schneider, Antonio Carlos Jobim, Edith Piaf, and Victor Jara. Ríos also invokes Walt Disney cartoons, the music of Chopin, and the Vietnam Veterans' Memorial in Washington, D.C. Ríos treats these references not as if they were foreign influences that displace the local myths of Nogales but rather as integral constituents of its everyday life. He presents them as they are interpreted locally and suggests that they illuminate Mexican American culture. He does not treat the popular culture he refers to as if it were the mirror of an alien reality.

As in previous books, here too the narrator and the characters understand everything that occurs in their lives—such as leaves falling from a tree or a person feeling sad—as the result of the will of an invisible entity. But in *The Lime Orchard Woman* for the first time the narrator tries to outsmart this agency. In "Secret Prune" the narrator discovers by accident the flavor of the seeds hidden in a prune's pit; he concludes that this is:

> . . . The pretend taste
> Carnivals had been hiding as a gift
> For patience, thirty-one years.
> There in prunes, in their middle.
> The one place no one would look.

The force (or forces) that moves things and plots events is not just external to human beings. In "Sculpting the Whistle," the narrator observes that "the machine is in us," a part of us that we do not control. Instead of negating the power of this mysterious agency, the poet rejoices in uncovering its secret designs and from time to time performs a small trick on it. "One Winter I Devise a Plan of My Own" relates the story of one of his successful attempts at asserting his independence from the all-powerful agent. Observing how the wind organizes leaves into mounds after they fall, he plots an innocent ruse:

> Pretend I'm searching for a coin or key,
> Then jump the biggest mound, and bruise it, bad.
>
> Now they have got to climb back on my trees.
> Today I've tricked the captain of the leaves.

A reflection on failure and death thus turns into a celebration of humanity in which limitations, misunderstandings, and even fate yield occasions to rejoice and inspiration to live more fully.

Ríos' next two books mark a clear break with his previous work. The autobiographical voice wanes in the first one, *Teodoro Luna's Two Kisses,* published in 1990, and disappears completely from the other, *Pig Cookies,* published in 1995. Moving away from the neighborhood of his personal experience seems to have freed Ríos from a sense of responsibility to adhere to personal experiences in the content of his writings and to aesthetic realism in their formal construction. *Teodoro Luna's Two Kisses* and *Pig Cookies* recreate a time before the poet's birth, the first half of this century; a place that mirrors Ríos' native town but on the other side of the border, Nogales, Mexico; and a mythic family, the Lunas. In these books, Ríos' singular brand of magical realism comes to fruition, finding extraordinary significance in waste materials. The leftovers from candles, or cookies that do not quite conform to the mold that they are cast in, are treated as the seeds of legend and art, while historic events like the Mexican Revolution or the Great Depression are dealt with in matter-of-fact language that makes them look like the most common of occurrences.

David Barber, writing in *Poetry* in 1993, characterizes Ríos' style in *Teodoro Luna's Two Kisses* as that of a "full-time fabulist who moonlights as a surrealist to make ends meet." Ríos offers a qualification when he describes his style as a surrealism that cherishes the reader. In an interview with Deneen Jenks in 1992 Ríos explained, "Magical Realism, as opposed to surrealism, evokes that same surrealist juxtaposition of two dissimilar things. But rather than putting that surrealist image in your lap and saying here it is, you do something with it, magical realism stays with you and brings you back." Leslie Ullman, in her 1991 review of *Teodoro Luna's Two Kisses* for the *Kenyon Review,* identifies in Ríos' style "a profound trust in, and affection for human nature—for the foibles and flights of fancy that keep us alive, unique, and which live beyond us as they are embellished and passed along."

Teodoro Luna's Two Kisses is the first of Ríos' books to be published by a multinational publishing house: W. W. Norton and Company. The book is organized around the lives of Anselmo and Teodoro Luna, two brothers who live in a frontier town on the United States–Mexico border during the first half of the twentieth century. The book is divided into three parts that dramatize an initial opposition between Anselmo and Teodoro and the way they eventually establish a strong connection. Anselmo is a Catholic priest who exercises his soul through a demanding routine of restraining his appetites and cultivating detachment from the world. Teodoro is a womanizer devoted to sensual pleasures. He is a man full of vital energy who celebrates his body and the bodies of the women he meets. Although only two of the poems tell stories about Anselmo's life, as a whole the first part of the book is devoted to expressing his religious vision of the world and the contradictions he encounters in his everyday life. The poems in the first part represent a metaphysical conception of the universe in which absences (the untold, the invisible, the imperceptible) are the ultimate explanation for events that take place in the material world.

The opening poem of the collection casts in this metaphysical light a topic that Ríos has examined since his very first book of poems: the sources and effects of the gradual decomposition of the body. ''The Used Side of the Sofa'' contains a powerful image of the idea that the body deteriorates day by day:

> She left her footprints,
> Then her feet,
> As she later could feel
> Nothing under her.
> When she sat then rose
> She left an indentation.
> A part of her
> Too comfortable,
> Not following so easily
> The rest of her.

Unlike Ríos' first poems on this topic, this poem does not contemplate the way things decompose for their own sake. It suggests the remedies that a person may apply to conjure up the ineffable presence of one who is absent:

> It was better simply
> To say nothing
> So that she did not feel
> The need to respond.

The poem sees in the respectful silence of living people evidence that a parallel reality lurks in the traces people leave in everyday objects after they have used them.

Anselmo Luna personifies the belief that the transcendent world can be perceived when one looks attentively at the small failures and the waste materials of life. Shadows formed by the smoke of candles in his church are, for Anselmo, as much a proof of the existence of God as the fact that a spatula disappears from the kitchen right at the moment when the breakfast eggs are starting to burn in the pan. A wind entering through the kitchen window, a collar that forces the wearer to look down, a persistent illness, the unstoppable growth of a beard, or the way in which a rough surface sands another one smooth, all serve in different poems as signs of the pervasive presence of invisible forces working to shape the world.

The second section of *Teodoro Luna's Two Kisses* explores a kind of devotion rather different from Anselmo's, the one professed by one body to another in the form of love and sexual desire. Teodoro Luna, who dominates this section, is presented as the man who ''invented the making of love,'' a man, we are told in ''Mr. Luna and History,'' whose mouth ''had the habit of women.'' The effect of desire in Ríos' poems is to transform desired persons into the image of the person who desires them or vice versa. Thus ''Marvella, for Borrowing'' portrays a woman who becomes all the men who have ever desired her:

> And the men grew thinner
> Because they looked too hard,
> And each long whistle they made
> Rudely was one inch too much of the rooster soul.
> Those noises became indentations under clothes,
> Spaces in place of protrusions
> Marvella in her turn
> Became with so many appendages
> A hundred men.

Desire has the opposite effect on Teodoro Luna who, as a result of uncontrollable desire, dissolves into all the women he has ever loved:

> A perfect diamond is invisible in water.
> How Mr. Luna died is not known,
> Nor what happened to his body.
> It is said he gave some of himself each time,
> From the inside and the out,
> Awake but also in dream.
> It is said he became a thousand women.

Teodoro Luna's Two Kisses reworks a topic that has been present in literature since the Middle Ages: the similarities and differences between divine love and profane love. The names of the characters indicate at the outset that the position the book defends is that each kind of love feeds on the other. Anselmo, the representative of divine love, is named after St. Anselm, the archbishop of Canterbury at the end of the eleventh century, who was well known for having had romantic adventures before becoming a priest. The representative of profane love, Teodoro, whose name means love for God, negates love for God by his behavior. In the third part of the book, Ríos explores the possibility of a synthesis between the two brothers and what they stand for. The first poem in this part announces with its long title—"Teodoro Luna Confesses after Years to His Brother, Anselmo the Priest, Who Is Required to Understand, But Who Understands Anyway, More Than People Think"—that the two brothers do achieve a certain meeting of the minds.

The transformations derived from understanding that the two loves represented by the brothers are paradoxical in their nature are not limited to the brothers' relationship but figure in other poems as well. Although Teodoro's confession starts with his explaining his desire, what he really wants to confess is his realization that in desiring women he also becomes the object of his desire:

> Only I am the woman, do you understand,
>   Anselmo?
> Caught in the circling rope. I am the woman.

Every human action portrayed in this final part of the book seems to contain the seed of its opposite. In "Uncle Christmas" the drinking habit of an uncle figures as a religious act and so makes him into the "Christ of the beers." In "Half Hour of August" a body, which symbolizes a person's identity, breaks into innumerable fragments and then reforms in the shape of a different person. In "A Dish of Green Pears" a body reveals the irrevocable double condition of being human:

> This man's skin is a drum's covering.
> A drum skin, smooth on the one side,
> An unfinished rot

> Of leather drippings
> And misalignments underneath.

Even the narrator's voice transforms itself into its other; it starts out sounding masculine, telling the story of a woman, and finishes sounding feminine, telling the story of a man. Form, structure, and message collaborate in creating an organic whole out of the apparently dissimilar fragments of *Teodoro Luna's Two Kisses*.

During the late eighties and early nineties Ríos' poetry began to appear frequently in national magazines such as the *New Yorker,* the *American Poetry Review,* and *Ploughshares.* The composer James DeMars arranged a number of Ríos' poems into a cantata that opened to great success in Carnegie Hall in 1992. With a Research and Creativity Grant he received from the Arizona State University Graduate College, Ríos was able to continue his collaboration with DeMars for an opera entitled *Curtain of Trees.* In 1992 he won the Pushcart Prize for his story "The Other League of Nations."

Pig Cookies is a collection of thirteen short stories set in the Mexican town of Nogales during the first half of the twentieth century. The stories are all written in the third person: Ríos here abandons totally the autobiographical style he employed in at least some stories or poems in all his earlier books. The protagonists of *Pig Cookies* live during the period that saw the Mexican Revolution, the expulsion of Chinese immigrants from the United States, the Great Depression, and World War II. The stories relegate these historic events to a remote background while highlighting those ordinary people and aspects of life that never made it into contemporary newspapers, especially the small tragedies and happy incidents that marked the lives of the inhabitants of Nogales.

Intertwined with the new material in these stories are references to Ríos' previous books. For example, Lázaro Luna, a sensitive storyteller with the charisma of a shaman—who serves as a link between all the stories in *Pig Cookies*—is the brother of Anselmo and Teodoro Luna from *Teodoro Luna's Two Kisses*. The story "Champagne Regions" constitutes an elaboration of the poem "Shoreline Horses" from *The Lime Orchard Woman*. But the intertextual connections between *Pig Cookies* and Ríos' previous work extend beyond these kinds of allusions. *Pig Cookies* shares several themes with Ríos' other books. It also shares with Ríos' earlier writing, especially his poems, an acute attention to metaphor and to the way words sound. The stories in *Pig Cookies* are, in fact, nearly prose poems.

The book explores the importance of storytelling in the lives of four men who are at odds with the unwritten but stern etiquette that rules the community of Nogales. Mr. Lee is a Chinese immigrant who hides inside an old radio to avoid being deported; Noé is a butcher who becomes a strongman in the circus; José Martínez is a carpenter who would rather tell a good story than make a cabinet; and Lázaro is the man who has performed every job in the village but who is most occupied with his embarrassment about his own feelings and his brothers' actions. The other Luna brothers would never feel themselves the discomfort about people's opinions that Lázaro does. Although different stages of these characters' lives appear in several of the stories, the chronological order is broken; the perspective from which the characters are seen changes, too, from story to story. This narrative strategy prevents the reader from adopting a judgmental attitude toward the actions or personalities of the characters. Ríos presents each character from two points of view in particular: the community's and each character's own intimate conscience.

The lives of the four men are shaped by relationships that are made impossible because of the interposition of the community. In "Susto" Noé's clumsy expression of his love for his neighbor Mariquita appears to be, in the eyes of his townspeople, a brutal form of physical abuse. José's jokes and tricks on Rosa in "Spiced Plums" end up forcing him into marrying her, not out of love but out of fear of transgressing a local tradition. "A Trick on the World" presents the only successful love story in the book. The protagonists, Mr. Lee and Chuyita, have to resort to trickery and secrecy to avoid the local racial prejudice that would separate them. Lázaro's shyness in front of the women he loves makes him unable to form any lasting relationship. Ironically the people in town think that the real truth is that he is a womanizer.

Like the chorus in a Greek tragedy, the community of Nogales speaks in a single voice in these stories. The community sees the world through the same eyes, speaks a "truth" rooted in custom and in the need to fit in with the group. The confrontations between the four main characters and the community trace an emotional map of masculinity. Throughout the book all the characters accept the manners that are imposed on them and have only the recourse of running away, marrying, or whimsically posturing to avoid submitting to the constraints of those manners. By the end of the book, however, Lázaro, approaching old age, decides to break the cycle. He vows to make public his love for Mariquita, a love they kept secret because they knew the rest of the town would surely disapprove of it, given the difference in age between them. The final paragraph of the book records Lázaro's decision this way:

> He would come to see her the next time at the front door, and in front of everybody.
>
> This is what he said to her now without words, this is what he intended. This is what he said to her with the mouths of his eyes, before he could get close enough to use breath: he was coming here today to tell her, here was the beginning of their story.

Lázaro's decision to make their secret public implies a challenge to the community and its manners. Lázaro thus ruptures the townspeople's control over the lives of individuals and breaks new ground for future stories.

In 1996 Ríos and his wife, María Guadalupe, lived in Phoenix, Arizona, with their nine-year-old son, Joaquín. He continued to teach at Arizona State University and to present his poems and short stories in workshops throughout the States. These activities brought together the poet and his public, following Ríos' commitment to be an ''artist-citizen.'' He understood his creative work as a double process. On the one hand, he composed his stories and poems in private. On the other hand, he approached people with his work and—as he explained to Deneen Jenks—''let them see some sense of personal inspiration.'' Going out in the community as an artist also carried for Ríos the responsibility to listen. It is from this listening that most of Ríos' stories came in the past; that is, both the topics of the stories and the language in which they were cast. The works resulting from this process of listening have been praised as visionary in such publications as the *American Book Review,* which writes: ''In fifty years, when the revolutions of American language are clear to us, most of the poetry of the 1980s will pale beside Ríos' . . . Ríos is 'onto something new' in his poetry—in the way that real poets of any time always are.''

Ríos' work illuminates the experiences of people who reside on the very cusp of territories separated by real or imaginary frontiers. His determination to remain on the uncomfortable borderline between different cultures and opposite experiences shows not only the possibility but also the necessity of exploring ''what's unheard of.'' Staying within the limits of everyday life, Ríos discovers a stubborn reality that refuses to acknowledge the borders imposed on it; he extracts from that reality universal truths by detailing the peculiarities of the Chicano experience.

Selected Bibliography

WORKS OF ALBERTO ÁLVARO RÍOS

POETRY
Elk Heads on the Wall. Arizona: Mango Press, 1979.
Sleeping on Fists. Story, Wyo.: Dooryard Press, 1981.
The Warrington Poems. Arizona: Pycarantha Press, 1989.
Whispering to Fool the Wind. New York: Sheep Meadow Press, 1982.
Five Indiscretions. Riverdale-on-Hudson, N.Y.: Sheep Meadow Press, 1985.
The Lime Orchard Woman. Riverdale-on-Hudson, N.Y.: Sheep Meadow Press, 1988.
Teodoro Luna's Two Kisses. New York: Norton, 1990.

POEMS IN ANTHOLOGIES AND MAGAZINES
''Nani.'' ''The Baby Manuelito.'' ''Morning.'' ''A Man Then Suddenly Stops Moving.'' ''Returning to the Cat.'' In *Agua Fresca: An Anthology of Raza Poetry.* Edited by Estevan Antonio Rodríguez. Tucson, Arizona: Oreja Press and Pajarito Publications, 1979.
''Horses Which Do Not Exist.'' *Paris Review,* 28:270 (Winter 1986).
''The Corner Uncle.'' *North American Review,* 272:71 (March 1987).
''Saints and Their Care.'' *American Poetry Review,* 17:47 (May–June 1988).
''Animals and the Noon Street.'' ''Remembering Watching Romy Schneider.'' ''The Vietnam Wall.'' ''City Dance.'' ''Noise and Hard Laughing in the Forties.'' ''England Finally, Like My Mother Always Said We Would.'' ''Burying Them.'' ''La La at the Cirque.'' ''Our Joe.'' ''Nikita.'' ''I Can Describe the Field.'' ''How She Comes after Me.'' ''Piece for Flute and Clarinet.'' ''One Winter I Devise a Plan of My Own.'' ''Stepping over the Arm.'' ''Mr. Palomino Walks by Again.'' ''The Annual Headline, Second Page.'' ''The Curses of Green and Night.'' ''The Hot-Kiss Fifties.'' ''Like This It Is We Think to Dance.'' *Journal of Ethnic Studies,* 16, no. 2:69–94 (Summer 1988).
''Sculpting the Whistle.'' ''Edith Piaf Dead.'' ''Leav-

ing Off.'' ''Shoreline Horses.'' *Prairie Schooner*, 62:109–114 (Fall 1988).

''Marvella, for Borrowing.'' ''Teodoro Luna's Old Joke.'' *Ploughshares*, 15, no. 4:179–182 (Winter 1989–1990).

''The Good Lunch of the Oceans.'' *American Poetry Review*, 119, no. 2:56 (March–April 1990).

''Mr. Luna in the Afternoon.'' *New Yorker*, May 21, 1990, p. 118.

''Mexico, from the Four Last Letters.'' ''Indentations in the Sugar.'' *Kenyon Review*, 12, no. 3:116–118 (Summer, 1990).

''The Influenzas.'' *New Yorker*, September 10, 1990, p. 48.

''Mr. Luna and History.'' *Paris Review*, 32, no. 116:139–140 (Fall 1990).

''What Is Quiet in the Spelling of Wednesday.'' *American Poetry Review*, 20, no. 3:41 (May–June 1991).

''Passing Late in the Day's Afternoon a History.'' ''Half Hour of August.'' *New England Review*, 13, nos. 3–4:279–285 (Spring–Summer 1991).

''Domingo Limón.'' ''In My Hurry.'' ''Common Crows in the Winter Tree.'' *Prairie Schooner*, 68, no. 4:12–19 (Winter 1994).

SHORT STORIES

The Iguana Killer: Twelve Stories of the Heart. New York: Blue Moon and Confluence Press, 1984.

''All-weddings.'' *Ohio Review*, 45:77–85 (Winter 1990).

''Trains at Night.'' *Ploughshares*, 16, nos. 2–3:238–244 (Fall 1990).

''The Other League of Nations.'' *Hayden's Ferry Review*, no. 8 (Spring–Summer 1991).

''Waltz of the Fat Man.'' *Kenyon Review*, 13, no. 3:7–13 (Summer 1991).

''Triton Himself.'' *North American Review*, 277, no. 3:34–38 (May–June 1992).

''Outside Magdalena, Sonora.'' *Ploughshares*, 20, no. 1:176–187 (Spring 1994).

Pig Cookies: And Other Stories. San Francisco: Chronicle Books, 1995.

ESSAYS

''Becoming and Breaking: Poet and Poem.'' *Ironwood*, 12, no. 2:148–152 (Fall 1984).

''Chicano/Borderlands Literature and Poetry,'' In *Contemporary Latin American Culture: Unity and Diversity.* Edited by Gail C. Guntermann. Tempe, Arizona: Center for Latin American Studies, Arizona State University, 1984. Pp. 79–93.

''West Real.'' *Ploughshares*, 18, no. 1:1–5 (Spring 1992).

''Remembering Pig Cookies.'' *Prairie Schooner*, 68, no. 4:9–11 (Winter 1994).

''Translating Translation: Finding the Beginning.'' *Prairie Schooner*, 68, no. 4:5–8 (Winter 1994).

CRITICAL STUDIES

Argüelles, Iván. Review of *The Lime Orchard Woman. Library Journal*, 114, no. 3:61 (February 15, 1989).

———. Review of *Teodoro Luna's Two Kisses. Library Journal*, 115, no. 15:81 (September 15, 1990).

Barber, David. ''Habits of Mind: *Teodoro Luna's Two Kisses.*'' *Poetry*, 162, no. 4:224–227 (July 1993).

Figueroa, Laura. ''Review of *Pig Cookies and Other Stories.*'' *Hispanic*, 8, no. 4:80 (May 1995).

Kaganoff, Penny, and Genevieve Stuttarford. Review of *The Lime Orchard Woman. Publishers Weekly*, 235, no. 1:96 (January 6, 1989).

Madueño, Amalio. Review of *Teodoro Luna's Two Kisses. Hispanic*, 90 (January–February 1991).

Muske, Carol. ''Disc Jockeys, Eggplants and Desaparecidos: *Five Indiscretions.*'' *New York Times Book Review*, February 9, 1986, p. 28.

Needham, George. ''Review of *Pig Cookies and Other Stories.*'' *Booklist*, 91, no. 17:1553 (May 1, 1995).

O'Brien, Michael. Review of *Teodoro Luna's Two Kisses. Literary Review*, 34, no. 3:419 (Spring 1991).

Olzewski, Lawrence. ''Review of *Pig Cookies and Other Stories.*'' *Library Journal*, 120, no. 8:134 (May 1, 1995).

Rosaldo, Renato. ''Fables of the Fallen Guy.'' In *Criticism in the Borderlands: Studies in Chicano Literature, Culture, and Ideology.* Edited by Hector Calderón and José David Saldívar. Durham, N.C.: Duke University Press, 1991. Pp. 84–93.

Saldívar, José David. ''Towards a Chicano Poetics: The Making of the Chicano Subject, 1969–1982.'' *Confluencia: Revista Hispánica de Cultura y Literatura*, 1, no. 2:10–17 (Spring 1986).

Scofield, Sandra. ''Review of *Pig Cookies and Other*

Stories.'' *New York Times Book Review,* September 17, 1995, p. 25.

Ullman, Leslie. "Solitaries and Storytellers, Magicians and Pagans.'' Review of *Teodoro Luna's Two Kisses. Kenyon Review,* 13, no. 2:179–193 (Spring 1991).

INTERVIEWS

Cárdenas, Lupe, and Justo Alarcón. "Entrevista con Alberto Ríos.'' *Confluencia: Revista Hispánica de Cultura y Literatura,* 6, no. 1:119–128 (Fall 1990).

Jenks, Deneen. "The Breathless Patience of Alberto Ríos.'' *Hayden's Ferry Review,* 11:115–123 (Fall–Winter 1992).

—ADRIÁN PÉREZ MELGOSA

Leslie Marmon Silko

1948–

POET, NOVELIST, SHORT-STORY writer, story-teller, and occasional filmmaker, Leslie Silko has had a major impact on the reclaiming of Native American myth, culture, and history. A central figure in the Native American literary renaissance of the seventies, Silko occupies a prominent place among her contemporaries N. Scott Momaday, James Welch, Paula Gunn Allen, Simon J. Ortiz, and Carol Lee Sanchez. Although not a prolific writer—she has written only one book of poetry, two novels, and a multigenre collection that includes poems, stories, and autobiographical fragments—Silko has, since the publication of *Ceremony* in 1977, become a vital force in contemporary American literature. Earlier she had published a few stories that were anthologized and her volume of poems, *Laguna Woman* (1974).

Ceremony was the first important novel published by a Native American woman. In 1978, the poet James Wright, who had met Silko in 1975 at a writers' conference in Michigan, wrote to her after he had read *Ceremony*. His passionate response typifies the effect Silko's first novel had on her readers:

> Now I have finally had the chance to read *Ceremony,* and I am moved to tell you how much the book means to me. In some strange way it seems inadequate to call it a great book, though it is surely that, or a perfect work of art, though it is one. I could call *Ceremony* one of the four or five best books I have ever read about America and I would be speaking the truth. But even this doesn't say just what I mean.
>
> I think I am trying to say that my very life means more to me than it would have meant if you hadn't written *Ceremony*. But this sounds inadequate also.

Others also greeted this novel with great praise. In a review for the *New York Times Book Review,* Frank MacShane said that it established Silko "without question as the most accomplished Indian writer of her generation"; he found the novel to be "one of the most realized works of fiction devoted to Indian life that has been written in this country." Peter G. Beidler, in a review of *Ceremony* for *American Indian Quarterly,* linked Silko to Momaday and Welch, asserting that "*Ceremony* will surely take its place as one of a distinguished triumvirate of first novels by contemporary American Indians."

In most of her work Silko draws on Laguna traditions, rituals, and stories, recirculating this material by suggesting that the old must be re-imagined, re-created, and sustained in the present. Old stories, which become new stories as they are retold, help us to live in the moment; their currency serves to endorse a view of time as nonlinear or cyclical. Ignoring a clear division between the distant past and the present, Silko culls from both oral and written traditions in an effort to restore a sense of wholeness to a world that seems devoid of spirituality, dangerously corrupt, emphatically chaotic, and often without any discernible meaning. For Silko, the Anglo-American culture she finds herself in threatens continually the very survival of Native American culture and its values.

Tayo, the central character in *Ceremony,* asks a question that Silko repeatedly articulates and attempts to answer in much of her work: ''I wonder what good Indian ceremonies can do against the sickness which comes from their wars, their bombs, their lies?'' In her art Silko seeks to counter the sense of perpetual loss and fragmentation exemplified by Tayo's question. To this end, she searches for a renewed and sustained connection to the land, to natural forces, and to the rituals and ceremonies that give us access to the natural order of things. In addition, she revitalizes the Laguna Pueblo stories she has inherited by recirculating them. These gestures, she posits, will lead to wholeness and health and will serve to preserve Native American ways of life. As she noted on the dust jacket of *Ceremony:*

> This novel is essentially about the powers inherent in the process of storytelling. . . . The chanting or telling of ancient stories to effect certain cures or protect from illness and harm have always been part of the Pueblo's curing ceremonies. I feel the power that the stories still have to bring us together, especially when there is loss and grief.

During the war, Tayo relies on stories to sustain himself and the other soldiers:

> He made a story for all of them, a story to give them strength. The words of the story poured out of his mouth as if they had substance, pebbles and stone extending to hold the corporal up, to keep his knees from buckling, to keep his hands from letting go of the blanket.

When writing to Wright on July 28, 1979, Silko also commented on the power stories have in our daily lives:

> I believe more than ever that it is in sharing the stories of our grief that we somehow can make sense out. . . . At Laguna whenever something happens (happy or sad or strange), that vast body of remembered stories is brought forth by people who have been listening to the account of this recent incident.

In 1981 Silko published *Storyteller,* a volume of stories, anecdotes, poems, and photographs ''dedicated to the storytellers as far back as memory goes and to the telling which continues and through which they all live and we with them.''

Born in Albuquerque in 1948, of Laguna Pueblo, Plains Indian, Mexican, and Anglo-American descent, Leslie Marmon Silko grew up on the Laguna Pueblo Reservation in northern New Mexico, surrounded by her extended family. The reservation was not far from the Los Alamos uranium mines and the Trinity site, where the first atom bomb was detonated in 1945. Living in the wake of this near-apocalyptic incident had a profound effect on Silko. In an interview with Per Seyersted in 1978 (published in 1981), Silko commented on the occasion:

> The Pueblo people have always concentrated upon making things grow, and appreciating things that are alive and natural, because life is so precious in the desert. The irony is that so close to us, in Los Alamos, New Mexico, scientists began the scientific and technological activity which created the potential end to our whole planet, the whole human race. The first atomic bomb was exploded in New Mexico, very close by us. To me it is very striking that this happened so close to the Pueblo people, but I suppose it is just one of those accidents of history.

Silko's two novels, *Ceremony* and *Almanac of the Dead* (1991), explore ''accidents of history'' in which Native American peoples and cultures are threatened with extinction owing to Anglo-American senseless actions or are severed from a healthy relationship with the land and things that

LESLIE MARMON SILKO / 559

grow. Both novels also deal with the delicate negotiations in which Native Americans must continually engage with mainstream white America in order to survive. In *Ceremony,* Tayo's Grandma witnesses the detonation of the A-bomb and notes, ''I thought I was seeing the sun rise again. . . . You know, I have never understood that thing I saw.'' Tayo, who knows that the laboratories where the bomb was created exist on land the government took from the Pueblos, sees all people ''united by a circle of death that devoured people in cities twelve thousand miles away, victims who had never known these mesas, who had never seen the delicate colors of the rocks which boiled up their slaughter.''

Silko first attended Laguna Day School, where students were forbidden to use the Laguna language, and then Manzano Day school, a Catholic private school in Albuquerque, to which she commuted. In 1969, she received a B.A. in English from the University of New Mexico. In an interview with Laura Coltelli in 1985 (published in 1990), Silko dates her love of reading and books to the first grade, but goes on to say: ''The fifth grade is when I really started actually writing secretly; but it wasn't until I was nineteen and got to the university, that the two things [reading and writing] just fell into place.''

While in college, Silko published her first story, ''The Man to Send Rain Clouds'' (1969), which, like many of her subsequent stories, was based on a real-life incident at Laguna. Later reprinted in *Storyteller,* the story describes the death of an old man and the belief that he will thus be able to send the community much-needed rain clouds; instead of being taken from the community by his death, he is reimagined as a spirit associated with the bringing of rain. (There are frequent droughts in this part of New Mexico, heightening the importance of the rituals associated with the bringing of rain.)

Leon, who finds old Teofilo's dead body, persuades a Catholic priest to participate in the Indian funeral by supplying holy water to be sprinkled on the grave. The priest is clearly made uncomfortable by this ritual, in the absence of administering last rites and a funeral mass, but is also joined to this community by his participation in their ritual: ''He sprinkled the grave and the water disappeared almost before it touched the dim, cold sand; it reminded him of something—he tried to remember what it was, because he thought if he could remember he might understand this.'' Leon, in turn, embraces the priest's ability to join them in their ritual, recognizing that the Indians need the holy water to complete their own ceremony: ''He felt good because it was finished, and he was happy about the sprinkling of the holy water; now the old man could send them big thunderclouds for sure.''

Creating new, but no less sustaining rituals within the Native American community, as a means of surviving in this historical moment, marks much of Silko's writing, allowing her to acknowledge the force of the past without relinquishing her engagement with the power of change in the present. Catholic ritual, which has been absorbed by so many of the Laguna Pueblos, can be combined with Pueblo ritual, enriching their Native American traditions in the process. As A. LaVonne Ruoff points out in ''Ritual and Renewal: Keres Traditions in the Short Fiction of Leslie Silko'': ''For Leslie Marmon Silko (Laguna), the strength of tribal traditions is based not on Indians' rigid adherence to given ceremonies or customs but rather on their ability to adapt traditions to ever-changing circumstances by incorporating new elements.'' And, as Betonie, a Navajo medicine man in *Ceremony,* tells Tayo at the Gallup Ceremonial: ''But after the white people came, elements in this world began to shift; and it became necessary to create new ceremonies. I have made changes in the rituals. The people mistrust this greatly, but only this growth keeps the ceremonies strong.''

Between 1969 and 1971 Silko attended law school at the University of New Mexico; she dropped out upon receiving a National Endowment of the Arts Discovery grant, which allowed her to focus exclusively on her writing. For the next few years (1974–1976) she taught intermittently at Navajo Community College in Tsaile, Arizona. Later in the 1970s, she taught at both the University of Arizona and the University of New Mexico, often commuting between the two institutions.

During this period, Silko turned her attention to writing a one-act play, based on her story "Lullaby." It was performed in 1976 in San Francisco but has not been published. She also tried her hand at filmmaking: she was commissioned by Marlon Brando and Jack Beck to write a script depicting the expedition of Francesco Coronado in 1540 from a Pueblo perspective. It was sent to Hollywood in 1977 and adapted by Harry Brown. It has, however, not been produced. In 1979–1980, with the help of a grant from the National Endowment for the Humanities, Silko and Dennis W. Carr did a film adaptation of a Laguna Pueblo narrative "Estoy-eh-muut and the Kunideeyahs (Arrowboy and the Destroyers)." In 1981 Silko received a MacArthur Foundation fellowship, which enabled her to give up teaching. By this time she was engaged in writing her very long novel, *Almanac of the Dead,* which was eventually published a decade later.

Although Silko published poems and stories in the early 1970s, winning both the *Chicago Review* and the *Pushcart* prizes for poetry in 1973, her first book was a chapbook of poems entitled *Laguna Woman,* put out by the Greenfield Review Press. Many of these poems were later reprinted in 1981 in *Storyteller,* Silko's collection of previously published stories and poems, retellings of traditional Laguna stories, family reminiscences and anecdotes, and photographs.

The eighteen poems that make up *Laguna Woman* draw on Native American myths and rituals as a way of remembering the past and bringing it into the present. "Slim Man Canyon," for example, begins with the line "700 years ago," and ends with the affirmation that in this moment the speaker can ride

past cliffs with stories and songs
painted on rock.
700 years ago.

The final line of the poem duplicates the first, calling attention in the form of the poem to the cyclical nature of life and to a faith that life as it has been known will endure:

tall sky and flowing water
sunshine through cottonwood leaves
the willow smell in the wind

Similarly, "Prayer to the Pacific" posits a faith in the future by looking back to a mythic time. The speaker travels to the ocean from the Southwest to discover the "gift from the ocean." Rain clouds are said to drift from the west, to be a gift from the ocean. This present becomes associated with another story, a myth concerning the origin of Indian life: thirty thousand years ago Indians were said to have been transported across the ocean from China, carried on the backs of sea turtles. Hence, "from that time / immemorial, / as the old people say," rain clouds came from the west, as a gift from the ocean.

In still other poems Silko celebrates the energy of animals' lives, which endure quite apart from human intervention. In "Preparations," she vividly evokes the "solemn and fat" crows feasting on dead sheep whose "guts and life [are] unwinding on the sand." Capturing the meticulous work of these creatures as they systematically and artfully dismember and devour the sheep, Silko ends the poem with a spare, almost otherworldly image of the process of completion:

Bones, bones
Let wind polish the bones.
It is done.

In this final image we have a sense of both finitude and eternity.

In "Four Mountain Wolves," the wolves are associated with eternity, with centuries passing, with living through the years, and yet they are rooted in a perpetual present as they move through a barren winter landscape. We see a gray mist wolf traveling over the deep snow crust, "Lonely for deer gone down to the valley / Lonely for wild turkey all flown away," a "swirling snow wolf" who shatters "gray ice dreams of eternity" and a "grey fog wolf" who is commanded to "call to the centuries as [he passes]." A human presence is denied until the end of the poem, when the speaker merges her identity with that of the lean wolf:

where miles become faded in time,
the urge the desire is always with me
the dream of green eyes wolf
as she reaches the swollen belly elk
    softly
her pale lavender outline
startled into eternity.

Although Silko has not published another volume of poems, she has continued to write them, often including them in her fiction. *Ceremony,* for example, begins with an untitled poem about an Indian creation myth. There are three sections. In the first we see Thought-Woman sitting by herself contemplating; as she thinks about people and things, they start to appear. She thinks of her sisters

and together they created the Universe
this world
and the four worlds below.

We are told that she is thinking of this story, at which point the speaker allies himself—Silko's storyteller here is male—with Thought-Woman:

"I'm telling you the story / she is thinking." In the second section of the poem, the storyteller speaks, asserting the importance of having stories: "You don't have anything / if you don't have the stories." This male storyteller is pregnant with these stories:

He rubbed his belly.
 I keep them here
    [he said]
Here, put your hand on it
  See, it is moving.
  There is life here
  for the people.

Thought-Woman returns in the third section to state that "the only cure . . . / is a good ceremony." By framing *Ceremony* in this way, Silko suggests that being an author is a sacred trust, which involves creating, naming, and storytelling—and a search for the right ceremonies. Later, in *Storyteller* and *Almanac of the Dead,* Silko also included poems. As a consequence, her work has increasingly become known for its blurring of the boundaries between prose and poetry.

Between 1976 and 1978, Silko lived in Ketchikan, Alaska, where her husband, John Silko, worked as the supervising attorney for Alaska Legal Services and she wrote *Ceremony.* Wright remarked that when he read *Ceremony* he felt that he was "almost hearing the landscape itself tell the story." In a letter to him dated November 1, 1978, Silko responded:

You pointed out a very important dimension of the land and the Pueblo people's relation to the land when you said it was as if the land was telling the stories in the novel. That is it exactly, but it is so difficult to convey this interrelationship without sounding like Margaret Fuller or some other Transcendentalist. When I was writing *Ceremony* I was so terribly devastated by being away from the Laguna country that the writing was my way of re-making that place, the Laguna country, for myself.

When Silko published *Ceremony,* it served to put her on the Native American literary map. Heralded as a great success and compared to Momaday's *House Made of Dawn* (1968) and Welch's *Winter in the Blood* (1974), *Ceremony* is the story of a shell-shocked, mentally deranged World War II veteran, Tayo, who journeys toward recovery, wholeness, and health in a world that is fraught with danger and sickness on every front. Tayo's healing takes place gradually, as he learns to reclaim and regain access to ancient tribal rituals, customs, and wisdom. Unable to look forward without first reconnecting himself to his roots, to what is usable from the ancient past, he learns in the process that the old ceremonies must be adapted to fit the world in which he lives. He also discovers that he must come to terms with his own past, with the memories that threaten to engulf him and have the capacity to blot out the present and his desire for rootedness in the moment.

Tayo struggles to deal with the effects of the war on his psyche; when he returns he finds it very difficult to fit back into society. Scarcely present at all, he cannot keep his memories in order or distinguish between recent events and more distant ones. The different threads of his history are often tangled in the narrative, as Silko blurs distinctions between Tayo's recent and distant past and the present. Tayo's quest for health and sanity, then, involves both embracing ancient ways and understanding his own history. Only by doing both can he abandon linear time for a world in which there are "no boundaries, only transitions through all distances and time."

Tayo is of mixed heritage and feels his "outsider" status keenly. The son of a Laguna Pueblo mother and a white father he will never know, Tayo is abandoned at the age of four, when his mother leaves him with her sister and her family:

"He clung to her [his mother] because when she left him, he knew she would be gone for a long time." This loss of maternal love and connection permeates the text. When his mother later dies, Tayo associates her death with a drought: "He remembered when his mother died. It had been dry then too." Tayo grows up with his aunt, her husband, Robert; his uncle, Josiah; his grandmother; and his cousin, Rocky. His aunt raises him and Rocky together, but she never lets Tayo forget that he is "other" and not part of the family. She wears the shame she feels about her sister's behavior like a talisman. Tayo remains "her dead sister's half-breed child."

Tayo and Rocky have different temperaments, desires, intuitions, and goals; while Tayo watches and tends to the speckled cattle with Josiah, who enjoys a healthy relationship with the land, Rocky reads magazines and aspires to be an athlete on the whites' playing fields. "Rocky understood what he had to do to win in the white outside world." His mother encourages Rocky to win in this world: "She could see what white people wanted in an Indian, and she believed this way was his only chance." When Rocky and Tayo go deer hunting with Robert and Josiah, Rocky cannot fully participate in the ritual: "Rocky turned away from them and poured water from the canteen over his bloody hands. He was embarrassed at what they did."

In contrast, Tayo is fully present: "They said the deer gave itself to them because it loved them, and he could feel the love as the fading heat of the deer's body warmed his hands." While Rocky looks toward the future, Tayo values the old rituals. When they both enlist in the army, Tayo decides to go in order to protect Rocky; when Rocky dies, Tayo feels guilty for surviving. When he returns, he feels there has been some mistake: "Rocky was the one who was alive . . . Rocky was there in the college game scores on the sports page of the *Albuquerque Journal.* It was him, Tayo, who had died, but somehow there had been a mistake with the corpses, and somehow his was still unburied.''

Boundaries are also blurred concerning Josiah's death. During the war Josiah had also died, having been hit by a car. Tayo is plagued, however, because during the war he had imagined that Josiah was with them in the jungle and that he, Tayo, ''had watched him die, and he had done nothing to save him.'' Tayo both witnesses and becomes implicated in Rocky's and Josiah's deaths; to survive these losses, he must make sense of his own survival. Most important, he must untangle the past from the present:

> He could get no rest as long as the memories were tangled with the present, tangled up like colored threads from old Grandma's wicker sewing basket when he was a child, and he had carried them outside to play and they had spilled out of his arms into the summer weeds and rolled away in all directions, and then he had hurried to pick them up before Auntie found him. He could feel it inside his skull—the tension of little threads being pulled and how it was with tangled things, things tied together, and as he tried to pull them apart and rewind them into their places, they snagged and tangled even more.

Tayo's inability to keep the past separate from the present causes him pain and makes him feel transgressive—if he knew how to use the past he would be able to sew together the threads; he would be able to tell a story and to heal himself.

When Tayo initially returns from the war he cannot keep past events from impinging on the present; thus, he has no access to himself, to his history, to his story. Nor can he untangle the different voices that emerge to compete with one another: loud voices, Japanese voices, Laguna voices, Josiah's voice, and his mother's voice. Hospitalized for his condition, he feels invisible and retreats into this state of anonymity: ''They saw his outline but they did not realize it was hollow inside.'' Invisibility is his only defense; as he becomes visible, he begins to remember, to feel—memories emerge, and he is in pain again.

There are also visible signs of sickness around him. ''The drought years had returned again, as they had after the First World War and in the twenties, when he was a child and they had to haul water to the sheep in big wooden barrels in the old wagon.'' Tayo feels responsible for this barrenness; although he knows he did not kill anyone in the war, he feels ''he had done things far worse, and the effects were everywhere in the cloudless sky, on the dry brown hills, shrinking skin and hide taut over sharp bone.''

His friends are also out of step with their surroundings. Harley, who had been at Wake Island and had received a Purple Heart, is on a burro he cannot control. He doesn't recognize that his attempts at controlling the burro are futile; his resistance keeps him from becoming ''part of the wind.'' Tayo, on the other hand, gives himself up to the motion of the mule he is on: ''He let himself go with the motion of the mule. . . . Above the wind, sometimes he could hear Harley cussing out the burro, telling it what he would do if he had a gun.'' Tayo's flexibility prefigures his final transformation and healing at the end of the novel, whereas Harley's inability to adapt himself to his surroundings leads to his untimely demise.

Tayo's health returns gradually as he reengages with the land, natural forces, and tribal rituals and ceremonies. His transformation occurs in stages. He meets Old Ku'oosh and Betonie, both of whom are medicine men who have been summoned to minister to his sickness. These encounters lead him to search for Josiah's spotted cattle, which had been stolen while Tayo was away at war. While searching for the missing cattle he meets Ts'eh, who seems to share an identity with Spider Woman (a Navajo Indian spirit associated with creation, Thought-Woman, who ''named things and as she named them they appeared'') or some primal female creative force. Tayo's time with her serves to reconnect him to himself, the land, and the ancient ways.

However, he must first encounter the two medicine men.

Old Ku'oosh, a Laguna medicine man, is called in by Tayo's grandmother after Tayo returns from the veteran's hospital. "He spoke softly, using the old dialect full of sentences that were involuted with explanations of their own origins, as if nothing the old man said were his own but all had been said before and he was only there to repeat it." Tayo has a difficult time understanding him, straining "to catch the meaning, dense with place names he had never heard." The medicine man tells him about a cave northeast of Laguna where rattlesnakes go to restore their life forces; he notes that maybe Tayo does not know about these things. He then tells Tayo that the world is fragile:

> It took a long time to explain the fragility and intricacy because no word exists alone, and the reason for choosing each word had to be explained with a story about why it must be said this certain way. That was the responsibility that went with being human, old Ku'oosh said, the story behind each word must be told so there could be no mistake in the meaning of what had been said; and this demanded great patience and love.

Tayo is tormented with thoughts that he may have killed someone without knowing it; Old Ku'oosh reassures him that such a thing could not have happened, but, Silko reminds us, Ku'oosh has no real comprehension of "white warfare—killing across great distances without knowing who or how many had died." Silko includes a poem about the cleansing ceremonies Indians had to go through after scalping their enemies. If they did not engage in these rituals,

> everything would be endangered.
> Maybe the rain wouldn't come
> or the deer would go away.

Old Ku'oosh leaves Tayo with some of the ingredients used in the ancient ceremonies—herbs for tea and a bag of blue cornmeal—and acknowledges that there are some things that cannot be cured anymore.

Tayo continues to believe that he has injured the world and is responsible for the current drought because, when he was in the jungle with Rocky, he had "prayed the rain away": "It took only one person to tear away the delicate strands of the web, spilling the rays of sun into the sand, and the fragile world would be injured. Once there had been a man who cursed the rain clouds, a man of monstrous dreams." We are reminded that before Tayo went to war he had visited the spring in the narrow canyon; as he listened to the water "he imagined with his heart the rituals the cloud priests performed during a drought." He watched a spider drink and thought of Spider Woman, who knew how "to win the storm clouds back from the Gambler so they would be free again to bring rain and snow to the people." Having access to these stories gives Tayo strength, but by the time he meets Old Ku'oosh he has lost his connection to these narratives.

Tayo is later sent to see a Navajo medicine man, Betonie, who lives near the Gallup Ceremonial grounds and participates in the annual Gallup Ceremonial. Like Tayo, Betonie is of mixed heritage; he is also not a conventional medicine man because he believes that the ceremonies do and must change: "But long ago when the people were given these ceremonies, the changing began, if only in the aging of the yellow gourd rattle or the shrinking of the skin around the eagle's claw, if only in the different voices from generation to generation, singing the chants." Change is vital and essential; the rituals must be modified to suit this world. As Betonie reminds Tayo: "You would do as much for the seedlings as they become plants in the field."

Betonie prompts Tayo to talk about his experiences during the war, pointing out to him that he saw Josiah in the Japanese faces because "thirty thousand years ago they were not strangers.'' Alluding to the belief that Native Americans originally came from Asia, Betonie encourages Tayo to embrace this memory from the war. He must, in short, embrace his own history along with that of his community. He also tells Tayo not to see himself as cut off and separate from white people: ''They want us to separate ourselves from white people, to be ignorant and helpless as we watch our own destruction.'' Maintaining a sense of humor, he tells Tayo that Indians, or Indian witchery, invented white people. Tayo holds on to this story, deriving strength from it.

After this introduction in Gallup, Betonie, his helper, and Tayo depart on a regenerative journey to the mountains. As the three move through this healing landscape, Tayo ''could see no signs of what had been set loose upon the earth: the highways, the towns, even the fences were gone.'' Betonie and his helper do a sandpainting ceremony; Tayo initially participates by sitting in the center of the white corn sandpainting. After the painting is complete, however, Betonie cuts Tayo across the top of his head and then, ''lifting him up by the shoulders, they guided his feet into the bear footprints, and Betonie prayed him through each of the five hoops.''

After the ritual Tayo sleeps and dreams of Josiah's stolen spotted cattle; when he wakes, he wants to leave right away to find them, recognizing that ''there were no boundaries; the world below and the sand paintings inside became the same that night.'' This lack of boundaries signals the beginning of his healing, though his quest is not complete. ''He could feel the ceremony like the rawhide thongs of the medicine pouch, straining to hold back the voices, the dreams, faces in the jungle in the L.A. depot, the smoky silence of solid white walls.'' Betonie, who knows what Tayo must find, then sends him off alone to find the spotted cattle, a woman, and a mountain.

While searching for the cattle Tayo meets Ts'eh, with whom he makes love; the next day she sends him on his journey toward the cattle and up the mountain of which Betonie had spoken. Rooted in the present, Tayo ''had forgotten all the events of the past days and past years''; no longer plagued by the past intruding on the present, the ''ride into the mountain had branched into all directions of time. He knew then why the oldtimers could only speak of yesterday and tomorrow in terms of the present moment.''

While on the mountain he meets a mountain lion, who is considered to be the hunter's helper; following him, Tayo is led to the cattle, only to be stopped in his pursuit by several white men who accuse him of rustling. Tayo becomes physically ill, and the white men decide it would be too much trouble to drive him to the local jail. ''He lay there and hated them. Not for what they wanted to do with him, but for what they did to the earth with their machines. . . . He wanted to follow them as they hunted the mountain lion, to shoot them and their howling dogs with their own guns.'' Shortly after this incident Tayo meets up with Ts'eh again, and she takes him to the cattle and teaches him about gathering roots and plants. His time with her is a ceremony in and of itself—one that recalls him to himself and to the possibility of loving: ''Their days together had a gravity emanating from the mesas and arroyos, and it replaced the rhythm that had been interrupted so long ago . . . when he cried now, it was because she loved him so much.''

Leading him to a rock painting that has almost faded, Ts'eh reassures him that ''as long as you remember what you have seen, then nothing is gone.'' She brings Tayo back to himself through her respect for rituals and traditions and through her faith in the power of recovering one's own history. She empowers him to hold on to all the stories and to embrace change. The ceremony, however, is not complete until he leaves her and journeys back to tell Old Ku'oosh and the other medicine men in the kiva (a large room used for religious and other purposes) about his time with her. Tayo's healing leaves them all blessed:

"You have seen her
We will be blessed
again."

Silko's next book, *Storyteller,* which includes some of her previously published stories and poems, family reminiscences in the form of stories, her autobiographical untitled prose narratives and untitled free verse, and family photographs, begins with the premise that telling and retelling stories can be healing. Like ceremonies, which necessarily change as they are performed again and again, stories are kept alive in their retellings.

I know Aunt Susie and Aunt Alice would tell me stories they had told me before but with changes in details or descriptions. The story was the important thing and little changes here and there were really part of the story. There were even stories about the different versions of stories and how they imagined these differing versions came to be.

And like ceremonies, the stories exist for the well-being and survival of the community and the individual. Tribal memory, like one's personal history, must be revisited and reimagined perpetually. Such a revisiting becomes a group effort that must be sustained by individual members of the community. Thus, Silko simultaneously transmits stories once told by others and authors them herself. In so doing, she pays homage to both oral and written tradition—to listeners, readers, storytellers, and writers.

The second, untitled, poem in the book pays tribute to Silko's Aunt Susie, who went to the Carlisle Indian School and attended Dickinson College in Carlisle before returning to Laguna. Silko notes that she transmitted:

an entire culture
by word of mouth
an entire history.

Keeping the oral tradition alive meant that each person had to listen and remember. Silko remembers how her aunt conveyed the story, what words and phrases "she used in her telling." Remembering the telling itself allows Silko to keep the "long story" alive: "I write when I still hear / her voice as she tells the story." Retelling one of Aunt Susie's stories about a little girl who drowned herself because her mother could not give her any *yashtoah,* the hardened crust on cornmeal mush, Silko keeps the oral tradition alive—both by telling the story again and by commenting on Aunt Susie's role as an effective storyteller.

Silko, in short, is listener *and* author, implying that these stories depend on both to survive. Aunt Susie's voice—the great tenderness, the deep feeling, the mournful tone, the excitement and wonder—must be preserved with the narrative. Similarly, she includes a short poem, describing Grandma A'mooh reading to her and her sisters from a book. Reading to attentive listeners, who will recount the experience to other listeners, becomes creative in its own right and likened to storytelling:

she always read the story with such animation and
    expression
changing her tone of voice and inflection
each time one of the bears spoke—
the way a storyteller would have told it.

Another way that Silko keeps the stories from becoming fixed and frozen and makes remembering a collective and collaborative enterprise is by including photographs at intervals throughout her text. For Silko, the photographs provide links to the stories she heard; they become part of the stories. As she wrote to Wright on July 5,1979:

I have discovered, though, since I began looking through my grandma's collections of old photographs, that much of what I "remember" of places and people is actually a memory of the photograph of the place and person, but that I had forgotten the photograph and remembered it as if I had been told about it. There were always many stories that accompanied the evenings we spent with the tall Hopi basket full of photographs. We would ask Grandpa or Grandma to identify people we did not recognize, and usually we would get a story of some sort along with the person's name. I suppose that may be why I have remembered these old photographs *not* as visual images but as the words that accompanied them.

The photographs function as an archive for Silko, allowing her to recover personal and tribal history.

Along with the photographs, Silko includes short narratives about her family; sometimes they accompany a photograph. One of Grandpa Hank reading by himself is paired with a short piece about his generosity and connection to those around him. Silko describes how the Navajo people would come back every year to the same houses for Laguna Feast; an old man from Alamo used to visit her grandfather regularly, bringing him gifts. In return, her grandfather would lovingly walk around his store gathering up things for his friend. Silko remembers the last time the old Navajo man came:

> He came into the store and looked for Grandpa where Grandpa always stood, behind his desk in the corner. When he didn't see him, the old man asked for him and then we told him, ''Henry passed away last winter.'' The old Navajo man cried, and then he left. He never came back anymore after that.

The next photograph is also of her grandfather; this time he is standing beside a car. Silko gives another vignette about his life, focusing on the missed opportunities. While at Sherman Institute, an Indian school in Riverside, California, he had been ''fascinated with engineering and design and wanted to become an automobile designer.'' His teachers had told him he could not

do it: ''So when Grandpa Hank came home from Sherman he had been trained to be a store clerk.'' Eventually he opened his own store, and Silko notes: ''He never cared much for storekeeping; he just did what had to be done. When I got older I was aware of how quiet he was sometimes and sensed there was some sadness he never identified.''

Making the sadness visible in the moment allows Silko to reconnect her grandfather with his passion for cars: ''He subscribed to *Motor Trend* and *Popular Mechanics* and followed the new car designs and results of road tests each year. In 1957 when Ford brought out the Thunderbird in a hardtop convertible, Grandpa Hank bought one and that was his car until he died.'' Later in *Storyteller,* Silko included two untitled poems about Grandpa Hank driving; in one he is taking a group of archaeologists to the top of Katsi'ma, Enchanted Mesa, and in the other he is seen out motoring on Sundays: ''I remember looking very hard out the window of the car / at the great dark mesa and the rolling plains below it.''

Silko also quotes from some of her own letters in *Storyteller.* In one to a friend, Lawson F. Inada, she includes a lyrical description of flowers blooming because there had been rain that spring: ''So many of these plants had never bloomed in my lifetime and so I had assumed these plants did not bloom; now I find that through all these years they were only waiting for enough rain.'' Seeing the flowers reminds her of the stories she had grown up with about ''meadows full of flowers'' and suggests the stories she will now tell: ''I will remember this September like they remembered the meadows and streams''; her listeners, in turn, will continue the cycle, remembering her stories by telling their own.

Much has been written about Silko's ''Yellow Woman'' section of *Storyteller,* which includes the title story, poems, reminiscences, and photographs. In *Spider Woman's Granddaughters,*

568 / AMERICAN WRITERS

Paula Gunn Allen provides a good description of Yellow Woman:

> Yellow Woman, like the tradition she lives in, goes on and on. She lives in New Mexico (or that's what they call it at present), around Laguna and other Keresan pueblos as well. She is a Spirit, a Mother, a blessed ear of corn, an archetype, a person, a daughter of a main clan, an agent of change and of obscure events, a wanton, an outcast, a girl who runs off with Navajos, or Zunis or even Mexicans.

Silko's retelling is important, because her narrator, who is unnamed, imagines that she must be the Yellow Woman. The narrator both writes herself into this powerful and empowering story and asserts her right to be a storyteller and a transgressor.

Her mobility, coupled with her leaving her family and the familiar, becomes self-expressive and creative, leading to the potential for self-discovery. As with the Yellow Woman's story, self-discovery is possible because she has a transgressive sexual encounter with someone; in her story he is named Silva, but we are made to infer that he is a surrogate for the *ka'tsina* spirit with whom the Yellow Woman goes away. Like Tayo's encounter with Ts'eh, Silko's narrator's union and time spent with Silva gives her a new sense of her surroundings, access to the potential for a deeper understanding of the landscape and its forces. Her time on the mountain is like a ceremony; when she returns to her "real" world she will bring a new vision to her family and community, though the price of her return is to abandon the sensual and sexual awakening she has experienced on the mountain with Silva. Transgression in this instance is silenced and becomes part of the fabric of conventional life.

Storyteller may well be remembered for the powerful short stories Silko includes in the collection. In keeping with the theme of the Yellow Woman story, some of her most compelling stories in the volume are about characters who trans-gress or are thwarted by others' transgressions. In the title story we find an Eskimo woman who, like the Yellow Woman figure, temporarily leaves her community to experience, in this case, white culture. She attends a Gussuck school for a time before being sent home for refusing to speak English—"she went because she was curious about the big school where the Government sent all the other boys and girls."

She had gone there in order to escape her home with her grandmother and the old man. Her grandmother's joints were "swollen with anger" because of what she has witnessed; and the Eskimo woman "knew what he [the old man] wanted." The old man wants her to continue having sex with him and to listen to his stories so that she will eventually find her own narrative, recognizing its relationship to those that came before. The Eskimo woman can also escape her grandmother's anger only for a short time; her grandmother's anger becomes her own as she learns about the death of her parents. (Her parents had been sold fuel by a Gussuck storekeeper, who had told them it was alcohol they could drink.)

This story becomes hers as she seeks revenge by luring the Gussuck who tends the store out onto the ice, where he dies. When questioned by an attorney, she responds: "It began a long time ago . . . in the summertime. Early in the morning, I remember, something red in the tall river grass." When she is in jail, she also refuses to pretend the incident was an accident: "I will not change the story, not even to escape this place and go home. I intended that he die. The story must be told as it is." Silko is content to expose the clash between the Eskimos and the Gussucks without attempting to resolve the dissonance. The Gussucks will never understand the story or why it has to "be told, year after year as the old man had done, without lapse or silence."

The most poignant tale in the collection is "Lullaby," a wrenching account of a Native

American couple who first lose their oldest son, Jimmie, in the war and then have their next two children, Danny and Ella, taken from them to be treated for tuberculosis by white doctors. Ayah is particularly bitter because she had unwittingly signed the papers that had allowed the children to go. They return briefly, only to leave again forever. The story, which is told from the mother's point of view, encompasses a day that is permeated by her memories, which surge up into the present, refusing to stay in the past. It is snowing when the story opens, and by the end we cannot be certain that Ayah and Chato, her husband, will survive the night. Nevertheless, a peace and resignation accompany them as Ayah mothers Chato, tucking a blanket around him as she once had done for her lost children.

The story begins with Ayah's meditation on the loss and the memories she is left with:

> The sun had gone down but the snow in the wind gave off its own light. It came in thick tufts like new wool—washed before the weaver spins it. Ayah reached out for it like her own babies had, and she smiled when she remembered how she had laughed at them. She was an old woman now, and her life had become memories.

Wrapped in her dead son's blanket, she thinks of her mother weaving and of her grandmother "spinning a silvery strand of yarn." In "*Storyteller:* Grandmother Spider's Web," Linda Danielson points out that the image of weaving is an empowering one for Ayah, linking her to the mythic power of Spider Woman, who in Navajo tradition is associated with weavers.

As Ayah waits to die, we are given her memories and a chronicle of her losses. She remembers her son Jimmie's birth and the day she learned from the army that he would not be coming back. Chato had translated for her: "He was taller than the white man and he stood straighter too." Chato's strength is established, only to be taken away later. Silko makes his gradual decline

visible: we learn that when he broke his leg, the white rancher "wouldn't pay Chato until he could work again"; eventually he was told "he was too old to work" anymore. Still later we see Chato drinking excessively, unable to take care of himself, and in failing health. When Ayah goes to the bar to fetch him her strength, in contrast to his, is highlighted: "In past years they would have told her to get out. But her hair was white now and her face was wrinkled. They looked at her like she was a spider crawling slowly across the room. They were afraid; she could feel the fear."

We see Ayah's fierce courage as well when the white doctors come to take her two younger children away. She grabs the children and flees to the hills. When the doctors return the next day she is forced to relinquish them—she had, Chato reminds her, signed a paper agreeing to this agreement. "It was worse than if they had died: to lose the children and to know that somewhere, in a place called Colorado, in a place full of sick and dying strangers, her children were without her." Wrenched from their mother and their culture, the children can never really return again. Unlike the young woman in "Storyteller," the children have no way to cross back, to return to their culture. They come to visit and hardly recognize their mother; on their last visit, Ayah does not try to pick her daughter up, and when she speaks to her son, "he spoke English words with the Navajo." Silko does not comment directly on Ayah's despair or the irreparable damage caused by this separation; she merely says Ayah "did not say good-bye." Stoicism and silent resignation characterize her stance throughout the story.

The story ends as it began, with an image of the snowstorm. Ayah and Chato are curled up in the snow in a barn, and we suspect that they are either waiting to die or will die owing to the severe weather conditions. Ghosts appear everywhere as Ayah sings a lullaby and cannot "remember if she had ever sung it to her children, but she knew that her grandmother had sung it and her mother had sung it.'' The song functions much as the image of weaving does at the beginning of the story to reunite Ayah with her mother and grandmother, positing faith that there will be others who will sing and weave, who will create and preserve the traditions.

A decade after publishing *Storyteller,* Silko published *Almanac of the Dead*—a long, complicated, and tortured novel reminiscent of Thomas Pynchon's work in its critique of paranoia and the relentless exploitation of human life in contemporary America. As Elizabeth Tallent noted in the *New York Times Book Review:* "This wild, jarring, graphic, mordant, prodigious book embodies the bold wish to encompass in a novel the cruelty of contemporary America, a nation founded on the murder and deracination of the continent's native peoples.'' Unlike *Ceremony* and *Storyteller,* in which clashes between Anglo-American and Native American values are merely made visible for the reader and finally accepted as inevitable, in *Almanac of the Dead,* Silko argues that nothing less than human survival is at stake in this perpetual conflict. People are at war in her novel. Native American resistance, which almost becomes a character in the novel, culminates in a growing plot to reclaim North America as the only way to reestablish the right ways of living, seeing, and feeling. Lecha, a Native American psychic who has been entrusted with one of the tribal almanacs that tells of the coming takeover of Anglo-American culture, muses on this impending apocalyptic event at the end of the novel:

> Lecha had claimed certain human beings sensed danger and began reacting without being conscious of what they were preparing for. They had no idea others like themselves existed as they worked alone with feverish plots and crazed schemes.
> . . . How many of these Chicanos and these Indians had ever heard the old stories? Did they know

the ancient prophecies? It all seemed quite impossible, and yet one only had to look as far as Africa to see that after more than five hundred years of suffering slavery and bloodshed, the African people had taken back the continent from European invaders.
> . . . Lecha warned that unrest among the people would grow due to natural disasters. Earthquakes and tidal waves would wipe out entire cities and great chunks of U.S. wealth. The Japanese were due to be pounded by angry earth spirits, and the world would watch in shock as billions of dollars and thousands of lives were suddenly washed away. . . . The old almanac said "civil strife, civil crisis, civil war.'' Allies of the United States would decline to intervene or send military aid.

Silko prepares her reader for this massive offensive by chronicling the relentless evil, maniacal cruelty, and all-pervasive destruction in every facet of Anglo-American life. As Alan Cheuse noted in a review for the *Chicago Tribune:* "European-American society is portrayed in these pages as an endless skein of pornography, drug addiction, heinous racist criminality, bestial perversion, white-collar crime, Mafia assassinations and the fouling of the earth and air and water.''

It is difficult to unravel the many plotlines, despite the fact that some of the narratives are intertwined. There are, according to Tallent, over seventy characters in the novel. A partial retelling of the first major plot begins to capture the texture and tone of Silko's horrific vision in this novel. The book opens with Seese, a former topless dancer, who is tending to Lecha, a Native American psychic she had seen on television. Seese is in search of her baby, who has been kidnapped, and to this end has enlisted the help of Lecha, who asks Seese to take care of her. The father of Seese's child, David, is a photographer who is also the lover of Beaufrey, a despicable character, whom Cheuse aptly describes as a "moral monster who traffics in operating room pornography (films of sex-change operations, surgical torture and abortions).'' Beaufrey has had David and Seese's baby kidnapped; he makes a film of the baby being killed and dismembered. Serlo, who is also involved with Beaufrey, shows David the color negatives:

> David did not doubt that Beaufrey had videotapes and enlarged color photographs of autopsies and organ harvests of Caucasian infants. David simply refused to believe the tiny cadaver in the images was that of his infant son, Monte. That simply was not possible because the cadaver had been considerably larger than his baby.

When David dies in a horseback riding accident shortly after this incident, Beaufrey, who witnesses the event, ''was grinning.''

There is a soap opera quality to the various plots and the extravagant lives Silko's characters lead. Actions are rendered with great theatricality; people are depicted as hollow and without any interiority. Nothing is too gruesome or graphic to be named and described in this novel; the weight of this brutal vision of life in our time is enormous. At times one feels numbed by the cataloging of atrocities, despair, and injustices. No one is immune or spared; all are implicated. It is difficult to imagine what Silko will write next, given the apocalyptic finality of this book.

Despite the dark vision of *Almanac of the Dead,* Silko's canon as a whole balances lightness and darkness with a remarkable faith in the complexity and richness of all human interactions. Wright captures this quality of her work magnificently in one of his letters to her:

> Tell me, Leslie: do you know [Alfred] Sisley and his work? Your writings have such a startling power of light and clarity that you remind me of him. That is, one side of your work reminds me of him. You also have something that he does [not] express so strongly: a sense of darkness and human entanglement.

Selected Bibliography

WORKS OF LESLIE MARMON SILKO

NOVELS
Ceremony. New York: Viking, 1977; New York, Signet, 1978.
Almanac of the Dead. New York: Simon & Schuster, 1991; New York, Penguin Books, 1992.

POETRY
Laguna Woman: Poems by Leslie Silko. Greenfield Center, N.Y.: Greenfield Review Press, 1974.

ESSAYS
''Language and Literature from a Pueblo Indian Perspective.'' In *English Literature: Opening Up the Canon.* Edited by Leslie A. Fiedler and Houston A. Baker, Jr. Baltimore: Johns Hopkins University Press, 1981. Pp. 54–72.
''An Old-Time Indian Attack Conducted in Two Parts.'' In *The Remembered Earth: An Anthology of Contemporary Native American Literature.* Edited by Geary Hobson. Albuquerque: University of New Mexico Press, 1981. Pp. 211–216.
''Landscape, History, and the Pueblo Imagination.'' *Antaeus,* 57:83–94 (Autumn 1986).

COLLECTED WORKS
Storyteller. New York: Seaver Books, 1981.

CORRESPONDENCE
Wright, Anne, ed. *The Delicacy and Strength of Lace: Letters between Leslie Marmon Silko and James Wright.* Saint Paul, Minn.: Graywolf Press, 1986.

BIOGRAPHICAL AND CRITICAL STUDIES

Anderson, Laurie. ''Colorful Revenge in Silko's *Storyteller.*'' *Notes on Contemporary Literature,* 15:11–12 (September 1985).
Antell, Judith. ''Momaday, Welch, and Silko: Expressing the Feminine Principle through Male

Alienation. *American Indian Quarterly* 12:213–220 (Summer 1988).

Beidler, Peter G. "Book Reviews: *Ceremony*." *American Indian Quarterly* 3:357–358 (Winter 1977–1978).

Cheuse, Alan. "Dead Reckoning." *Chicago Tribune-Books,* December 1, 1991, p. 3.

Danielson, Linda J. "*Storyteller:* Grandmother Spider's Web." *Journal of the Southwest,* 30:325–355 (Autumn 1988).

Graulich, Melody, ed. *"Yellow Woman": Leslie Marmon Silko.* New Brunswick, N.J.: Rutgers University Press, 1993.

Gunn Allen, Paula. *Spider Woman's Granddaughters: Traditional Tales and Contemporary Writing by Native American Women.* Boston: Beacon Press, 1989.

————. *The Sacred Hoop: Recovering the Feminine in American Indian Traditions.* Boston: Beacon Press, 1986.

Hirsch, Bernard A. " 'The Telling Which Continues': Oral Tradition and the Written Word in Leslie Marmon Silko's *Storyteller*." *American Indian Quarterly,* 12:1–26 (Winter 1988).

Lincoln, Kenneth. *Native American Renaissance.* Berkeley: University of California Press, 1983.

MacShane, Frank. "American Indians, Peruvian Jews: *Ceremony*." *New York Times Book Review,* June 12, 1977.

Ruoff, A. LaVonne. "Ritual and Renewal: Keres Traditions in the Short Fiction of Leslie Silko." MELUS, 5:2–17 (Winter 1978).

Ruppert, Jim. "Story Telling: The Fiction of Leslie Silko." *Journal of Ethnic Studies,* 9:53–58 (Spring 1981).

Seyersted, Per. *Leslie Marmon Silko.* Boise: Boise State University Western Writers Series, no. 45, 1980.

Tallent, Elizabeth. "Storytelling with a Vengeance." *New York Times Book Review,* December 22, 1991, p. 6.

INTERVIEWS

Barnes, Kim. "A Leslie Marmon Silko Interview." *The Journal of Ethnic Studies,* 13:83–105 (Winter 1986).

Coltelli, Laura. "Leslie Marmon Silko." In her *Winged Words: American Indian Writers Speak.* Lincoln: University of Nebraska Press, 1990.

Evers, Lawrence J., and Dennis W. Carr. "A Conversation with Leslie Marmon Silko." In *Sun Tracks: An American Indian Literary Magazine,* 3:29–33 (Fall 1976).

Fisher, Dexter. "Stories and Their Tellers: A Conversation with Leslie Marmon Silko." In his *Third Woman: Minority Women Writers of the United States.* Boston: Houghton Mifflin, 1980.

Jahner, Elaine. "The Novel and Oral Tradition: An Interview with Leslie Marmon Silko." *Book Forum: An International Transdisciplinary Quarterly,* 5:383–388 (1981).

Seyersted, Per. "Two Interviews with Leslie Marmon Silko." *American Studies in Scandinavia,* 13:17–33 (1981).

—CELESTE GOODRIDGE

Neil Simon

1927–

NEIL ("Doc") SIMON stands alone as by far the most successful American playwright of this century and most probably in the history of the American theater. His legendary feats include having four works run on Broadway simultaneously, a record which ties that of Avery Hopwood in 1920 and which also recalls the productivity of Clyde Fitch at the turn of the century. Simon's bicoastal writing career includes plays and musicals, as well as screenplays. Since 1961 he has averaged almost a play a year for the New York stage. Ironically, however, this overwhelmingly successful, multimillionaire writer has been virtually ignored by literary critics, who routinely dismiss him as a writer of popular comedies that cater to the tastes of a well-established and loyal audience. As of 1996, only two book-length studies of Simon exist: Edythe M. McGovern's *Not-So-Simple Neil Simon,* published in 1978, which offers an introduction to Simon's early career and includes a preface by the playwright himself; and Robert K. Johnson's *Neil Simon,* published in 1983, an overview of both Simon's work and life. Unfortunately, neither of these works is able to provide the kind of in-depth, scholarly analysis that the volume and quality of Simon's output merits. Neither do the few journal essays that have appeared add substantially to our understanding of this most prolific dramatist. While theater critics have written on productions of his work staged all over the world, and Simon has granted many interviews both at home and abroad, his oeuvre remains essentially uncharted territory, ripe for exploration from any number of scholarly perspectives.

Neil Simon draws extensively on his personal and family experiences for his plays. Although he has repeatedly insisted that his dramas are not strictly autobiographical, one can make strong and direct connections between Simon's life and his art simply by juxtaposing the two. In the early phases of his playwriting career, Simon culled details from his memories of his first jobs and marriage; over time he has reached even farther back for inspiration, to his childhood and the lives of his parents and family. In a 1988 interview with Patricia Bosworth, Simon acknowledged, "It's possible to trace my entire life through my plays. Most of them come out of what I've been thinking or feeling at a given time."

Marvin Neil Simon was born on July 4, 1927, to Irving and Mamie Simon in New York City, where Irving worked in the garment industry. Simon grew up during the Depression in the Washington Heights section of Manhattan (which is located at the northern end of the island). His father was not a strong presence at home, since he and Simon's mother had a troubled marriage: Irving was, in fact, frequently absent for long stretches of time. The family often suffered financially as a result, so Mamie had to find ingenious ways to support her two sons, Danny—Neil's elder brother—and Neil himself. In interviews, Simon speaks of her strategies for supporting the boys, which included working as a clerk in the now-defunct department store Gimbels; running poker games in their home in exchange for a cut of the profits; and taking in lodgers such as the butchers who paid their rent in lamb chops. In 1986 Simon told William A. Henry, III, about the painful ''yo-yo'' cycle of separation and reunion that marked his family's life. On other occasions he has recalled his close relationship with his older brother, who clearly served as surrogate father throughout Simon's youth. Although the exact origin of the moniker is unclear, Danny seems to have been responsible for his brother's nickname ''Doc''—which still sticks—as well as for Simon's first paying job and the brothers' professional entry into show business as a writing team in 1946.

Simon speaks enthusiastically of his early exposure to both the theater and film. He told David Sterritt in 1985, ''When I was a kid, going to the theater was the most exciting thing you could do. Going to the movies was the most *exotic* thing you could do.'' He counts among his theatrical influences Kaufman and Hart, Garson Kanin, Tennessee Williams, and Arthur Miller but feels even more indebted to the films of Charlie Chaplin, Laurel and Hardy, and Buster Keaton. In 1965 Simon told Tom Prideaux of ''being dragged out of movies for laughing too loud'' as a child. To several interviewers he has recounted the story of his falling off a ledge from laughing so hard at an outdoor screening of a Chaplin film.

As a teenager Simon commuted to DeWitt Clinton High School in the Bronx, from which he graduated in 1944. Because America was in the midst of World War II, Simon joined a reserve training program, hoping to become an air force pilot. But instead of giving him orders to report to some distant locale, the military sent Simon to study ''basic engineering techniques'' at New York University. (So Simon explained to Alan Levy in 1965.) After a year, Simon was briefly stationed at Lowry Field in Colorado, where his principal task was to write for the base newspaper.

After the war, Simon secured a job in the mailroom of Warner Brothers' New York offices through Danny, who was working in the Warner Brothers publicity department at the time. But the Simon brothers had set their sights on writing careers. When they heard that Goodman Ace at CBS was developing new talent for radio, they quickly pursued the lead and received an overnight writing assignment as a test of their skills. Alan Levy explains that their job was to come up with a routine for ''a movie review to be recited by a Brooklyn usherette.... The movie under surveillance was a Joan Crawford picture and the line that landed the Simons in radio was 'She's in love with a gangster, who is caught and sent to Sing Sing and given the electric chair, and she promises to wait for him.' '' The brothers went on to write for such radio comics as Robert Q. Lewis, Jan Murray, and Phil Foster before making the transition to work in television in 1948. This period in Simon's life, complicated by the experience of moving out of his childhood home, informs his first play, *Come Blow Your Horn*, first produced in 1961 (throughout this essay, dates given for Simon's plays are for first productions; publication dates for these works can be found in the bibliography). The play tells the story of two brothers' attempts to establish their own personal and professional lives.

Danny and Neil worked as writers during what has come to be known as the ''Golden Age'' of television. In the early 1950s, the brothers wrote for Tallulah Bankhead, Phil Silvers, Jerry Lester, Jackie Gleason, Sid Caesar, and Red Buttons.

During the summers of 1952 and 1953 they were hired to write comedy revues at the Tamiment resort in the Poconos in Pennsylvania. It was there that Neil Simon met his first wife, Joan Baim, a dancer who was employed in the children's camp connected with the vacation center. They were married in 1953 and subsequently had two daughters, Ellen and Nancy. Simon partly based his play about newlyweds in New York, *Barefoot in the Park* (1963), on the early days of his marriage to Joan.

In 1956, the Simon brothers ended their writing partnership. Danny moved to Hollywood to work in film, while Neil remained in New York, continuing to write for television programs, including the *Sid Caesar Show,* the *Phil Silvers Arrow Show,* the *Phil Silvers Show,* and the *Garry Moore Show.* In interviews, Simon speaks of the great impact this work had on the style and technique of his playwriting. Two jobs in particular stand out for Simon, as he explained to Jackson R. Bryer in 1991: "*Your Show of Shows* was writing sketches and *[Sergeant] Bilko* was like a half-hour movie; so I was learning the dramatic form." Simon received Emmy Awards for his work on both the *Sid Caesar Show* and the *Sergeant Bilko* series. He later reflected on the work he did for Caesar in *Laughter on the 23rd Floor* (1993), a play about television comedy writers.

During the late 1950s, Simon admitted to Bryer, he had made a few "abortive attempts" at playwriting. But it was only when Jerry Lewis hired him to come to California to write a television special that Simon found the time he needed to devote to a stage script. Lewis had hired him for six weeks, but Simon completed the script in ten days. Lewis told him to do what he liked until rehearsals began, so Simon spent three weeks drafting *Come Blow Your Horn.* The play, he recalled for Richard David Story in 1991, subsequently "went through twenty drafts . . . and was optioned by twenty-five producers"

before it was finally mounted, first in summer stock at the Bucks County Playhouse in Pennsylvania and then on Broadway.

Simon's dramatic output following the moderate success of *Come Blow Your Horn* most closely resembles a train that leaves the station, full steam ahead, and has yet to halt, despite a few near derailments. During the period from 1961 to 1973, Simon emerged as America's foremost comic playwright, with a string of successes including the Tony Award–winning *Odd Couple* (1965), *Plaza Suite* (1968), *Last of the Red Hot Lovers* (1969), and *The Sunshine Boys* (1972). During this same period, Simon wrote the books for a number of musical comedies: *Little Me* (1962), *Sweet Charity* (1966), and *Promises, Promises* (1968). He also branched out into film, writing original screenplays such as *After the Fox* (1966) and *The Heartbreak Kid* (1972). In addition, he adapted some of his own hit plays—like *The Odd Couple* (1968) and *Plaza Suite* (1971) —for the movies. Even this partial list of what Simon wrote at this time supports the point made by the critic Walter Kerr in 1970: Simon "treats his craft as a profession" and "is a steady and possibly compulsive worker."

In 1973, Simon lost his first wife to cancer, a blow from which he has never fully recovered. Later that same year, he married actress Marsha Mason, whom he met when she auditioned for his play *The Good Doctor.* Simon soon realized, however, that he had not fully dealt with Joan's death. His mourning and struggle to understand his loss affected not only his new marriage but also his writing. Different facets of this transitional period are manifest in *God's Favorite* (1974), which questions fate and faith, and *Chapter Two* (1977), which dramatizes the beginning of his life with Mason. Simon and Mason divorced in 1982, but during their marriage, Mason proved to be a muse for Simon. He wrote five screenplays for her, including *The Goodbye Girl* (1977), *Chapter Two* (1979), and *Only*

When I Laugh (1981)—each of which won her an Oscar nomination for best actress.

Simon began another pivotal period in his playwriting career with *Brighton Beach Memoirs* in 1983. This play became the first work in a trilogy that also includes the Tony Award–winning *Biloxi Blues* (1985) and *Broadway Bound* (1986). These three plays are related to the very successful *Lost in Yonkers* (1991), which won both a Tony Award and a Pulitzer Prize. All four works stand out for the way they draw on Simon's childhood and adolescence and frankly acknowledge the subculture of his youth as an inspiration. In these plays for the first time, Simon openly depicts Jewish characters and gives details of the Jewish experience in America during the years immediately before, during, and after World War II.

In 1987, shortly after the opening of *Broadway Bound,* Simon married the former actress and model Diane Lander, but the relationship was rocky, and they quickly divorced the next year. After a period of reconciliation, they remarried in 1990, and Simon officially adopted Lander's daughter Bryn. Significantly, Lander insisted in their prenuptial contract that Simon "not write about her or her daughter in her lifetime." Knowing Simon's predilection for dramatizing details from his life, Lander explained in an interview with David Richards in 1991 that she "didn't want [Simon] observing the relationship. I wanted him to live it. I thought if I took away his ability to write about it, he might treat it differently."

In the 1990s, Simon struggled with work that did not enjoy as much success as most of his previous writing: *Jake's Women* (1992), a play that drew on Simon's relationships with women he had known at different points in his life; the musical version *The Goodbye Girl* (1993); and *Laughter on the 23rd Floor* (1993). In 1995, Simon produced a new installment in his "hotel series," the not-yet-published *London Suite,*

which caused quite a stir not on account of the play itself but because of Simon's decision to produce it off Broadway, in a smaller and less costly venue than would be possible on Broadway. In interviews connected with this production, Simon claimed to be working on his autobiography, and he seemed sanguine about the prospect of doing more work for the Off-Broadway theater.

Interviewers often ask Simon how he writes: does he start with an outline, a theme, or something else? Echoing Pirandello's famous discussion of his *Six Characters in Search of an Author,* Simon explained in a 1978 interview in *American Film* that outlining had thus far been useless for him: "I [have] found [that] . . . characters start . . . to move off in their own directions." The playwright has said that it is the discovery of a "dilemma" that drives his writing. In a lengthy interview with James Lipton for the *Paris Review* in 1992, Simon revealed that he had incorporated his "anatomy" for comic dramaturgy into his autobiographical *Broadway Bound:*

> Stan keeps asking Eugene for the essential ingredient in comedy, and when Eugene can't answer, Stan says, "Conflict!" When he asks for the *other* key ingredient, and Eugene can only come up with, "*More* conflict?" Stan says, "The key word is *wants*. In every comedy, even drama, somebody has to want something and want it bad. When somebody tries to stop him—that's conflict." By the time you know the conflicts, the play is already written in your mind. All you have to do is put the words down.

Simon also acknowledged to Lipton two other elements central to his development of a play: envisioning its physical environment and establishing the existence of an "anchor" character who can serve as a sort of "Greek chorus." The anchor is "the character who either literally talks to the audience or talks to the audience in a sense. . . . [to] express the writer's viewpoint." It should not surprise us that the Simon character who functions most effectively in this capacity is the autobiographical figure Eugene Jerome from the trilogy that begins with *Brighton Beach Memoirs.*

Simon's work in radio and television comedy has had a decisive influence on his dramaturgy. It is easy to see that Simon has carried over to his stage work certain established comic techniques from radio and television—like the running gag or the zingy one-liner. But it is equally important to recognize how his early assignments for radio and television shaped the very way he writes. Simon told Lipton that "construction" is his greatest strength, a skill that can be closely related to the tight structure that is typical of media production formats. Equally significant is Simon's speed of composition—evidenced by the example of *Come Blow Your Horn.* How to write fast is what Simon learned from the relentless pace of the television seasons, which demanded thirty-nine continuous weeks of new material from him. Television also taught him to revise: as he explained to Clive Hirschorn in 1977, in television, one repeatedly has to "re-write a scene until it works as well as it possibly can."

Simon often works on multiple projects simultaneously, and he sometimes takes years to finish a given piece. That does not mean that he writes less or less quickly: Frequently he will start a play, then put it away in a drawer for a time before producing a final draft. But in between he goes on "writing" all the while. As he suggested to James Lipton, "in the back of [his] mind, there's a little writer who writes while [he is] doing other things." Simon's preferred method for developing a play is to have a read-through of an early draft with actors and a director and then to rework as much as necessary before rehearsals begin. He also likes to have the freedom to keep refining a play during the rehearsal period. Simon's close relationship with such prominent directors as Mike Nichols and Gene Saks has

bolstered his faith in this procedure: he tends to rely on directors' instincts about what works or fails on stage.

Simon describes his dramaturgical process as very personal. In fact, he told Lipton that his "greatest weakness" lies in his inability to write "outside of [his] own experience." Yet his facility for adapting that experience has clearly contributed mightily to his commercial success. Simon creates in his plays "what he calls 'photographs' taken from his own life," wrote Richard Gilman in 1967. Like a photographer, Simon sees himself as standing apart from the life around him. He speaks often of his role as an "observer" and of having thought when he was a child that he was "invisible" because he rarely participated in family conversation. In his plays from the decade 1985–1995—especially *Lost in Yonkers* and, earlier, the trilogy, *Brighton Beach Memoirs; Biloxi Blues;* and *Broadway Bound*— Simon reveals more about his troubled childhood. In his interview with Lipton, Simon claimed that "one of the main reasons" he writes plays is for "catharsis." "It's like analysis without going to the analyst," he explained. "The play becomes your analysis." In that same interview, Simon described writing as a kind of exorcism, usually to dispel "painful" experiences; he said his plays are extended "monologues" about his life. Thus it is not surprising that Simon also claimed that he "become[s] *everybody*" in his plays.

Some of the most perceptive commentary on Neil Simon comes not from theater critics or scholars but from his fellow stage artists, particularly Thomas Meehan, author of the book for the musical *Annie.* Reviewing the first half of Simon's career in 1978, Meehan characterized the "world" of Simon's plays as

peculiarly unreal . . . everyone [in it] . . . is capable of coming up with rapid comic ripostes. . . . [It is] an isolated world, too, where such concerns as politics . . . barely exist, but where everyone is instead interested only in his or her own personal problems, which usually have to do with marriage and sex. But not with money—money is almost never a problem in the world of Neil Simon. . . . [It is] a world, in short, that can be found only on the stage.

The isolation that Meehan speaks of is particularly significant. Simon's plays are hermetic, almost claustrophobic in the way they contain their characters and action. The light and breezy quality of his first two plays does not necessarily require weightier content; even the early plays, which supposedly tackle more serious topics, rarely escape the confinement of the domestic framework with which Simon appears to feel most comfortable.

It is a world that we may relate to one of the two classical traditions of comedy. If Simon eschews the political themes of Aristophanic Greek comedy, he draws directly on the conventions of such dramatists as Menander, who epitomizes the New Comedy, which emerged after 336 B.C. and was carried over from Greece to Rome. This form features stock characters in ''timeless'' situations—generational conflict, marital discord, the quest for sex and money—and rarely focuses on anything beyond the domestic sphere.

The plot of Simon's first play, *Come Blow Your Horn* (1961), perfectly exemplifies this New Comic tradition. The irascible father, Mr. Baker, disapproves of his son Alan's work habits, lifestyle, and girlfriends. The younger son Buddy at first appears to be his brother's opposite in taste and habits, yet both brothers are trying to escape their parents' control. Their scatterbrained mother wants to reconcile father and sons but only creates comic confusion. Although Alan tricks his father in family business matters (all to his father's ultimate good) and sows his wild oats with worldly women, in the end he chooses to marry a nice girl and arrives at, more professional attitude toward the family wax fruit business. This conclusion, in which family harmony is restored and the characters revert to socially sanctioned behavior, typifies plays in the tradition of the New Comedy.

In *Come Blow Your Horn* and in other plays, Simon uses familiar character types and time-honored sources of dramatic conflict to construct a comedy that progresses efficiently and predictably. The audiences' familiarity with Simon's format, derived from the ancient comic traditions, adds to their enjoyment of his humor. Again, much of the humor in his earliest plays derives from radio and television formulae for one-liners and running gags. Some of Simon's detractors feel that unless the comedy actually derives from the plot, the play is not so skillfully written. Such critics scorn those plays in which action is created or dialogue is generated purely for the sake of setting up a laugh line or some other comic business. But Simon's wit is well matched to his audience, as this exchange from *Come Blow Your Horn* demonstrates:

BUDDY: . . . I just can't get excited about making wax fruit.
ALAN: Why not? It's a business like anything else.
BUDDY: It's different for you, Alan. You're hardly ever there. . . . You're the salesman, you're outside all day. Meeting people. Human beings. But I'm inside looking at petrified apples and pears and plums. .They never rot, they never turn brown, they never grow old . . . It's like the fruit version of *The Picture of Dorian Gray.*

Simon's allusion to the novel by Oscar Wilde demonstrates his feel for an educated but not elitist audience—one that will appreciate the association of an artifact of ''high'' culture with one devised for the American masses.

In his second play, *Barefoot in the Park* (1963), Simon gets considerable comic mileage out of the setting, a newlywed couple's sixth-floor walk-up apartment. Toward the end of the play, one of the characters who has struggled repeatedly with the ascent remarks, ''I feel like we've died . . . and gone to heaven . . . only we had to climb up.'' High-brow critics generally panned this play; Simon himself in a 1979 interview with Lawrence Linderman readily admitted that this second work is ''a soufflé.'' He acknowledged to Clive Hirschorn that *Barefoot in the Park* ''relies more on its one-liners than on any intrinsic texture the text might have.'' (We could well apply both observations to a number of Simon's plays.) Typically Simon speaks quite frankly about his occasional flops and about basic conceptual flaws in his writing. In interviews, the playwright often quotes from Walter Kerr's review of *The Star-Spangled Girl* (1966): ''Neil Simon . . . hasn't had an idea for a play this season, but he's gone ahead and written one anyway.''

Simon's original inspiration for *The Star-Spangled Girl* was the interaction he had observed between two individuals of strongly opposed political views who nevertheless shared a sexual attraction; he wondered about the dramatic possibilities suggested by this potentially conflicted relationship. But, as he explained to Hirschorn, ''instead of using these two types in the play, I chose two other types completely. I invented a story about a couple of young guys living at Berkeley University, and how their lives are disrupted by the arrival of an attractive young girl.'' Unfortunately, Simon had no real experience on which to base these characters, the setting, or the situation. The play suffered as a result. To Hirschorn, Simon acknowledged that to ''write convincingly'' he had to know the world he was creating on stage. This may be why Simon has rarely strayed beyond dramatizing his New York milieu.

The Star-Spangled Girl may have been a sort of watershed in failing to convey some genuine concern for politics and social issues: it seems to have driven Simon permanently away from engaging such themes in any thoroughgoing way.

Despite the fact that the plot necessitates that the two male characters, Andy Hobart and Norman Cornell, have political convictions—they spend their time working on a leftist publication—Simon seems incapable of making their political concerns really matter to our sense of who they are. The *sexual* politics of the play present another problem: the title character, a stereotypical ''dumb blonde'' named Sophie who spouts empty jingoistic diatribes, is subjected to blatant sexual harassment by Andy and Norman; Simon tries to portray it as good-natured humor. *The Star-Spangled Girl* may offer the clearest example of Simon's unquestioningly conventional portrayal of gender. Helen McMahon, in an essay from 1975, called Simon's early work ''chauvinistic, to say the least,'' but Simon himself seems oblivious to the idea. He claimed to Lipton that many of his female characters are ''stronger [and] more interesting . . . than the men'' in his plays. He appears totally unaware of the social contexts in which he frames his female characters and reduces them to ineffectual wives, mothers, or girlfriends.

The issue of gender roles is at the heart of *The Odd Couple* (1965), probably Simon's best-known work. The play raises questions about homosociality and homophobia; it might be understood as an oblique depiction of homosexuality. Interestingly, Simon did not conceive of the basic idea for the play himself: his brother Danny did, based on his own personal experience. But Danny found that he couldn't get anywhere with his ''story about two divorced men living together and [how] the same problems they each had with their wives repeat with each other.'' So, as Simon explained to Richard Meryman in 1971, Danny allowed Neil to pursue the story line. What Simon created was a relationship between two men that mirrors the contemporary popular image of the white, middle-class, American marriage. Felix Ungar fills the ''feminine'' role: he cooks and cleans compulsively;

he is emotional and dependent. Oscar Madison, on the other hand, is all guy: he's a slob, he's irresponsible and inconsiderate, and he can't understand why Felix behaves as he does. Supposedly, the two are best friends, but both the dialogue and the action seem to hint at a closer tie.

Simon's lines for Oscar and Felix continually —and ironically—invoke marriage. Consider this exchange from the first act of the play, when Oscar suggests they share his apartment:

FELIX: Why do you want me to live with you?
OSCAR: Because I can't stand living alone, that's why! For crying out loud, I'm proposing to you. What do you want, a ring?

Simon then quickly complicates the situation by having Felix unwittingly substitute his wife's name for Oscar's: "Good night, Frances," Felix tells Oscar at the close of act 1. In act 2, scene 1, Felix remarks that he hasn't "even *thought* about women in weeks" and claims that since his marriage broke up he doesn't "even know what a woman looks like." At the opening of the next scene, Oscar "playfully" announces, "I'm home, dear!"—as if Felix were his wife. But their arrangement deteriorates, thanks primarily to a disastrous double date with the Pigeon sisters, and Oscar decides he wants out:

> It's all over, Felix. The whole marriage. We're getting an annulment! Don't you understand? I don't want to live with you any more. I want you to pack your things, tie it up with your Saran Wrap and get out of here.

While the audience may laugh precisely because of the similarity of the men's interaction to that of a married couple, we must also question why the playwright has developed the conceit of a marriage (and breakup) between men.

Simon's presentation of these two diametrically opposed, "straight" characters who clearly have a relationship modeled on a stereotypical heterosexual marriage creates the opportunity for highly nuanced analysis of gender, sexuality, and relational paradigms in American culture. Significantly, Simon's other work features a number of gay male characters (for example, James Perry in *The Gingerbread Lady*), but these figures are often portrayed in terms of clichés, which indicates interesting tensions between Simon's overt dramatic choices and complicated feelings of which he may not be so aware. His gay characters seem unreal, but Felix and Oscar, cloaked in heterosexuality, paradoxically are both more believable—and intriguing.

In 1985, supposedly at the request of actresses who saw in *The Odd Couple* a great opportunity for women's comic roles, Simon gave it what Linda Winer—in her review—called a "sex-change operation." Simon turned Felix and Oscar into Florence and Olive and attempted to put a feminist spin on his original play. While the critics deemed it a qualified success, the revision did not take off as had the first version. Howard Kissel pointed out in his review,

> Until the feminist revolution is complete and all the mannerisms associated with sexual identity . . . have been obliterated, a certain inequity will exist in the theater. We will, I'm afraid, invariably find it funnier to see men imitating women's behavior than vice-versa.

From a theoretical standpoint, however, the two *Odd Couple* plays may represent some of the most interesting work Simon has ever done, for they invite critical speculation about popular conceptions of and responses to gender roles. Simon made fairly few changes in his script for the version of the play he wrote for women: he simply changed a few details to suit the new sexual identity of his characters and updated some of the cultural references. The upshot is that he put us in a position to study exactly how he—and also his audience—may treat the two sexes differently in the same situations.

* * *

Although Simon has never referred to these works as such, the three comedies *Plaza Suite* (1968), *California Suite* (1976), and *London Suite* (1995) form a series sharing structure, themes, style, and even characters. Each play consists of a series of scenes that function as one-acts (three for *Plaza Suite* and four for the other two), which are linked by being set in the same hotel room. Simon set each act in a different style, ranging from farce to tragicomedy, and in each he covered familiar ground: marital discord, generational conflict, and social foibles of various kinds. Simon did not intend to write *Plaza Suite* as an evening of one-acts. But, as he explained to Michael Sommers in 1995, "after he hit upon the curtain line for the first act, he felt that enough of the . . . story had been told," so he decided to create separate companion pieces to fill out the bill. Afterward he grew fond of the form: "In the playlet," he told Rowland Barber in 1976, "you can get straight to the big scenes, the crucial moments, the immediate laughs."

Plaza Suite's three scenes include "Visitor from Mamaroneck," "Visitor from Hollywood," and "Visitor from Forest Hills." "Mamaroneck" chronicles the disintegrating marriage of Karen and Sam Nash. In the hope of rekindling their romance, Karen has reserved the suite she *believes* they spent their honeymoon in twenty-four (or, as Sam thinks, twenty-three) years earlier. But Sam's affair with his secretary, which Karen suspects and Sam finally admits, renders a renaissance of their relationship unlikely. To capture the midlife crises facing both husband and wife, Simon alternates farcical, physical humor with verbal pathos. Sam explains that he is driven to try to reclaim his youth through fanatic attention to his body (exercise, diet, and so on) and an affair with a younger woman—all because his dreams of success and a wonderful family have been fulfilled. He claims "I just want to do it all

over again . . . I would like to start the whole damned thing right from the beginning." Simon highlights the irony of this situation by leaving the conflict between Karen and Sam unresolved. But he gives the audience a clear image of a relationship that has gradually, almost imperceptibly dissolved.

In "Visitor from Hollywood" Simon also attempts to balance humor with sadness. Jesse Kiplinger, a famous Hollywood producer who has come to New York for a brief stay, has contacted his high-school sweetheart, Muriel Tate, and asked her to visit him in his hotel room. Muriel has never left the world of Tenafly, New Jersey, and has settled into an empty life as a wife and mother; she regularly seeks vicarious excitement by following the exploits of her old beau in the movie magazines. Jesse, equally disenchanted with the emptiness of life in Hollywood, wants to recapture the innocence of his youth through an affair with Muriel. Simon lays out the fantasy that each character brings to their reunion; then he dramatizes how unlikely it is that the dreams of either one might ever be realized. Neither Jesse nor Muriel really hears the other. The impossibility of their communicating generates both comedy and sorrow: Simon presents these two as meeting only in the language of ephemeral, and so phony, romance.

Simon continues to explore the theme of frustrated romance and failed marriage in the final scene of *Plaza Suite,* "Visitor from Forest Hills." This part of the play tells the story of Norma and Roy Hubley, whose daughter Mimsey is to be married at the hotel. The pretext for the scene is Mimsey's having locked herself in the bathroom, refusing to come out for the wedding. As her parents try to communicate with her, they slowly come to see their own foibles. It is no surprise when we learn that Mimsey is "afraid" of what she and her fiancé, Borden, are "going to become"—the duplication of her parents. Here again, amidst the farcical humor of ruined stockings, ripped tuxedos, and exaggerated personalities, Simon inserts perennial familial concerns. But he has had little success in generating genuine audience sympathy for the three sets of couples in *Plaza Suite* because of his superficial characterizations. Many of the figures in the play lack depth; they border on caricature or stereotype, and the troubles in their lives are equally clichéd. For a critic like Edythe M. McGovern, the familiarity of the characters and their situations translates to the idea that *Plaza Suite* (and other of Simon's plays) have a universal appeal. Other critics, however, see Simon's work as just limited.

In *California Suite* and *London Suite* Simon continues his seriocomic explorations of familial and marital crises. In the former, he develops two characters, Diana and Sidney Nichols, who are much more complex and distinctive than the characters in *Plaza Suite*. The fact that Simon revives Diana and Sidney for *London Suite* suggests that he realized that they are especially effective. Simon does not fully escape clichés in either of the two later "suites," but Diana and Sidney's stories come the closest to achieving a genuine combination of humor and sorrow. When we first meet them, Diana, an actress nominated for an Academy Award, has traveled from England to Hollywood for the ceremony, accompanied by her husband Sidney. Simon composed brisk dialogue for them—brittle repartee in the British style. It is, of course, almost inevitable that Diana does not win the Oscar, and the piece unflinchingly displays the unraveling of the bright demeanor and wit we first encounter in her and Sidney. At the core of their marriage lies an insoluble problem, hinted at early on and later revealed fully when Diana, in despair, has gotten drunk: Sidney is gay, and their caring for each other can never resolve the sexual and emotional gulf between them. Simon achieves genuine poignancy in the closing lines of the play:

DIANA: I love you, Sidney. (*SIDNEY leans over and kisses her with warmth and tenderness*) Don't close your eyes, Sidney.

SIDNEY: I always close my eyes.

DIANA: Not tonight . . . Look at *me* tonight . . . Let it be *me* tonight.

When Simon revives Diana and Sydney for *London Suite,* he presents them as being reunited after a separation of many years. Sidney has left England and is living on an island with his male lover. Diana has gone on to considerable financial and commercial success as an actress in American television. Their apparently casual, warm reunion, however, ends as close to tragedy as Simon can reach: after trying to evade making the revelation for some time, Sidney finally admits that he has AIDS. Diana immediately resolves to bring Sidney home with her for medical care and extends her hospitality to include Sydney's companion, if he wishes to come. What initially drove Diana and Sydney apart, ironically, finally brings them back together, with the inevitability of Sidney's death heightening the emotional impact of the scene's conclusion. Simon succeeds with Diana and Sidney for the key reason that they are complex, full characters whose conflicts derive from intrinsic elements of who they are; their situation never fails to appear to be genuine. Since he is able to go far beyond avoiding caricature with Diana and Sydney, Simon is able to accomplish in their segments of *California Suite* and *London Suite* a more natural blend of emotional responses than he does in most of his other work.

All the plays in the "hotel series"—including *London Suite*—have farcical elements. These are significant not only in themselves but for their relationship to *Rumors,* Simon's full-length farce in the French and English tradition, which was produced in 1988. While nowhere near as exemplary of the genre as, say, Michael Frayn's *Noises Off, Rumors* does demonstrate Simon's ability to do sustained work in a style that is both restrictive and demanding. He himself has described *Rumors* to Bryer and to Lipton as "the most dangerous" and "the most difficult" play he has ever written. In an interview with the *New York Times Magazine* in 1988, he explained that "with a farce the plot has to get more complicated, funnier and wilder every second." Many reviewers of the play felt that Simon was too overwhelmed by the form to create an interesting or successful plot, characters, or dialogue, however. The shorter sequences of the three hotel "suites" remain Simon's most successful attempts at writing farce.

While *Last of the Red Hot Lovers* (1969) is structured like the hotel plays, it is closer thematically to the two plays Simon wrote immediately after completing it: *The Gingerbread Lady* (1970) and *The Prisoner of Second Avenue* (1971). Each of these dramas conveys a dark comic tone; each features a desperate central character adrift in the turmoil and impersonality of life in Manhattan. Strangely, however, the first two plays also appear to be among the most hermetic of Simon's works, despite their dependence on a sense of urban angst. Simon does not represent the vibrant political and artistic culture of New York; instead he only uses the city as a flat backdrop to the personal lives of his apartment-dwelling characters. Paul D. Zimmerman, reviewing *Last of the Red Hot Lovers* for *Newsweek* in 1970, pointed out that the play "speaks in the idiom of middle-class New York, respects the pieties of that class and seeks truth within the comfortable confines of a militantly middle-class way of life"—a statement that applies equally to *The Gingerbread Lady.* Both plays refer only rarely to the world outside the middle-class home.

In each act of *Last of the Red Hot Lovers,* Barney Cashman tries to have a brief affair with a different woman, but he fails at each attempt because of conflicts that arise between him and the female characters. By staging the action in Barney's mother's apartment—Barney expects his mother to be out doing volunteer work twice a week until 5:00 P.M.—Simon underscores the bathetic nature of these abortive encounters, the consummation of any one of which would be a first for Barney. Barney is suffering a certain midlife crisis. Like Sam Nash and Jesse Kiplinger in *Plaza Suite,* Barney senses that life is passing him by too uneventfully: "Life must go on . . . But while it's going on, shouldn't it be better than just 'nice'?" he wonders. Simon explained in his interview with Linderman that this "is a little bit of the way I was feeling when I wrote [the] play because I was then in my early 40s and here was this whole sexual revolution going on, and a lot of it had skipped by me." The sexual politics of *Last of the Red Hot Lovers*—particularly the treatment of male predation, which verges on rape in the final act—now appear highly problematic, however. In this case, as in others, Simon's work reminds us of the radical changes in American sexual mores between the 1960s and the 1990s.

While *Last of the Red Hot Lovers* explores sexual desperation, *The Gingerbread Lady* focuses on Evy Meara's debilitating struggle with alcoholism and her desperate friends' failures to help her. *The Gingerbread Lady* represents one of Simon's few attempts to write predominantly serious plays, but many reviewers and audiences found it too great a departure from Simon's comic style. The 1971 *Life* magazine feature by Richard Meryman detailed the entire rehearsal and production process for the play, which Simon initially intended to close after the out-of-town tryout in Boston. However, he then decided to try to revise the ending to imbue the work with greater optimism, and in doing so, Simon claims, he discovered the principal theme for the play: "For the first time, I saw it was a play about these three adult misfits who somehow managed to screw up their lives. And the only one who had any strength was [Evy's] 17-year-old daughter [Polly] because she had not yet really been kicked around by life. So Evy would derive her strength from the kid at the end of the play.''

Unfortunately, Simon's revision compromised the dramaturgical integrity of the piece, since it called for a predicable final, upbeat scene of reconciliation between mother and daughter—and so further strained the already implausible character of the young woman, Polly, who suffers throughout from irritating perkiness. Robert K. Johnson suggests in his study of Simon that the playwright ''has never . . . created a thoroughly convincing preadult.'' However, the real issue is that Simon cannot fathom or portray young *women:* for example, the character Libby Tucker in *I Ought to Be in Pictures* (1980) is only somewhat more believable than Polly. By contrast, Simon's quasi-autobiographical portrait of Eugene Jerome in the *Brighton Beach* trilogy, as well as the two boys in *Lost in Yonkers,* shows real depth and understanding.

Simon achieved a much better balance of comic and dramatic tones in *The Prisoner of Second Avenue* (1971), a play with ongoing relevance for its revealing examination of the psychological impact of corporate downsizing, especially white-collar unemployment. After losing his job in advertising, Mel Edison becomes a ''prisoner'' in his Manhattan apartment—trapped by the economic impact of his persistent unemployment on his family, its lifestyle, and his sense of self. Simon explores the feelings of emasculation Mel experiences when his wife becomes their sole means of support, and he portrays with grim humor the growing paranoia Mel evinces as he senses that his world is closing in around him. Simon also uses an unusual device to close each scene: a voice-over news report, which emanates from the television, chronicling the deterioration of New York City through crime, unemployment, domestic strife, and other urban ills. *The Prisoner of Second Avenue* thus engages social and

cultural issues that are patently absent from most of Simon's work.

The play also features quintessentially Simonesque running gags, such as the Edisons' ongoing battle with their neighbors over noise, but these gags work successfully and naturally here because they suit the nightmare context of the urban setting. Simon strikes a false note with the introduction of Mel's siblings, who hold a family council about his deteriorating mental condition, but this mistake of Simon's does not detract from the main thrust of the play. *The Prisoner of Second Avenue* is unlike many of Simon's comedies, which seem only to reflect their immediate moment and therefore age poorly. Because it is more fully engaged with depth of character and real, ongoing social issues, *The Prisoner of Second Avenue* emerges as a text worth careful study, one with continuing currency for the theater.

Audiences, critics, and artists alike responded enthusiastically to Simon's 1972 hit *The Sunshine Boys.* As Martin Gottfried noted in his review, with this play Simon had discovered ''a real reason to write a play—an appreciation of old-time comics.'' As with all Simon's plays, the plot here is thin: two elderly vaudeville performers, who have gone their separate ways after the acrimonious dissolution of their act, are asked to reunite for a television special on the history of American comedy. The play chronicles the ups and downs of their reunion. Simon's characters Al Lewis and Willie Clark are closely modeled on the real vaudeville team of Joe Smith and Charlie Dale, who started performing together shortly before World War I. But as Daniel Walden notes in his essay ''Neil Simon's Jewish-Style Comedies,'' Simon's use of the names of the famous American explorers Lewis and Clark also ''reminds us of the great performers of the past and the way they carried on through thick and thin, often beyond the time when they should have quit.'' Smith and Dale were famous for their Dr. Krankheit sketch, and Simon builds a barely disguised version of this comedy routine into his play as the scene the performers must rehearse for the television special.

The Sunshine Boys evolved, Simon explained to Bryer, from Simon's desire "to write . . . about two partners in business"; as "in a lot of [his] plays, [he positioned those] two people . . . in major confrontation with each other, like in *The Odd Couple*." Simon told Bryer that part of his fondness for the "old codgers" he created came from their interaction: "They really didn't know after a while whether what they were saying was funny or was from the act, because they talked in life in the same rhythms that they did in the act for forty-five or fifty years." The realistic relationship between the protagonists, their speech patterns, their background, and the situations in which Simon placed them allows the piece to flow smoothly. The humor of the play appears integral to the characters and action, rather than imposed upon them by the playwright. The integrity of character, dialogue, and theme gives *The Sunshine Boys* a stylistic and structural coherence that is rare in the Simon canon.

Simon's next play, *The Good Doctor* (1973), is an adaptation of short stories by Chekhov. To Linderman Simon acknowledged that he had "always written in the New York idiom, and this [play] gave [him] a chance to deal differently with language." He had been reading Chekhov's story "The Sneeze" during his wife Joan's battle with cancer—as he searched for ways to take his mind away from the pain and stress his family was undergoing—and decided to dramatize some of the Russian writer's fiction as a series of vignettes. However, as he explained to Bryer, he discovered that some of his first vignettes—based directly on Chekhov—didn't play well out of town, "so [he] wrote [his] own Chekhov pieces" to make a full-length production. Edythe McGovern compares Simon to other master playwrights, including Molière, Shaw, and Ben Jonson. But Simon is really not in the same league as any of these writers, nor can he be compared to Chekhov, one of the greatest modern dramatists. *The Good Doctor* is light and whimsical; it features the broad physical comedy that is a Simon trademark, as well as some gentler, character-based humor. But the play reveals none of the depth, precision of dialogue and portraiture, or grasp of cultural context that marks Chekhov's writing as being at the pinnacle of theatrical creativity. Rather, Simon has simply imposed his style on folkloric clichés about Russian character and setting.

His technique in the much later play *Fools* (1981) is remarkably similar, although this play has a single plotline and set of characters as well as a standard two-act structure. In both *Fools* and *The Good Doctor*, Simon uses a narrator figure who addresses the audience directly, standing in for the voice of the playwright. While this technique facilitates some narrative continuity within each play, it is also a sign of Simon's uneasiness with any dramatic material not of his own time and place: writing about a culture or a history that is distant, he seems to feel the need to maintain some special contact with the audience.

Like *The Good Doctor*, *Fools* features a mythologized Russian setting, with clichéd folk characters. Most critics felt Simon was attempting in *Fools* a piece in the mode of Shalom Aleichem, but the result is closer to the superficial American musical theater than to any genuine product of Yiddish culture. Frank Rich, in his review of *Fools*, likened the play to the work of George Abbott, the famous director of splashy Broadway musicals, and T. E. Kalem described *Fools* as "Anatevka-*cum*-Brigadoon." The plot alone suggests the level of humor: a young man arrives to save a village where all the inhabitants believe they live under a curse that makes everyone stupid. Simon does inject a bit of philosophical inquiry into the second act, where he explores the ideology of education and the control of knowledge, but otherwise the play demands little more of the audience than the characters would think they could handle themselves.

In the aftermath of his wife Joan's death in 1973, Simon composed two plays that are very different from one another but equally cathartic: *God's Favorite* (1974) and *Chapter Two* (1977). The first helped Simon confront his loss on religious and mythic (that is, symbolic) levels, while the second was so close to literal autobiography as to verge on "docucomedy." Many critics were baffled by *God's Favorite,* Simon's version of the biblical story of Job; it is probably the least typical of any of Simon's plays. Some critics could only think to compare *God's Favorite* with *J.B.* (1958), the controversial but highly successful Archibald MacLeish dramatization of the same epic. Few found any humor in Simon's contemporary rendition, which is set in the Long Island home of wealthy businessman Joe Benjamin and which depicts Joe's own personal test of faith as a series of increasingly horrific events. The apocalyptic style of *God's Favorite* bears little resemblance to the usual comic realism of Simon's plays. It recalls Thornton Wilder's *The Skin of Our Teeth* (1942), another theatrical extravaganza that questions fate by drawing an analogy between contemporary experience and an Old Testament narrative. But *God's Favorite* is not as masterful as Wilder's play.

In *Chapter Two,* Simon presented in thinly disguised form the more quotidian trials of his courtship and marriage to his second wife, Marsha Mason. As Thomas Meehan observed in 1978:

> Besides being autobiographical, *Chapter Two* is like the best of Simon's earlier comedies in that it is set in New York and is peopled by bright, wisecracking, upwardly mobile Manhattanites, middleaged and middle-class, who . . . are for the most part simply trying to survive modern times and modern marriages in a world they never made.

We can link *Chapter Two* to the other dramas about relationships that also depict segments of Simon's life: *Come Blow Your Horn, Barefoot in the Park,* and sections of the hotel plays, to name just a few. Like *The Odd Couple* and many of Simon's other plays, *Chapter Two* centers on a conflict between two characters. What distinguishes *Chapter Two* from these other plays is that the connection between its creator's life and the world of the play has been obvious to the public from the moment it was first produced. By the time Simon wrote this comedy, he was already well established as America's most prolific and successful dramatist, and Mason was on her way to stardom. That he would share his life with his audience must have had great appeal for them; that he could process the most painful event of his life so publicly suggests a tantalizing psychological insight to those who would analyze Simon's career.

Simon started writing *Brighton Beach Memoirs* (1983) nine years before he finished it—which makes this play the most extreme example of Simon's often lengthy process of composition. He told Bryer that during the interval between beginning and finishing *Brighton Beach Memoirs* "somehow the play had been written in my head" and he finished drafting it very quickly. The timing of its inception should not surprise us: the original idea for the play came to Simon at the same time that Joan became ill and died, a period when Simon was, naturally, reflecting on his own life and hers. Simon had not originally thought of the play as the first in a series; however, he claims that after reading the review of it in the *New York Times* by Frank Rich, who expressed hope for a second installment of the story, Simon decided to write a sequel. The success of *Biloxi Blues* (1985, which won the Tony Award for Best Play), motivated him to continue the saga with *Broadway Bound* (1986).

Simon calls these plays "semi-autobiographical" because, he explained to Lipton, "[They are] based on incidents that happened in my life—but they're not written the way they happened.'' Referring specifically to *Brighton Beach Memoirs* he continued,

> if I [had] meant it to be autobiographical I would have called the [central] character Neil Simon. He's not Neil. He's Eugene Jerome. That gives you greater latitude for fiction. It's like doing abstract painting. You see your own truth in it, but the abstraction is the art.

Simon agreed with a critic who observed that *Brighton Beach Memoirs* is ''about the family I *wished* I'd had instead of the family I *did* have.'' He added, ''It's closer to [Eugene O'Neill's] *Ah, Wilderness* than my reality.'' By the time Simon wrote *Broadway Bound,* both his parents had passed away, and he felt he could be more honest about his family life: ''I didn't pull any punches with that one,'' he told Lipton.

The three semi-autobiographical plays cover the period of time preceding the moment represented by *Come Blow Your Horn.* But they feel like they are about a more distant time because the playwright imbues them with such nostalgia for the bittersweet era of his youth. *Brighton Beach Memoirs* dramatizes Eugene Jerome's adolescence, with particular emphasis on his developing sense of sexuality—hardly a surprising narrative line for a Simon play. *Biloxi Blues* chronicles what happens when Eugene enlists in the army during World War II and goes to Biloxi, Mississippi, for basic training. *Broadway Bound* returns us to New York and focuses on the early attempts of Eugene and his brother, Stan, to break into show business.

The trilogy represents Simon's first overt dramatization of ethnicity and its connection to politics and history. Eugene's mother reminisces about her family's heritage; referring to *her* mother, she recalls,

> The day they packed up and left the house in Russia, she cleaned the place from top to bottom. She

said, ''No matter what the Cossacks did to us, when they broke into our house, they would have respect for the Jews.''

Because World War II is the backdrop to *Brighton Beach Memoirs* we learn about other family members escaping persecution in Poland. In *Biloxi Blues,* we are made aware of prejudice at home: Eugene observes both anti-Semitism and homophobia in the American military. The final installment of the trilogy stresses financial disparities in postwar America. Simon introduces a new character, Eugene's ''Grandpa,'' Ben, as the voice of class consciousness; thus he makes *Broadway Bound* strongly echo Clifford Odets' *Awake and Sing!* (1935) through the use of a grandfather character with beliefs reminiscent of the socialist ideology of the time.

When Eugene and Stan's first successful writing effort is broadcast on the radio, Simon interjects this telling exchange between the younger writer and his grandfather:

BEN: To me, comedy has to have a point. What was the point of this?
EUGENE: To make people laugh.
BEN: That's not a point. To make people *aware,* that's a point. Political satire, that's what you should have written. You could change half the world with political satire. Think about that sometime.
EUGENE: Political satire? We're lucky we came up with a few good jokes.

With this, Simon seems to be answering all those critics who wish he were a writer more engaged with politics than ''mere'' entertainment. A few moments later, Eugene also reveals what underlies much of his humor: about one part of a sketch he wrote with Stan he acknowledges, ''To me it was just a joke. . . . Only I didn't know I was so angry.'' Indeed, much of Simon's writing seems rooted in anger, particularly at the unhappy home that, ironically, sparked his creativity.

Although Simon claims that *Lost in Yonkers*—which was produced five years after *Broadway*

588 / AMERICAN WRITERS

Bound—is not one of his semi-autobiographical plays, it shares a biographical foundation with the pieces in his trilogy. Like Arty and Jay Kurnitz, he and his brother "were parceled out to live with relatives when their parents separated." And as in the three plays about Eugene Jerome, *Lost in Yonkers* is set during World War II, which allows Simon to allude in it to the history of American Jews, to the Holocaust, and to the culture from which he emerged. Here again, though, politics is not really at the fore. Gene Saks, who directed the first production of *Lost in Yonkers,* pointed out to Richard David Story: "You could say the play's about a lot of things. . . . But Neil's not making a case for a play about social issues." He added, "What we're both interested in is how human beings affect each other." Simon told Lipton that he liked to think of the characters in *Lost in Yonkers* as "Dickensian," but he may have granted them a bit too much literary value. Rather, one might say that Simon created with this play his best fusion to date of character-based comic drama, American history, and social commentary. This combination positioned the play well within the conventions of American theater and helped it earn the Pulitzer Prize for drama in 1991.

Since his phenomenal success with the trilogy and *Lost in Yonkers,* Simon has continued to produce at his usual pace, generating three new plays (*Jake's Women* [1992], *Laughter on the 23rd Floor* [1993], and *London Suite* [1995]), a musical (the adaptation of his own film, *The Goodbye Girl* [1993]), an original screenplay (the disastrous *Marrying Man* [1991]), and the screen adaptation of *Lost in Yonkers* (1992). Most of these projects have not been as successful as his endeavors of the mid-1980s, but the work is all of a piece with everything Simon has produced previously in his career: it all draws on his own personal experience.

Jake's Women could just as well have been called "Doc's Women." Once again employing a writer/narrator figure as the title character, Simon builds a play around what are essentially memories and fantasies of a man's relationships with various types of women: wives, a daughter, a sister, a girlfriend, a psychiatrist. The play is extremely self-referential and self-conscious; for example, when wife Maggie explains that she is leaving Jake, she remarks, "We started off with a marriage and ended up with a monologue," a line that obviously alludes to the fact that Simon routinely dramatizes details from his life.

The play has an interesting premise: Jake compulsively writes scenarios about the women in his life, but the women always retain a certain autonomy and turn the scenes to their own purposes, in a fashion again reminiscent of Pirandello. Jake's sister Karen, for example, segues seamlessly from sympathetically commiserating with Jake on the death of his first wife to the remark: "This is another good speech. Give me more lines like this. This is a woman you could like." Yet after a while, the novelty of this dramaturgical technique wears off, and Simon seems to have nowhere to go with his plot, ending the play on a contrived, optimistic note. Simon came close to abandoning the piece after an initial tryout proved a dismal failure, but after substantial revision and recasting, he brought the play to Broadway. Like *The Gingerbread Lady* and *God's Favorite, Jake's Women* struck many as atypical Simon, and the critical views were decidedly mixed. Nevertheless, the play demonstrates that Simon was still in the 1990s exploring dramatic form, even within the parameters of autobiography, geography, and the themes that have dominated his career.

Over the years, Simon has cultivated and expanded the audience for his stage plays in part through his work in other media, specifically the musical theater and film. These other forms share the distinction of being collaborative in a way that Simon's dramatic work is not. When Simon signs on to a musical, he joins a composer and lyricist, his contribution being the "book" (the spoken dialogue). In the movies, Simon's screenplays provide plot and language; the major impact of a film, however, derives from the way it is directed and edited. In interviews, Simon expresses a primarily negative opinion of his participation in such collaborative ventures; he says that he feels that a great deal of time goes into work that ultimately displays comparatively little of his input. He told Bryer, "I would say, generally speaking, that when a play opens, 95 percent of what's up there is what I approved of. With a film, I'm at the mercy of the director, and what comes out on the screen is about 10 percent of what I approved of." Simon claims to prefer writing original screenplays to adapting his own drama for the cinema but says he finally enjoys writing for the theater most. In his 1979 interview with Linderman he avowed, "Playwriting is still the most important aspect of my life, because when I'm writing a play, what I visualize is exactly what the audience sees. Unless you direct a film, it's really out of your hands." Nevertheless, between 1963 and 1992, Simon generated 24 screenplays, earning four Oscar nominations—for *The Odd Couple, The Sunshine Boys, California Suite,* and *The Goodbye Girl.*

Although Simon has worked on fewer musicals, his feelings about that experience seem to be remarkably similar to those he expresses about film. Much of his frustration with musicals is directly related to his dramaturgical process—specifically his penchant for revision. He told Reed Johnson in an interview in 1995, "A musical takes two years of your time, and it's not your show. I really don't feel like collaborating anymore. If a song doesn't work, I can't fix it; if a lyric doesn't work, I can't fix it."

Despite his negative feelings, Simon's achievement in both musicals and film is noteworthy.

The musical *They're Playing Our Song* (1979) and the film *The Heartbreak Kid* (1973)—to give just two examples—have already achieved "classic" status. Much of Simon's work in each field has proven to be highly rewarding artistically for the actors, directors, and creative staff involved in the projects. However, the collaborative nature of both film and musical theater requires that a critic who would assess Simon's achievement in these areas analyze more than just the book or screenplay by Simon; these aspects of his career remain virtually uncharted.

Simon's status as a comic playwright is unparalleled, yet this categorization has also diminished his work in the eyes of many critics who believe that only serious drama proves dramaturgical skill and artistic merit. An examination of Simon's plays, however, shows the evolution of his comedic techniques toward a more nuanced form of humor, which Simon himself readily acknowledges. He has long been aware and slightly resentful of the critics' dismissing him specifically because he writes comedy. To Bryer he claimed he "wanted to write . . . drama and tell it as comedy" and that he is "always looking for a comic idea that has a dramatic subtext to it." But he has also realized he cannot control his audience or the critical response he gets. He explained to Erstein that even though he felt *Plaza Suite,* for example, "was serious, it was getting more laughs than I wanted it to get. Sometimes I write funny without meaning to write funny."

Early in his career, Simon earned a reputation as a "gag factory" and a "joke machine," which is directly attributable to his work as a comedy writer in television. Zimmerman made that connection in his review of *Last of the Red Hot Lovers:* he pointed out that "Doc['s] . . . ability to string together four or five laugh lines with seeming ease . . . has survived in Simon the playwright." Alan Levy highlighted another Simon "trademark," "repetition," which is related to the use of "runs"; that is, sustained comic bits that build momentum through repetition. One of the clearest examples of such a "run" comes in *Barefoot in the Park,* where Simon has character after character enter out of breath from having climbed six flights of stairs. Tom Prideaux noted that Simon often uses gags "to build up character." Gerald Berkowitz, on the other hand, suggested that:

> Simon is at his best, and safest, when he sticks to the surface. The characters, events and dialogue of his plays are there to produce laughter, and they rarely get more complex or sharply drawn than is necessary to that end. Certainly Simon never seems overly concerned about realism of characterization. Almost every play has its resident caricature.

The diverging views of Prideaux and Berkowitz represent the range of criticism Simon got early on in his theatrical career—critical differences that followed his writing until the appearance of the *Brighton Beach* trilogy.

The central issue appears to be how critics perceive the balance between serious matters and comedic form, dialogue, and situation in Simon's work. The view of Jack Kroll, expressed in a 1974 review of *God's Favorite,* is condescending in a way that is typical of many critics:

> As with all funny guys, Simon's real subject is the pain of it all. But . . . he does not detonate human experience into grenades of laughter whose shrapnel rips up the pomposity of homo sap. Instead, Simon trivializes experience with a shower of one-liners that tickle, sometimes hit a vulnerable spot, but never draw blood.

When Simon was awarded the Pulitzer Prize for *Lost In Yonkers* in 1991, though, a strategic shift took place in the critical reception of his work. Critics began to take a tone of more uniform praise, in keeping with the dramaturgical cohesivness found in the style, theme, action, and characters of these plays. Significantly, perhaps, this critical transition coincided with Simon's decision to portray more fully and explicitly his class background and ethnicity, specifically his Jewish cultural heritage. The plays based on his family history—*Brighton Beach Memoirs, Biloxi Blues,* and *Broadway Bound*—reveal Simon's ability to reach a level of poignancy absent in his earlier work.

For decades Simon's critics have claimed that Simon's characters are just like the types of people who make up his audience. But the critics have also made the somewhat contradictory assertion that Simon's plays are universal in their appeal. Zimmerman expressed a widely held view when he wrote, "You don't have to be Jewish to love Neil Simon because, for all the ethnic center of gravity in his plays, his characters speak a language open to all." Meehan, however—challenging the notion that "Simon deliberately panders to the Broadway audience by writing only about people they can identify with"—argued that Simon "writes about such people because of who he is." Meehan suggests that Simon's concerns naturally resonate with those of his audience precisely because he and they do have much in common, specifically cultural and ethnic heritage.

Early in his career, Simon claimed to Erstein he shied away from ethnic specificity in his plays because he was advised to by the producer Saint-Subber. "He used to talk to me about archaic terms like 'the carriage trade.' He said the carriage trade wouldn't like this, saying they seemed Jewish. So 'Barefoot in the Park,' for instance, turns out to be neuter in a way. It's neither Jewish nor gentile. . . . But when I got to plays that it mattered that they were Jewish and I didn't say it, then I think I was couching it a little bit. Playing it safe." For his later plays, Simon has drawn directly on Jewish culture, and his audiences have been highly receptive. Speaking of the trilogy and its companion piece, *Lost in Yonkers,*

Simon acknowledged to Bryer, "[T]he humor comes out of the Jewish culture as I know it." He added, however, that he was unconscious of invoking his Jewishness when he wrote those plays. Rather, he said, "[The culture is] so deeply embedded in me and so inherent in me that I am unaware of its quality." Jewish ethnicity simply inheres in his writing, and is often represented most fully by actors who also derive from this heritage.

There are a few scholarly pieces that focus on Jewish culture in Simon's plays, including two by Daniel Walden: "Neil Simon: Toward Act III?" (1980) and "Neil Simon's Jewish-Style Comedies" (1983). What seems key to contemporary critical perspectives on this topic is a re-examination of the concept of "universal" as it is applied to the drama, coupled with an analysis of the audiences for Simon's work. Given the increasingly narrow subset of Americans who attend the theater, and the belief by many that a significant portion of that audience comprises people of Jewish background, it seems problematic to speak of universals. It is equally important to understand how the theater audience has evolved with regard to a number of parameters, including class, race, ethnicity, and gender, among others. In other words, the invocation of the term "universal" can be seen to be quite exclusive, as historically it included only those who are Caucasian of middle- to upper-class status and of European heritage. What is eminently clear is that Simon appeals strongly to his audience, and that, for the most part, his drama resonates with their interests, outlook, and values. Whether this resonance can be applied more broadly—into the realm of what is genuinely "universal"—remains to be firmly established.

In any event, it appears that, over the decades, Simon has developed a loyal audience—one that *may* identify with his characters' ethnicity or perhaps *may* respond to the "universals" he dramatizes, such as "leaving home, falling in love,

being unfaithful" (typical plot developments in his plays pointed out by Bosworth). In interviews, Simon repeats an anecdote from early in his career about an "elderly Negro porter" backstage at *Come Blow Your Horn,* who "howl[ed] with glee" at the play because the character of the father was identical to his own. For Simon, such events demonstrate the broad appeal of his work—which is also borne out by the international success of his plays.

It seems fitting to end this examination of Neil Simon by looking at *Laughter on the 23rd Floor.* Here Simon looked back to the beginning of his career, to his days as a staff writer for Sid Caesar. Simon dedicated the work "To Sid Caesar and the Writers: Mel Brooks, Mel Tolkin, Larry Gelbart, Sheldon Keller, Danny Simon, Gary Belkin, Lucille Kallen, Selma Diamond, Tony Webster, Carl Reiner, and all the others I've missed." When one reads this list of names and thinks of the subsequent (meteoric) careers of artists like Brooks, Gelbart, and Reiner, one realizes how remarkable—and crazy—the environment was in which Simon did his apprenticeship. Unfortunately, he was not fully capable of capturing the manic quality of this world in the play, in part because he had never learned how to orchestrate group comedy (e.g., *Rumors*) successfully, his forte remaining the two-character comic agon. While it is tempting to focus on trying to match the identities of Simon's former colleagues to the characters in the play, it is clear that Simon's emphasis was not on individuals but on the ensemble. One consequence is that *Laughter on the 23rd Floor* is more heavily dependent on staging and acting than many of Simon's other plays, which are humorously effective even for the reader.

Perhaps most frustrating here, however, is Simon's tap dance around the serious historical issue of McCarthyism, which he uses to frame the action by having his characters repeatedly express concern over McCarthyism's rampant blacklisting and accusations of communist sympathies. The disastrous impact of anticommunist fervor on the American entertainment industry in the 1950s is legendary. Simon had the opportunity to fully engage a political conflict that was integral both to his own personal story, in terms of his close working relationship with many artists who came under government scrutiny, suspicion, or persecution, and to the history of his profession, but he chose only to touch upon it, despite its real relevance to those upon whom the play is based.

Since Simon has explored so much of his own biography in the theater, it remains to be seen where his theatrical imagination will take him. Perhaps that direction depends on what Simon has left to be angry about.

Selected Bibliography

WORKS OF NEIL SIMON

PLAYS

Bibliographical note: Most of Simon's theatrical work exists in acting editions published by Samuel French. However, for scholarly purposes, the trade editions are preferable. French editions will be cited only when no other version is available.

Come Blow Your Horn. Garden City, N.Y.: Doubleday, 1963.

Barefoot in the Park. New York: Random House, 1964.

The Odd Couple. New York: Random House, 1966.

The Star-Spangled Girl. New York: Random House, 1967.

Plaza Suite. New York: Random House, 1969.

Last of the Red Hot Lovers. New York: Random House, 1970.

The Gingerbread Lady. New York: Random House, 1971.

The Prisoner of Second Avenue. New York: Random House, 1972.

The Sunshine Boys. New York: Random House, 1973.

The Good Doctor. New York: Random House, 1974.

God's Favorite. New York: Random House, 1975.

California Suite. New York: Random House, 1977.

Chapter Two. New York: Random House, 1979.

I Ought to Be in Pictures. New York: Random House, 1981.

Fools: A Comic Fable. New York: Random House, 1981.

Brighton Beach Memoirs. New York: Random House, 1984.

Biloxi Blues. New York: Random House, 1985.

Broadway Bound. New York: Random House, 1987.

Rumors: A Farce. New York: Random House, 1990.

Lost in Yonkers. New York: Random House, 1991.

Jake's Women. New York: Random House, 1994.

Laughter on the 23rd Floor. New York: Random House, 1995.

London Suite. 1995.

COLLECTED PLAYS

The Comedy of Neil Simon. New York: Random House, 1971.

The Collected Plays of Neil Simon. Vol. 2. New York: Random House, 1979.

The Collected Plays of Neil Simon. Vol. 3. New York: Random House, 1991.

MUSICALS

Adventures of Marco Polo: A Musical Fantasy. Written in collaboration with William Friedberg. Music by Clay Warnick and Mel Pahl. New York: Samuel French, 1959.

Heidi. Written in collaboration with William Friedberg. Adapted from the novel by Johanna Spyri. Music by Clay Warnick. New York: Samuel French, 1959.

Little Me. Adapted from the novel by Patrick Dennis. Music by Cy Coleman. Lyrics by Carolyn Leigh. In *The Collected Plays of Neil Simon. Volume 2.* Revised version, 1982.

Sweet Charity. Based on the screenplay *Nights of Cabiria* by Federico Fellini, Tullio Pinelli, and Ennio Flaiano. Music by Cy Coleman. Lyrics by Dorothy Fields. New York: Random House, 1966.

Promises, Promises. Based on the screenplay *The Apartment* by Billy Wilder and I. A. L. Diamond.

Music by Burt Bachrach. Lyrics by Hal David. New York: Random House, 1969.

They're Playing Our Song. Music by Marvin Hamlisch. Lyrics by Carol Bayer Sager. New York: Random House, 1980.

The Goodbye Girl. Music by Marvin Hamlisch. Lyrics by David Zippel. 1993.

SCREENPLAYS

After the Fox. 1966.
Barefoot in the Park. 1967.
The Odd Couple. 1968.
The Out-of-Towners. 1970.
Plaza Suite. 1971.
The Last of the Red Hot Lovers. 1972.
The Heartbreak Kid. 1973.
The Prisoner of Second Avenue. 1975.
The Sunshine Boys. 1975.
Murder by Death. 1976.
The Goodbye Girl. 1977.
The Cheap Detective. 1978.
California Suite. 1978.
Chapter Two. 1979.
Seems Like Old Times. 1980.
Only When I Laugh. 1981.
I Ought to Be in Pictures. 1982.
Max Dugan Returns. 1983.
Lonely Guy. 1984.
The Slugger's Wife. 1984.
Brighton Beach Memoirs. 1986.
Biloxi Blues. 1988.
The Marrying Man. 1991.
Lost in Yonkers. 1992.

CRITICAL STUDIES

Barber, Rowland. "A Californian Named Neil Simon Heads for Broadway." *New York Times,* June 6, 1976.

Berkowitz, Gerald M. "Neil Simon and His Amazing Laugh Machine." *Players,* 47:111–13 (February 1972).

Bosworth, Patricia. "Simon Says." *Vanity Fair,* May 1988.

Erstein, Hap. "King of Comedy's Serious Work." *Insight,* March 18, 1991, pp. 56–57.

Gilman, Richard. "The Human Comedian." *Newsweek,* January 9, 1967, pp. 70–71.

Gottfried, Martin. "Theatre: 'The Sunshine Boys.' " *Women's Wear Daily,* December 22, 1972.

Henry, William A., III. "Reliving a Poignant Past." *Time,* December 15, 1986, pp. 72–78.

"In the Works." *New York Times Magazine.* Part 2, *The New Season,* September 11, 1988.

Johnson, Reed. "High Comedy." *Detroit News,* January 6, 1995.

Johnson, Robert K. *Neil Simon.* Boston: Twayne, 1983.

Kalem, T. E. "Nudniks." *Time,* April 20, 1981.

Kerr, Walter. "The Theater: Neil Simon's 'Star-Spangled Girl.' " *New York Times,* December 22, 1966.

———. "What Simon Says." *New York Times Magazine,* March 22, 1970.

Kissel, Howard. " 'The Odd Couple.' " *Women's Wear Daily,* June 12, 1985.

Kroll, Jack. "The Patience of Joe." *Newsweek,* December 23, 1974, p. 56.

Levy, Alan. "Doc Simon's Rx for Comedy." *New York Times Magazine,* March 7, 1965.

McGovern, Edythe M. *Not-So-Simple Neil Simon: A Critical Study.* Van Nuys, Calif.: Perivale Press, 1978.

McMahon, Helen. "A Rhetoric of American Popular Drama: The Comedies of Neil Simon." *Players,* 51:10–15 (October–November 1975).

Meehan, Thomas. "The Unreal, Hilarious World of Neil Simon." *Horizon* 21:70–74 (January 1978).

Meryman, Richard. "When the Funniest Writer in America Tried to Be Serious." *Life,* May 7, 1971.

Prideaux, Tom. "The Odd Couple." *Life,* April 9, 1965.

Rich, Frank. "Theater: 'Fools' by Simon." *New York Times,* April 7, 1981.

Richards, David. "The Last of the Red Hot Playwrights." *New York Times Magazine,* February 17, 1991.

Sommers, Michael. "Simon Suite." *Sunday Star Ledger,* April 2, 1995.

Sterritt, David. "Off Screen, Neil Simon Offers Gentle Quips Rather than Barbed One-Liners." *Christian Science Monitor,* April 29, 1985.

Story, Richard David. "Broadway Rebound." *New York,* February 18, 1991, pp. 47–51.

Walden, Daniel. "Neil Simon's Jewish-Style Comedies." In *From Hester Street to Hollywood: The Jewish-American Stage and Screen,* edited by

Sarah Blacher Cohen. Bloomington: Indiana University Press, 1993. Pp. 152–166.

———. "Neil Simon: Toward Act III?" *MELUS,* 7, no. 2:77–86 (1980).

Winer, Linda. "On Stage: A Snappy Female 'Odd Couple.' " *USA Today,* June 12, 1985.

Zimmerman, Paul D. "Neil Simon: Up from Success." *Newsweek,* February 2, 1970, pp. 52–56.

INTERVIEWS

Bryer, Jackson R. "An Interview with Neil Simon." *Studies in American Drama, 1945–Present,* 6, no. 2:153–176 (1991).

———. "Neil Simon." In *The Playwright's Art: Conversations with Contemporary American Dramatists.* Edited by Jackson R. Bryer. New Brunswick, N.J.: Rutgers University Press, 1995. Pp. 221–240.

"Dialogue on Film: Neil Simon." *American Film,* 3:33–48 (March 1978).

Hirschhorn, Clive. "Make 'Em Laugh: Neil Simon in Interview." *Plays and Players,* 24:12–15 (September 1977).

Linderman, Lawrence. "Neil Simon: A Candid Conversation about Humor and Success with the Sunshine Playwright." *Playboy,* February 1979.

Lipton, James. "Neil Simon: The Art of Theater X." *Paris Review,* 34:166–213 (Winter 1992).

The author wishes to express gratitude to Simon's publicist, Bill Evans, for providing information on the playwright; to Sherry Keller for her research assistance; and to David Faulkner for his editorial suggestions.

—J. ELLEN GAINOR

Wallace Stegner

1909–1993

WALLACE STEGNER LEFT behind him a written legacy that few writers have matched. A true man of letters, he earned acclaim during his eighty-four years as a short-story writer, essayist, novelist, historian, biographer, autobiographer, critic, and teacher. Along the way, among other awards, he received the O'Henry Memorial Award for short stories (three times), the Pulitzer Prize, the National Book Award, and the *Los Angeles Times'* Robert Kirsch Award for lifetime literary achievement. Of course, these facts are the superficial markers of a fruitful career. What we want is the life and thought of Wallace Stegner the artist.

Better to begin with the text that might be thought of as the "continental divide" in Stegner's literary geography, *Wolf Willow: A History, a Story, and a Memory of the Last Plains Frontier.* Published in 1962, at the midpoint of his publishing career, *Wolf Willow* records the history of the region where Stegner spent his formative years (from ages five to twelve). It provides not only a sampling of the various genres within which Stegner wrote but also an exposure to the prominent themes running through much of his work: the search for identity and origins, the need for historical continuity, the importance of place and of community, the relationship between human beings and the land, and the West as a shaping environment. The subtitle of the book—"A History, a Story, and a Memory of the Last Plains Frontier"—serves nicely to structure our discussion. In Stegner's writing the three categories of history, story, and memory do not represent clear-cut divisions in his thinking, but rather strands consciously interwoven to create as nearly as possible a "true" picture of individual and cultural identity.

Turning to Stegner's essay "Fiction: A Lens on Life" (in *One Way to Spell Man,* 1982), we might also add a fourth category: concept. Stegner argues that a "serious fiction writer . . . is not a dealer in concepts." But Stegner the essay writer *is* such a dealer. He puts forward such ideas as that found in "Born a Square" (in *The Sound of Mountain Water,* 1969): the western writer is in a box "booby-trapped at one end by an inadequate artistic and intellectual tradition, and at the other end by the coercive dominance of attitudes, beliefs, and intellectual fads and manners destructive of his own." Or, as an advocate for environmental preservation, he asserts: "We simply need that wild country available to us, even if we never do more than drive to its edge and look in. For it can be a means of reassuring ourselves of our sanity as creatures, a part of the geography of hope" ("Coda: Wilderness Letter" in *The Sound of Mountain Water*). Or, as a self-reflective writer, he proclaims: "A writer . . . is a synthesizer, a blender, and everything he has ever heard or seen or read or known is potentially there, available for the creation of his story'' (''On Steinbeck's Story 'Flight' '' in *Where the Bluebird Sings to the Lemonade Springs,* 1992). But rather than open a fourth category and plumb Stegner's essays in their own right, I'll take Stegner at his word when he says the writer's ''ideas, the generalizations, ought to be implicit in the selection and arrangement of the people and places and actions'' in his fiction (''Fiction: A Lens on Life'').

As Merrill and Lorene Lewis have pointed out, the ''quest for identity, personal and regional, artistic and cultural'' has been at the center of Stegner's writing. It would be more accurate to say that his central concern is to construct a *unified* identity. In a discussion of Wallace Earle Stegner the continental divide is an apt metaphor. As Stegner points out in *Wolf Willow,* the divide does not merely send continental waters flowing in different directions; it separates histories, tribes, and cultures. Stegner grew up on the divide formed by the Cypress Hills region of Saskatchewan, where his family settled in 1914 when he was five years old. Stegner himself was marked by the divide in ways that would remain with him. In his writing, divides mark the line between West and East, frontier and civilization, America and Europe, youth and age, masculine and feminine, wilderness and development.

All these dichotomies might be subsumed under two. First is the divide between past and present. Growing up in the West, Stegner always felt as though he had no ''usable past'' to draw upon, to use the phrase he borrowed from Nathaniel Hawthorne. In a sense, living in a frontier culture in the twentieth century, his present was already past or, rather, the past was his present. In 1893, Frederick Jackson Turner had already declared the American frontier closed. Yet, as a boy in Canada, Stegner was living a frontier existence. Moreover, the history taught to a frontier boy like himself was always imported from the centers of civilization, disconnected from the life he was living. Much of his work aims to create some sense of continuity between past and present.

The second great divide thematized in his work separates two opposing ways of life on the American frontier. On the one hand are those people inspired by the vastness of the West and a usually unrealistic dream of riches, the energetic individualists, contemptuous of the law, who in their pursuit of the life of ease often become the land's rapers and pillagers. On the other hand are those people, like the Mormons, who settle the land in cooperative groups. They bring civilization but also the danger of an ordering impulse so strong as to stifle individual action and imagination. Both groups share an unbounded faith in progress' taming hand. Both are often disappointed by an unforgiving environment that resembles in very few ways the eastern regions of the United States—from which both kinds of settlers take their models for settlement. Stegner finds the archetypes for the two groups in his father and mother, George Stegner and Hilda Paulson, his prototypes for Bo and Elsa Mason of *The Big Rock Candy Mountain* (1943).

Stegner appreciates the positive traits of both his individualistic father and his community-minded mother, but he leans toward the latter. He knows that to survive in the West one must learn the importance of cooperation and cherish the benefits of home and community. Still, his father and what he represents never completely relinquish their hold on Stegner's imagination. Throughout his career, he grapples with his attraction to elements of both worldviews and strives to find harmony between the two.

Ultimately, Stegner's two thematic projects may be one. As he says in ''History, Myth, and the Western Writer'' (in *The Sound of Mountain Water*), ''In a way, the dichotomy between the past and present is a product of two forces frequently encountered in both western fiction and the Western: the freedom-loving, roving man and the civilizing woman.'' In Stegner's own work, to find a way to harmonize the perspectives passed on to him by his parents would also be to make clear, if not smooth, his own path from innocent, ''savage'' youth to worldly, wise, cultured adulthood.

Wolf Willow begins in the realm of individual memory. Although Stegner tells Richard Etulain that the autobiographical elements in *Wolf Willow* are adjunct to the historical thrust of the work, he underscores the importance of individual memory in a passage ringing with the lyricism of William Wordsworth, Ralph Waldo Emerson, and Walt Whitman:

> Lying on a hillside where I once sprawled among the crocuses . . . I feel how the world still reduces me to a point and then measures itself from me. Perhaps the meadowlark singing from a fence post—a meadowlark whose dialect I recognize—feels the same way. All points on the circumference are equidistant from him; in him all radii begin; all diameters run through him; if he moves, a new geometry creates itself around him.

The circular imagery points us to the chapter's title, ''The Question Mark in the Circle.'' Paradoxically, at the center of the circle, Stegner is both the source of order and the void. In *The Writer in America* (1952), Stegner says that it is the job of the artist ''to bring order where no order was before him.'' Stegner's double task is to fill the void and to give it order.

During his first five years, young Stegner had already experienced much that would find its way into his writing, most important, the tension between the two very different approaches to living embodied in his father and mother. George was the embodiment of the restless mobility enforced by the western environment, a gambler, a bootlegger, a ''boomer,'' pursuing one fading mirage of the American dream after another; Hilda

longed for nothing more than a stable home within a community in which she could raise her children.

Wallace Stegner was born February 18, 1909, in Lake Mills, Iowa, when his parents, who were living at that time in North Dakota, were visiting the home of Hilda's parents. The family migrated from North Dakota, where George and Hilda had met and married, to the Seattle area when Stegner was about two and a half years old. When George's plans to take the family to Alaska to cash in on the gold rush fell through, he and Hilda split up for a time. In 1913, Hilda's best option seemed to be to put her two sons in an orphanage. Eventually, dissatisfied with the home's treatment of her children, she removed them and retreated to her father's home in Lake Mills.

Eventually, George lured Hilda to an uneasy reconciliation in Saskatchewan with what would later prove to be a false vision of rootedness. There, in the ''raw new non-town of Eastend,'' Stegner tells us in ''Finding the Place: A Migrant Childhood'' (in *Where the Bluebird Sings*), ''the real film [of memory] begins . . . the shaping years of my life.'' These first years he would eventually flesh out in the semiautobiographical *The Big Rock Candy Mountain.* By age eleven, when the Stegners left Eastend, Stegner had experienced one-half of his divided identity—the half molded by the primitive, uncultured existence of frontier life, the hardships of land and climate. During his Canadian years, listening to the wild ''moan and mourn,'' Stegner says in ''Finding the Place,'' that he learned that ''as surely as any pullet in the yard, I was a target.''

For the life emerging from those early years, aside from Stegner's own writings, the principal biographical sources are Merrill and Lorene Lewis' brief monograph for the Western Writers Series (1972), Forrest G. and Margaret G. Robinson's addition to Twayne's United States Authors Series (1977), and Etulain's interviews

(1983). As for Stegner's own writings, both non-fiction and fiction have something to contribute. Most of what passes for nonfictional autobiography is found in the hard-to-classify *Wolf Willow* and in various essays, many of which have been collected in *The Sound of Mountain Water* and *Where the Bluebird Sings to the Lemonade Springs*. (The essays of *One Way to Spell Man* focus on the craft of writing and on the West and its artists.)

Briefly, the facts are these. Following the Stegners' six years in Saskatchewan and a stopover in Great Falls, Montana, they headed to Salt Lake City in 1921. This move marked the break from the provincial life of the frontier to the civilized life of a more urban setting, which meant two things for young Stegner. First, it was the chance to belong to a stable community, despite his family's moving between countless different Salt Lake homes in the span of nine years. Mormon society did not appeal to Stegner on religious grounds, but the Mormon social life open to non-Mormons touched Stegner's need for human connection. Second, though it was not New York or San Francisco, Salt Lake City provided culture and the chance to join the larger world. As a young boy, small and picked on, Stegner had taken refuge in libraries. Salt Lake City offered an environment more favorable to his contemplative temperament than life on the frontier.

Eventually, the University of Utah, which he entered in 1925 at the age of sixteen, pointed him in the direction of a literary career. There, in freshman English, he studied with the novelist Vardis Fisher. Upon graduating in 1930, Stegner followed the opportunity that dropped into his lap and entered the graduate program in English at the University of Iowa, where Norman Foerster had just set up the School of Letters. Under this program one could get a master's degree by writing a creative project. Stegner's thesis consisted of three short stories.

Although this period in his life witnessed rapid personal growth and much success, it was also marred by family tragedy. He had already pulled up roots during his sophomore year, following his parents to Los Angeles and enrolling briefly at the University of California at Los Angeles. He returned to the University of Utah, however, and in the same year that he finished his degree at Utah and entered Iowa, his brother, Cecil, died suddenly of pneumonia. In the midst of his graduate program, Hilda became ill with cancer, so in 1932, after two years at Iowa and a period at the University of California at Berkeley (where he had enrolled to be closer to his ailing mother), Stegner left school to join his parents. In 1933 Hilda died after a protracted period of suffering, leaving Stegner greatly angered at what he perceived to be his father's inadequate response to his mother's ordeal. He relived and attempted to work through much of this episode in *The Big Rock Candy Mountain* and, later, in *Recapitulation* (1979).

Upon returning to Iowa in 1934, Stegner married Mary Stuart Page and took a teaching job at Augustana College in Rock Island, Illinois. Offered a position at the University of Utah in 1935, Wallace took his new bride back to Salt Lake City, where he completed his degree with a dissertation on one of John Wesley Powell's fellow explorers, the literary naturalist Clarence Earl Dutton.

Stegner launched his literary career by winning the Little, Brown novelette prize with *Remembering Laughter* in 1937 and started his family with the birth of his only child, a son, Page. A teaching job at the University of Wisconsin followed. He also chose this time of transition to begin his first big novel, *The Big Rock Candy Mountain*. Within the next five years he published one novella, *The Potter's House* (1938); two short novels, *On a Darkling Plain* (1940) and *Fire and Ice* (1941); and one history, *Mormon Country* (1942) before bringing out his first major novel.

During this same period (in 1939), Stegner was also invited to teach at Middlebury College's Breadloaf writers' conference in Vermont, where he formed lasting friendships with Bernard De-Voto and Robert Frost. That same year he purchased the Vermont farm in Greensboro that became a summer refuge for him and his wife for much of the rest of his life. The year 1940 was another with high and low points. Stegner was hired for the Harvard creative writing program, but that same year his father committed suicide. In 1943 Stegner published *The Big Rock Candy Mountain,* his biggest and best novel to date, and in 1944 he acted on his success, leaving Harvard to work on a series on racial and religious intolerance for *Look* magazine, an assignment that became, instead, the book *One Nation* (1945). For this work Stegner received the Anisfield-Wolfe Award for best book of the year on race relations.

In 1945 Stegner was appointed to the English Department at Stanford University in Palo Alto, California, where he founded the highly successful Stanford Creative Writing Program. With this move Stegner satisfied his longing to return to the West and found long-term stability, maintaining his home in Los Altos, California, until his death in 1993. Stanford provided what most writers need: the economic freedom and intellectual support necessary to write. Along with the Pulitzer Prize–winning *Angle of Repose* (1971) and the National Book Award–winning *Spectator Bird* (1976), Stegner published during his time at Stanford the novels *Second Growth* (1947), *The Preacher and the Slave* (1950) (reissued in 1969 as *Joe Hill: A Biographical Novel*), *A Shooting Star* (1961), *All the Little Live Things* (1967), and *Crossing to Safety* (1987). His two books of short stories, *The Women on the Wall* (1950) and *The City of the Living and Other Stories* (1956) (all of which were gathered together in 1990 as *Collected Stories of Wallace Stegner*), also came out after his appointment to Stanford. His pri-

mary histories and biographies published after 1945 include *Beyond the Hundredth Meridian: John Wesley Powell and the Second Opening of the West* (1954), *The Gathering of Zion: The Story of the Mormon Trail* (1964), and his biography of Bernard DeVoto, *The Uneasy Chair* (1974).

Throughout his life Stegner also satisfied his own version of the wanderlust he inherited from his father. A Rockefeller Fellowship funded a worldwide tour in 1950–1951. His visit to Japan on this trip resulted in the publication of *The Writer in America,* lectures on the history and contemporary status of American literature. In 1954 he lived in Denmark and traveled to Norway, the home of his maternal ancestors, as part of a comparative project on village democracy that was to include what he had learned on his trip to Eastend the year before as well as his knowledge of Vermont's history. The revised project did not include Denmark or Vermont and resulted ultimately in *Wolf Willow,* but the Denmark excursion eventually bore fruit in *The Spectator Bird* some twenty years later. During 1955, while he was a fellow at the Center for Advanced Studies in the Behavioral Sciences at Stanford, he traveled to Saudi Arabia to do research for *Discovery! The Search for Arabian Oil,* which was serialized in *Aramco World Magazine* from January 1968 to August 1970 and issued in book form in 1971.

There were also trips to Europe (a year as writer-in-residence at the American Academy in Rome in 1960, for example) and Africa during these years. But as much as anything, Stegner enjoyed traveling the roads of America. Several of his experiences on these trips found their way into the many essays he wrote. In addition to the collections mentioned earlier, in 1984 Stegner collaborated with his son, Page, and the photographer Eliot Porter on *American Places,* a region-by-region look at ''how the American people and the American land have interacted, how they have shaped one another.'' As a natural outgrowth of his experiences growing up and living in the West, he became an increasingly active environmentalist, serving in 1961 as a special assistant to the secretary of the interior under President John F. Kennedy and on the National Parks Advisory Board from 1962 to 1966. His environmental beliefs found expression in such essays as ''A Capsule History of Conservation'' and ''A Letter to Wendell Berry'' (in *Where the Bluebird Sings*).

Sadly, Stegner's love for traveling by road through the western landscape—the landscape of his heart—may have been what ended a still vibrant, productive life. In *The Sound of Mountain Water* he wrote, ''It seems to me sometimes that I must have been born with a steering wheel in my hands, and I realize now that to lose the use of a car is practically equivalent to losing the use of my legs.'' On April 13, 1993, Stegner died from injuries sustained in a car crash in Santa Fe, New Mexico.

These are the facts about Wallace Stegner. The stuff of memory is more rounded, more fleshy, and getting at it is more difficult, as *Wolf Willow* shows us. Stegner's return for the first time in almost forty years to Saskatchewan is a lesson in sensual recall à la Marcel Proust's *Remembrance of Things Past*. Amid the changes he sees, something familiar in the form of an unidentified scent tugs at him, demanding recognition. All at once he has it:

> It is wolf willow . . . that brings me home. . . . The perspective is what it used to be, the dimensions are restored, the senses are as clear as if they had not been battered with sensation for forty alien years. . . . The sensuous little savage that I once was is still intact inside me.

Again and again in Stegner's fiction this process of remembering occurs, a function of the shaping power of the physical environment. The act of remembering, though, is not without anxiety.

Stegner consciously avoids returning to the old summer homestead on the Saskatchewan-Montana border, preferring to explore the house and town where his family spent their winters. He fears he might ''find every trace of our passage wiped away—that would be to reduce my family, myself, the hard effort of years, to solipsism, to make us as fictive as a dream.''

Ironically, what Stegner does record is also steeped in the fictive. As he noses his way through Whitemud in search of the ''sensuous savage self'' he was in youth, he thinks, ''I half suspect that I am remembering not what happened but something I have written.'' Indeed he *has* written these memories in *The Big Rock Candy Mountain*, the saga of the Mason family, Bo, Elsa, and their sons, Chet and Bruce. The name of the town he has returned to in *Wolf Willow*—Whitemud—is in fact the fictional name for the real town of Eastend. It is Bruce Mason's boyhood town, not Wallace Stegner's. But we make that distinction at our peril. In *Where the Bluebird Sings*, speaking of his story ''The Colt'' (which was incorporated into *The Big Rock Candy Mountain*), Stegner says ''The story is an approximation only.'' But when he talks of the story's ending, he coyly blurs his pronouns: ''In the very thrill of leaving, it struck him—me—all of a sudden *what* he and I were leaving.'' An aging Bruce Mason experiences this same overlapping of personae in *Recapitulation*.

Memory, then, is not an act of passive recall stimulated by the watchful senses. Individuals are always at least partial creators of their memories, adding their own brush strokes to the foundation of fact. Memory is discriminating, the rememberer a creative (and, one might add, moral) agent. One could say of memory, as Stegner does of fiction in his essay of the same title, that it is a ''lens on life,'' not a mirror. It does not merely reflect life; it frames and clarifies the image. The formative facts of existence—accident, luck, the reality of elevation and aridity, the contingencies of life that are beyond human control—are necessary elements in Stegner's universe. They are the chaotic demanding order, eliciting the hard work of memory, of history, and of story. They push; we push back.

Finally, if the divide between past and present confronting Stegner is an obstacle to be bridged by memory, it is also positive and productive. Stegner may have lived, as he tells Etulain, a ''life of the senses'' as a boy in Saskatchewan, but to quote Wordsworth, the divide of time and age provides ''abundant recompense'' to the adult looking back. Touring Whitemud in *Wolf Willow*, Stegner revises his childhood memories to fit reality. ''It is a lesson in how peculiarly limited a child's sight is,'' he says. ''He sees only what he can see. Only later does he learn to link what he sees with what he already knows, or has imagined or heard or read, and so come to make perception serve inference.'' As Stegner works through memories both individual and cultural, we learn that it is in the face-off between the child's view and that of the adult, the frontier of yesterday and the civilization of today, that we find true insight.

The transition from memory to history in *Wolf Willow* takes place in the essay ''The Dump Ground.'' In a frontier town, Stegner argues, there is no local history. The history is that of a former world and another place that the settlers bring with them as one of the tools of settlement—the wrong tool. Stegner has more than once quoted his friend Robert Frost's famous line from ''The Gift Outright'': ''The land was ours before we were the land's.'' The town dump, containing both what the community ''has to throw away and what it chooses to,'' bears witness to that process of a people becoming the land's, and the history of that people arises from their contact with that land.

The dump ground is a doubly fitting introduction to Stegner's historical projects. First, it illustrates figuratively the necessity of digging for the real history of the West (often part of what a community chooses to throw away), cutting through what Stegner calls in ''History, Myth, and the Western Writer'' ''mythic petrifaction''—the solidifying of the stereotypical western hero in the American consciousness into an image taken as fact. The dump ground also illustrates how the mind of the novelist-turned-historian works. In the essay ''One Way to Spell Man'' (in his book of the same name), Stegner distinguishes between the scientist and the artist, saying that the scientist (here meaning one kind of historian) values objectivity and verifiability and eschews ambiguity. The artist, on the other hand, attempts to ''make use of all the cultural moss that words gather, all the suggestive coloration and patina of language.'' In *Wolf Willow*, when Stegner concludes that ''the town dump was our poetry and our history,'' he is in effect describing the combination he strives for in his histories.

The Robinsons, taking their cue from Stegner himself, describe his historical method as the search for the ''middle ground.'' One of the literary tools Stegner uses is what he calls in his biography of DeVoto ''history by synecdoche,'' whereby through careful selection of key events and figures the historian can represent the entire sweep of a period. Such an approach lends itself well to a dramatic, narrative history, and Stegner enthusiastically follows DeVoto's advice to the historian Garrett Mattingly: ''When you get a scene, play it!' ''

Stegner's first big historical project (actually a bit history, a bit sociology) was *Mormon Country*. Stegner tells Etulain that *Mormon Country* was ''almost pure nostalgia.'' The book begins like a novel, focusing on the lives of two young people in love who might live in any small town across America. Stegner creates a sense of the typicality of this pair despite their differences as Mormons from the rest of America. Thus, he begins to cut through myth and stereotype.

Written as part of Erskine Caldwell's American

Folkways series, *Mormon Country* is divided into two parts, the first focusing on Mormon history and society, the second on the so-called Gentiles, or non-Mormons, of the region, a division that reflects the split between the two settlement options of Stegner's parents. Midway through the section on the Gentiles, opening the chapter on the famous Wild Bunch, Stegner pauses to summarize: "So there are three varieties of Gentiles—mountain men, railroad men, and miners—who have left their mark in one way or another on the Mormon Country." Among the other varieties who came, Stegner singles out the "cattle man and the inevitable concomitant, the rustler and outlaw." Mountain man, railroad man, and miner all represent in some way antagonists to a healthy community. The mountain man is the icon of rugged individualism. The railroad man is transience personified. And the miner is the paradigmatic get-rich-quick rapist of nature. The Mormons, on the other hand, pioneer in well-organized groups, build orderly towns, plant trees, reap the benefits of the railroad by trading with those passing through or by exporting their own products, and avoid falling prey to the lure of mining's potential riches.

As Stegner himself acknowledges, the Gentiles make for more interesting reading: "The Mormons are not, as Mormons, a colorful people. . . . The colorful episodes of Mormon history are likely to have been furnished by the apostates, by the Gentiles, by the cowpunchers and all the floating and reckless elements on the fringes of the region." There are deeper implications for his own project when Stegner says of the Mormons and the Gentiles, "They clashed, and in many ways they still clash, yet in a curious way they were necessary to each other." Although the Mormons embody cooperation, community spirit, and productive rather than destructive settlement, Stegner needs the untamed wildness of the Gentiles and of the lapsed Mormons to help carry the book.

Although Stegner is a self-proclaimed realist, and while, as a historian, he is out to deflate the myths of the cowboy West, he knows his story needs a little romance and myth. So he gives us the Wild Bunch and the miner-turned-desperado Rafael Lopez. And Stegner does what he can to enliven the Mormon section with, for example, the legend of the ghostly "perpetual patriarchs."

Stegner breaks down the dichotomy between Gentile and Mormon with a "hybrid" figure representing each of the two cultures. One of the "Two Champions" of Mormon history on whom Stegner focuses is J. Golden Kimball, whose bluntness and spicy language gave the Mormons "their heritage." In fact, "he *was* their heritage, a salty combination of zealot and frontiersman, at its very best." As for the Gentiles, there is the explorer Jedediah Strong Smith, who "was all man" but who was also "more than the brute some of his followers were." Indeed, "he was an intelligence." *Mormon Country* succeeds because of the combination of romance and realism, legend and fact, wildness and order, Gentile and Mormon that Stegner holds in tension.

In 1964 Stegner returned to Mormon country in a more straightforward history, *The Gathering of Zion,* focusing more narrowly on the exodus of the Mormons from Nauvoo, Illinois (and elsewhere), to the city in the desert. Stegner writes to cut through the Mormon enthusiast's "stylized memory of the trail." Stegner's growth as a historian over the more than twenty years between his Mormon books is apparent. The overt dichotomous structure separating Mormon and gentile has been integrated into a more fluent and linear narrative; the stark contrast between the two groups has modulated to something more subtle. If the basis for *Mormon Country* was personal nostalgia, Stegner has tried to dissipate it here by relying on journals written by the pioneers themselves. Letters and journals also come to play an important role in Stegner's fiction, as they do here, as a way of achieving both intimacy and authorial detachment.

Though muted, the distinction between Mormons and gentiles remains. It emerges most clearly in Stegner's emphasis on the women on the Mormon hegira. "Their women," he says in the final line of the introduction, "were incredible." But it is not only the women who keep us mindful of the gendered nature of the division between gentile and Mormon, between the rugged, ruthless, manly individualists and the more feminine community-oriented types in Stegner's writing. The mass of the Mormon men, because of their obedience to their faith, are described several times in what are traditionally and stereotypically feminine attitudes. For example, Parley Pratt, chastised by Brigham Young, "took the rebuke with meekness." Stegner adds, "It is a constant astonishment to an outsider how submissive even the apostles could be to this man [Brigham Young]." Bearing up under suffering and tribulation—a sort of passiveness that Stegner reminds us was a part of the Mormon faith that helped them reach Zion—was also his mother's (and Elsa Mason's in *The Big Rock Candy Mountain*) role in life.

Falling chronologically midway between Stegner's two Mormon works is perhaps his best history, *Beyond the Hundredth Meridian*. The book tells the story of John Wesley Powell's two expeditions down the Colorado River and his subsequent efforts to establish intelligent federal control and administration of the western lands. Like Stegner, Powell was a myth buster, a realist. Opposed to Powell are those who viewed the West through glitter-filled eyes, like those of William Gilpin, the first territorial governor of Colorado. Gilpin was one of the fathers of the "Garden West" myth, proclaiming that the West would be the new and fertile seat of America's rapidly expanding empire. Powell understood the West's arid reality.

Although he is cast in opposition to "Gilpinism," Powell is really a middle-ground figure, standing between the untamed individualist and the completely "sivilized" (as Huck Finn would have put it) social being. As a historical subject he represents the middle ground also. Stegner, the narrative historian, makes the most of Powell's first trip down the Green and Colorado river system through the canyon country of Utah and Arizona. But Powell's second trip down the Colorado somehow "doesn't make a story," says Stegner; there is no "dramatic tale." In the two expeditions, Powell's life story has both the titillation of a one-armed man clinging desperately to the outcropping of a canyon wall he has climbed with more eagerness than caution and the less thrilling, slower account of the careful organizer, trying to create a centralized and more equitable control of a region threatened by the profit-driven lusts of monopolists and land speculators. In one figure Stegner has a subject representing the best of both his parents: a risk-taking advocate for community.

The artists in Stegner's histories also negotiate this mixed terrain between romance and realism. Powell himself was a nineteenth-century realist who, Stegner writes, "might on occasion be led to follow Twain's . . . advice to [Rudyard] Kipling: 'Young man, first get your facts and then do with them what you will.'" Powell's double temperament is revealed, says Stegner, in his choice of complementary illustrators for the reports of his various explorations, the idealizing romantic Thomas Moran and the realist William Henry Holmes.

One might expect Stegner to give preference to the less romanticized work of Holmes over that of Moran. After all, Stegner emphasizes in *Beyond the Hundredth Meridian* the need for artists to attune their eyesight to the western landscape's "new palette." Yet despite the fact that Stegner praises Holmes for contributing "to the clarification of the Plateau Province something in

604 / AMERICAN WRITERS

the line of Powell's own ambition: art without falsification," we must read that assessment in light of the illustrations reproduced for the book in what amounts to a pictorial essay. The last of this portfolio is not a sketch by Holmes, but a drawing by Moran placed alongside a photograph by E. O. Beaman. The caption points out the weaknesses of the photograph and ends in a defense of Moran's artistic license. In the text, Stegner says of Moran what would serve well enough as a description of his own views on writing: "Realism was for him a means to an end, not an intention or a philosophy. . . . he proceeded from facts but attempted to transcend them."

Powell's moral dimension as well as his realism speaks to Stegner. According to Powell, Stegner writes, "The world worked toward unity, toward cooperation, . . . toward ethics and conscience and representative government"—and not by accident. Powell "believed more fervently that government should undertake research for human good. He understood scientific knowledge to be not only abstract but practical. Its immediate end was policy implemented by legislation, and its ultimate end was the improvement of man's lot and of man himself." In other words, Powell's belief in benevolent and effective federal bureaucracy—anathema to a West raised on a self-image of rugged individualism—was a belief in the power and moral imperative of mankind's ability to improve the human condition. In Powell we see a reflection of Stegner's faith in the rememberer's active shaping of memory, the historian's transcendence of facts, and the literary artist's refusal to be only a mirror of reality.

In "The Law of Nature and the Dream of Man: Ruminations on the Art of Fiction" (*Where the Bluebird Sings*), Stegner suggests that few fiction writers write autobiographies because they "have already written their autobiographies piecemeal, overtly or covertly, and go on doing it every working day." Without making the "vul-

gar error," as Stegner calls it in conversation with Etulain, of reading Stegner's fiction as thinly veiled autobiography, we can make the case that Stegner's oeuvre illustrates the ambiguous relationship between an author's life and his literary production. The Robinsons argue that the shift in perspective in Stegner's short stories from third to first person (from the "Brucie" Mason persona of *The Big Rock Candy Mountain* to that of Joe Allston, who appears in *All the Little Live Things* and *The Spectator Bird*) marks the evolution of authorial detachment necessary for aesthetic success. Kerry Ahearn contends, in his essay "Stegner's Short Fiction," that Stegner's maturing vision "develop[s] the themes of self-exploration by taking account of a pluralistic society, portraying that pluralism and granting some validity to all the voices speaking." The two arguments are versions of the same insight, and both are connected to Stegner's negotiation of a path between the various coordinates represented by the lives of his parents. Over the course of his career, Stegner's "fictional autobiography" works to bridge that gendered divide between individualism and community spirit to arrive at a more complex and nuanced view of the world and each individual's place in it.

The better of the two short stories in *Wolf Willow*—extensions of the book's historical project—is the long, well-crafted "Genesis," the initiation to manhood of a young Brucie-like figure. Rusty Cullen, the would-be cowboy-knight, learns during a blizzard that being a man is not a matter of "heroic deeds: singlehanded walks to the North Pole, incredible journeys, rescues, what not." In this country it's more to do with brotherhood.

The other *Wolf Willow* story, "Carrion Spring," is important for its metaphorical image of the husband and wife. "They were a couple that, like the slough spread out northwest of them, flowed two ways, he to this wild range, she back to town and friends and family." A similar image appears in the story "Two Rivers" (in *The Women on the Wall*), a story later incorporated into *The Big Rock Candy Mountain* with the characters transformed into Bo and Elsa Mason and their son Bruce. At the end of a "swell day" of picnicking with his parents, the boy recalls the early childhood memory of a "river that was half cold and half warm," or, as his mother puts it, a "place where one river from the mountains ran into another from the valley, and they ran alongside each other in the same channel." This image of confluence contains both the coldness of his father and the warmth of his mother. In the context of the story such harmony is part of an idyllic moment in the past that has been briefly resurrected. In the context of *The Big Rock Candy Mountain* things fall apart. Over time the order, unity, and harmony will break down under the pressure of the river's flow and turbulence.

However, Stegner eventually found aesthetic success in something like the river's ambiguous turbulence. As in his stories, Stegner's search for a point of view offering a balanced and complex perspective, sympathetic to multiple standpoints culminated in the self-critically ironic stance of Joe Allston in *All the Little Live Things* and his sophisticated, educated, worldly-wise and world-weary analogues such as Charlie Prescott in "He Who Spits at the Sky," Burns in "Something Spurious from the Mindinao Deep," and especially Lyman Ward in *Angle of Repose*. "The Traveler," selected as the first in the *Collected Stories of Wallace Stegner,* is a good choice for explicating more precisely the direction of Stegner's narrative development. The plot is simple and straightforward. A traveling salesman's car breaks down "in its middle age" along a snowy, deserted country road. After making the futile "efforts that the morality of self-reliance demanded," he walks to a nearby farmhouse, where he finds an anxious young boy hitching up a horse and sleigh in order to go for help for his unconscious, ailing grandfather. The traveler vol-unteers to go instead, leaving the boy to watch the sick man. As the traveler, who was once himself an orphan raised on a farm by his grandparents, drives off, he looks back over his shoulder at the boy "to fix forever the picture of himself standing silently watching himself go."

Clearly, this gem of a story is about the continuity of identity, a continuity created by the strength of the traveler's active imagination and memory superimposing the image of his former self over that of the boy in the present moment. He was once the boy on the frontier who ached to follow "roads that led to unimaginable places." The maturing Stegner knows that civilization is only in some ways an improvement over the frontier life. Progress—in the form of the car—fails the salesman "in mid-journey." His sample cases are filled with drugs that represent "not only a value but a danger." And when he comes to the farmhouse, he comes face to face with the ultimate destination, death, which no drug can cure. Confronted by the fact of the dying grandfather, a vision of his future self, he realizes "that here, as at the car, he was helpless."

Ironically, he is changed by circumstances "from a man in need of help to one who must give it." His own salvation is in his contact with the boy—with himself. Yet even as he steps back to a simpler time, a time of horse-drawn sleighs, he learns that the "ways a man fitted in with himself and with other human beings were curious and complex." And the fit is always tenuous. As he starts down a "road he had never driven . . . towards an unknown farm and an unknown town," in the midst of this epiphany of self-recognition, he understands that this feeling of continuity is forever in need of reconstruction. Amidst the chaos of chance and the complexity of human relations, identity is the "most chronic and incurable of ills."

"The Traveler" takes as its theme the importance of perspective. Insight comes with time and the ability to look back on one's past as though looking at the life of another. (Given the importance of this chronological perspective in Stegner's work, it is worth noting how often he recycles material or returns to a previously worked subject.) Likewise, understanding between individuals is a function of the ability to see from the other's perspective—to have, as Stegner tells us in *Wolf Willow,* the "sympathy" his mother had and his father lacked. We often see both kinds of perspective at work in Stegner's fiction, with the chronological perspective used as the framework within which his characters grope for those ephemeral moments when one is able to see through the eyes of another. When such a moment happens what we get is both continuity across time and unity of separate individuals—community.

During his life Stegner published thirteen novels, ranging in length from the novella *The Potter's House* to the near-epic *Angle of Repose.* In terms of quality, one finds a similar range. I want to focus on the best of Stegner's novels—*The Big Rock Candy Mountain,* the two Joe Allston novels (*All the Little Live Things* and *The Spectator Bird*), *Angle of Repose,* and *Crossing to Safety,* turning only briefly to some of the others for what they contribute to his development.

Stegner began writing *The Big Rock Candy Mountain,* perhaps the most autobiographical of his novels, in 1937, the year he published *Remembering Laughter.* In the introduction to *Where the Bluebird Sings,* he says of his father, "Out of his life I made a novel." To Etulain he says that the story "Buglesong" (in *The Women on the Wall*), which was incorporated into the novel and there focuses on Brucie Mason, was "pure autobiography." The autobiographical nature of *The Big Rock Candy Mountain* is both its strength and its weakness. Because *Big Rock* is so closely linked to Stegner's personal experience, the characters are more vivid and alive than in his previous novels. On the other hand, since Stegner was so close to the source material, finding the distance (the perspective) he needed to give it an aesthetic finish turned out to be beyond his capability at that time. So close was he to the events of the story, he tells Etulain, that he did not know how the book was supposed to end until his father committed suicide.

Even with its weaknesses, *The Big Rock Candy Mountain* is, for several reasons, Stegner's strongest novel up to that point in his career. For one thing, there is its scope. The book follows the Mason family—Bo, Elsa, and their sons, Chet and Bruce—as they migrate from North Dakota to Washington to Saskatchewan and Salt Lake City. It ends with Bruce in his twenties burying his father, having already lived through the deaths of both Elsa and Chet.

Second, there is, generally speaking, an improved subtlety of characterization, strengthened by the novel's episodic structure. Each family member takes center stage, some for longer periods than others, but each is fleshed out believably and, for the most part, sympathetically. Even Bo, whose violently energetic and futile search for the Big Rock Candy Mountain forces his family to endure hardship and continuous flux, earns our admiration—at times. The six well-crafted short stories that appear in chapters 4 and 5 play a big part in realizing all four Masons.

Howard Mumford Jones, reviewing the novel in Arthur's *Critical Essays on Wallace Stegner,* described it as a "vast, living, untidy book." Its untidiness lies in the uneven balance of the perspectives presented in the novel. The first third of the narrative is told through Elsa's eyes, the last third through Bruce's. The remainder of the novel is split between Bo and Chet. But in terms of interpersonal dynamics, the book falls roughly into two, with the Bo-Elsa (George-Hilda) dynamic taking up the first half of the novel and an oedipal conflict between Bruce and Bo occupying the second half. Bo comes off as the loser in either case, but it is Bruce's viewpoint that really wrenches the narrative off track.

During the heavy-handed eighth section, when

Bruce is trying to write through his feelings about his cancer-stricken mother, sounding like a thinly disguised Stegner, he confesses, "I suppose I have always hated him," and adds, "probably not always with justice." The Bruce-Bo conflict drags the novel down because Bruce never convinces himself or us of the truth of that afterthought. Whatever is admirable in Bo earlier in the book, when Elsa dominates the narration, degenerates to the merely pitiable once Bruce takes control of the novel. Ironically, in taking so strenuously the side of Elsa over Bo, Bruce and the novel fail to embody the qualities she represents. Looking at Bo through Elsa's eyes we can find something to love. Seen through Bruce's eyes, Bo is just a reflection of Bruce's bitterness.

Wallace Stegner as Bruce Mason imagines at the conclusion what resolution would be:

> Perhaps it took several generations to make a man, perhaps it took several combinations and recreations of his mother's gentleness and resilience, his father's enormous energy and appetite for the new, a subtle blending of masculine and feminine, selfish and selfless, stubborn and yielding, before a proper man could be fashioned.

Unfortunately, in this novel at least, imagination is not strong enough to carry it off. What it will take is the healing perspectives of time and a novelistic perspective that heals.

Stegner's first novel, *Remembering Laughter,* won the Little, Brown novelette prize, and for its simple elegance it was a deserving choice. It fares better in terms of point of view than *Big Rock.* This may be because Stegner adopted for his plot a story from his wife's family history. Even though Alec Stuart, boyish and untamed, resembles in some ways Bo Mason–George Stegner, distance gives us the George Stegner of whom his son remarks to Etulain, "He could be enormously entertaining, he could be very funny, he knew all kinds of ballads, he could be a good egg." Alec, even after his infidelity with his wife's sister, the event that chills the home for the next twenty years, is the most sympathetic of the three characters by the novel's end. With the distance offered by someone else's story, Stegner's critical gaze falls on Alec's wife, Margaret, and her puritanical rage for civilized order, perhaps the extreme version of Elsa Mason's desire for a stable home.

On a Darkling Plain is the first of Stegner's novels to exploit the Saskatchewan frontier region of his boyhood. It is an initiation story set on the Saskatchewan frontier, this time during the 1918 influenza epidemic. Like Rusty in "Genesis," twenty-year-old Edwin Vickers, would-be poet and disillusioned World War I veteran, is initiated not into an individualistic, heroic manhood, but into a healing sense of community.

The novel is interesting for what it says about Stegner's attitudes toward an imperfect world and the role of the novelist in that world. In *The Writer in America,* Stegner charts the descent of American literature from its height in Twain's "shirt-sleeved and democratized idealism" through the "sudden plunge" to gloom and pessimism after 1890 through the postwar decades of the "lost generation"—the generation of writers immediately preceding Stegner's own. In much of their work, he writes, "they were celebrating a purely personal nihilism, a dramatized and rather pathetic personal rebellion, or a highly literary and mannered despair, in the manner of Hemingway, F. Scott Fitzgerald, Edna St. Vincent Millay, Eugene O'Neill and others." *On a Darkling Plain* responds to the despairing attitude of that generation. With none of the literary tricks of style or structure employed by his predecessors, Stegner tells the rest of the world that there is hope even after horror, "that in the comradeship of ruin there was a tempering of the spirit; the resiliency of humanity under the whip was justification for all its meanness." In Vickers, Stegner shows us that we can bear a "life too painful to bear" and that it is our moral duty to do so.

Fire and Ice is the last time we see Stegner as

an apprentice novelist. At Wisconsin, Stegner met members of the Young Communist League, who struck him, he tells Etulain, as "people who were committedly, frantically, tensely political." The novel's protagonist, Paul Condon, is a firebrand in his school's Young Communist League. Embittered by his own impoverished upbringing, Paul is too much of an impassioned individualist to remain contented within the organization. His attempted rape of a wealthy student socialite leads to his realization that "I couldn't really accept the ready-made answers and the opportunist methods. . . . I'm gradually getting the idea that there's more in a man's life than economics." Fortunately for him, the woman does not press charges, and Paul leaves school to "start all over again." As a possible attack on social realism, the novel is an aesthetically weak response, a reflection rather than a critique of the formulaic, unsophisticated thought it takes aim at.

Stegner's follow-up to *The Big Rock Candy Mountain* was *Second Growth.* Tightly structured, with three alternating narrative threads, the novel is notable for its attempt to incorporate those insights Stegner picked up working on *One Nation* for *Look* magazine (one of the narratives concerns the attempt of a Jewish couple to integrate into the small New England town of Westwick). But the three narratives are not equally compelling, the best being that concerning young Andy Mount. His move from a cultural backwater to the larger civilization lies closest to Stegner's own experience. In this novel, as in *Remembering Laughter,* the energy and willingness to change of a George Stegner or a Bo Mason wins out over the narrow security of the permanently settled, that is, over a stagnated Hilda-Elsa vision of home and community.

The Preacher and the Slave is a mostly solid historical novel about Joe Hill, the legendary songster for the Industrial Workers of the World who was convicted on circumstantial evidence and executed for murder, that dramatically shifts perspective, much as *The Big Rock Candy Mountain* does. Joe is an individualist and a dreamer—another Bo Mason in some ways—and the combination leads to his willing martyrdom.

In Gus Lund, the Lutheran minister and friend of Hill who takes over the narrative, we are given a figure for the writer struggling with a narrative at the point where knowledge and understanding of the subject break down, a figure that recalls Bruce Mason. But Lund's relative detachment —he has nothing against Joe—makes Lund's narrative intrusion more palatable. In both novels the abrupt shift in perspective indicates Stegner's groping for something like what he describes in his essay "The West Authentic: Willa Cather" (in *The Sound of Mountain Water*). Stegner sees in the narrator of *My Ántonia* (1918), Jim Burden, a perspective that "permits Miss Cather to exercise her sensibility without obvious self-indulgence." The tactic also lets us "see the essential theme from two points [that of Jim and of Ántonia], and the space between those points serves as a base line for triangulation." We could call Stegner's aim intimate detachment, a position standing both inside and outside. In *The Preacher and the Slave* his solution is still awkward.

Stegner's next novel, *A Shooting Star,* was not published until eleven years after *The Preacher and the Slave*. Sabrina Castro, born to a wealthy New England family living in the foothills of the San Francisco Bay Area, struggles after an affair, which opens the novel, to build some meaning into her life. By the novel's end, having discovered herself pregnant by her former lover, Sabrina resolves to raise her child at home, work for the betterment of the local community, and create the connection she never had with her own mother. In this novel, Stegner definitely tilts toward Elsa Mason's communalism.

A Shooting Star is the first of four novels set in California, a region that is only marginally a part of Stegner's West. As he says in "The West

WALLACE STEGNER / 609

Coast: Region with a View'' (in *One Way to Spell Man*), ''The West Coast as a region shows a blurred image.'' Part of Sabrina's problem is her feeling of rootlessness—the rootlessness of California, captured in the ''cheap and frantic glitter of everything'' and the labyrinthine sameness of the suburbs, all a part of the ''fog [that] lay over the whole Peninsula, over the whole of California, over the whole of America, over the whole twentieth century, . . . still, dense, settling.''

Also for the first time in a Stegner novel, the community-individualist conflict centers on the environmental issue—land development versus preservation. Opposing each other over the use of a tract of land owned by Deborah Hutchens, Sabrina's mother, are two men, two alternatives of masculinity. Sabrina's brother, Oliver, is virility personified. Willing to have his mother declared legally incompetent to get his way, ''he was . . . what, on one limited side, this civilization came to.'' On the other side is Leonard Mac- Donald, the husband of one of Sabrina's lifelong friends: a high school English teacher, a family man, and a community servant. Sabrina and the novel come down on the side of Leonard.

Leonard serves the same purpose in this novel as Gustave Lund did in *The Preacher and the Slave*. Both provide an outside perspective helping us get behind the masks of their respective characters. Wise Leonard is another stand-in for Stegner himself. Although Leonard is not the occasion for another disturbing shift in perspective, even Sabrina gets ''infuriated'' at ''his air of omniscience.'' In *A Shooting Star*, Stegner is still struggling to find the perspective that will allow him to comment without artificially intruding into the novel. His answer is Joe Allston.

All the Little Live Things marks the novelistic debut of Allston, the ironic, self-critical, retired literary agent who first appeared in the story ''Field Guide to the Western Birds'' (in *The City*

of the Living). He relates a tale of moral ambiguity set in the late 1960s. The locale, which Joe refers to as ''Prospero's Island'' is again Stegner's northern California. Caliban is a hippie named Jim Peck who has squatted on a part of Allston's property with the latter's grudging permission. An antiestablishment college-aged youth, Peck sets up a sort of Swiss Family Robinson–Brook Farm, on which he engages in all the latest fads of youthful rebellion and enlightenment. Miranda is Marian Catlin, the young wife and mother who lives next door to the All- stons. Pregnant and afflicted with a cancer that is for the moment in remission, she professes a faith in the value and naturalness of ''all the little live things,'' no matter their destructive potential; pain as a form of pleasure (it heightens one's sense of being alive); and the progress of the natural world (including humankind) toward perfection.

To Joe, Peck is the king of misrule and disorder, but he is also a reminder of Joe's own rebellious son, Curtis, who died—perhaps killed himself—in a surfing accident. In Peck, Joe sees all the mistakes of his son repeated and amplified. In both, he sees his own ''foolishness made manifest.'' As for Marian, loving her like a daughter, Joe sees her ''philosophy of acceptance'' and willingness to countenance Peck's anarchy as its own kind of dangerous foolishness. In Joe's Manichaean worldview, evil is real and must be fought.

The novel's horrific climactic scene seems to confirm Joe's pessimistic view of the world. On her way to the hospital to die, Marian is forced to watch her husband, John, kill a horse that has slipped through the gaps in a plank bridge and broken three legs. Yet at the last, Marian has won over Joe, despite the gruesome trip the hospital and his witnessing of Marian's painful death. Joe reflects: ''Would I forgo the pleasure of her company to escape the bleakness of her loss? Would I go back to my own formula, which was twilight sleep, to evade the pain she brought with her? Not for a moment. . . . I shall be richer all my life for this sorrow.''

In Joe Allston, Stegner has finally found a way to unify perspective without losing the richness of multiple points of view. An ironic narrator's viewpoint is itself multiple. Irony requires first that we see things as others in the novel see them, that is, straight. Over that view we read the narrator's critical spin. But what I have described as a chronological process actually happens simultaneously. In the ironic narrator, Stegner can, in effect, unite past and present. Such a narrator heightens complexity and ambiguity when he places his own naïveté under scrutiny.

Joe describes the condition of humanity as being ''infected with consciousness and the consciousness of consciousness.'' It may be true that Stegner's early characters and narrators were ''infected'' with consciousness. But ''consciousness of consciousness'' is not infection; it is the cure. Only through such critical self-awareness are Joe and, by extension, the reader able to appreciate and hold in productive tension the complexities of life. In a way, Joe also unites the poles represented by Stegner's parents: individualism and the spirit of community. The ironic view is the view of an individualist, because the ironist must stand apart from those he comments upon. But if he is also self-critical, as Joe is, his own position gets subverted. Joe simultaneously stands insistently apart from those he comments on and in sympathetic self-examination is drawn to those same people.

A Joe Allston–like figure is our filter for the Pulitzer Prize–winning *Angle of Repose*. Lyman Ward, a crippled, retired historian living in Grass Valley, California, travels back in time, riding the vehicle of his grandmother's art, journals, and letters, to find answers to his own life in superficial California in 1970. Like Allston, he is cynical about the live-for-the-moment, anything-goes popular culture. He is also bitter about his wife, who has succumbed to that culture and left him for another man. Unlike his son, Rodman, Lyman believes in ''time . . . and in the life chronological rather than in the life existential.'' He seeks in the Victorian past the connection and continuity that has escaped him in the present.

The problem confronting Lyman in listening to the voices of the past is a function of what he calls, borrowing from science, the ''Doppler effect'': ''The sound of anything coming at you—a train, say, or the future—has a higher pitch than the sound of the same thing going away.'' Apostrophizing to his grandmother, Susan Burling Ward, Lyman laments, ''I would like to hear your life as *you* heard it, coming at you, instead of hearing it as I do, a sober sound of expectations reduced, . . . hopes deferred or abandoned, . . . griefs borne.'' Of course, the inevitably warped retrospective view gives the artist the room to create a truth that spans the present and the past. Stegner values that.

The history Lyman is writing is one that Stegner might have written. To the degree that it is western history, Lyman focuses on ''real'' people rather than on what Rodman refers to as ''colorful stuff.'' He is demythologizing, as Stegner had in his own histories. But Lyman insists, ''I'm not writing a book of Western history. . . . I'm writing about something else. A marriage,'' he says. ''A masculine and a feminine. A romantic and a realist. A woman who was more lady than woman, and a man who was more man than gentleman.'' Although he did not see it initially, Stegner acknowledges to Etulain that *Angle of Repose* is the ''boomer husband and the nesting wife, although with variations,'' a revision of *The Big Rock Candy Mountain*.

The ''variations'' are revealing. The later book is markedly more evenhanded in its treatment of the couples involved. Whereas Bo Mason is clearly and vehemently the ''bad guy'' in *Big Rock,* in *Angle* the blame for a marriage that nearly breaks and then settles into the ''angle of repose'' lies more with Susan than with Oliver Ward, despite Lyman's clear sympathy for his grandmother. Oliver has his faults, but as Stegner says of John Wesley Powell in *Beyond the Hundredth Meridian,* he is an ''honest man'' with an ''uncomplicated ambition to leave the world a little better for his passage through it.''

A related variation is in the romantic-realist dichotomy. In *Big Rock,* Bo is the dreamer, the lawbreaker, the romantic figure. Elsa, as an advocate of the home and a well-regulated community, represents something closer to the realism of everyday life. In *Angle of Repose,* Oliver is the realist suited to his environment, equipped with a ''physical readiness, his unflusterable way of doing what was needed in a crisis.'' Confronted by the rugged new landscape and the primitiveness of the frontier, Susan's response, conversely, is to gloss things with a ''literary flourish,'' to recast experience as scenes from a *Century* magazine piece. For her, life copies art. In fact, it is her desire for the life of East Coast civilization and culture that leads to her romance with Frank Scrgent and the inadvertent death of her daughter, Agnes. Between *Angle of Repose* and *The Big Rock Candy Mountain,* the gendered associations of romance and realism get reversed. The result is a more sympathetic male figure and, paradoxically, a more realistic female figure.

Angle of Repose succeeds for some of the same reasons *Remembering Laughter* succeeded. Stegner was able to filter his own experience through the story of another. The bitterness toward his father is blunted, the saintliness of his mother scuffed. This is not to fall into the trap of reading Lyman Ward as speaking with Wallace Stegner's voice: quite the opposite. It is to acknowledge that in the fictional character of Lyman Ward, Stegner finds a way to work through issues important to him *without* using his own voice—he finds detachment.

This detachment is also partly due to Stegner's basing Susan's story on the real-life experiences of Mary Hallock Foote. So deep is his indebtedness to the Foote papers (housed at Stanford) that Stegner was accused implicitly, if not directly, of plagiarism by Mary Ellen Williams Walsh in her 1982 essay ''*Angle of Repose* and the Writings of Mary Hallock Foote: A Source Study.'' To Etulain, Stegner explains, ''As far as I am concerned the Mary Hallock Foote stuff had the same function as raw material, broken rocks out of which I could make any kind of wall I wanted to.''

Williams Walsh's other charge is that Stegner has slandered Foote in those places where he *does* deviate from Foote's life story. This is an important consideration, but it misreads the focus of *Angle of Repose.* It is not the story of Susan Burling Ward; it is about Lyman Ward's attempt to work through the ills of his own life through his grandmother. He does not merely record his grandmother's turbulent years, but rather creates them at critical points; just as Stegner does not merely record his memories in *Wolf Willow,* but instead writes them. Lyman tells us flatly, ''What went on on that piazza? I don't know. I don't even know they were there, I just made up the scene to fit other facts that I do know.''

Stegner's National Book Award winner, *The Spectator Bird,* takes us back to Joe Allston. Once again he is engaged in his pastime of ''bird''-watching, and, as usual, one of the birds is himself. Stegner accentuates the sense of detached self-observation that was apparent in *All the Little Live Things* by having Joe read to his wife, Ruth, the journals he wrote on their, for him, ''therapeutic'' journey to his maternal homeland in Denmark. The trip was taken partly in response to his still-unresolved feelings about the death of his son, Curtis, but now, at age seventy, with friends passing on and his own body deteriorating, death has become a more pressing and intimate concern.

In Denmark, Joe hopes to find some clue to his own unhistoried identity as well as some way of reestablishing the continuity of his life that was obliterated by Curtis' death. When he meets and falls in love with the woman on whose family estate his mother once lived, the Countess Astrid Wredel-Krarup, Joe plays "with a daydream in which she fills with affection and loyalty a place left empty and sore by my failure with my son." Ultimately, of course, the daydream proves to be just that.

Stegner might have used the title of his final novel, *Crossing to Safety,* for this book. Joe's journey back to Denmark in search of his mother's birthplace is a search for security. The searches for love, home, mother, and even death (Joe suspects that Curtis didn't fall off his surfboard, but let go) are all versions of the same quest for sanctuary. Perhaps most important, the act of telling the story is a crossing to safety. In every case, crossing to safety means breaking the boundaries of the self, but Joe is a proponent of order. He is enough of an individualist to find tearing down the ego's fences frightening. Denmark, however, provides a lesson against an inward-turning, selfish order. The eugenic experiments of the aristocratic Rødding men are expressions of people obsessed with boundaries and purity. Their inbreeding is an attempt to maintain the genetic line and to stave off the ultimate disintegration of self, death. Eigel Rødding's brave new farm is "civilization" without the "wildness." Joe confesses to Eigel, "As an American I have to stand up for hybrid vigor."

Appropriately, the story of this champion of both order and wildness takes place in an atmosphere of half-light—the ambiguous white nights of Denmark, the death-in-life existence of the aged, and the hazy world between past and present, between thought and act (hence Stegner's allusions to *Hamlet*). Joe's moment of indiscretion with Astrid represents both a reaching out to another human being and a violation of the rules necessary to a well-ordered community. As the latter, it cannot be written of in Joe's journal,

so this attempt to establish connection and continuity becomes a break in continuity, a gap in the narrative.

Paradoxically, the way to some sense of unity for Joe is through reading his journal to Ruth. Initially his problem was that "in the recollections that the diary brought back, I wasn't quite spectator enough." He comes to see his experience as a "story about someone else," which allows him to reconnect with his wife and himself. Still, the novel ends on a satisfyingly ambivalent note. When the Allstons step to the back of their house to look, as a sort of confirmation of their reestablished connection, for a lunar rainbow like the one they had once seen, Joe knows there will not be one. And there is no rainbow.

One cannot bring back the past; one can only rewrite it in a way one can live with. In his penultimate novel, *Recapitulation,* Stegner tries to do just that—rewrite the past in a way he can live with. He returns to dangerous ground. Ambassador Bruce Mason is back in Salt Lake City for the burial of an aunt—his father's sister—and finds himself trying to come to terms with the broken relationships of his youth, especially the antagonistic one he had with his father. Unfortunately, in returning to the town and subject matter of his own youth, it is as though Stegner returned to the problems of the immature writer. He ventures back to Salt Lake City and the life of Bruce Mason without the armor of Joe Allston and comes up short. At one point Bruce thinks to himself, "His childhood had been a disease that had produced no antibodies. Forget for a minute to be humorous or ironic about it, and it could flare up like a chronic sinus." Unfortunately, Mason is continually forgetting to be "humorous or ironic," and the split between the adult Mason and the young Bruce becomes ponderous.

The problems with *Recapitulation* are not simply a function of the narrative strategy. There is also the difficulty of integrating previously written short stories. "Maiden in a Tower" (in *The City of the Living*), retailored as the first chapter in *Recapitulation,* is the story of Kimball Harris, a character in the manner of Henry James, who returns to a haunt of his youth and recalls his failure to "rescue" his "maiden in distress." In the opening to the novel, Harris is refigured as Bruce Mason and the episode sets up expectations that go unfulfilled. The woman in the story, Holly, virtually drops out of the novel, but, like Herman Melville's Bulkington in *Moby-Dick,* remains as a burr on the surface of the narrative.

Stegner is still too close to his material (the wound is clearly still open even ten years after *Recapitulation* in Stegner's epistle to his mother, "Letter, Much Too Late" in *Where the Bluebird Sings*). He even violates the old creative writing seminar maxim "Show, don't tell." The characters, including Mason and his young alter ego, Bruce, rarely come alive. Toward the end of the novel, Mason thinks, "Memory, sometimes a preservative, sometimes a censor's stamp, could also be an art form." Stegner made this point before, in *Wolf Willow,* for example. One only wishes that in *Recapitulation* the artist had been as skillful.

The sculptor of memory finds redemption in Stegner's last novel, *Crossing to Safety.* Stegner writes in *Where the Bluebird Sings,* "Of all the books I ever wrote, *Crossing to Safety* is in some ways the most personal. It is, in fact, deliberately close to my own experience, opinions, and feelings, which are refracted through a narrator not too different from myself." It is the story of four people—the narrator, Larry Morgan; his wife, Sally; and their lifelong friends, Sid and Charity Lang. At one point in the novel, driving northeast from Madison, Wisconsin, to the Langs's house in the Vermont countryside, Larry thinks, "Exhilarated, going the wrong way on a one-way historical street, I rattled back toward the begin-

nings of the Republic, toward the ancestral East that had never figured in my life."

In one sense, the novel itself is a journey against the flow of Stegner's own writing. His subject has generally been the West and westering. As Jackson J. Benson suggests, however, this is an eastering narrative. It is a trip to a different landscape, back to the civilization and culture longed for by Elsa Mason and Susan Ward. Yet the same issues that informed Stegner's novels of the West are present here, too. There is the tension between men and women representing, on the one hand, individualism and unfettered freedom and, on the other, organization and order. There is the dichotomy between romance and realism. There is the promotion of family and community, of strength through suffering, of sympathy, and of survival.

Sid and Charity are wealthy easterners who adopt as much as befriend their western colleagues. The four meet at the University of Wisconsin, where both Larry and Sid are pursuing careers, each in his own way. Larry is a writer supporting his calling by teaching. Sid is a would-be poet trying, at Charity's insistence, to publish scholarly articles to ensure academic promotion. Although neither career goes just as planned, the friends stay together through babies, Larry's success, Sally's crippling bout with polio, and the group's eventual geographical separation. Charity is the latest in a family matriarchy, and the plot turns on her need to organize and control her life and the lives of those around her; this compulsion is the "serpent" in the two couples' Garden of Eden. She clamps the lid on Sid's (in her mind) frivolous romanticism. At the novel's end she, dying of cancer, goes so far as to orchestrate her own exit from life (much as Marian Catlin does in *All the Little Live Things*), forcing Sid to submit to her will one last time by letting her go to the hospital without him. As she tells him, "I can't stand it when you break *down*!"

It is a testament to Stegner's growth as an artist that with all her faults Charity is not a mere symbol, as Margaret Stuart is in *Remembering Laughter,* nor a cardboard villain, as Bo Mason is much of the time. She is a sympathetically realized character whom we come to love and whom we will miss at the novel's close. After a day of sightseeing in Italy, a day of extreme highs and lows, Larry asks Sally, "When you remember today, what will you remember best, the spring countryside, and the company of friends, or Piero's Christ and that workman with the mangled hand?" She answers, "All of it. . . . It wouldn't be complete or real if you left out any part of it, would it?" Stegner succeeds in *Crossing to Safety* because he has put in "all of it."

Stegner has also harnessed the power of perspective. At the beginning of the novel, Larry characterizes the four friends as hoping "to define and illustrate the worthy life" according to their own capacities. Larry is the realist, Sid the romanticist. Sally's strength is "sympathy, human understanding"; Charity relies on "organization, order, action, assistance to the uncertain, and direction to the wavering." As a writer, Larry is a lot like Charity: "I moved with the freedom of a god. I controlled the climate. . . . I could anticipate, even plan, every event, and predict, even dictate, every consequence. . . . I ran my New Mexico mornings about the way Charity had always tried to run the life of the Lang family." Larry is a successful novelist, but if he is to become a Wallace Stegner, he will need to learn, as Stegner knows and shows here, that if a writer is to invent people and then "make them see a little better," his job is not merely to impose order but to do so with sympathy.

In the chapter of *Wolf Willow* entitled "The Making of Paths," Stegner recalls lovingly his joy at the sight of the paths and trails around the family's prairie homestead in Saskatchewan, created by the mundane movements of everyday family life. "They were ceremonial, an insistence not only that we had a right to be in sight on the prairie but that we owned and controlled a piece of it." These trails, so much like writing, were the product of sweat and toil, but their creation was also an "intimate act, an act like love."

Stegner's career as a writer might best be seen in this light—as the making of paths for all of us. The project has been an important one. Stegner asks, "How does one know in his bones what this continent has meant to Western man unless he has, though briefly and in the midst of failure, belatedly and in the wrong place, made trails and paths on an untouched country and built human living places, however transitory, at the edge of a field that he helped break from prairie sod?" Thanks to him we can begin to answer that question. As with all paths, the one he has carved out with memory, history, and story is not straight nor perfectly level nor without stones to trip on, but the path Wallace Stegner has engraved on the literary landscape takes us home.

Selected Bibliography

WORKS OF WALLACE STEGNER

NOVELS
Remembering Laughter. Boston: Little, Brown, 1937.
The Potter's House. Muscatine, Iowa: Prairie Press, 1938.
On a Darkling Plain. New York: Harcourt, Brace, 1940.
Fire and Ice. New York: Duell, Sloan and Pearce, 1941.
The Big Rock Candy Mountain. New York: Duell, Sloan and Pearce, 1943.
Second Growth. Boston: Houghton Mifflin, 1947.
The Preacher and the Slave. Boston: Houghton Mifflin, 1950. Reprinted as *Joe Hill: A Biographical Novel.* Garden City, N.Y.: Doubleday, 1969.

A Shooting Star. New York: Viking, 1961.

All the Little Live Things. New York: Viking, 1967.

Angle of Repose. Garden City, N.Y.: Doubleday, 1971.

The Spectator Bird. Garden City, N.Y.: Doubleday, 1976.

Recapitulation. Garden City, N.Y.: Doubleday, 1979.

Crossing to Safety. New York: Random House, 1987.

SHORT FICTION

Much of Stegner's fiction has been reprinted in prize collections and anthologies. For a good accounting of such reprints see Nancy Colberg's descriptive bibliography.

"Pete and Emil." *Salt Lake Tribune,* December 9, 1934.

"Saskatchewan Idyll." *Monterey Beacon,* June 29, 1935, sec. 1.

"Home to Utah." *Story,* 9:28–42 (August 1936).

"Buglesong." *Virginia Quarterly Review,* 14:407–415 (July 1938).

"Goin' to Town." *Atlantic,* June 1940.

"The Chink." *Atlantic,* September 1940.

"Butcher Bird." *Harper's,* January 1941.

"In the Twilight." *Mademoiselle,* November 1941.

"Two Rivers." *Atlantic,* June 1942.

"Chip off the Old Block." *Virginia Quarterly Review,* 18:573–590 (October 1942).

"The Colt." *Southwest Review,* 28:267–279 (Spring 1943).

"Hostage." *Virginia Quarterly Review,* 19:403–411 (July 1943).

"The Berry Patch." *Atlantic,* September 1943.

"The Volcano." *Harper's,* September 1944.

"Balance His, Swing Yours." *Rocky Mountain Review,* 10:32–38 (Autumn 1945).

"Saw Gang." *Atlantic,* October 1945.

"The Women on the Wall." *Harper's,* April 1946.

"Beyond the Glass Mountain." *Harper's,* May 1947.

"The Sweetness of the Twisted Apples." *Cosmopolitan,* March 1948.

"The Double Corner." *Cosmopolitan,* July 1948.

"The View from the Balcony." *Mademoiselle,* July 1948.

The Women on the Wall. Boston: Houghton Mifflin, 1950.

"The Admirable Crighton." *New Yorker,* June 15, 1946.

"The Blue-Winged Teal." *Harper's,* April 1950.

"The Traveler." *Harper's,* February 1951.

"Pop Goes the Alley Cat." *Harper's,* February 1952.

"Impasse." *Woman's Day,* February 1953.

"The City of the Living." *Mademoiselle,* January 1954.

"Maiden in a Tower." *Harper's,* January 1954.

"The Volunteer." *Mademoiselle,* October 1956.

"Field Guide to the Western Birds." In *New Short Novels 2.* New York: Ballantine Books, 1956.

The City of the Living and Other Stories. Boston: Houghton Mifflin, 1956.

"He Who Spits at the Sky." *Esquire,* March 1958.

"Something Spurious from the Mindinao Deep." *Harper's,* August 1958.

"Genesis." *Contact,* 2:85–167 (April 1959).

"The Wolfer." *Harper's,* October 1959.

"Carrion Spring." *Esquire,* October 1962.

"Amicitia." *Sequoia,* 31:16–25 (Centennial Issue 1987).

Collected Stories of Wallace Stegner. New York: Random House, 1990. Contains all of the stories from *The Women on the Wall* and *The City of the Living* plus "Genesis" and "Carrion Spring" from *Wolf Willow.*

NONFICTION

Many of the essays and chapters in the following books were published elsewhere originally.

Clarence Earl Dutton: An Appraisal. Salt Lake City: University of Utah Press, 1935.

Mormon Country. New York: Duell, Sloan and Pearce, 1942.

One Nation. With the editors of *Look.* Boston: Houghton Mifflin, 1945.

The Writer in America. Kanda, Japan: Hokuseido Press, 1952. Contains "Fiction: A Lens on Life," "The American Literary Tradition," "Contemporary Trends," "New Climates for the Writer," "Some Problems," "Literary Journalism," and "The Internationality of Literature."

Beyond the Hundredth Meridian: John Wesley Powell and the Second Opening of the West. Boston: Houghton Mifflin, 1954.

Wolf Willow: A History, a Story, and a Memory of the Last Plains Frontier. New York: Viking, 1962. Contains "The Question Mark in the Circle," "History is a Pontoon Bridge," "The Dump Ground," "First Look," "The Divide," "Horse and Gun," "Half World: the Métis," "Company of Adventurers,'' ''Last of the Exterminators,'' ''The Medicine Line,'' ''Law in a Red Coat,'' ''Capital of an Unremembered Past,'' ''Specifications for a Hero,'' ''Genesis,'' ''Carrion Spring,'' ''The Town Builders,'' ''Whitemud, Saskatchewan,'' ''The Garden of the World,'' and ''The Making of Paths.''

The Gathering of Zion: The Story of the Mormon Trail. New York: McGraw-Hill, 1964.

Teaching the Short Story. Davis, Calif.: University of California, 1965.

The Sound of Mountain Water. Garden City, N.Y.: Doubleday, 1969. Contains ''The Sound of Mountain Water,'' ''The Rediscovery of America: 1946,'' ''Packhorse Paradise,'' ''Navajo Rodeo,'' ''San Juan and Glen Canyon,'' ''Glen Canyon Submersus,'' ''The Land of Enchantment,'' ''Coda: Wilderness Letter,'' ''At Home in the Fields of the Lord,'' ''Born a Square,'' ''History, Myth, and the Western Writer,'' ''On the Writing of History,'' ''The West Synthetic: Bret Harte,'' ''The West Authentic: Willa Cather,'' ''The West Emphatic: Bernard DeVoto,'' and ''The Book and the Great Community.''

Discovery! The Search for Arabian Oil. Beirut: Middle East Export Press, 1971.

The Uneasy Chair: A Biography of Bernard DeVoto. Garden City, N.Y.: Doubleday, 1974.

American Places. With Page Stegner and Eliot Porter. Edited by John Macrae III. New York: E. P. Dutton, 1981.

One Way to Spell Man. Garden City, N.Y.: Doubleday, 1982. Contains ''This I Believe,'' ''One Way to Spell Man,'' ''Fiction: A Lens on Life,'' ''To a Young Writer,'' ''The Writer and the Concept of Adulthood,'' ''Excellence and the Pleasure Principle,'' Good-bye to All T—t!'' ''That New Man, the American,'' ''The Provincial Consciousness,'' ''The West Coast: Region with a View,'' ''Making a Myth,'' ''A. B. Guthrie,'' ''Walter Clark's Frontier,'' ''A Desert Shelf,'' ''Ansel Adams and the Search for Perfection,'' and ''The Gift of Wilderness.''

20–20 Vision: In Celebration of the Peninsula Hills. Palo Alto: Green Foothills Foundation, 1982; distributed by Western Tanager Press.

The American West as Living Space. Ann Arbor: University of Michigan Press, 1987.

Where the Bluebird Sings to the Lemonade Springs: Living and Writing in the West. New York: Random House, 1992. Contains ''Finding the Place,'' ''Letter, Much Too Late,'' ''Crossing into Eden,'' ''Thoughts in a Dry Land,'' ''Living Dry,'' ''Striking the Rock,'' ''Variations on a Theme by Crevecoeur,'' ''A Capsule History of Conservation,'' ''Coming of Age: The End of the Beginning,'' ''On Steinbeck's Story 'Flight,' '' ''George R. Stewart and the American Land,'' ''Walter Clark's Frontier,'' ''Haunted by Waters: Norman Maclean,'' ''The Sense of Place,'' ''A Letter to Wendell Berry,'' and ''The Law of Nature and the Dream of Man: Ruminations on the Art of Fiction.''

COLLECTIONS EDITED BY STEGNER

Stanford Short Stories, 1946. Edited with Richard Scowcroft. Stanford, Calif.: Stanford University Press, 1947.

This Is Dinosaur, Echo Park Country and Its Magic Rivers. New York: Knopf, 1955.

Twenty Years of Stanford Short Stories. Edited with Richard Scowcroft and Nancy Packer. Stanford: Stanford University Press, 1966.

The Letters of Bernard DeVoto. Garden City, N.Y.: Doubleday, 1975.

BIBLIOGRAPHY

Colberg, Nancy. *Wallace Stegner: A Descriptive Bibliography.* Lewiston, Idaho: Confluences Press, 1990.

BIOGRAPHICAL AND CRITICAL STUDIES

Ahearn, Kerry. ''Heroes vs Women: Conflict and Duplicity in Stegner.'' *Western Humanities Review,* 31:125–41 (Spring 1977).

———. ''Wallace Stegner and John Wesley Powell: The Real—And Maimed—Western Spokesmen.'' *South Dakota Review* 15:33–48 (Winter 1977–1978).

———. ''Stegner's Short Fiction.'' *South Dakota Review,* 23:70–86 (Winter 1985).

Arthur, Anthony. *Critical Essays on Wallace Stegner.* Boston: G. K. Hall, 1982. In addition to a selection of reviews of various Stegner works (including Howard Mumford Jones's review of *The Big Rock*

Candy Mountain), the volume contains the following essays: David Dillon interview (cited below); Joseph M. Flora, "Vardis Fisher and Wallace Stegner: Teacher and Student"; Robert Canzoneri, "Wallace Stegner: Trial by Existence"; Forrest Robinson and Margaret Robinson, "Wallace Stegner: *The Preacher and the Slave* and *A Shooting Star*"; Jamie Robertson, "Henry Adams, Wallace Stegner and the Search for a Sense of Place in the West"; William C. Baurecht, "Within a Continuous Frame: Stegner's Family Album in *The Big Rock Candy Mountain*"; Kerry Ahearn, *The Big Rock Candy Mountain* and *Angle of Repose*: Trial and Culmination"; Barnett Singer, "The Historical Ideal in Wallace Stegner's Fiction"; Lois Phillips Hudson, "*The Big Rock Candy Mountain*: No Roots—and No Frontier"; Richard W. Etulain, "Western Fiction and History: A Reconsideration"; Sid Jenson, "The Compassionate Seer: Wallace Stegner's Literary Artist"; Audrey C. Peterson, "Narrative Voice in Wallace Stegner's *Angle of Repose*"; Mary Ellen Williams Walsh, "*Angle of Repose* and the Writings of Mary Hallock Foote: A Source Study"; and Merrill Lewis, "Wallace Stegner's *Recapitulation*: Memory as Art Form."

Benson, Jackson J. " 'Eastering': Wallace Stegner's Love Affair with Vermont in *Crossing to Safety*." *Western American Literature,* 25:27–33 (May 1990).

———. "Finding a Voice of His Own: The Story of Wallace Stegner's Fiction." *Western American Literature,* 29:99–122 (August 1994).

Burrows, Russell. "Wallace Stegner's Version of Pastoral." *Western American Literature,* 25:15–25 (May 1990).

Clayton, James L. "From Pioneers to Provincials: Mormonism As Seen by Wallace Stegner." *Dialogue,* 1:105–14 (Winter 1966).

Eisinger, C. E. "Wallace Stegner: The Uncommitted." In his *Fiction of the Forties.* Chicago: University of Chicago Press, 1963.

Ferguson, J. M., Jr. "Cellars of Consciousness: Stegner's 'The Blue-Winged Teal.' " *Studies in Short Fiction,* 14:180–182 (Spring 1977).

Flora, Joseph M. "Stegner and Hemingway As Short Story Writers: Some Parallels and Contrasts in Two Masters." *South Dakota Review,* 30:104–119 (Spring 1992).

Gamble, David E. "Wallace Stegner and the Gift of Wilderness." *North Dakota Quarterly,* 56:99–110 (Fall 1988).

Hairston, Joe B. "Wallace Stegner and the Great Community." *South Dakota Review,* 12:31–42 (Winter 1974–1975).

Hicks, Granville. "Fiction That Grows from the Ground." *Saturday Review,* August 5, 1967.

Lewis, Merrill, and Lorene Lewis. *Wallace Stegner.* Boise: Boise State College, 1972.

Mason, Kenneth C. "*The Big Rock Candy Mountain*: The Consequences of a Delusory American Dream." *Great Plains Quarterly,* 6:34–43 (Winter 1986).

Mosely, Richard. "First-Person Narration in Wallace Stegner's *All the Little Live Things.*" *Notes on Contemporary Literature,* 3:12–13 (March 1973).

Olsen, Brett J. "Wallace Stegner and the Environmental Ethic: Environmentalism As a Rejection of Western Myth." *Western American Literature,* 29:123–142 (August 1994).

Rice, Rodney P. "Wallace Stegner and Tom Wolfe: Cowboys, Pilots, and The Right Stuff." *Notes on Contemporary Literature,* 21:5–7 (March 1991).

Robinson, Forrest G., and Margaret G. Robinson. *Wallace Stegner.* Boston: Twayne, 1977.

Ronda, Bruce A. "Themes of Past and Present in *Angle of Repose*." *Studies in American Fiction,* 10:217–226 (Autumn 1982).

South Dakota Review 23 (Winter 1985). Wallace Stegner Number. Contains the following essays: John R. Milton, "Literary or Not"; James D. Houston, "Wallace Stegner: Universal Truths Rooted in a Region"; Wendell Berry, "Wallace Stegner and the Great Community"; Edward Loomis, "Wallace Stegner and Yvor Winters as Teachers"; Gary Topping, "Wallace Stegner and the Mormons"; T. H. Watkins, "Bearing Witness for the Land: The Conservation Career of Wallace Stegner"; Forrest G. Robinson, "A Usable Heroism: Wallace Stegner's *Beyond the Hundredth Meridian*"; Kerry Ahearn, "Stegner's Short Fiction"; Melany Graulich, "The Guides to Conduct that a Tradition Offers: Wallace Stegner's *Angle of Repose*"; and John R. Milton, interview cited below.

Tyburski, Susan J. "Wallace Stegner's Vision of Wilderness." *Western American Literature,* 18:133–142 (August 1983).

Tyler, Robert L. "The I.W.W. and the West." *American Quarterly,* 12:175–187 (Summer 1960).

Zahlan, Anne Ricketson. "Cities of the Living: Disease and the Traveler in the *Collected Stories by Wallace Stegner.*'' *Studies in Short Fiction,* 29:509–515 (Fall 1992).

INTERVIEWS

Dillon, David. ''Time's Prisoners: An Interview with Wallace Stegner.'' *Southwest Review,* 61:252–267 (Summer 1976).

Etulain, Richard. *Conversations with Wallace Stegner on Western History and Literature.* Salt Lake City: University of Utah Press, 1983.

Ferguson, Suzanne. ''History, Fiction, and Propaganda: The Man of Letters and the American West. An Interview with Wallace Stegner.'' In *Literature and the Visual Arts in Contemporary Society.* Edited by Suzanne Ferguson and Barbara Groseclose. Columbus: Ohio State University Press, 1985.

Fletcher, Peggy, and L. John Lewis. ''An Interview with Wallace Stegner.'' *Sunstone,* 5:7–11 (January–February 1980).

Henkin, Bill. ''Time Is Not Just Chronology: Interview with Wallace Stegner.'' *Massachusetts Review,* 20:127–39 (Spring 1979).

Lathem, Edward Connnery. *Wallace Stegner on the Teaching of Creative Writing: Responses to a Series of Questions.* Hanover, N.H.: Montgomery Endowment, Dartmouth College, 1988.

Robinson, Forrest G. ''Conversation with Wallace Stegner.'' *South Dakota Review,* 23:107–118 (Winter 1985).

White, Robin, and Ed McClanahan. ''An Interview with Wallace Stegner.'' *Per Se,* 3:28–35 (Fall 1968).

—MARK S. BRALEY

Mark Strand

1934—

Mᴀʀᴋ Sᴛʀᴀɴᴅ's ᴄʟᴏꜱɪɴɢ words in his 1994 book on the painter Edward Hopper may serve as a first word on the poet himself:

> In Hopper's paintings we can stare at the most familiar scenes and feel that they are essentially remote, even unknown. People look into space. They seem to be elsewhere, lost in a secrecy the paintings cannot disclose and we cannot guess at. It is as if we were spectators at an event we were unable to name. We feel the presence of what is hidden, of what surely exists but is not revealed.

Strand's poems reveal a world that, like Hopper's, is ostensibly remote, unfamiliar, and secretive. His poems pay witness to an elusive reality with their own otherworldly spaces. Strand is the vatic poet of our moment. His lyric prophecies and oracular visions establish him as a modern symbolist, an heir of Ralph Waldo Emerson and Wallace Stevens. At the same time, he has fashioned for himself a style of language and vision that is uniquely his own. The Mark Strand signature is widely recognized: a plain-style vocabulary and straightforward syntax; lyric and narrative elements that recall documentary or journalistic reportage; a meditative tone that suggests allegorical or surrealist intentions; an otherworldly and often humorous and ironic quality; allusions to and echoes of other poets and their work; and broad but spare landscapes, simple contrasts such as light and dark, single rooms, one or two characters, and one or two happenings. All these elements combine to suggest more abstract truths that precise details or historical particulars might obscure.

Strand's poetic world is essentially psychological. His poems are allegorical ruminations on the nature and condition of the self as it discovers its place in a world of lack, absence, and desire. Strand's province is the darker side of the human psyche, where we know ourselves as divided, anxious, vaguely culpable, and where we find ourselves both astonished and paralyzed by our simple being in the world, by the mere consciousness of our having selves. In "The One Song" (*Darker,* 1970), Strand articulates the weight that the most basic aspects of life can have on the psyche:

> I prefer to sit all day
> like a sack in a chair
> and to lie all night
> like a stone in my bed.
>
> When food comes
> I open my mouth.
> When sleep comes
> I close my eyes.

His poems give voice to that estranged self, and in so doing they form a mythology that invokes the modernist negations of opposition, fragmentation, dissociation, and erasure. The critic Harold Bloom referred to Strand as "a dark child of [Wallace] Stevens." Indeed, he shares with his avowed mentor an intense regard for imaginative vision and a penchant for representations of reality as stark and diminished. He is heir to the wintry and meditative clarities of mind that we associate with Stevens, whose late-Romantic perceptions of reality are accomplished by a series of subjective negations and self-effacements. In a century dominated by the ironic mode, Strand is one of our great ironists. He speaks for the *undermined* self, the self caught up in a compromising struggle for control over its own identity.

Revelations of the self as impoverished and limited are one motif in Strand's oeuvre. Another motif concerns the world of poetic vision and its embodiment in poetry. This motif is the reforming powers of the imaginative word. For Strand, encountering a poem is an experience of a particular nature. In "Slow Down for Poetry" (1991), he writes,

> The way poetry has of setting our internal houses in order, of formalizing emotions that are difficult to articulate, is one of the reasons we still depend on it in moments of crisis and during those times when it is important that we know in so many words what we are going through.

Poetry helps us to interpret and control experience and its effects. It gives us room. During the 1960s and 1970s, when conspicuously formal verse was treated with skepticism if not disdain, Strand was praised for a formal acuity and finish. Often stunning in its marriage of simplicity and invention, Strand's poetry reveals a great trust in the unique properties and functions of the poem as a poem. In the ghostly sleight of hand of his plain style, readers have long detected a fertile, self-reflexive interest in the mere fact of poetic speech and all that can be accomplished there.

These then are Strand's two main motifs—the limited self, the imaginative word—and the poet has developed them so closely that much of the time they are harmonious.

Although Strand takes as his subject the restless and diminished self, its failings and its experiences of paralysis and guilt, his poems have little in common with the confessional school or any other of the dominantly self-centered poetic traditions. In the more explicitly autobiographical poetry of such poets as Robert Lowell, John Berryman, and Anne Sexton, expressions of personal crisis are legion. But Strand's poems are really only biographical in the sense that they express a mythologized self, a deeper and truer self that is at once elusive, immanent, and potential and part of a reality and condition that underlies our everyday existence. His poems are an expression not only of the lives we live, but also of a potential life. His instances of struggle and alienation are universal parables. In this consideration, Strand's work is connected to an Emersonian line that passes through Wallace Stevens to such poets as John Ashbery and W. S. Merwin. Like them, Strand celebrates not a mere descent into the ordinary and the particular, but a transformation of it into myth, into a vision of the commonplace as more deeply strange than we conventionally imagine. Readers, then, ought not to look here for biography in the usual sense: we learn little about what actually happened in Strand's life, whom he knew, what he did, or where he had been. The poems are very respectful of their maker's privacy. At the same time, it is clear that these poems arise from important experiences and thoughts about them. Personal memory, for example, may have inspired the meditations on childhood that appear in *The Story of Our Lives* (1973) and *The Late Hour* (1978), but what Strand finally brings to light is metamorphosis and translation.

* * *

Mark Strand was born in Summerside, Prince Edward Island, Canada, on April 11, 1934, but lived there only as an infant. His father, Robert Joseph Strand, was a man of great intuition and intelligence, but insecure means. He was an itinerant professional, a salesman, who held no less than twenty jobs in the first few years of his son's life. By the time Strand was a young man, he had lived in Halifax, Montreal, Philadelphia, Cleveland, New York City, Croton-on-Hudson, Colombia, Peru, and Mexico. Summers were spent with his aunt in Nova Scotia, at Seabright, at French Village, and at Hackett's Cove, places that later came together in the poet's mind as a mythologized vision of home. His parents were bookish, but intellectually insecure and somewhat emotionally aloof. They were charmed by their son's manifest artistic temperament— Strand's mother, Sonia Apter Strand, felt that she could see a painter in her son's eyes when he was only a year old. As Strand grew into what he calls an absentminded adolescent, they encouraged his art with the hope that it would not detract him from a more stable professional career. Strand describes his youth as having been characterized both by a sense of responsibility for his parents' happiness and well-being and by a certain inward imaginative existence that was his private domain. The ideals and permanent values of the interior life served even then as an antidote to itinerancy and the precarious emotional environment in which he lived.

Strand entered college in the mid-1950s, though he never felt that he was cut out to be a good student in the conventional sense. He received his B.A. at Antioch College in 1957, having studied under Nolan Miller and read a good deal of poetry. He recalls being moved by the meditative quality of the poems of Wallace Stevens and by the technical authority of many of the poets included in *New Poets of England and America* (1957), an anthology edited by Donald Hall, Robert Pack, and Louis Simpson that he carried around with him at school.

It was as a painter that Strand first tried to develop his talents. He went to Yale in 1959 and studied painting under Joseph Albers. However, it was not long before he felt that he was not destined to be a successful visual artist, and so he turned his hand to poetry. In 1960, as a Fulbright scholar, he traveled to Italy to study nineteenth-century Italian poetry, and met his first wife, Antonia Ratensky (a daughter, Jessica, was born to them). He returned to America and completed his M.A. in 1962 at the University of Iowa, where he then took a position as an instructor of English until 1965. It was there that he published his first book of poems, *Sleeping with One Eye Open.* Divorced from his first wife, in 1976 he married Julia Runsey Garretson, with whom he had a son, Thomas Summerfield.

In a certain sense, Strand's professional career resembles his father's. The thirty years following his first book brought much travel and many teaching positions. He taught at Yale, Harvard, Princeton, Brandeis, Columbia, Wesleyan, and the universities of Washington, Virginia, and California (Irvine), before settling for thirteen years at the University of Utah in Salt Lake City. He received many fellowships (including a Guggenheim and a Rockefeller) and prizes (including one from the National Institute of Arts and Letters), and was awarded a MacArthur Foundation fellowship in 1987. He was named Poet Laureate of the U.S. Library of Congress in 1990, and as of 1995 held a position in the Writing Seminars at Johns Hopkins University.

The characteristic features of Strand's poetry are in evidence in even his earliest poems. *Sleeping with One Eye Open* was published in 1964 in a limited edition of 250 copies. The title is significant and derives from the epigraph of the book, John Fletcher's ''Let one Eye his watches keep / While the Other Eye doth sleep.'' The quotation points to the fine line between the states of waking and dreaming, the external objective world of reality and the internal subjective worlds of human consciousness. Poems like "The Whole Story" and "The Tunnel" play at the edges of the solipsistic universe where the real world beyond wavers like a mirage. In "The Whole Story," we begin with a traveler and a companion:

> I nudge you and say,
> "That's a fire. And what's more,
> We can't do anything about it,
> Because we're on this train, see?"
> You give me an odd look
> As though I had said too much.

But the nature of the supposed journey and the reason for the speaker's curious observation remain a mystery throughout the poem, and what little we do seem to understand at the beginning (that there is a traveler, a companion, a fire outside the window) is eroded. By the end, our sense of a solid reality, of reliable relations between truth and illusion, has been replaced with a sense that the world "out there," beyond the window, may or may not exist and that the traveler who seems to be riding through that oddly inaccessible landscape may or may not be alone.

The reader of Strand's poetry comes quickly to recognize that the reality we inhabit in the world of the poem makes for a very special case. In "The Tunnel," a man sees another man in front of his house, becomes anxious, and in various discreet ways tries to get him to leave. When he fails, he digs a tunnel out of the house:

> I come out in front of a house
> and stand there too tired to
> move or even speak, hoping
> someone will help me.
> I feel I'm being watched
> and sometimes I hear
> a man's voice,
> but nothing is done
> and I have been waiting for days.

Like most of Strand's environments, the environment of "The Tunnel" is made up of the most basic elements: the interior of a house and the property surrounding the house. There are two people, one inside and one outside. By the end of the poem, the man who feels watched and who attempts to escape seems to have taken the place of the man in front of the house who was watching. But he has gotten nowhere. He is watchful of himself and therefore divided (that is, both watching and watched), trapped in a circle from which he cannot tunnel free. The poem dramatizes a state of paranoid self-consciousness. Any feeling we might have had at the beginning of the poem that there is a real world out there beyond the window is gradually replaced by a feeling of paranoia and a restless desire to get away.

The narrative of a poem like this is clearly unfolding on a level different from everyday lived experience. The simplicity of the story underlines its function as symbolic allegory, for the more straightforwardly and nonchalantly the events are narrated (a man posting suicide notes on his window, tunneling out of his house), the more we are forced to conclude that they are part of an alternative reality where such things are possible, one that is stranger, less recognizable, than the one we believe we inhabit. Strand's readers have tried to characterize that alternative reality and have found it useful to think of his work in terms of a surrealist aesthetic, though we need to be very careful with how we use this term.

Surrealist artists try to express the alternative and liberating logic of the dream state, of the unconscious. They think of poems and paintings as gateways, the artist's job being to represent the dream state by an effective use of poetic narrative and image pattern, which would initiate artist and audience alike into secret, preconscious orders. Surrealism has evolved continually since its first inception in the 1920s in France, and there are many exponents. A neo-surrealist movement became popular in the United States in the 1960s—through such poets as James Wright, W. S. Merwin, Galway Kinnell, and Robert Bly (almost all of whom went on to other things). Their search for what Bly called the "deep image" spoke to a generation that pursued various mind-expanding, altered states as a challenge to the historical and political realities of the decade.

Strand has been numbered among the surrealists, though for him especially it is a slippery and rather inadequate term. His own surrealist influences are more painterly than literary. Critics have pointed to the presence of such artists as René Magritte in his early work, and Strand has declared an allegiance to some visual artists who skirt the edge of what we would consider surrealist art (such as Balthus and Edward Hopper). Some of the relevant influences among the writers he admires are Bruno Schulz, Franz Kafka, Italo Calvino, and particularly the Argentinian writer Jorge Luis Borges (whom he has translated). But Strand would not identify these writers, or himself, as surrealist. Lance Olsen prefers the term "literary fantasy" when characterizing Strand's poetic universe. He argues that the poetry produces "a psychological state characterized by daydreaming, hallucination, and a disregard for 'consensus-reality' . . . a mode of consciousness that in the end expresses all the liberation and all the terror of the schizophrenic who can never find release from the fantasmagoria of his own mind." Olsen argues that Strand's poems seek to "overthrow 'reality' by generating . . . autistic worlds of phobia, oppression, entrapment, and guilt" and that "at most his poems maintain a fragile awareness of the external universe." Strand himself was reluctant to make rigid distinctions between what is realistically observed and what is imagined. He said to David Brooks in an interview, "To a certain extent, we all depend on free association, and we all use the suggestions that come from our unconscious." He preferred to speak instead of those

works which seem to deal in a "twilight zone of experience."

If we see surrealism as based on a destructive principle (the undoing of a "consensus-reality") that promotes the apparent chaos and disorder of the unconscious, then Strand would make a poor candidate as one of its practitioners. His subjects are strictly determined by the law and condition of the reality they find themselves in. Whereas in conventional surrealism we often feel that subjects are liberated into a state where anything can happen, Strand's subjects experience their place in a finished order that is not theirs to control or influence.

If the poet's subjects are seen to have little control over their fate in these early poems, the poet himself certainly does exercise control. In *Sleeping with One Eye Open,* reality is not surreal, but it does give the impression of having been conspicuously put together or constructed. The poet's world appears to be made up of stagecraft:

> Someone is always carting
> The scenery off to the wings
> And I,
> Set free from all the places
> I have never really been,
> Move on beyond the curtains
> Of a closing night . . .
>
> We take the props
> and fixtures of our days
> With us into the dark.

These scenes have less to do with the unconscious than with a painted and fabricated reality, a product of artifice. With the knowledge that all the world is a movable stage comes the experience of estrangement and detachment from all that is and the feeling that everything in this world is subject to the poet's sleight-of-hand transformations. Strand is testing his powers as the artificer of a poetic universe. As he says in "The Map," he offers

A diagram
Of how the world might look could we
Maintain a lasting,
Perfect distance from what is.

Strand's second book, *Reasons for Moving* (1968), introduced him to a much wider audience and secured his reputation as an important new poet of his generation. He preserved four poems from his first collection, including the title poem, ''A Reason for Moving,'' here renamed ''Keeping Things Whole.''

In this poem, Strand describes an inescapable anxiety about the space he takes up in the world:

We all have reasons
for moving.
I move
to keep things whole.

There may be wholeness and plenitude, but that ''field'' is always outside of and beyond the poet, who experiences himself as an absence, a hole, within it. Strand puns on the last word of the poem. His impossible task—the word itself shows us this—is to take the ''hole'' out of the ''whole,'' to reassert plenitude and identity by removing himself as the displacing figure of absence. Strand's identity is in a sense the negative expression of the Hebrew God's own name for himself as he revealed it to Moses: ''I am that I am.'' For Strand, ''Wherever I am / I am what is missing.'' Instead of being wholly at one with himself, Strand quietly suggests that he is a simple mirror (''I am / I am''), an expression of human doubleness, of our penchant for reflection and self-scrutiny.

It is with *Reasons for Moving,* Richard Howard argues, that Strand first narrates for himself Rimbaud's discovery that ''je est un autre'' ('' 'I' is an other''). Strand takes this doubleness as the essence of our humanity. We watch ourselves, and in watching we experience a strange alienation and detachment from who and where we are.

The style and narrative design of the poems are characterized by a direct, unembellished language. Richard Howard writes that most lines in *Reasons for Moving* ''are coincident with the simplest declarative statements. . . . The generally short lines . . . construct a simple report of things seen with all the odd exactitude of a documentary film.'' Events are described, laid out, like simple objects on a table. They suggest still lifes even as they further the narrative, as in ''The Accident'':

A train runs over me.
. . . .
[The engineer] wipes my forehead,
. . . .
He whispers in my ear
. . . .
He talks
. . . .
Back home he sits
. . . .
He sees me sprawled
. . . .
He rushes
from the house
. . . . . .
He puts his head
down next to mine
. . . .
I listen to the wind.

Many of the poems employ a species of primer-book syntax:

The poems are gone.
The light is dim.
The dogs are on the basement stairs and coming up.

Sentences and lines are often coterminous, complete in themselves:

I cannot sleep.
I cannot stay awake.
The shutters bang.
The end of my life begins.

Strand's plain style lends his poems an apparent directness and urgency that would seem to argue an open, ingenuous, and strong moral intent. Wayne Dodd and Stanley Plumly talk about "the sense of a great transparency in the language," as though in his pared-down diction and syntax the poet were trying to get outside the poem's metaphorical evasions. Yet Strand is nothing if not a master stylist who understands the deeper rhetorical effect of working in primary colors. In their exaggerated simplicity, his poems suggest a self-consciousness about intentionality. Even the poem "The Babies," which directly solicits the reader, avoids conviction:

> Let us save the babies.
> Let us run downtown.
> The babies are screaming.
> . . . .
> Let us not wait for tomorrow.
> Let us drive into town
> and save the babies.
> . . . .
> Let us hurry.
> Let us save the babies.
> Let us try to save the babies.

Our sense of the poem's apparently earnest call-to-action is attenuated by the exaggerated simplicity of the refrain; it is as though the poem were bringing to our attention a strangeness in the appeal.

There is an underlying humor in much of Strand's work, and often his most tragic poems flirt with the absurd, leaving the reader in doubt as to the purpose and nature of the poem. His style, moreover, suggests the unreal tragedy of cartoon caricature: our attention is drawn away from what is happening to the rhetorical impact of the caricature itself. Strand's style demonstrates well the poetics of irony that is so dominant in our century: the further you go with an effect and the more pronounced it is, the more self-conscious, duplicitous, and tongue-in-cheek your content will appear. Strand's plain style,

then, points in two directions. In the end-stopped lines one senses the cogency of the poem's logic, which appears complete and at one with itself. The resemblance to documentary reportage and the ordinary diction suggest an urgency and directness that seems incompatible with the typically evasive surfaces of poetic language. Yet these same features, in their extremity, suggest an element of self-parody that compromises their initial impact on the reader. The cogency, urgency, and directness are part of a larger ironic effect; they play the role of the straight man in the poem's attempt to mean something. Strand's poems—like the characters we find in them—often seem to be watching themselves function as poems. They are shy about their identity and manifest the same duplicity of self that is at the heart of Strand's concern.

With one eye turned toward metaphysical and psychological concerns, and the other toward the nature and function of poetic language, it is not surprising that Strand's poetry is quite removed from the contemporary fashions of politically and socially activist poetry. His work is more revelatory than prescriptive, more focused on revealing things as they are than on telling us how to live and what to do. A poem like "The Babies" parodies the very sense of social engagement that it appears to solicit. This effect is in keeping with Strand's use of poetic language. Though he learned much from Walt Whitman, Strand shows little taste for the Whitmanesque vision of the poet as someone who can address an entire nation about concerns of national identity and destiny. His conception of the poet's role and relationship to an audience is considerably more modest and self-effacing:

> I don't believe poetry is for everyone any more than I believe roast pork is for everyone. Poetry is demanding. It takes a certain amount of getting used to, a period of initiation. Only those people who are willing to spend *time* with it really get anything out of it. . . . I think all you can do is

address yourself to ideas and issues that you yourself are concerned about.

The history of Strand's development as a poet is the history of his reading. Regarding his early work, critics point to the importance of Theodore Roethke and Elizabeth Bishop for simplicity of manner, Richard Wilbur for elegance and form, the stories of Borges and the poetry of Carlos Drummond de Andrade for a sense of the fantastical and phantasmagoric. In *Darker* (1970), Strand revealed a new and strong interest in the eighteenth century English poet Christopher Smart (an interest that he shared with his contemporary plain stylist W. S. Merwin). Smart's long poem-journal *Jubilate Agno* (1758–1763) is a litany of prayers, meditations, and prophecies. Its long lines and high supplicatory tone, its invocation of myth and biblical history, its penchant for maxim and apothegm, its meandering and discontinuous narrative line, are all evident in the major poems of Strand's new book. Experimenting with Smart's manner and voice, Strand said to David Brooks, "was one of the ways in which I broke the tyranny of writing those pseudo-narratives that I was writing in *Reasons for Moving*." He was ready for a change: "I wanted some kind of rhetorical accretive effect in my poetry, rather than the plain, narrative, reductive, pinched thing I had been doing."

Strand's lines have become longer, more spacious, and make their impression through repetition and refrain rather than through the concentrated chessboard rhetorical strategies of his earlier lyrics. "The New Poetry Handbook," by its very title, promises a new manner and style, one that suggests an axiomatic wisdom based on fixed principles. But the title again is ironic. In "Notes on the Craft of Poetry," Strand writes that he is very wary of any formalizing of the rules of poetic creation. The "Handbook," on one level, makes light of the

rise of the creative writing workshop in American colleges and universities and of the notion that good writing can be taught. Strand's precepts are anything but commonplace and prescriptive, and they invoke exactly the sorts of mysteries that a "handbook" ought to be solving: "If a man lets his poems go naked / he shall fear death," and "If a man fears death, / he shall be saved by his poems."

The tone here is as representative for this volume as the envoi "Eating Poetry" was in *Reasons for Moving*. "Eating Poetry" invokes a detached, fantastical, and wholly literary world, one that is made of poems and the reading of poems. The poem suggests a potential menace in the extreme solipsism of the speaker: he says, "I romp with joy in the bookish dark," without showing much concern for the meaning and impact of his reckless abandon. But in this new envoi, Strand seems attentive to just these concerns of meaning and effect. His prescriptive handbook points to those mysteries that lie beyond the reach of the language in which they are embodied. The poem exists not to solve those mysteries, but to suggest their force. With its use of supposition and a repetitive cause-and-effect construction (if this, then that), "The New Poetry Handbook" would seem to argue that poems can have an actual effect, that there are real consequences for our actions as readers and writers. When we consider the potential that Strand's vision in this book has for highlighting our impotence in the contemporary world, and when we think of his own reluctance to claim a political and social advantage for his poems, this tacit expression of the supplicatory and conjuring powers of verse takes on a subversive meaning and authority of its own.

In *Darker* we also witness a change in focus. The poems are, for one, darker. Death is a conspicuous presence here, a good deal more so than in the earlier poems. Richard Howard writes that "Strand is both nervous and morbid, and a con-

sideration of finality is his constant project.''
What Strand says in ''My Life'' is true of the
book in general:

> I grow into my death.
> My life is small
> and getting smaller.

In ''The Sleep,'' Strand lists the varieties of repose that we experience, and ends with the most
intimate and personal:

> And there is the sleep that demands I lie down
> and be fitted to the dark that comes upon me
> like another skin in which I shall never be found,
> out of which I shall never appear.

Coupled with the awareness expressed
throughout these poems that ''The future is not
what it used to be'' (''The Way It Is'') is a
clearer vision of the self as existing, by its very
nature, everywhere in chains. We are caught up
in ourselves, in all senses of the word, self-
absorbed, entangled, trapped. Behind many of
these poems is a Chekhovian vision of a long
row of days, each one the same, each one showing us the limits of who we are and who we may
be. Strand summarizes such a life in ''The Hill'':

> One foot in front of the other. The hours pass.
> One foot in front of the other. The years pass.
> The colors of arrival fade.
> That is the way I do it.

In the best of moments, our impotence can be
a kind of grim repose. Strand writes in ''Coming
to This,''

> Coming to this
> has its rewards: nothing is promised, nothing is
> taken away.
> We have no heart or saving grace,
> no place to go, no reason to remain.

But at other times he experiences our condition
as a form of imprisonment. ''The Remains,'' for

example, suggests an identification between the
self and a Möbius strip:

> I empty myself of the names of others. I empty my
> pockets.
> I empty my shoes and leave them beside the
> road. . . .
> Time tells me what I am. I change and I am the
> same.
> I empty myself of my life and my life remains.

The use of refrain and repetition, as in a continuous litany, represents our sense of coming and
going back to the same facts and the same conditions. In ''Giving Myself Up,'' Strand seems to
''give up'' on losing himself:

> I give up my eyes which are glass eggs.
> I give up my tongue.
> I give up my mouth which is the constant dream of
> my tongue.
> I give up my throat which is the sleeve of my voice.

Throughout *Darker*'s expressions of our general condition, we notice a heightened note of the
personal and intimate, particularly in the third
and last section of the book, ''My Life by Somebody Else.'' Although there is no increased appetite in these poems for personal information or
factual detail, there is something less allegorical,
less fabular, about them. The events they attend
to seem more immersed in the credible details of
the ordinary world. Family, for example, makes
an appearance in '' 'The Dreadful Has Already
Happened' '':

> The relatives are leaning over, staring expectantly.
> They moisten their lips with their tongues. I can
> feel
> them urging me on. I hold the baby in the air.
> Heaps of broken bottles glitter in the sun.
>
> A small band is playing old fashioned marches.
> My mother is keeping time by stamping her foot.
> My father is kissing a woman who keeps waving
> to somebody else. There are palm trees.

In *Darker* we begin to leave behind those poems that seem to remove or estrange us from our familiar world. More and more Strand will be staying closer to home, showing us what is most otherworldly about it.

Critics generally agree that Strand's next book marked a turning point. "The career of Mark Strand appears to have two distinct phases," Peter Stitt wrote in 1983. "In what we may call the later poems . . . Strand writes concretely of remembered places and people. In the early poems . . . the real world is held very much at arm's length." *The Story of Our Lives* (1973) is generally considered the first in this next stage, and though reviews of the book were somewhat mixed, there was no doubt in readers' minds that it represented a departure. Robert Miklitsch called it "one of the most original books of poetry to appear in years." Strand himself talked of it more as a transitional work. There is more evidence here of actual personal experience than we are accustomed to seeing in his poems.

"Elegy for My Father," for instance, resembles the earlier poems in its struggle on an existential level with experiences of loss and grief. At the same time, it conveys the feeling of a personal conversation. It is as though the poet were addressing his observations directly to his father:

> Why are you going?
> *Because nothing means much to me anymore.*
> Why are you going?
> *I don't know. I have never known.*
> How long shall I wait for you?
> *Do not wait for me. I am tired and I want to lie
>   down.*
> Are you tired and do you want to lie down?
> *Yes, I am tired and I want to lie down.*

We don't get the feeling here that Strand is being more revealing or more personal to us, but rather that he is being more personal or open towards himself and his own memories and reflections, and that we are overhearing for a moment a quiet conversation that he is having with his own inner voices.

The title of the book is significant. Most of Strand's poems are stories of a sort, parables, exempla, lyrical vignettes, and cameos. *The Story of Our Lives* is the first book that offers a series of extended narratives. There are only eight poems in the book as a whole, and the four longer poems (including "Elegy for My Father") average eight pages in length. We may have previously encountered the characters whose stories are told—they feel self-conscious, limited, and unable to act or change who they are—but Strand goes much further than merely to recount, this time in longer stories, a litany of our inertias. *The Story of Our Lives* is also the first of Strand's works that seems to be looking hard for a window of opportunity and of transcendence. These poems not only tell stories about our lives, but also reveal our lives as being stories themselves. We have seen, even as early as *Sleeping with One Eye Open,* how Strand has an intuitive sense of our reality as constructed, fabricated, written. He has not until now, however, turned to the relations between living and storytelling in his search for a means of liberation and self-creation.

In the title poem, the characters find themselves living their lives as though they were writing and reading them. They have a simultaneous sense of freedom and imprisonment. They feel the power that their words have in a world of words:

> We sit beside each other on the couch,
> reading about the couch.
> We say it is ideal.
> It is ideal.

At the same time, they experience a curious separation from themselves, finding everything they do, as they do it, already written. They feel the weight of that text, the weight of being caught inescapably in a world of words. They are incapable of writing their lives beyond the writing that they must read. The book that they live is both their redemption and their curse. They read in the end:

> *The book would have to be written*
> *and would have to be read.*
> *They are the book and they are*
> *nothing else.*

"The Untelling" offers a similar story, but from the perspective of memory. A character recalls a scene from early childhood: a luminous moment at evening, a lake, a lawn, a child with his young cousins, uncles, and aunts stretched out on the grass, a woman "in a long yellow dress," a man running across the grounds holding a piece of paper (these are in fact transformed fragments of Strand's earliest memory). The poet sitting at his desk over a sheet of blank paper trying to recreate the reality of the scene. He tries out various versions, plying and manipulating the elements of his story, but finds something always missing, always vanishing ahead of his approach:

> It bothered him,
> as if too much had been said.
> He would have preferred
> the lake without a story,
> or no story and no lake.
> His pursuit was a form of evasion:
> the more he tried to uncover
> the more there was to conceal
> the less he understood.
> If he kept it up,
> he would lose everything.

What is required, then, is a curious kind of "untelling" that would communicate what cannot be spoken. That telling might be a poem like this one that untells, retells, erases, and recreates different versions of the vanishing past. But the poem's most lasting impression—which is also perhaps its most effective way of untelling its

story—is its blurring of the boundaries between the real life of the storyteller and the imagined life of the story. The teller's life seems to become a version itself of what he has told even as he tells it. The self and the poem, the life written and the life lived, become deeply enmeshed, mutually limiting and liberating. "It is the act of telling itself," Robert Miklitsch writes, "the lost self cast into the form of the imagined self, into the world of the poem, that is meaning." The imagined self cast into the world of the poem: this double projection is how Strand's poems bring an element of open space and possibility to the lives that we imagine for ourselves.

The Late Hour and *The Monument* (both published in 1978) represent two alternative lines of development that issued from *The Story of Our Lives*. One development was in the direction of personal memory, the other was in the direction of literature, its function in our lives.

The Late Hour contains more of what we might call personal poems than any other of Strand's books. Though they are not autobiographical in the strict sense, there are poems entitled "My Son" (modeled after a poem by Carlos Drummond de Andrade) and "For Jessica, My Daughter." The section entitled "Poor North" contains a series of childhood reminiscences and reflections. These explore sensations of loss and desire, the vulnerability and impermanence of memory; they search for traces of memory in the lived moment, its simultaneous presence and absence there. In "Pot Roast," for example, Strand emphasizes the solidity of memory, and in "The Garden," its mercurial nature:

> And now
> I taste it again.
> The meat of memory.
> The meat of no change.
> I raise my fork in praise,
> and I eat.
> . . . . .

Even as you lean over this page,
late and alone, it shines; even now
in the moment before it disappears.

These are lovely and quiet poems, recalling something of the still waters of childhood that they speak of. The poems are more open, relaxed, and approachable—Strand called them "less riddling" in his interview with Brooks—and in a sense sadder in their evocation of the luminous ordinariness of our lives. They are the signs of the deeper and more spacious elegiac cadences of his later poems.

Yet Strand had reservations about these poems. He said to Katharine Coles,

> I never felt that poems about my childhood and my family were my poems or poems I really wanted to write. They were poems that were generated by the atmosphere of American poetry at the time. Lots of poets I admired were writing about their childhoods. So I wanted to be a member of the childhood club. But I discovered I didn't have much of a gift for it.

The gift he pursued in *The Monument* was in an altogether different literary direction: translation.

Strand had been active as a translator throughout his career, but was particularly so in the 1970s, publishing *New Poetry of Mexico* (1970), *18 Poems from the Quechua* (1971), *The Owl's Insomnia, Poems by Rafael Alberti* (1973), *Souvenir of the Ancient World, Selected Poems of Carlos Drummond de Andrade* (1976), and *Another Republic: 17 European and South American Writers* (1976). The strong allegorical and otherworldly quality of the poems of Drummond de Andrade and the fiction of Borges played a significant role in his early development as a poet. But for Strand, the idea of translation itself was also important. Like the self that Strand wrote about—divided, self-conscious, both self and other—translations are in a sense texts that are not themselves: they are carried across from their original language into another state.

As translation means "to be borne across," to be translated, then, is to accomplish a kind of immortality, and this struggle for translation is the work of *The Monument*. Speaking to us of its desire to live beyond itself, the text calls out to the one who is projected into the future, the one who will make it into more than it is: "Tell me that my ugly tomb, my transcending gesture, my way into the next world, your world, my world made by you, you the future of me, my future, my features translated, tell me that it will improve." How fitting that many of the fifty-two untitled sections of the book include epigraphs and quotations and extended passages from other writers, which the present text variously seems to translate, measure up to, and weigh itself against. The work becomes a hall of mirrors, reflecting on itself as a text and on all the texts that lie within and beyond it.

The experiment of *The Monument* represents an important stage in Strand's development, for it suggests that the ideal or mythic self that we may imagine, the one that expresses who we are in the form of a possible life, is becoming increasingly defined by the aspirations, limits, and nature of the living text in which it is brought into being. In an interview with Grace Cavalieri, Strand revealed a personal stake in the significance and limitations of translation: "And so it's that I want to be translated—not just what I've written—but I want to be translated in such a way that I can live infinitely . . . I want not translation but continuous life."

Strand's *Selected Poems,* which appeared in 1980, included five new poems (including one of Strand's finest in the mode of transcendent reminiscence, "Shooting Whales"), but over nine years passed before the publication of Strand's next full book of poems, *The Continuous Life* (1990). For about five of those years, Strand felt that he was far away from poetry. The eighties were in part a period of retooling, but they were not by any means an inactive time.

For Strand, it was a decade of prose that saw the publication of three children's books, two books on art, and a volume of short stories. It is no negative comment on the works themselves if we see each of them as a continuation of the poetry by other means. Each work reinforces, in one way or another, our sense of what is central to Strand's poetic achievement. In *Mr. and Mrs. Baby and Other Stories* (1985), we recognize the journalistic, at times almost deadpan reportage, the elements of an otherworldly psychological allegory, and in particular the pervasive ironic and comic vision. The stories are a powerful indictment of materialism and consumerism in contemporary society. The children's book *Rembrandt Takes a Walk* (1986)—in which the Dutch painter ''comes down'' from his painting and accompanies a young boy in a walk through the city—reveals a continuing interest in the power of artistic vision to ''descend'' into our world, make itself manifest, and transform the conditions of our lives.

Strand, however, did not leave prose behind when he again began publishing books of poetry in the 1990s. He authored several fine essays, most notable of which are his ''Fantasia on the Relations between Poetry and Photography'' (1990) and his 1990 address as Poet Laureate to the Library of Congress, ''Views of the Mysterious Hill: The Appearance of Parnassus in American Poetry'' (published in 1991). One senses in essays such as these, and especially in his art criticism, that Strand is attempting in part to articulate the aspirations of his own art as he seeks to characterize the vision of those poets and artists he most admires.

Reviewers spoke enthusiastically of the Strand who reappeared in 1990 with *The Continuous Life*. Strand's voice had been enlarged somehow: his lines are roomier, more spacious, with more light and air in them; they reveal an expanded breadth of concern and vision. These poems are more holistic, more communal, more absorbed in the relations and struggles of everyday life. At the same time—and here once again is Strand's unique genius—the poems are more deeply immersed than ever before in the literature of the past. In an interview with Cavalieri, Strand spoke of ''rereading . . . Virgil and Robert Fitzgerald's splendid translation, and rereading the *Iliad* and the *Odyssey*'': ''They had a lot to do with my newer poems.'' Armed with neoclassical voices and allusions, Strand returned to and freshened his great theme—the desire to translate ordinary life and experience into the continuous life of song.

He describes this desire in ''The Idea'':

For us, too, there was a wish to possess
Something beyond the world we knew, beyond our-
    selves,
Beyond our power to imagine, something never-
    theless
In which we might see ourselves . . .

To those seeking themselves in what lies beyond them, Strand offers poetry. In *The Continuous Life* he has given his readers an extended opportunity to see themselves poetically. He has moved to embrace the ordinary in his poems, but not in such a way that our lives seem unreal there and falsely mimed in the distortions of art. Poetry for Strand is not a distortion of real life. Instead, it gives expression to a quality of permanence and repose that exists within real life. As his poetry comes closer to the ordinary, it shows more and more the poetry that is already a part of our days there.

Strand's publication in 1987 and 1994 of books of art criticism—individual studies of realist painters William Bailey and Edward Hopper—provides us with important clues to an understanding of the poetry he wrote during this period. Although Strand was himself trained as a painter, it was not until the appearance of these two books that readers had an opportunity to consider his craft in relation to his tastes and proclivities in the visual arts. Strand seems to be particularly drawn to those painters whose work evinces a tension between elements of ordinary narrative time (such as indications of age, season, movement, chronology) and tacit expressions of permanence in the particular moment portrayed. In *Hopper,* he writes, we find "two imperatives—the one that urges us to continue and the other that compels us to stay." And elsewhere: "Everything in this painting [*Ground Swell,* 1939] suggests an equilibrium has been reached between the depiction of passage and the more powerful accommodation of stillness." Many of Strand's favorite paintings seem to represent something of that equilibrium, where the passages of real time that we see represented in the moments of ordinary domestic routine seem to partake of the continuous life. He writes of a life that is both itself (ordinary, inexpressive, limited in time and space) and more than itself (representative, luminous, and permanent).

Many of Strand's 1990s poems seem to puzzle out the meaning of that crossing, that momentary accommodation of the infinite in our temporal lives.

Of course, poems too evoke the tension between time and timelessness: we have, on the one hand, the sequential time of word following word and, on the other, those elements of poetic language that seem to effect a kind of stillness or repose. Strand seems always conscious of the poem running out of time and pulling against its own tendency to come to an end. He often dramatizes that tension in the scenes and settings of *The Continuous Life,* perhaps no more so than in the title poem:

> . . . Tell the children to come inside,
> That your search goes on for something you lost—a
> name,
> A family album that fell from its own small matter
> Into another, a piece of the dark that might have
> been yours,
> You don't really know. Say that each of you tries

> To keep busy, learning to lean down close and hear
> The careless breathing of earth and feel its avail-
> able
> Languor come over you, wave after wave, sending
> Small tremors of love through your brief,
> Undeniable selves, into your days, and beyond.

It is by giving witness ("Tell," "Say"), Strand suggests, that the tension can be transformed. All our experiences of time—the past, the present, the future, continuity, permanence, loss, return, repetition, motion and stillness, progression and repose—become authentic through recognition and invocation. We can become conduits of a sort and make ourselves available to what timeless energies might pass through us.

The potential powers of a poem are such that it might give expression to, and perhaps in some way realize, this transformation into continuous life. The neoclassical "Orpheus Alone" speaks for that potential. As a pre-Homeric mythic figure, Orpheus attests to the continuous life of poetry. The various forms and fictions in which he has appeared make him an ideal figure with which to investigate relations of desire and time. The songs of this classical Ur-poet could redeem the dead and charm god and beast alike. We associate his music with the powers of transformation, or metamorphosis, but Strand has turned to him not to claim these powers as his own, but to review them in the light of twentieth-century skepticism and disbelief.

In his contemporary guise, Orpheus is alone and his role in the world somewhat changed. He might once have been able to take up the broken world

> and put in its place the world
> As he wished it would be, urging its shape and
> measure
> Into speech of such newness that the world was
> swayed.

But that is a poem "which no one recalls anymore." Instead, the greatest poem comes into the world, not as a magical force with transformative powers of its own, but as the world itself, in all its manifestations of permanence and mutability, death and birth. The greatest poem

> Came into the world as the world, out of the un-
> sayable,
> Invisible source of all longing to be; it came
> As things come that will perish, to be seen or heard
> A while, like the coating of frost or the movement
> Of wind, and then no more . . .
> . . . .
> . . . it came in a language
> Untouched by pity, in lines, lavish and dark,
> Where death is reborn and sent into the world as a
> gift,
> So the future, with no voice of its own, nor hope
> Of ever becoming more than it will be, might
> mourn.

If Orpheus' last poem changes the world, it changes it in such a way as to make it more of what it is, leaving its longings and perishables intact. The poem becomes transparent to the everyday world, and in so doing gives that world a voice of its own.

Dark Harbor: A Poem (1993)—divided into forty-five Roman-numeraled sections—is Strand's best book as of 1995. He wrote it very quickly, in a rush of creative energy, and in fact ended up publishing only about half of the poems that he had written. The poems do not form a narrative but circle around a set of themes or motifs. In *Dark Harbor,* Strand's engagement with the ordinary moments in our lives, and his transformation of them into myth, into islands of stillness and calm, is complete. Water is one of the dominant symbols in these poems, and even when there is no water mentioned or alluded to, we feel its presence, its influence as a metaphor of freedom and release. Section XIV has us at the edge of the everyday, floating just beyond the reach of its influence, as we prepare ourselves to depart into the myths we imagined we might live by:

> Why are so many of them crowded at the rail,
> With the ship still dozing in the harbor?
> And to whom are they waving? It has been
>
> Years since the stores in town were open,
> Years since the flag was raised in the little park,
> Since the cloud behind the nearby mountain moved.

The magic of these poems is that we find ourselves as readers already launched into something like the space these passengers seem to long for. Orpheus again is the poet's representative here, wandering quietly among nearly half of the poems in the book. It becomes clear to us that he is working in his accustomed place, halfway between this and a remoter world, and that once again he is trying to bring that more distant and timeless realm back to life.

For Orpheus, song is life; the journey out into the dark harbors of experience is also a journey out to the end of the poem, a journey to the end of singing. Strand's poems have always seemed conscious of their own closed spaces, but here they seem particularly so, as passages from I, XI, XXXII, and XXXVIII attest:

> . . . for the ash
> Of the body is worthless and goes only so far
> . . . the particular way our voices
> Erased all signs of the sorrow that had been,
> Its violence, its terrible omens of the end?
>
> An understanding that remains unfinished, unen-
> tire,
> Largely imperfect so long as it lasts
>
> A fragment, a piece of a larger intention, that is all.

The note of lamentation or complaint in the phrases ''goes only so far,'' ''omens of the end,'' ''so long as it lasts,'' and ''that is all'' makes it almost seem that, as the poem concludes, it cannot help but draw discreet attention to the fact of its own imminent extinction. Yet, by using something like picture windows on the interior walls of the dissipating structure, Strand also shows a way beyond it.

Strand's work in the 1990s is increasingly absorbed in echo and allusion. Few other poets writing in English today so constantly suggest to the reader the tug of other voices, that sense of the ear reaching after some half-remembered expression, line, or phrase. Listen, for example, to Strand's variation in section II of Richard Wilbur's "the heaviest nuns walk in a pure floating / Of dark habits": "everyone dreams of floating / Like angels in sweet-smelling habits." This sort of aural cue can be found everywhere in the book. Strand's echoes of Stevens and W. B. Yeats, of Ovid, Dante, and Milton, enlarge the poem within its own space. For Strand, the presence of other poets in a poem do not weight it down or burden it, but rather open it up. When we hear echoes of other poets that we cannot quite name, we have a feeling of entering into spaces we did not know existed. They are in a sense unreal spaces, invisible and remote, except for that feeling of the mind casting off, being drawn away toward an unsuspected voice. As we read toward an inevitable conclusion, we feel we are already elsewhere, already listening to a choir of voices that is not a part of time, in which each voice has its permanent place.

And so these poems deliver on the promise of their subject. Throughout *Dark Harbor,* we are witness to groups of lost souls wandering in circles, trying to rise above their own shadows and not being able to, having to leave but wanting to remain, setting out into their dark harbors while trying to wrest from that remoteness and melancholy a sense of liberation and permanence. But in Orpheus' song and journey, that dark harbor is already an afterworld. We find ourselves participating, feeling nostalgia for the simple places and affections of our days and recognizing the sting of regret for lost chances and things that we left unsaid. In section XLV, Orpheus sings,

. . . there were many poets
Wandering around who wished to be alive again.
They were ready to say the words they had been
    unable to say—

Words whose absence had been the silence of love,
Of pain, and even of pleasure.

As Orpheus sings, the sufferings of the underworld become the accomplishments of our own restless passage in time—our aimless wandering, our straining against the shades of ourselves. Just as the poems echo into unseen rooms, we feel the enlargements of that afterlife, break through to it as we depart. And yet we are still here, not on the fatal river Styx, but on a darkening harbor. Strand's orphic enchantments simply return us to where we are, and help us to long for the things that we have in this world as we pilot among them.

Strand is a poet of mystery and the unknown. In all their craft and evocation, the poems harbor their mysteries and allow us to suspend ourselves within them for a while as we look to understand the relations between lived experience and the mythic shapes we give to it in poetry. He began his career attempting to invoke those mysteries, in part, through a form of modernist psychological irony—trying to give the self away or make nothing of it in order to transcend its limitations. Now he has become heir apparent to Wallace Stevens' "interior paramour"—that dweller in the imagination—looking to find safe haven for that self in the beguiling inward spaces of the poem and struggling to understand what it might mean to dwell in them. Strand's concluding remarks on Edward Hopper began this essay. We might end with the poet's concluding remarks on the painter William Bailey; lines that certainly summarize the achievement of Mark Strand himself at the end of the twentieth century: "His reality transcends our common experience, it has no visible moment of inception. His paintings are grandiose and hieratic, self-contained, and secre-

tive. . . . They present us with a version of time-lessness, of things disposed to perfection.''

Selected Bibliography

WORKS OF MARK STRAND

POETRY

Sleeping with One Eye Open. Iowa City: Stone Wall, 1964.
Reasons for Moving. New York: Atheneum, 1968.
Darker. New York: Atheneum, 1970.
The Story of Our Lives. New York: Atheneum, 1973.
The Late Hour. New York: Atheneum, 1978.
The Monument. New York: Ecco, 1978.
Selected Poems. New York: Atheneum, 1980; Knopf, 1990.
The Continuous Life. New York: Knopf, 1990.
Dark Harbor: A Poem. New York: Knopf, 1993.

PROSE

The Contemporary American Poets: American Poetry since 1940. Edited by Mark Strand. New York: New American Library, 1969.
Art of the Real: Nine American Figurative Painters. Edited and introduced by Mark Strand. New York: C. N. Potter, 1983.
Mr. and Mrs. Baby and Other Stories. New York: Knopf, 1985.
William Bailey. New York: Abrams, 1987.
The Golden Ecco Anthology: 100 Great Poems of the English Language. Edited by Mark Strand. Hopewell, N.J.: Ecco, 1994.
Hopper. Hopewell, N.J.: Ecco, 1994.

UNCOLLECTED PROSE

"Landscape and the Poetry of Self." *Prose,* 6:169–183 (Spring 1973).
"Notes on the Craft of Poetry." In *Claims for Poetry.* Edited by Donald Hall. Ann Arbor: University of Michigan Press, 1982.
"Fantasia on the Relations between Poetry and Pho-tography." *Grand Street,* 9:96–107 (Winter 1990).
"Slow Down for Poetry." *New York Times Book Review,* September 15, 1991, pp. 1, 36–37.
"Views of the Mysterious Hill: The Appearance of Parnassus in American Poetry." *Gettysburg Review,* 4:669–679 (Autumn 1991).

MANUSCRIPT PAPERS
Lilly Library, University of Indiana, Bloomington.

TRANSLATIONS

18 Poems from the Quechua. Cambridge, Mass.: H. Ferguson, 1971.
New Poetry of Mexico. Selected and annotated by Octavio Paz, Ali Chumacero, Jose Emilio Pacheco, and Homero Aridjis. Edited and with translations by Mark Strand. New York: Dutton, 1970.
The Owl's Insomnia. Poems by Rafael Alberti. New York: Atheneum, 1973.
Souvenir of the Ancient World: Selected Poems of Carlos Drummond de Andrade. New York: Antaeus, 1976.
Another Republic: 17 European and South American Writers. Edited by Charles Simic and Mark Strand. New York: Ecco, 1976.
Travelling in the Family: Selected Poems. By Carlos Drummond de Andrade. Edited by Thomas Colchie and Mark Strand, with additional translations by Elizabeth Bishop and Gregory Rabassa. New York: Random House, 1986.

BIOGRAPHICAL AND CRITICAL STUDIES

Angel, Ralph. "In the Shadow Theatre." Review of *The Monument. American Poetry Review,* 21:49–50 (May/June 1992).
Armand, Octavio. "Writing as Erasure, the Poetry of Mark Strand." Translated by Carol Maier. In *Strand: A Profile.* Edited by Frank Graziano. Iowa City: Grilled Flowers, 1979. Pp. 49–63.
Benfey, Christopher. "The Enigma of Arrival." Review of *Dark Harbor: A Poem. New Republic,* March 8, 1993, pp. 34–37.
Bensko, John. "Reflexive Narration in Contemporary American Poetry: Some Examples from Mark

636 / AMERICAN WRITERS

Strand, John Ashbery, Norman Dubie, and Louis Simpson.'' *Journal of Narrative Technique,* 16:81–96 (Spring 1986).

Berger, Charles. ''Poetry Chronicle: Amy Clampitt, Louise Gluck, Mark Strand.'' Review of *The Continuous Life. Raritan,* 10:119–133 (Winter 1991).

Bloom, Harold. ''Dark and Radiant Peripheries: Mark Strand and A. R. Ammons.'' *Southern Review,* 8:133–149 (January 1972).

Bradley, George. ''Lush and Lean.'' Review of *The Continuous Life. Partisan Review,* 58:562–565 (Summer 1991).

Brennan, Matthew. ''Mark Strand's 'For Her.' '' *Notes on Contemporary Literature,* 13:11–12 (January 1983).

Brooks, David. ''The Genuine Remains.'' In *Strand: A Profile.* Edited by Frank Graziano. Iowa City: Grilled Flowers, 1979. Pp. 67–75.

Cole, Henri. Review of *The Continuous Life. Poetry,* 158:54–57 (April 1991).

Crenner, James. ''Mark Strand: *Darker.*'' *Seneca Review,* 2:84–89 (April 1971).

Donaldson, Jeffery. ''The Still Life of Mark Strand's Darkening Harbor.'' *Dalhousie Review,* 74:110–124 (Spring 1994).

French, Roberts W. ''Eating Poetry: The Poems of Mark Strand.'' *The Far Point,* 5:61–66 (1970).

Graziano, Frank, ed. *Strand: A Profile.* Iowa City: Grilled Flowers, 1979.

Howard, Richard. ''The Mirror Was Nothing without You.'' In his *Alone with America: Essays on the Art of Poetry in the United States since 1950.* Enlarged Edition. New York: Atheneum, 1980.

Jackson, Richard. ''Charles Simic and Mark Strand: The Presence of Absence.'' *Contemporary Literature,* 21:136–145 (1980).

Kirby, David. ''The Nature of No One.'' *Times Literary Supplement,* September 15, 1978, p. 1009.

Kirby, David K. *Mark Strand and the Poet's Place in Contemporary Culture.* Columbia: University of Missouri Press, 1990.

McMichael, James. ''Borges and Strand, Weak Henry, Philip Levine.'' *Southern Review,* 8:213–224 (January 1972).

Miklitsch, Robert. ''Beginnings and Endings: Mark Strand's ''The Untelling.'' *Literary Review,* 21:357–373 (Spring 1978).

Olsen, Lance. ''The Country Nobody Visits: Varieties of Fantasy in Strand's Poetry.'' In *The Shape of the Fantastic: Selected Essays from the Seventh International Conference on the Fantastic in the Arts.* Edited by Olena H. Saciuk. New York: Greenwood, 1990. Pp. 3–8.

Stitt, Peter. ''Stages of Reality: The Mind/Body Problem in Contemporary Poetry.'' *Georgia Review,* 37:201–210 (Spring 1983).

INTERVIEWS

Bacchilega, Christina. ''An Interview with Mark Strand.'' *Missouri Review,* 4:51–64 (Summer 1981).

Brooks, David. ''A Conversation with Mark Strand.'' *Ontario Review,* 8:23–33 (Spring/Summer 1978).

Cavalieri, Grace. ''Mark Strand: An Interview by Grace Cavalieri.'' *American Poetry Review,* 23:39–41 (July/August 1994).

Coles, Katharine. ''In the Presence of America: A Conversation with Mark Strand.'' *Weber Studies,* 9:8–28 (Fall 1992).

Cooper, Philip. ''The Waiting Dark: Talking to Mark Strand.'' *Hollins Critic,* 21:1–7 (October 1984).

Dodd, Wayne, and Stanley Plumly. ''A Conversation with Mark Strand.'' *Ohio Review,* 13:54–71 (Winter 1972). Revised and reprinted in *American Poetry since 1960: Some Critical Perspectives.* Edited by Robert B. Shaw. Cheadle, Great Britain: Carcanet, 1973.

Graziano, Frank. ''An Interview with Mark Strand.'' In *Strand: A Profile.* Edited by Frank Graziano. Iowa City: Grilled Flowers, 1979. Pp. 27–48.

Miller, Nolan. ''The Education of a Poet: A Conversation between Mark Strand and Nolan Miller.'' In two parts. *Antioch Review,* 39:106–118 (Winter 1981) and 39:181–193 (Spring 1981).

Vine, Robert, and Robert von Hallberg. ''A Conversation with Mark Strand.'' *Chicago Review,* 28:130–140 (Spring 1977).

—*JEFFERY DONALDSON*

May Swenson

1913–1989

MAY SWENSON ONCE said (in a 1978 interview with Karla Hammond) she did not mind being classified as a nature poet as long as it was understood that for her "nature includes everything: the entire universe, the city, the country, the human mind, human creatures, and the animal creatures." While a great many of her poems are about birds, the seasons, waves, clouds, and other natural phenomena, Swenson also wrote poems about New York City, space shuttles, making love, going to the dentist, baseball, God, and DNA. Truly, "the entire universe" is Swenson's purview, and the oeuvre in which it is represented is a richly eclectic one. Yet all Swenson's poems are linked by a common element—her endeavor to perceive and record the world with clarity, precision, and most of all, freshness. In her essay "May Swenson: The Art of Perceiving" (1969), Ann Stanford called Swenson "the poet of the perceptible": "She is the exemplar of that first canon of the poet—*Behold!*" Swenson steers clear of preconceptions, avoids conventional perspectives, and rejects standard categories and names, in an effort to discern the things of the world as if for the first time. Robert Lowell captured the essence of Swenson's work when he declared of *To Mix with Time* (1963) that "Swenson's quick-eyed poems should be hung with permanent fresh paint signs."

Swenson is also known as a meticulous crafter of poems. She is most famous for her shaped poems, which she called "iconographs," in which the actual shape of the poem on the page exemplifies or amplifies the poem's subject matter, but all of her poetry exhibits her visual inventiveness. Like E. E. Cummings, an early influence, Swenson was an amateur artist, and like Cummings, she was acutely concerned with the visual impact of the form of her poems. Thus, in Swenson's poetry, typographical arrangements of words, lines, and stanzas are carefully manipulated. Words are broken apart to reveal the words contained within them; spaces between words and even individual letters not only enforce pauses and create unexpected relationships between words but also form lines which visually slice the poems in pieces. Swenson's perceptions of the world are also conveyed through a dazzling array of poetic devices: metrical variations, rhyme (usually internal and frequently off-rhyme), repetition of words, assonance, consonance, alliteration, and onomatopoeia. Swenson's extravagant use of these devices along with her unusual word combinations point to her close reading of Gerard Manley Hopkins, while her omission of punctuation in her early poems, the unusual use of punctuation in later poems, and her use of capitalization for emphasis have led many critics to compare Swenson to Emily Dickinson.

Swenson's poetry is paradoxical in several ways. Her fascination with formal experimentation is curiously coupled with a firm belief in the spontaneity of the creative process: she insisted that she never had a predetermined plan for her poems but just let them evolve their own forms. The high level of artifice in Swenson's poetry also involves a paradox, for through it she seeks to simplify and strip away, to penetrate to the truth of the thing being observed or described. In her essay "The Poet as Anti-Specialist," Swenson describes poetry as "a craving to get through the curtains of things as they *appear,* to things as they *are,* and then into the larger, wilder space of things as they *are becoming.*" This explanation is clearly indebted to Hopkins' poetic theory: Hopkins believed that the goal of the poet is to recognize, through an intense act of perception he called "instress," the unique and dynamic design that constitutes the individual identity of an object or person—which Hopkins termed "inscape." Swenson's career can be characterized as a continual pursuit of the inscapes of the world —large and small, simple and complex.

That pursuit began in Logan, Utah, where Swenson was born on May 28, 1913, the eldest of Anna Margaret and Dan Arthur Swenson's ten children. Her parents were Swedish immigrants who came to Utah after converting to Mormonism. A teacher of mechanical engineering at Utah State Agricultural College (now Utah State University), Swenson's father was a skilled carpenter who inspired Swenson's devotion to careful craftsmanship. As a teenager, she began to write poems by typing her thoughts on her father's typewriter, and significantly, it was the look of the words on the page that convinced her that what she had produced was poetry. While attending Utah State, Swenson wrote for the college newspaper and published poems in the literary magazine. After earning a B.S. degree in 1934, Swenson stayed in Utah for a few years, working part-time for the *Logan Herald Journal* and other local newspapers, but she decided in 1936 to move to New York City to pursue her dream of being a writer. While Swenson justified the move to her family in professional terms, it was also a personal necessity. In the 1930s, it was not easy for any young woman to choose a career over marriage. But for Swenson, the Mormon environment in which she was raised made her decision particularly difficult. Rejecting conventional expectations that she would marry and have a family also meant rejecting her parents' religion and separating herself from "the fold." While she later compared her move away from her family to her parents' own break with the country and religion of their parents, she knew that her decision to make poems her children (as she would sometimes playfully refer to them) was a disappointment to her parents. The weight of that disappointment was still in evidence years later in her poem, from *Iconographs* (1970), "I Look at My Hand":

> forgive me
> that I do not throw
>
> the replacing green
> trunk when you are ash,
> When you are ash, no
> features shall there be,
> tangled of you,
> interlacing hands and faces
>
> through me
> who hide, still hard,
> far down under your shades—
>
>   and break my root, and prune my buds,
>   that what can make no replica
>   may spring from me.

Arriving in New York during the Depression, Swenson did not find work easily; it was especially difficult to make a living as a writer. She supported herself with a series of editing and secretarial jobs, and in 1938 was hired by the Federal Writers' Project to record oral histories of Americans. In that same year, she began living with Anca Vrbovska, a poet who had recently emigrated from her native Czechoslovakia. Their turbulent relationship and Swenson's ongoing struggle to make a living (the government job did not last long) made the years from 1938 to 1948 unproductive ones for Swenson. Later, when Swenson's birth date was mistakenly printed as 1919, she decided to perpetuate the error, as a way to partially wipe out the decade in which she accomplished so little as a poet; it was not until after her death that her actual birth date became widely known.

In 1948, after her breakup with Vrbovska and a move to a new apartment on Perry Street in Greenwich Village, Swenson resolved to apply herself with renewed commitment to her writing. What is most impressive about Swenson's second decade in New York is her mastery of the business of being a poet. With unflagging energy, Swenson submitted and resubmitted her poems to every journal and newspaper she knew of, applied for grants and fellowships, and gave readings. Although this work was time-consuming and usually frustrating, it did eventually pay off. It also set a pattern that Swenson would follow the rest of her life: as Paul Gray remarked in a 1979 review for *Time* magazine, Swenson's "works have appeared nearly everywhere," making her "one of the most accessible of all living U.S. poets."

In 1950, after Swenson's poems first began to be published in *Saturday Review* and *New Directions in Poetry and Prose,* she was invited to spend two months at Yaddo, an artist's colony in Saratoga Springs, New York. It was there that her friendship with Elizabeth Bishop began, and there that she made other connections which led to the appearance of her poems in the *New Yorker* and, eventually, to the publication of her first book, *Another Animal,* in 1954. Published together with first volumes by two other poets under the general title of *Poets of Today, Another Animal* is a remarkably assured and distinctive debut. It was reviewed enthusiastically by John Ciardi and John Berryman, among others, and was nominated for a National Book Award. Although greeted as the work of a new young poet, it was actually the product of almost two decades of work.

The poems in *Another Animal* represent the beginning of what would become a lifelong exploration of the nature of perception. This exploration is not of an abstract or cerebral nature, however, but is a joyful, sensual quest founded in the desire to understand the world to its fullest, through touch and smell and taste, but most of all through sight. One of Swenson's greatest strengths is her ability to observe the world carefully and describe it precisely: in the poem called "Green Red Brown and White" she writes, "Bit an apple on its red / side   Smelled like snow / Between white halves broken open / brown winks slept in sockets of green." But Swenson is dissatisfied with the conventional conception of subject and object, for it creates a sense of separation between them which prevents the perceiving subject from penetrating to the reality or truth of the object perceived. In "An Opening," Swenson imagines herself "in a landscape limitless and free / all that my Eye encircles I become / Trees ponds pastures." Like Hopkins, who in such poems as "Binsey Poplars" and "The Alchemist in the City" sought to reduce himself to a "sleek and seeing ball" so as to enjoy "free long looking," Swenson yearns to remove the impediment of her own being in order to see and to know with more clarity. Thus in poems such as "Feel Like a Bird," "Beast," and "Another Animal," she transforms herself into the objects of her observation; in "Evolution," she is able to sense that "the stone / would like to be / Alive like me / the rooted tree / longs to be Free."

Magical transformations abound as human

and animal, animate and inanimate, overlap and dissolve into one another. Swenson turns a feeding horse into a swan; facial features arise out of a landscape. With "shamanism and sorcery," Swenson explores what Richard Howard has called "the mystery that only when a thing is apprehended as something else can it be known as itself." In her preface to *More Poems to Solve* (1971), Swenson emphasizes how effective a change in perspective can be and how unusual vantage points yield fresh, new views of familiar things: "something simple or ordinary may be seen as wonderful, something complex or opaque becomes suddenly clear." Like Marianne Moore, Swenson considers everything worthy of attention, nothing too trivial or small: in "Any Object," she declares "any Object before the Eye / can fill the space can occupy / the supple frame of eternity."

One of the most striking features of the poems in *Another Animal* is their reticence on subjects that Swenson considered private. In her endeavor to see precisely and clearly, Swenson obviously regarded her personal emotions and memories as impediments or as filters that warped rather than clarified vision. An erotic energy animates many of Swenson's poems, but as in "Sun," it is usually deflected away from humans toward either animals or the natural world. But the personal and the autobiographical do surface from time to time, usually with powerful results. In "Rusty Autumn," the changing of the seasons is linked with the passing of Swenson's childhood and the loss of the warm protection of her parents; to the autumnal landscape and to her mother Swenson cries, "Hold me mother though I am grown and you are old / and burning only for death." The desire to lie on nature's "flat breast," to merge with the grass and the leaves, is a central one in Swenson's poetry and is most beautifully expressed in "I Will Lie Down," one of a sequence of four brief poems about death that form the emotional center of *Another Animal:*

I will lie down in autumn
let birds be flying

Swept into a hollow
by the wind
I'll wait for dying

I will lie inert unseen
my hair same-colored
with grass and leaves

Gather me
for the autumn fires
with the withered sheaves

While this kind of physical disintegration is welcomed in "I Will Lie Down," in "Question," another poem in the sequence, Swenson uses the same incantatory rhythm to celebrate her body and mournfully anticipate her loss of it:

Body my house
my horse my hound
what will I do
when you are fallen

Where will I sleep
How will I ride
What will I hunt

Where can I go
without my mount
all eager and quick
How will I know
in thicket ahead
is danger or treasure
when Body my good
bright dog is dead

In this, one of Swenson's best poems, an exquisite tension is created as the poet's fantastic metamorphoses are juxtaposed with the stark reality of death.

Swenson's early poetic influences are not entirely assimilated in the poems of *Another Animal.* In a 1978 interview with Karla Hammond, Swenson revealed that early in her career she had been impressed by the fact that Moore did not write about emotions; in *Another Animal* she is clearly emulating Moore's objectivity. The influence of Cummings is evident, too, in Swenson's playfulness, her artful simplicity, and her attention to the placement of words on the page. Bishop is brought to mind by Swenson's meticulously detailed descriptions, and the presence of Hopkins and Dickinson is manifest. But while it is not unusual to find the traces of other writers in a poet's first volume, what is surprising is the degree to which Swenson's characteristic voice and style are already firmly established in *Another Animal*. The forms of the poems are typographically distinctive, with columns, slanted or zigzagging margins, lack of punctuation, and unusual spacings and capitalization. The rhythms of the poems are compelling; the language is simple yet rich in visual details and sound patterns. But most extraordinary is the calm yet powerful assurance of Swenson's unique poetic voice: unafraid to be childlike in her persistent questions and wide-eyed engagement with the world, she is, at the same time, sophisticated, witty, and intensely alert.

A number of the preoccupations central to Swenson's first volume are carried over to *A Cage of Spines* (1958). In ''The Centaur,'' the merging of inanimate with animate and animal with human reappears when Swenson recalls how, as a girl, she would pretend a willow branch was her horse, yet in riding that branch, she would become both rider and horse: ''Doubled, my two hoofs beat / a gallop along the bank, // the wind twanged in my mane, / my mouth squared to the bit. / And yet I sat on my steed // quiet, negligent riding, / my toes standing in the stirrups, / my thighs hugging his ribs.'' The polymorphous freedom of childhood is marvelously rendered as are the impending restraints of socialization, for when the disheveled May returns home, her mother chastises her: *''Why is your mouth all green?''* To which May coolly replies,

''Rob Roy, he pulled some clover / as we crossed the field.''

Swenson continued her experiments with unusual perspectives, most notably in ''Water Picture.'' In a pond in a city park, where ''all things are doubled,'' an ''arched stone bridge'' becomes an eye, ''with underlid / in the water,'' and by seeing through that eye, as it were, the reader's reality becomes that of an upside-down world. When a swan kisses her own reflection, however, the surface of the water is broken, and a new perspective emerges: ''all the scene is troubled: / water-windows splinter, / tree-limbs tangle, the bridge / folds like a fan.'' Sometimes the shifts in perspective are not so much visual as relational. In ''Almanac,'' the progress of a bruise on a thumbnail marks and is marked by significant events in the world at large: the poet notes that while a dark ''moon'' made by a hammer was traveling toward the nail's tip, ''an unmanned airship / dived 200 miles to the hem of space.'' When the moon/bruise has finally disappeared off the end of the nail, the poet tells us, ''Einstein (who said there is no hitching / post in the universe) at 77 turned ghost.'' All is relative: by looking at ''little and large together,'' linking the personal and the cosmic, Swenson disorients and delights her reader.

As in all Swenson's volumes, in *A Cage of Spines* there are many fine poems of natural description: ''Early Morning: Cape Cod'' and ''The Even Sea'' are striking for the beauty and clarity of their images. Swenson's continuing interest in typographical experiments is exemplified by the shaped poem ''Fountain Piece,'' a meditation on the tension between art and reality in which she describes a bird perching on the wing of a statue of an angel within a fountain. The shape of the poem on the page is suggestive rather than representational: it traces the outline of a statue or a fountain, as well as the curve of a bird's wing. Yet the meandering left margin of the poem might also be tracking the path of the water/tears that (the poem tells us) run down the angel's stone cheek.

In "Her Management," Swenson, recalling Hopkins, revels in the beauty of nature's rich and messy multiplicity, but she singles out for particular praise nature's refusal to "place, relate, or name / the objects of her hall." Similarly, in the riddle poems that form the literal and thematic heart of *A Cage of Spines,* Swenson adamantly refuses to name or categorize her poetic subjects. In an interview for the *New York Quarterly* in 1977, Swenson likened her method in her riddle poems to that of a painter, who observes an object in "its form and its particularity, its characteristics, what it does to him—his eye, the way he sees it," but is not really interested in labeling the object. So it is that in each riddle poem an object is fully described yet never named. But when the poem is "solved," as Richard Wilbur explained in a "Memorial Tribute" to Swenson in 1992, "the riddle is a revelation, giving us not only a name, but an object freed from clichés of perception and seen with wonder as if for the first time." Thus the reader is led to discover that the "red-haired beast" is fire, that the "seamless miracle" is an egg, and that "this nimble animal or five-legged star" is a hand.

Swenson collected her riddle poems (along with other "play-poems") in two volumes for young readers—*Poems to Solve,* in 1966, and *More Poems to Solve,* in 1971—because she thought children would enjoy "the pleasure of the unexpected, of discovery, and of solution." But the simplicity of these poems is deceptive; in their revelations of how much one relies upon names and how disorienting the world is when those names are withheld, they offer challenges to all readers. In fact, when Swenson's riddle poem "By Morning" was accepted for publication by the *New Yorker* in 1954, Howard Moss, the poetry editor, insisted upon adding "Snow" to the title (against Swenson's wishes) for fear that readers would not understand the poem without the name of its subject. Swenson's riddle poems are also important as exemplars of one of her key poetic strategies. Even in poems that are not explicitly riddles, she refuses to rely upon conventional designations or take any qualities for granted; she suggests, in fact, that throwing away labels is a way of seeing more clearly, of penetrating to the essence of the object under observation. Thus another paradoxical aspect of Swenson's poetry is that while she uses words as the tools of her trade, she is also distrustful of them: there is always the danger that words will reduce rather than expand meaning. Swenson's riddle poems allow her to circumvent the confines of language while letting her readers participate in the poetic process that she describes in the preface to *Poems to Solve* as "finding and recognizing, comparing and contrasting, shaping and naming, solving and enjoying."

While some of her early critics saw Swenson's riddle poems as perfect illustrations of her poetic method, others felt that they embodied just what was lacking in Swenson's poetry. In the 1950s and 1960s there was a general critical agreement that Swenson's fanciful and often humorous comparisons were delightfully clever. But, although William Stafford argued in a 1967 review that Swenson's conceits "open into something that looms beyond the material, something that impends and implies," other critics complained that the subject matter Swenson chose was too often trivial and the resultant poems, superficial. In 1959, John Hollander noted that "the conceit, rather than the poem, ends up all too often as her ultimate and most effective unit of expression." Swenson's punning playfulness, and her elaborate technical and typographical games, struck some critics as ways of avoiding deeper and more difficult terrain, and a few (most notably William H. Pritchard) dismissed Swenson as a poet with little to say.

Despite this mixed critical reception, the 1950s and 1960s were productive and rewarding decades for Swenson. Although she was not yet able to support herself through her poetry, she finally found a job that made use of her abilities as a writer—working as a manuscript reader at New Directions Press from 1959 to 1966. In 1957, she was the Robert Frost fellow at the Bread Loaf Writers' Conference, and in 1960 she was awarded a Guggenheim Fellowship. In 1960 an Amy Lowell Travelling Scholarship enabled her to travel throughout Europe with her friend Pearl Schwartz, and the poems that she wrote about Spain, France, and Italy are collected in *To Mix with Time* (1963), which includes other new poems as well as selections from her first two books.

To Mix with Time is a volume of enormous variety, in which Swenson experiments with form and covers a wide range of subject matter; the results are uneven, perhaps inevitably so, given the volume's ambitious scope. It begins with a number of poems in which Swenson's restless curiosity extends beyond the things of the world into an investigation of the nature of man, God, and the universe. Swenson's characteristic mode of insistent questioning here becomes metaphysical and epistemological; even so, Swenson asks her large questions with a wry lightness that recalls Dickinson. She also purposely leaves her questions unanswered, bringing up abstract conundrums only to break them apart, mock them, and ultimately leave them for the reader to solve: "Because / we think / we think / the universe / about / us. / But does it think, / the universe? / Then what / about? / About / us?" She continues her typographical experiments in these poems, using spaces between words, unusual line breaks, and columns to reflect her own hesitations and doubts as she struggles to "get / out of my / head and / into the / world." In "God," a poem about the human desire for some

kind of divine permanence, she splits the text into two columns:

They said there was a	Thing
that could not	Change
They could not	Find
it so they	Named
it	God

In this poem about reification, Swenson gives a visible demonstration of how words themselves are integral parts of the process.

Swenson continues to play with angles of perception in *To Mix with Time,* as in "When You Lie Down, the Sea Stands Up" and "Southbound on the Freeway," in which an alien from outer space concludes, "The creatures of this star / are made of metal and glass. // Through the transparent parts / you can see their guts." "The Contraption" is another variation on the riddle poem, in which the "solution" to what is being described is both a roller-coaster ride and life itself: "How / did the morning, the whole blue-and-white day / go by in what seems one swoop?" With "Landing on the Moon," Swenson begins her tradition of space poems, in which she celebrates the scientific advances of the space program and revels in the new perspectives it offers. In her essay "The Poet as Anti-Specialist," Swenson "confesses" her envy of astronauts, whose experiences yield a host of entirely new "sensations" and allow them "to escape the earth-ball, its tug, and one's own heaviness!" Swenson sees a parallel between the astronaut and herself, for she, through her poetry, is striving to free herself from a different kind of gravity—that created by conventional ways of being and seeing.

As in her first two volumes, Swenson offers several evocative depictions of New York City, yet significantly and strangely, it is a city without people. Like Hopkins, Swenson wishes to observe yet be unobserved and thus is uneasy in the presence of humanity; when she does write about humans, she usually does so indirectly, through her poems about animals or natural objects. So even in the midst of crowded city sidewalks, she avoids people, and turns her gaze instead towards garbage trucks or taxis or the weather. "Pigeon Woman," a vividly observed poem about a quirky woman who feeds the birds in front of the library, is a rare exception. "Snow in New York" is another kind of departure for Swenson; in it, the "I" is not merely a situating device but represents the poet herself, whose descriptions prompt personal meditations. As she walks down a street and sits in a restaurant, Swenson mingles together, with a kind of dream logic, the snow outside, the writing of poetry, and eating, until the image of "belts of time" recalls the conveyer belts going in and out of the kitchen, and Swenson is snapped back to the reality of the present moment: "But then I thought: / Snow in New York is like poetry, or clothes made of roses. / Who needs it, what can you build with snow, who can you feed? / Hoses / were coming to whip back to water, wash to the sewers the nuisance- / freight." But despite the emotional effectiveness of the fluid narrative structure and reflective tone of "Snow in New York," most of the poems in *To Mix with Time* are more static and tightly controlled and, as a result, more impersonal.

In many of her poems on nature in *To Mix with Time,* such as "Each Like a Leaf" and "The Exchange," Swenson returns to the calm, chanting rhythms, simple language, and short, often unpunctuated lines of her earliest style, with impressive results. In "Another Spring Uncovered" the transformation she describes is both natural and fantastic:

> Colors take bodies,
> become many birds.
> Odors are born
> as earliest buds.
> Sounds are streams,
> the pebbles bells.
> Embraces are
> the winds and woods.

In "The Crossing," human and animal quietly intersect:

> With stealthy wing
> the hawk crossed over
> the air I breathed
> and sank in some cover.
>
> Through water I drank
> the deer stepped slow
> without chinking a stone
> and slid into shadow.

It was surely these poems Bishop was referring to when she remarked that Swenson "is one of the few good poets who write good poems about nature . . . not just comparing it to states of mind or society."

But when Swenson applies her descriptive abilities to the sights and sounds of Europe, she is less successful. The European poems in *To Mix with Time* are longer and more prose-like than Swenson's usual style, and they suffer from what Barbara Gibbs, in a 1959 review in *Poetry,* described as "a self-imposed limitation, that of the surface, or mere existence, of things." Most of Swenson's reviewers have noted that one of the dangers of her method of detailed sensory observation is that it can produce poems which are purely descriptive, as is the case with several poems in *To Mix with Time.* Neither personally revelatory nor philosophically engaging, these poems offer the reader little to respond to other than a pleasing picture. Gibbs deemed this tendency particularly lamentable because she knew Swenson to be capable of writing poems in which "one is suddenly face to face with an emotion rather than a jubilant play of sense." But in interviews and in essays, Swenson rarely mentions emotion when discussing her poetry. In her interview with Hammond, she emphasized the "objectivity" of her poems, and says "I think of my poems as 'things' rather than messages made of words." She was fond of comparing the work

MAY SWENSON / 645

of the poet to that of the scientist; she emphasized that the goal of her careful attention to the surface of things was, like the scientist's goal, knowledge—not the expression or exploration of emotion.

Swenson's next volume, *Half Sun Half Sleep* (1967), is, like *To Mix with Time,* a wide-ranging and uneven collection; it concludes with Swenson's translations of six Swedish poets. A central difficulty of the collection is that the poems are arranged alphabetically; with no support from meaningful juxtaposition or context, each poem must stand on its own, yet many are not able to do so. The volume seems unfocused, the creation of a poet unsure of what her next move should be; the subjects and styles of most of the poems are familiar from previous volumes. "Motherhood" is a riddle poem of sorts, although it quickly becomes obvious that the unattractive mother with "her breasts two bellies / on her poked-out belly, / on which the navel looked / like a sucked-in mouth" is an ape. But the initial expectation of a human mother changes in delightful and touching ways the reader's response to the monkey mother. There are shaped poems such as "Out of the Sea, Early," which looks like a rising sun, and "The Lightning," in which a diagonal line of spaces cuts through the words of the poem. "The Little Rapids," reversing one of Swenson's previous images, turns the body into a landscape, with the heart figured as a waterfall.

Shifts in perspective continue to allow Swenson to transform the ordinary into the extraordinary. In "Flying Home from Utah," Swenson, looking out of an airplane window, observes the landscape as a giant would; then shifts her perspective to that of those on the ground who see the plane as an insect; and then, finally, summons an image of a leaf in her mind, and imagines the intricate world to be found on its veined surface: "One leaf of a tree that's one tree of a forest, /

that's the branch of the vein of a leaf / of a tree. Perpetual worlds / within, upon, above the world, the world / a leaf within a wilderness of worlds." In "While Seated in a Plane," Swenson longs to live among the clouds but concludes "one must be a cloud to occupy a house of cloud"; she resolves the difficulty by becoming a cloud in her imagination. "Gods | Children" couples Swenson's interest in the link between naming and creating with the metaphysical questioning that typifies *To Mix with Time.* The central question of the poem—"Are gods children?"—is characteristic of Swenson's style in that the seriousness of the query is tempered by Swenson's playful manipulations of the phrase "God's children."

The critical response to *Half Sun Half Sleep* was divided along predictable lines. Critics such as Karl Shapiro praised Swenson's joyful playfulness and love of language and declared "it hardly matters what her subject is." But Swenson's choice of subject matter and her reluctance to match the complexity of her poetic conceits with emotional or philosophical depth continued to disappoint other critics who felt she was misdirecting her considerable poetic talents. While Swenson emphatically declared all things to be of interest, slight poems like "After the Dentist" or "A Basin of Eggs" made her critics long for a recognition on her part of differences in scale and value. In addition, by this point in her career, the mannerisms and contrivances of Swenson's style had become familiar and, to some, tiresome. In *Half Sun Half Sleep,* poems such as "Colors without Objects" and "Flag of Summer" hold little interest except as exhibitions of Swenson's painterly ability to break the world down into shapes and colors. The schematic "Cardinal Ideograms," in which numerals from 0 to 10 are described as something else (for example, "3 Shallow mitten for two-fingered hand"), is, like the earlier "Parade of Painters" and her other inventory-like poems, more of a writing exercise than an actual poem; one finishes reading a work like this one with a sense of Swenson's ingenuity but little else.

The debate over the ends to which Swenson put her formal inventiveness intensified with the publication in 1970 of her next volume, *Iconographs*. In it, Swenson's choice of subject matter continues to be eclectic: she writes about, among other things, an old field jacket, the DNA molecule, the death of her father, a James Bond movie, a mobile outside the Smithsonian, and a ride on a turbojet. But what is remarkably new about this volume is the degree of boldness in Swenson's typographical experimentation. Here again we find techniques Swenson employed in earlier volumes, such as unusual lineation, slanted or zigzagging margins, and the splitting of poems into parts by spaces or literal lines drawn through the text. But many of the poems are rendered in a recognizable shape that exemplifies or amplifies the poem's subject: those shapes include a wave, a movie screen, a flag, a butterfly, a mobile, and a bottle. The novelty and visual impact of these poems have made *Iconographs* the volume for which Swenson is best known, but critical response was mixed. Some dismissed the shapes of these poems as merely distracting or irrelevant; others worried that Swenson was resorting to gimmickry in order to gain attention because people no longer seemed interested in poetry. The emphasis on the visual over the aural in *Iconographs* was deemed by some readers a crucial misunderstanding of the nature of poetry. Only a minority of critics agreed with Swenson that the shaped poems offered an exciting new dimension in which to experience poetry.

It is not surprising that a poet who emphasized the primacy of vision would strive to make a visual impact with her poems. In "A Note about *Iconographs*," Swenson explains that for her "words on a page are objects, too," that a poem has "an existence in space, as well as in time"; this belief is evident even in her earliest poetry.

But in *Iconographs*, she not only seeks to represent and recreate her visual experiences for her readers, but to do so while giving them an additional, entirely new visual experience—that of reading the shaped poem. Thus, in "The Mobile in Back of the Smithsonian," the curving shape of the poem changes on each page to represent the movement of the mobile as it turns; "Black Tuesday," a poem for Martin Luther King, is shaped like a flag at half-mast; and "Unconscious Came a Beauty" recreates the butterfly that is its subject by using the title to form antennae and its two "stanzas" to form wings.

But Swenson's "iconographs" are not pattern poems, like George Herbert's "Easter Wings" and "The Altar,"in which the shapes and the texts are created in conjunction with one another. Nor are they concrete poetry, in which the visual impact takes precedence over the meaning of the words. In "A Note about *Iconographs*," Swenson explains that she added the shapes after the texts of her poems were finished, an admission that lends some support to critics who feel that the shapes are extraneous to the meaning of the poems. Indeed, many of these poems were later reprinted without their shapes with no appreciable loss. As a result, the poems in this volume have been seen by some reviewers as exemplifying the conflict in Swenson between her cleverness and her artistry. But this is not to say that Swenson's experiment in *Iconographs* is a failure. As in the case of "Bleeding," one of Swenson's most powerful poems, the jagged slash which cuts the poems in two functions in important, even essential ways: it forces the reader to jump across it, in each line, breaking the rhythm of the poem. This broken rhythm, in turn, emphasizes the gulf that exists between the knife and the cut (the two "characters" in the poem), and, by implication, between men and women:

Stop bleeding   said the knife.
I would if I   could said the cut.

Stop bleeding   you make me messy with this blood.
I'm sorry   said the cut.
Stop or   I will sink in farther said the knife.
Don't   said the cut.
The   knife did not say it couldn't help it but
it   sank in farther.

As one reads the poem, there is a constant, visible reminder of the rupture created by the knife; the wound at the center of the poem emphasizes that the poem is not about healing but about an ongoing and violent conflict between the sexes.

As "Bleeding," with its impassioned feminist content, makes clear, *Iconographs* marks the beginning of a new era in Swenson's career. Because critical attention has focused primarily on the volume's formal innovations, its strikingly new subject matter—personal, passionate, and socially involved—is sometimes overlooked. Although Swenson does not abandon altogether the impersonality she has so carefully cultivated, it is mitigated by the number of poems in the volume in which she expresses strong feelings. One can only guess the reasons behind Swenson's admittance of previously taboo subjects into *Iconographs:* did she feel she could somehow hide her emotions within the shapes, or did the innovative forms inspire similar innovation in content? Whatever the answer might be, the paradox remains: Swenson's most formally innovative poems are also her most personally revelatory.

In two of the finest poems in the volume, "I Look at my Hand" and "Feel Me," Swenson writes with great intimacy about her relationship with her parents. In the latter poem, her father's dying words, "Feel   me to do right," initiate an emotional struggle as Swenson tries not only to find the "right" meaning in his words but to "feel" in the right way. In this poem, she exploits the ambiguity of language not to achieve her usual playful effects but to represent both the difficulty and the urgency of human communi-

cation. In "Women," as in "Bleeding," Swenson startles the reader by making an explicitly feminist statement with unabashed anger and bitterness. In this frequently anthologized poem, she compares women to rocking horses, waiting to be set in motion by men: "To be / joyfully / ridden / rockingly / ridden   until / the   restored / egos dismount and the legs stride away." This expression of personal politics is radically different from Swenson's usual mode of presenting her opinions obliquely, through metaphysical speculations or observations of nature. Similarly, her poems about the assassinations of Robert Kennedy and Martin Luther King Jr., while not remarkable when viewed in the context of the politically volatile 1960s, were, for Swenson, a significant departure.

The most momentous personal revelation in *Iconographs,* however, has to do with Swenson's sexuality. It is now generally known that Swenson was a lesbian, but throughout most of her life, Swenson, like Bishop, preferred to keep her sexual orientation a private matter. That reticence, coupled with (and perhaps partially responsible for) her preferred poetic mode of impersonality, proscribed any explicit engagement with human sexuality in her poetry in her first four volumes. Instead, in her characteristic manner, she approached the subject of sexuality indirectly, through descriptions of animals and plants. "Zambesi and Ranee," from *A Cage of Spines,* is rare in its specific applicability to Swenson's life, for although its ostensible subject is a lioness and a tigress who are caged together in a zoo, it is tacitly about lesbian couples: "The life these ladies lead, / upon a stage, repeats itself behind the walls / of many city streets." But in *Iconographs,* Swenson renounces her usual objectivity in a dramatic fashion with poems that are explicitly sexual, lesbian, and personal: "Wednesday at the Waldorf," "In the Yard," "The Year of the Double Spring," and most notably, "A Trellis for R."

The latter is a delicately beautiful love poem, in which a lover's physical features are individually described and admired while being figured iconographically as roses on a trellis.

By the time of the publication of *Iconographs,* Swenson had moved out of New York City and settled into a new home, in Sea Cliff, New York, where she lived for the rest of her life with R. Rozanne Knudson, an author of fiction for young readers. During the late 1960s and the 1970s, Swenson's reputation became firmly established. She was honored with numerous awards, grants, and fellowships, including a Rockefeller Foundation grant in 1967 and a National Endowment for the Arts Grant in 1974. During this same time period, she was a writer-in-residence at several universities, including Purdue University, the University of North Carolina, and the University of California at Riverside. She published an award-winning translation of works by the Swedish poet Thomas Transtström in 1972, and created two more books for young readers—*More Poems to Solve* in 1971 and, in 1976, *The Guess and Spell Coloring Book.*

In 1978, Swenson published *New and Selected Things Taking Place*—a volume with sixty-three new poems, as well as selections from her five previous volumes (arranged in reverse chronological order). Her desire to republish even her earliest poems is of interest, as is her refusal to revise her previously published poems in any way. She said in her interview with Karla Hammond that "it isn't a good idea to impose your older self on your younger self because you've become a different person. What you produced when you were young had better stay in that form or else be discarded." But significantly, a number of the poems from *Iconographs* reprinted in this volume *are* changed in that they are no longer in shaped form. The decision to place these poems in fairly standard stanzaic forms

seems to indicate that Swenson ultimately agreed with the critics who felt that the forms were superfluous. But she did retain some shaped poems from *Iconographs,* along with some of her earlier typographical experiments, and when viewed together in one volume, they reveal, on the one hand, an extraordinary range of formal innovation. On the other, these poems also attest to a remarkable consistency in Swenson's poetic project: in almost every poem, one can trace Swenson's attention to the visually perceptible, her complex verbal fashioning, her affinity with the natural world, her quirky perspective and playful sense of humor, and her objectivity. These elements continue to be central to the new poems, which are printed at the beginning of *Things Taking Place,* but in some cases they are employed in surprisingly fresh ways.

What is most immediately noticeable in *Things Taking Place* are the poems that feature Swenson's new, relaxed personal voice. While none of the poems in this volume has the revelatory impact of the passionate poems in *Iconographs,* there are several poems that are distinctively different from anything Swenson had done before. In them, Swenson's use of the first-person pronoun is no longer carefully guarded; her language is less tightly controlled, even informal at times; the lines of her poems are longer and looser, more proselike. Most significant, her characteristically detailed observations are no longer the product of aloof objectivity but arise out of her own subjective experience. In "Staying at Ed's Place," although careful not to disrupt the scene she's observing, Swenson is nevertheless obviously, physically, there in a way that is different from her usual detachment:

I like being in your apartment, and not disturbing
  anything.
As in the woods I wouldn't want to move a tree,
or change the play of sun and shadow on the
  ground.

MAY SWENSON / 649

The yellow kitchen stool belongs right there
against white plaster. I haven't used your purple
        towel
because I like the accidental cleft of shade you left
        in it.

The casualness of Swenson's new style in *Things Taking Place* does not preclude the use of her typical poetic devices, but she tends to employ them in an organic rather than ostentatious fashion. He poetic devices are an essential part of what she is expressing rather than mere exhibitions of technique. For example, in "Digging in the Garden of Age I Uncover a Live Root," Swenson underplays her usual intricate mixture of rhyme, alliteration, and consonance:

Flash of new trowel. Your eyes
green in greenhouse light. Smell of
your cotton smock, of your neck
in the freckled shade of your hair.
A gleam of sweat in your lip's scoop.
Pungent geranium leaves, their wet
smell when our widening pupils met.

Within these easygoing lines, Swenson's poetic devices augment rather than dominate the images and emotions being rendered.

In her interview with the *New York Quarterly,* which was conducted the year before the publication of *Things Taking Place,* Swenson emphatically states, "I'm through making shaped poems. . . . I took it as far as I could go. I had satisfied my eye enough." Although a few of the poems in the volume have unusual typographical layouts, most of the poems are broken up into recognizable stanzas, the length of the lines making them almost prose paragraphs. This development corresponds to another shift in Swenson's method at this time: *Things Taking Place* is far less contrived than earlier volumes; there are fewer puns, riddles, and other word games, and fewer schematic poems. Similarly, while Swenson continues to focus her attention on nature, it does not function primarily as a metaphor or

elaborate conceit or an arena for magical transformations; more often than not, it is simply what it is. In some cases, such as "Camping in Madera Canyon" or "From Sea Cliff, March," the resultant poems are pure descriptions, with no other level of meaning hidden beneath their beautiful surfaces. But when Swenson does go beyond the surface—as in "A Navajo Blanket"—the outcome can be spectacular. The poem begins with her characteristic focus on the observed object: "Eye-dazzlers the Indians weave. Three colors / are paths that pull you in, and pin you / to the maze." Yet once we have entered the blanket, as it were, the experience becomes one of the spirit, not the senses:

. . . Then, slipping free of zigzag and
hypnotic diamond, find your way out
by the spirit trail, a faint Green thread that
secretly crosses the border, where your mind
is rinsed and returned to you like a white cup.

Swenson is most successful when she finds subject matter which is substantial enough to stand up to, rather than be engulfed by, her imaginative powers. In *Things Taking Place,* those poems are most often the ones in which she confronts aging and death. She described them as "rather dark," and most of them are a departure from her typical mode of affirmative delight. Yet even in her first volume of poetry, *Another Animal,* it is evident that Swenson is fascinated with death and that autumn is the season she is drawn to most often. But whereas in her earlier work she hid behind metaphysics in her explorations of death, and focused on the surface of sensuous details in her poems about autumn, in *Things Taking Place* she is clearly thinking about her own death and using autumn to reflect upon her own feelings about aging. In "October," a beautiful and moving lyric in seven sections, Swenson intersperses her observations of the present with memories of the past. Moving in stately meters, Swenson's precisely rendered images are not static but carry the reader back in time and, finally, inward, to the poet's personal connection to the scene being observed:

> . . . Stand still, stare
> hard into bramble and tangle,
> past leaning broken trunks,
> sprawled roots exposed. Will
> something move?—some vision
> come to outline? Yes, there—
> deep in—a dark bird hangs
> in the thicket, stretches a wing.
> Reversing his perch, he says one
> "Chuck." His shoulder-patch
> that should be red looks gray.
> This old redwing has decided to
> stay, this year, not to join the
> strenuous migration. Better here,
> in the familiar, to fade.

Swenson's presence in this passage gives it a poignancy rarely achieved in her more objective poems; the reader does not have to be told that the final line expresses Swenson's resignation as well as that of the bird.

However, it is evident from the majority of poems in *Things Taking Place* that Swenson still feels more comfortable when camouflaged behind the details, withholding the true depths of her emotions. In "That the Soul May Wax Plump," a poem about the death of her mother, she describes her mother's corpse without betraying any sense of loss or love, without giving an inkling of what she feels about what she's writing:

> My dumpy little mother on the undertaker's slab
> had a mannequin's grace. From chin to foot
> the sheet outlined her, thin and tall. Her face
> uptilted, bloodless, smooth, had a long smile.

She goes on to describe her mother's final "regimen of near starvation," her belief "in evacuation, an often and fierce purgation, / meant to teach the body to be hollow, that the soul / may wax plump." Swenson's coolness is baffling and disturbing; the poet's conceit triumphs over the daughter's emotion.

Sven Birkerts, in a 1985 essay, characterizes Swenson's fluctuations between subjectivity and objectivity in *Things Taking Place* as "exhibiting that on-off quality that often accompanies a new poet's search for voice." Even though this is Swenson's sixth book of poetry and contains many poems that are "unquestionably the work of a mature and sophisticated artist," Birkerts sees it, paradoxically, as a kind of debut in which Swenson is struggling "to bring her own self forward." In an interesting fantasy poem, "The Wonderful Pen," Swenson imagines a pen that would connect directly to a vein in her arm and then choose "all the right words for my feelings." But when the pen runs dry and other fanciful inventions and forms of expression fail, Swenson decides to offer herself as the text to be read: "But I have a wonderful mind: Inventive. It is / for you to find. Read *me*. Read my mind." The poem betrays Swenson's fear of giving away too much of herself in her poetry, yet it also indicates her desire for her readers to experience, in some essential way, herself.

In the last decade of her life, Swenson's poetic achievement was recognized to be that of a major American poet, and she was honored in many ways. She was awarded an Academy of American Poets Fellowship in 1979 and in 1981 won the Bollingen Prize in Poetry (which she shared with Howard Nemerov). She served as chancellor of the Academy of American Poets from 1980 until her death and, in 1987, was a recipient of a MacArthur Fellowship. But the final years of her life were most remarkable for her sustained creativity. Instead of looking backwards and working on a volume of collected poems, Swenson chose instead to continue her investigations of perception and her experiments with poetic form.

The last volume of Swenson's poetry published in her lifetime, *In Other Words* (1987) (which appeared when Swenson was 74), is comprised entirely of new poems. A series of poems of impressive variety, *In Other Words* reveals that Swenson's penchant for playfulness did not diminish with age. Riddling descriptions and wordplay turn up throughout the volume, and Swenson devotes an entire section (entitled "Comics") to poems which are pure amusement. In "A Nosty Fright," the children's game of switching consonants is employed to depict the "frosty night" of Halloween and the possibility of a "nasty fright" that lies hidden among "the roldengod and the soneyhuckle, / the sack eyed blusan and the wistle theed." There is little of Swenson's typographical inventiveness in this volume, but she does experiment with different types of prose poems, including a "novel" called "Giraffe" in which the first chapter begins, "Giraffe is the first word in this chapter. Is is the second word," and so on, for twelve chapters. The final section of the volume is a bizarre thirty-three page allegorical poem/story, "Banyan," that follows the adventures of a white cockatoo who has escaped from a library in Florida and the ape/narrator who befriends her.

Most of *In Other Words,* however, is familiar. Swenson's customary subjects are all represented: there are poems on nature, the sea, animals (especially birds), and space travel. Swenson employs here the longer lines and narrative style she developed in *Iconographs* and *Things Taking Place* but, curiously, replaces the relaxed personal voice that emerged in those volumes with her earlier stance of omniscient objectivity. The return to reticence is matched by a resurgence of artifice, with Swenson reasserting her control over diction and syntax, as in this passage from "Waterbird":

> . . . Her beak, ferrule of a folded black
> umbrella, with neat thrust impales her prey.
> She flaps up to dry on the crooked, look-
> dead-limb of the Gumbo Limbo, her tan-
> tipped wing fans spread, tail a shut fan dangled.

The spirit of Bishop, who died in 1979, is strong in this volume, manifesting itself in the exotic quality of poems like "Waterbird" as well as in the two poems that are addressed to her directly. One of these, "In the Bodies of Words," is a powerfully simple and deeply felt elegy, in which the natural setting Swenson observes—the beach, sandpipers—recalls Bishop's poetry: encountering birds on the shore, she exclaims "your pipers, Elizabeth!" Swenson's insistent message to Bishop in this poem is especially moving because it is also clearly an attempt to reassure herself: "But vision lives! / Vision, potent, regenerative, lives in bodies of words. / Your vision lives, Elizabeth, your words / from lip to lip perpetuated."

But with the exception of "In the Bodies of Words," Swenson avoids the subjects which in the past yielded some of her finest poems—aging and death. In the absence of poems of personal expression, Swenson's strengths are best displayed in several poems of natural description, including "Goodbye, Goldeneye" and "Little Lion Face." The latter poem is a lusciously sensual and sexual poem in which the sunflower of the title is described as both flower and lover. However, Swenson's renewed interest in formal control also revives her tendency to latch onto trivial (and hence more malleable) subjects; Swenson can do things to subjects like a blood test or a house full of teddy bears, but they, in turn, give little back to Swenson or the reader. Linda Gregerson contrasts Swenson's conceits with those of the metaphysical poets, concluding that "hers are frictionless conceits for the most part . . . poetic figure delightfully embellishes but does not alter or explicate the underlying object of regard."

The scarcity of transformation or revelation in *In Other Words* can surely be traced, at least in part, to Swenson's physical and emotional retreat from her poems. But interestingly, it is in this volume that Swenson makes a startling personal appearance that is like no other in her oeuvre. For the first time in her career, Swenson turns her exacting eye upon herself and relentlessly, mercilessly, tells us what she sees:

> Her stomach poked out and sagged, partly hiding her slumped, hairless pudenda, and her flattened breasts hung, the left longer than the right. Shoulders were narrow, upper back hunched, skinny neck and nearly hairless head thrust foreward [sic]. Arms and lowers legs were thin, but the flaccid thighs, the buttocks and the coil of fat at the waist hung in jelly-like bags.

After describing the rest of her body, she moves on to her face:

> Her lips, string-like and crooked, pressed together sternly, and the mouthcorners hooked down to meet trenches of the slack jaws and corded neck. . . . the forehead with its limp fringe of square-cut hair, was hardly wrinkled at all. Although the earlobes had lengthened and creased, the small nose, which was upturned with round prominent nostrils, remained inappropriately childlike.

Standing next to Swenson, the old woman, is Swenson as a two-year-old girl, wearing a "starched white dress" and high-buttoned shoes, with "straight, fine hair, blond . . . cut square across the forehead above a tiny short nose." This haunting passage is embedded within the pages of "Banyan" and presented as a vision the ape and the cockatoo encounter; one finishes reading the passage without knowing exactly what Swenson wants to convey through this juxtaposition of young self and old or how she feels about it. But to be suddenly confronted, in the final poem of Swenson's final book, with a powerfully honest self-portrait of a woman who spent most of her career trying to efface herself, is both disturbing and strangely moving.

Swenson died December 4, 1989, in Oceanview, Delaware, of a heart attack two years after the publication of *In Other Words*. Since then,

three posthumous volumes have been published: *The Complete Poems to Solve* (1993) collects her two previous books of riddle poems; *The Love Poems of May Swenson* (1991) and *Nature: Poems Old and New* (1994) include poems from the seven volumes published in her lifetime, as well as poems collected from other sources and poems published for the first time. *Nature* provides an excellent introduction to Swenson's poetry, but it also reveals, through several important new poems, unexpected facets of Swenson that heighten the already paradoxical nature of her work. "The Truth Is Forced," a poem from 1961, is an unguardedly confessional poem unlike anything Swenson published in her lifetime. In it, she admits that her "most precious properties" are "distance, secrecy, privacy," but declares "Not able to be honest in person / I wish to be honest in poetry": "I am glad, indeed I dearly crave / to become naked in poetry / to force the truth / through a poem." Fittingly, this *ars poetica* was a private one, and the aim it articulates is one Swenson struggled with throughout her career. In another new poem, "Lying and Looking," Swenson celebrates her own body; the poem only provides an interesting contrast to the harsh assessment of her body Swenson offered in "Banyan" but also tempers the impression of physical aloofness fostered by Swenson's other published poems. One of the most remarkable poems in *Nature* is "Staring at the Sea on the Day of the Death of Another." This stately meditation on death figures the sea as a mausoleum and the waves as "countless shelves, / cradling the prone effigies of our unearthly selves"; Swenson calmly but chillingly concludes the poem with the observation that "One of them is mine / and gliding forward, gaping wide." "Staring at the Sea on the Day of the Death of Another" is one of Swenson's finest poems, yet it was never included in any of the seven volumes she published. The excellence of this poem and that of other new poems in *Nature* and *The*

Love Poems of May Swenson, as well as the knowledge that as of 1996 hundreds of Swenson's poems have yet to be published in book form, indicate that the full depth of Swenson's poetic achievement remains to be measured.

However, as each posthumous volume has appeared, critics have reviewed Swenson's career and attempted to evaluate her achievement, to ascertain her place in the field of contemporary poetry. After *The Love Poems of May Swenson* was published, critical attention began to focus on the importance of Swenson's sexual orientation. Swenson was wary of being classified as a lesbian poet; as she explained in a letter of refusal to the editors of a proposed anthology entitled *Lesbian Poetry,* she was fearful that any poem in "an anthology with that label as title will look as though it was 1. written by Lesbians, 2. about Lesbianism." Swenson's expression of dissatisfaction with the limitations of names here is consistent with her poetic practice. But as Sue Russell points out, in an essay on Swenson as a lesbian poet, Swenson was pleased when her poems were understood fully, in their proper context, and late in life, she did agree to appear in a volume entitled *Gay and Lesbian Poetry in Our Time* (1988). Ultimately Swenson's varied and wide-ranging poetry resists simple categorization, but the fact of her lesbianism adds an important dimension to some of her poems, one that continues to attract critical scrutiny. One particularly compelling question is the extent to which Swenson's sexual orientation may have determined or at least influenced her poetic impersonality.

In any final assessment of Swenson, a comparison to Bishop is perhaps inevitable. Of the same generation and close friends, they shared a passion for the natural world, an exactness of visual perception, a tendency toward personal detachment. But while Bishop's reputation has grown enormously in the years after her death, Swenson's following in the 1990s is comparatively small. However, if Swenson's aims and accomplishments are distinguished from, rather than measured by, those of Bishop her strengths are evident. As Mary Jo Salter noted in a piece in the *New Republic* in 1988, while Swenson's poems do not display the same depth or range of feeling as Bishop's, they surpass hers in the intricacy of their musical effects. Similarly, one should not use Bishop's naturalness as a standard by which to judge Swenson, who cultivated artifice. To appreciate fully the achievement of Swenson, one must look past the transient value of her flamboyant typography and her word games and her minor topical poems and focus on her strengths—her keen sight, her ceaseless curiosity, her inventiveness, her humor, her joy. The final paradox of Swenson's career is that her most powerful poems are also, in many ways, her simplest. The poems that linger in memory are those in which, following her favorite injunction to "look closer," Swenson breaks through the surface of things and finds the truth.

Selected Bibliography

WORKS OF MAY SWENSON

POETRY

Another Animal: Poems. In *Poets of Today.* Edited by John Hall Wheelock. New York: Scribners, 1954. Pp. 103–179.
A Cage of Spines. New York: Rinehart, 1958.
To Mix with Time: New and Selected Poems. New York: Scribners, 1963.
Poems to Solve. New York: Scribners, 1966.
Half Sun Half Sleep: New Poems. New York: Scribners, 1967.
Iconographs: Poems. New York: Scribners, 1970.
More Poems to Solve. New York: Scribners, 1971.
The Guess and Spell Coloring Book. Illustrated by Lise Gladstone. New York: Scribners, 1976.

New and Selected Things Taking Place. Boston: Little, Brown, 1978.

In Other Words: New Poems. New York: Knopf, 1987.

The Love Poems of May Swenson. Boston: Houghton Mifflin, 1991.

The Complete Poems to Solve. New York: Macmillan, 1993.

Nature: Poems Old and New. Boston: Houghton Mifflin, 1994.

PLAY

The Floor: A Play in One Act. First Stage, 6, no. 2:112–118 (1967).

SHORT STORIES

"Appearances." *New Directions in Prose and Poetry,* 13:69–82 (1951).

"Eclogue." *Paris Review,* 10:97–103 (Fall 1955).

"Mutterings of Middlewoman." In *discovery no. 5.* Edited by Vance Bourjaily. New York: Pocket Books, 1955. Pp. 96–118.

ESSAYS

"On Richard Wilbur's 'Love Calls Us to the Things of This World.'" *Berkeley Review,* 1:12–16. Reprinted in *The Contemporary Poet as Artist and Critic.* Edited by Anthony Ostroff. Boston: Little, Brown, 1964. Pp. 12–16.

"The Poet As Anti-Specialist." *Saturday Review,* January 30, 1965, pp. 16–18, 64. Reprinted as "The Experience of Poetry in a Scientific Age" in *Poets on Poetry.* Edited by Howard Nemerov. New York: Basic Books, 1966. Pp. 147–159.

"May Swenson on Becoming a Poet, and on Form." *Envoy,* 1:1–2 (Spring–Summer 1979).

MANUSCRIPT PAPERS

Swenson's manuscripts and correspondence from 1949 to 1980 are housed in the Modern Literary Manuscripts Collection. Special Collections of the Washington University Libraries, Saint Louis, Missouri.

BIBLIOGRAPHY

Gadomski, Kenneth E. "May Swenson: A Bibliography of Primary and Secondary Sources." *Bulletin of Bibliography,* 44:255–280 (December 1987).

TRANSLATED POETRY

Windows and Stones: Selected Poems, by Tomas Tranströmer. Translated with Leif Sjöberg. Pittsburgh: University of Pittsburgh Press, 1972.

CORRESPONDENCE

"Elizabeth Bishop—May Swenson Correspondence." *Paris Review,* 131:171–186 (Summer 1994).

BIOGRAPHICAL AND CRITICAL STUDIES

Berryman, John. "The Long Way to MacDiarmid." *Poetry,* 88:52–61 (April 1956).

Birkerts, Sven. "A Versatile Dance in the Mind." *Parnassus,* 12–13:317–334 (Spring–Summer–Fall–Winter 1985).

Ciardi, John. "Three Voices in Verse." *New York Times Book Review,* November 14, 1954.

Corn, Alfred. Review of *The Love Poems of May Swenson. Poetry,* 161:295–298 (February 1993).

George, Diana Hume. " 'Who Is the Double Ghost Whose Head Is Smoke?': Women Poets on Aging." In *Memory and Desire: Aging—Literature—Psychoanalysis.* Edited by Kathleen Woodward and Murray M. Schwartz. Bloomington, Indiana University Press, 1986. Pp. 134–153.

Gibbs, Barbara. "Five Recent Volumes." *Poetry,* 94:189–195 (June 1959).

Gray, Paul. "Four Poets and Their Songs." *Time,* June 25, 1979, pp. 69–72.

Gregerson, Linda. "A Cradle of String." *Poetry,* 154:233–238 (July 1989).

Hammer, Langdon. "Formal Feelings: New Books by Women." *Yale Review,* 83:121–141 (January 1995).

Hoffman, Daniel. "Poetry: Dissidents from Schools." *Harvard Guide to Contemporary Writing.* Edited by Daniel Hoffman. Cambridge: Harvard University Press, 1979. Pp. 564–606.

Hollander, John. "Poetry Chronicle." *Partisan Review,* 26:137–144 (Winter 1959).

Howard, Richard. "May Swenson." *Tri-Quarterly,* 7:119–131 (Fall 1966).

Johnson, Rosemary. "All Things Bright and Beautiful." *Parnassus,* 7:46–59 (Fall–Winter 1978).

Knudson, R. R. *The Wonderful Pen of May Swenson.* New York: Macmillan, 1993.

Malkoff, Karl. "May Swenson." In his *Crowell's Handbook of Contemporary American Poetry.* New York: Crowell, 1972. Pp. 309–313.

McElveen, Idris. "May Swenson." *Dictionary of Literary Biography.* Vol. 5, *American Poets since World War II.* Edited by Donald J. Grenier, Detroit: Gale, 1980. Pp. 309–318.

Ostriker, Alicia. "May Swenson and the Shapes of Speculation." *American Poetry Review,* 7:35–38 (March–April 1978). Reprinted in *Shakespeare's Sisters: Feminist Essays on Women Poets.* Edited by Sandra M. Gilbert and Susan Gubar. Bloomington: Indiana University Press, 1979. Pp. 221–232.

Pritchard, William H. "Poetry Chronicle." *Hudson Review,* 20:304–314 (Summer 1967).

Russell, Sue. "A Mysterious and Lavish Power: How Things Continue to Take Place in the Work of May Swenson." *Kenyon Review* 16:128–139 (Summer 1994).

Salter, Mary Jo. "No Other Words." *New Republic,* March 7, 1988, pp. 40–41.

Sanders, Charles. "Swenson's 'Snow in New York.'" *Explicator,* 38, no. 1:41–42 (1979).

Schulman, Grace. "Life's Miracles: The Poetry of May Swenson." *American Poetry Review,* 23:9–13 (September–October 1994).

Shapiro, Karl. "A Ball with Language." *New York Times Book Review,* May 7, 1967.

Smith, Dave. "Perpetual Worlds Taking Place." Poetry, 135:291–296 (February 1980).

Stafford, William. "A Five-Book Shelf." *Poetry,* 111:184–188 (December 1967).

Stanford, Ann. "May Swenson: The Art of Perceiving." *Southern Review,* 5:58–75 (January 1969).

Swenson, Paul. "May in October: Life and Death as Existential Riddles in May Swenson's Poetry." *Weber Studies,* 8:18–21 (Spring 1991).

Wheelock, John Hall. "A Critical Introduction." In his *Poets of Today.* New York: Scribners, 1954. Pp. 3–15.

Wilbur, Richard. "May Swenson: A Memorial Tribute." *Gettysburg Review,* 5:81–85 (Winter 1992).

Zinnes, Harriet. "No Matter What the Icons Say." *Nation,* February 28, 1972, pp. 282–283.

INTERVIEWS

Draves, Cornelia, and Mary Jane Fortunato. "Craft Interview with May Swenson." *New York Quarterly,* 19:14–27 (Autumn 1977).

Hammond, Karla. "An Interview with May Swenson: July 14, 1978." *Parnassus,* 7:60–75 (Fall–Winter 1978).

Hudson, Lee. "A Conversation with May Swenson." *Literature in Performance,* 3:55–66 (April 1983).

Lazarus, Arnold, and Rozanne Knudson. "Conversation with May Swenson." *Quartet,* 4:9–27 (Winter 1969).

—*JANE ELDRIDGE MILLER*

Anne Tyler

1941—

SOMEWHERE IN THE course of most of Anne Tyler's novels a character will suddenly look at the situation that has developed and ask, "How did I get into this?" Macon Leary of *The Accidental Tourist* (1985) finds himself back home with his brothers and sister, his marriage and his leg broken, and thinks, *"What have I gone and done?"* In *Dinner at the Homesick Restaurant* (1982) Luke Tull, running away from home, finds himself hitching another ride near Richmond: "All at once . . . what was Luke *doing* here? What could he be thinking of?" *Ladder of Years* (1995) finds Delia Grinstead, having walked away from a family vacation, in an unfamiliar town, thinking, *"Oh, God, . . . how am I going to get out of this?"* The reader caught up in the effortless narrative, is astonished that these essentially passive characters have been led into outrageous, outlandish, or simply impossible situations by a logical series of events. It is Tyler's gift that she can make us see the plausibility of lives and actions that, viewed from the outside, we might dismiss as strange, eccentric, or downright crazy.

By 1996, Tyler had published thirteen novels, one every two to three years since 1964. In addition, she had written over fifty short stories, which, while they had won prizes and been anthologized, had not been collected into a volume. She had also reviewed books extensively for such publications as the *New Republic*, *National Observer*, *New York Times Book Review*, and *Washington Post*. In 1993 she published a children's book, *Tumble Tower*, which was illustrated by her daughter Mitra.

Over the years Tyler built a following of readers and critics (including John Updike), received many awards (including the Pulitzer Prize and a National Book Critics Circle Award), and was elected to the American Academy and Institute of Arts and Letters. However, her work only began receiving the scrutiny of scholars in the mid-1980s. Relatively few scholarly articles and books were written by 1996, allowing for much discussion of her work to come.

Anne Tyler is an intensely private writer who chronicles the private lives of families. She explores these lives with sympathy, gentle humor, and quiet acceptance, never condemning. Tyler's themes evolve from the intricacies of relationships lived within the fine old houses of the posh section of Baltimore, Roland Park; downtown row houses; and houses in between. She focuses on the tension between the desire to escape and the desire to return home, on the problem of taking responsibility for one's own and others' actions, and on the fine line between endurance and hopelessness. She returns to these themes again and again, each time approaching them from a different perspective. As her art deepened and matured, so did her exploration of these themes. Rarely, however, does she give the reader an absolute answer; no one narrative voice speaks with authority.

Born in Minneapolis, Minnesota, on October 25, 1941, the daughter of Quakers, Lloyd Parry Tyler and Phyllis Mahon Tyler, Tyler spent much of her first ten years in experimental Quaker communities, including one in Celo, North Carolina, near Asheville. When she was eleven, the family moved to Raleigh, North Carolina. In her 1980 essay ''Still Just Writing,'' Tyler remembers feeling like an outsider in her new middle-class world: ''I had never used a telephone and could strike a match on the soles of my bare feet. All the children in my new school looked very peculiar to me, and I certainly must have looked peculiar to them.'' At sixteen Tyler entered Duke University, younger than most freshmen, and found a mentor in Reynolds Price, who taught her writing. After graduating Phi Beta Kappa with a major in Russian in 1961, Tyler continued her studies in Russian at Columbia University (1961–1962). Returning to Duke in 1962 as a Russian bibliographer in the library, Tyler married Iranian-born Taghi Mohammad Modarressi, a medical resident in psychiatry, in 1963. From 1964 to 1965 they lived in Montreal, Canada, where Modarressi completed his residency at McGill University and Tyler worked in the McGill Law Library. In 1967 they moved to Baltimore, Maryland, where they still lived in 1996. Modarressi is a child psychiatrist and novelist; they have two adult daughters, Tezh and Mitra.

As the years went by, Tyler became increasingly reclusive. She did not give readings or go on television; she conducted interviews by mail. She kept her life private, her writing a solitary activity. In ''Still Just Writing'' she explains,

> I feel I am only holding myself together by being extremely firm and decisive about what I will do and what I will not do. I will write my books and raise the children. Anything else just fritters me away. I know this makes me seem narrow, but in fact, I *am* narrow.

However, she made many valuable statements about her work in written interviews, in some cases compelled to explain matters her critics had failed to understand. As might be expected, she sometimes changed her mind about issues over the years, so that earlier statements and interviews are not as reliable as later ones.

Tyler's desire for solitude—her distance from her readers, critics, and fellow writers—combines with other isolating factors in her background (moving from a commune to a middle-class world, going to college at an early age, marrying a man from another culture, living in Canada for several years) to explain her typical narrative stance. As Frank Shelton has pointed out, she views her characters with both compassion and distance. In ''Still Just Writing'' she describes her understanding of her relationship to her characters: ''I have given up hope, by now, of ever losing my sense of distance; in fact, I seem to have come to cherish it.'' That distance, though, is coupled with understanding: ''it just seems to me that even the most ordinary person, in real life, will turn out to have something unusual at his center.'' And so Tyler explores those ordinary lives, ''buttressing my inside world, where people go on meaning well and surprising other people with little touches of grace.''

If Morning Ever Comes (1964), Tyler's first novel, was praised by critics mostly for the youth of its author rather than for the intrinsic merits of the text itself. Subsequently, Tyler herself stated her dislike for the book, saying in an interview with Wendy Lamb that *If Morning Ever Comes* ''should be burned,'' that it is ''formless and wandering and should never have been published.'' As a result, critics who so choose can treat it quickly, if at all, and move on to the later work. However, in terms of both narrative technique and theme this novel is a precursor of the work to come.

Tyler's narrative technique in *If Morning Ever Comes* is one that she uses often. While the novel covers a short period of time (Thursday to Tuesday), flashbacks and storytelling fill in the preceding years so that we understand how the current situation arose. People tell stories that others do not remember; they explain their actions by telling stories from the past.

Ben Joe Hawkes, the one man in a family of six sisters, a mother, and a grandmother, believes that he must be the sole support, financially and emotionally, of all the women in the family partially because of his guilt over his father's death. He has entered Columbia Law School, not because he wants to be a lawyer but because he thinks practicing law will make him enough money to support his family. However, he is mistaken in thinking his family is dependent on him: they send him money weekly for his expenses, and when he returns home to Sandhill, North Carolina, for a weekend his sisters are so independent that he feels he hardly exists for them.

He returns home because of what he perceives as a crisis: his sister Joanne has left her husband, Gary, because she is afraid that she will repeat the mistakes her parents made in their marriage. Ben Joe can do nothing to help, though, so while he is home, bored with his family and his alienation from it, he spends time with a former girlfriend, Shelley Domer, and eventually invites her to marry him and move to New York. Within this small plot, we find various themes that recur in Tyler's works: the pull toward home and revulsion from it, guilt over a family member's death, and the attempt of a family to adapt to the absence of a father and husband.

When Ben Joe and Shelley actually leave on the train to marry in New York, the reader can't help but wonder what will become of them. They, like so many characters in Tyler's novels, seem to be marrying for the wrong reasons. Ben Joe hopes to protect his wife and son-to-be just as he had hoped to protect his sisters. He falls asleep on the train and dreams of "Shelley and his son like two white dancing figures . . . they were suspended a minute . . . and then they danced off again and he let them go; he knew he had to let them." He realizes that "one part of them was faraway and closed to him, as unreachable as his own sisters," and that he, too, has that place that is inaccessible to others. Ben Joe's realization of every person's essential separateness may allow him a chance at happiness in his marriage in that he will be able to respect the privacy of those closest to him. Tyler does not predict; she shows us her characters and allows us to decide.

Tyler disowned her second novel, *The Tin Can Tree* (1965), just as she had her first. Once again, the critics seemed amazed that a woman so young could write so mature a novel; however, the novel does raise questions that Tyler works out more effectively in later works. Six-year-old Janie Rose Pike has been killed in a tractor accident. Her family, which occupies one-third of a three-family house, tries to deal with her death. The novel is a third-person narration from the points of view of Joan Pike, a cousin who is living with Janie Rose's family, and James Green, who lives at the other end of the house and has been dating Joan.

The basic issue in the novel is Mrs. Pike's guilt over her daughter's death. She feels that she neglected Janie Rose in favor of her brother, Simon; however, instead of lavishing attention on Simon after his sister's death, she ignores him, provoking him eventually to run away from home. Perhaps the most moving scene in the novel comes when Mrs. Pike, trying to regain some sense of normalcy, resumes her work as a seamstress. Joan has enlisted the help of one of Mrs. Pike's customers and of Simon in an attempt to distract Mrs. Pike, since being a seamstress invites the kind of chatting one would find at a hairdresser's. As Simon recounts a bit of gossip, Mrs. Pike seems to be moving out of her grief and guilt, until a random phone call from a radio station reminds her poignantly of her daughter: "She had crumpled up against her sewing machine, leaning her forehead against the wheel of it and clenching both fists tightly against her stomach. . . . Mrs. Pike only rocked back and forth, and Simon and Joan stared at the floor."

While the death of Janie Rose and its effects are at the center of the book, other relationships are also important. At the other end of the house from the Pikes live the brothers James and Ansel Green. James is a photographer, a sort of artist figure, while Ansel is a hypochondriac who irritates everyone else in the novel. Unlike most of Tyler's eccentrics, Ansel is very hard, if not impossible, to like, and one is hard-pressed to understand why James puts up with him until James's own sense of guilt about his family becomes clear. When contemplating whether or not he could ever marry Joan, James thinks,

> he could go after her and say, "Come back. And will you marry me?" in his *mind* he could say that, but not in real life. In real life he had Ansel, and would have him always because he couldn't walk out on that one, final member of his family that he hadn't yet deserted.

So James will endure the situation, never having a family of his own. Endurance is a quality Tyler admires, but the reader is not persuaded by James's reasons.

Joan shows similarities with other Tyler characters. She can pack everything she owns into two suitcases. She is respectful of others' privacy, living in the Pike home as if she were a guest, always confining her personal belongings to her own bedroom, never intruding on others. Joan runs away just before Simon does, and her attempt is as abortive as his. However, Simon's message has been heard: his mother realizes his need for her. Joan's message, on the other hand, has not been heard. Only Ansel and Simon were even aware that she had left; there is no change in her relationship with James.

The celebration upon Simon's return that concludes the novel is not convincing. As Joan takes a picture of the entire group from all three portions of the house, she thinks,

> whole years could pass, they could be born and die, they could leave and return, they could marry or live out their separate lives alone, and nothing in this finder would change. They were going to stay this way, she and all the rest of them, not because of anyone else but because it was what they had chosen, what they would keep a strong tight hold of.

The foreshortened lives of the characters, their unresolved difficulties, their family problems, their unfulfilled potential—all these limitations make Joan's positive assertion hard to believe.

Tyler's third novel, *A Slipping-Down Life* (1970), is perhaps her most bizarre. Evie Decker, an overweight seventeen-year-old, carves the name of a local rock singer into her forehead with fingernail scissors as a way of getting his attention, an incident based on an actual occurrence during Elvis Presley's career. The novel covers the year in which Evie becomes aware of Bertram "Drumstrings" Casey, carves his name in her forehead, marries him, and leaves him, returning alone and pregnant to her family home, after her father dies of a heart attack.

Rather than portray Evie's impulsive action as a mistake that could lead only to disaster, Tyler shows how even this eccentric behavior can have positive consequences, as Evie slowly learns to assert herself and to take some control over her life. For instance, as she waits for her father in her hospital room after cutting "Casey" in her forehead, Evie says to her friend Violet, "I believe this might be the best thing I've ever done . . . Something out of character. Definite. Not covered by insurance. I'm just sure it will all work out well." Ironically, she may be right. She goes on, "While I was walking through that crowd with the policeman, I kept thinking of my name: Evie Decker, *me*. Taking something into my own hands for once. I thought, if I had started acting like this a long time ago my whole *life* might've been different.''

At this moment she sees the value of taking the initiative, of no longer waiting for things to happen to her. Later, she lapses into her old, passive ways, staying at home in her bathrobe and refusing to return to school. But when she eventually does decide to return, it is in her own way. First, she pushes Violet into telling her what her schoolmates are saying about her. Violet describes their attitude: ''Like when someone has crossed over where the rest of them haven't been. Getting pregnant, or dying, or that boy in the band who shot himself.'' Evie then makes sure that her classmates will continue to think of her as having crossed over: she calls Drum Casey, insists that he come see her, and then has him take her to school, late, in ''a red taffeta party dress.''

Just as Evie develops a plan for returning to school in a shocking way, she also develops a plan to further Drum's career and forcefully pushes it through. To get more publicity, she sits up front in the Unicorn roadhouse every weekend to lure curiosity seekers. Hearing that a revival preacher is using her as an example of what is wrong with the world, Evie insists that she and Drum attend the next revival meeting, photographer in tow. She later cooks up a scheme to have Drum supposedly kidnapped by his fans. Her methods are extreme, but she does have drive and determination.

As Evie develops her ability to take charge, Drum Casey becomes increasingly passive. Fired from his job and thrown out of his family home, Drum spends his nights sleeping on Evie's front-porch swing until he asks her to marry him, his rationale being that he does like her and that he wants to be married and have a place of his own. They elope and then settle into a tar-paper shack in the middle of tobacco fields. Ironically, Drum proves to be interested in homey things while Evie becomes increasingly independent. Over Drum's objections, she takes a job at the library in order to provide a steady source of money. She also becomes pregnant, again without his consent. At the end of the novel, Evie returns from her father's deathbed to find Drum in bed with Fay-Jean, the trashy girl who had first taken Evie to the Unicorn. Evie leaves Drum and returns to her father's home.

The narrative stance of the novel is not to predict what will become of Evie nor to label her. She has, some characters think, caused her father's heart attack because of her bizarre behavior; she has married on impulse and left her husband; she will, it seems, raise her child alone. Instead of condemning her, though, Tyler offers the possibility that she will do quite well, that she has taken some control over her life and may now act in a mature way, not as an impulsive child.

The Clock Winder (1972), Tyler's fourth novel, is the first to be set in Baltimore. Elizabeth Abbott, from Raleigh, North Carolina, arrives in Baltimore and becomes the handyman for helpless Mrs. Emerson, who has been unable to handle the many daily tasks around the house since her husband's death. Elizabeth, who had been awkward at home, finds here that she can do any task necessary.

The novel covers a decade, from Elizabeth's first arrival at the Emersons' house in 1960, some three months after Mr. Emerson's death, to a visit to the family home by Peter Emerson and his new wife, P. J., in 1970. We see the action mostly from Elizabeth's point of view, but some sections are narrated from the points of view of Peter and his sister, Margaret.

The main issue in *The Clock Winder* concerns taking responsibility for one's actions. Elizabeth tries to go through life without making choices and without influencing anyone because she fears the consequences. As she explains to Margaret, "Just before the finish line I think no, what if I'm making a mistake? . . . Things are so permanent. There's damage you can't repair."

However, even in her passivity she manages to hurt people who care about her. Timothy, another son of the Emersons, in an attempt to make Elizabeth take him seriously, threatens suicide; Elizabeth reaches for the gun, which fires and causes Timothy's death. Tyler never makes clear who was responsible for the shooting. Later, Elizabeth acquiesces to her parents and consents to marry Dommie Whitehill, a sweet young man who has loved her for years. She realizes the morning of the wedding that she cannot go through with it and leaves Dommie at the altar, hurting him deeply and publicly.

Only when Andrew Emerson, who feels Elizabeth was responsible for his brother's death, threatens to shoot her does Elizabeth realize that she is powerless to change some events, a realization that frees her from her fear of taking action. As Andrew aims the gun at her, she thinks back to Timothy's death: "she had never been sure what she should have done instead." The bullet grazes her arm, and when the others reach her, she is laughing. While Dr. Felson dresses her wound, she thinks, "Now we are even, no Emersons will look at me ever again as if I owe them something; now I know nothing I can do will change a bullet in its course." Furthermore, her wounding takes her out of her role as an observing caretaker and brings her into the Emerson family. After the visit to the doctor, she climbs into the car "among a tangle of other Emersons."

As Tyler's skill grew, she developed the trait of having various characters see events from their own points of view, without including an authorial voice to tell the reader what to believe. For example, the only outsider in the Emerson house in the last scene, P. J., evaluates the family this way:

That little closed-up family of yours is closed around *nothing,* thin air, all huddled up together scared to go out. Depending on someone that is like the old-maid failure poor relation you find some places, mending their screens and cooking their supper and fixing their chimneys and making peace—oh, she ended up worse off than *them.*

To some extent, this is Tyler's evaluation as well. She has said that she thinks the ending is a sad one, with Elizabeth settling for less than she could have had out of life. But, she admits, Elizabeth does what is happiest for her, even if that happiness means looking after a house and a passive, dependent family. P. J.'s analysis is thus no more trustworthy than anyone else's. The ending of *The Clock Winder,* then, like the endings of so many Tyler novels, is ambiguous.

Celestial Navigation (1974) a novel that Tyler has called her favorite, explores the difficulty of living an ordinary life while being an artist. Jeremy Pauling, an agoraphobic artist, lives in his mother's boarding house and remains there as an out-of-touch landlord after her death. The novel spans roughly a decade, from the death of Jeremy's mother in 1960 to his final rift from his family in 1971, with a short epilogue added. During this time Jeremy grows as a person and as an artist through his relationship with Mary Tell, but they are ultimately unable to remain together.

In this novel Tyler further develops her technique of offering differing points of view and evaluations of people and events. For the first time, Tyler uses first-person narrators. The narrator changes chapter by chapter, beginning with Amanda Pauling, Jeremy's bitter, self-righteous older sister, and then alternating among Jeremy, Mary, and Miss Vinton, one of the boarders. Only Jeremy's chapters are in the third person, appropriately so since he is inarticulate.

Jeremy spends his time creating "pieces," two-dimensional collages made of scraps of paper and cloth. As his relationship with Mary grows and then dies, Jeremy's art takes on a third dimension and increases in size. At the beginning of the novel, Amanda describes Jeremy's art: "Well, they're surely not *pictures*. Not even regular collages, not that intricate, mosaic-like way he does them." She goes on, "Little people made of triangles of wrapping paper and diamonds of silk. No definite outlines to them. Something like those puzzles they have in children's magazines—find seven animals in the branches of this bush. I couldn't see the point of it." Amanda, impatient and jealous, expresses the perspective of those who don't understand artistic endeavor: What's the point? However, she does give us a sense of the complexity of Jeremy's creations, a view we do not get from Jeremy. What we can see through Amanda's dismissive description is the intricacy and richness of Jeremy's work. At the end of the novel, Miss Vinton gives us a brief look at what his "pieces" have become: "great towering beautiful sculptures."

This change in his work is directly connected to his relationship with Mary Tell. Mary moves into Jeremy's boarding house with her daughter, after running away from her husband with John Harris, who promises to leave his wife but doesn't. As Mary's life is falling apart, Jeremy asks her to marry him. Unable to think of any other way to support herself and her daughter, Mary agrees—but to a sham marriage, since her first husband has refused to give her a divorce. She and Jeremy have five more children, which is a problem critics have with the novel: it is hard to believe that Jeremy is capable of sexual intercourse. The change in his art more convincingly reflects the change he is undergoing—his willingness to act, in spite of his phobias, because of his love for Mary. He is growing; sadly, Mary, in an attempt to protect him, does not encourage these steps.

The relationship is doomed to failure because Jeremy continues to feel the need to pull away from too much human contact and because Mary wants to protect him too much. The final blow comes when Jeremy realizes that the children are more important to Mary than he is. Visiting them at the boatyard where Mary and the children are living after leaving him, Jeremy is about to row out with the children to a sailboat when Mary asks him not to take them. He knows he is inept; he also knows that Mary has been rowing out to the sailboat with the children regularly. He thinks, "Of course he shouldn't take them. He knew that too. But to have her stand there telling him that, saying she was willing for him to go himself but not to take the children!" He returns to the boardinghouse without his family, the relationship severed.

The artist's paradoxical need for both distance and closeness is not resolved in this novel. Jeremy has clearly grown as an artist through his relationship with Mary Tell, but he cannot give himself to her fully and remain an artist. He can use the relationship as a source for his inspiration, but still must pull away, distance himself, in order to produce his art. Tyler's evocation of this artistic problem reflects her own need for privacy and perhaps explains why this novel would be her favorite.

Searching for Caleb (1976) is the story of the search for Caleb Peck, who left his family in 1912 and has not been seen since. In 1973, his brother, Daniel, and granddaughter Justine (who has married her first cousin Duncan) succeed in finding him, but the end of the search does not bring what they had expected.

The novel begins with Duncan and Justine Peck moving to Caro Mill, Maryland, and it ends with their moving out almost a year later. These two moves are the last in a long sequence. Within the framework of the year spent in Caro Mill, the novel includes Peck family history going back to 1870. The long span of this narration allows Tyler to explore the complexities of a family that is insular, resentful, and suspicious of outsiders, that bolsters itself with good manners and family rituals.

It is only many years later, when Laura Peck, Caleb's mother, dies that Daniel starts his search for his lost brother. He is wary of his relatives, who think of Caleb as "a deserter." To Daniel, Caleb "is still a member here," even though Caleb does not want to be. Daniel explains to Justine, the only other member of the family who expresses an interest in Caleb, "I would give all the remaining years of my life if I could set eyes on him again . . . only this time, paying closer *attention.*" He does give the rest of his life, traveling with Justine, who is "the only one who would hop into the car with him at a moment's notice."

Once Caleb has been located, Daniel writes him a typical Peck letter, mixing love and reproach, and then waits for an answer—which does not come. Disappointed, he complains,

> You think I shouldn't say how I feel. . . . In my childhood I was trained to hold things in, you see. But I thought I was holding them until a certain *time.* I assumed that someday, somewhere, I would again be given the opportunity to spend all that saved-up feeling. When will that be?

When he suffers a fatal heart attack later that day, his last words are, "Well . . . I had certainly hoped for more than *this* out of life."

This disappointment in life may be what Duncan has been fiercely trying to avoid. He is critical of his family, living his life in reaction to his family members, doing what they do not do, always seeing the worst in any gesture they make. Pecks drive black V-8 Fords; Duncan drives a green Graham Paige. Pecks are successful in business; when Duncan's odd business ventures turn unaccountably successful, he loses interest and moves to a new business, uprooting Justine and their daughter, Meg, each time. He worries about the effect on Justine of their frequent moves: "Sometimes he remembered that she had

not always been this way, though he couldn't put his finger on just when she had changed. Then he wondered if she only *pretended* to be happy, for his sake."

Justine *has* changed, from a quiet, orderly child destined to be just like her cousins to a fortune teller in constant motion, unconcerned about her appearance or others' opinions of her. She eventually recognizes that in her life with Duncan she has accepted his demands for move after move, rushing ahead without considering the effect on either herself or her daughter. Justine evaluates her life after her grandfather's funeral: "She had been so quick and brash, so loud, so impatient . . . where was the old slow, tender Justine?" She then realizes that "what she had mislaid was Justine herself."

Once Justine rescues Caleb from the home for the indigent where he has been committed, she discovers that Caleb cannot replace her grandfather, that he is different from every Peck she has ever known. She reflects that all the years he has spent away from the family have changed him: "he had gone by degrees, traveling only where led, merely proving himself adaptable, endlessly adaptable." She then realizes that she has done exactly the same thing. Justine, like Caleb, has allowed herself to go along with anyone who asked until she has lost herself. However, after her grandfather's death, Meg's marriage, and Caleb's escape, she cannot continue the annual moves; she needs some stability. As the only other way of life she knows is that of her family, she and Duncan pack to return, defeated, to Baltimore.

Before they take that step, though, Caleb sends them a thank-you note, the typical Peck "bread-and-butter" letter. This confirmation that he is a Peck after all somehow frees Justine to find a compromise between the stagnation of the Pecks who have remained at home and the endless movement she and Duncan have shared. Justine will become the fortune teller and Duncan the mechanic for Alonzo Divich's carnival, which travels a circuit around the area and has a permanent home in a pasture in Parvis, Maryland. They can thus move with the carnival and still have a home base, still be part of a community. This compromise—in effect, running away with the circus—appears to be perfectly reasonable: a credit to Tyler's ability to avoid condemning her characters while showing their motivations for what they do.

Earthly Possessions (1977), for which Tyler received a citation for literary excellence from the American Academy and Institute of Arts and Letters, is the first of her novels to feature one character as a first-person narrator. Charlotte Emory, the narrator, is at a bank in Clarion, Maryland, withdrawing money with which to leave her husband, Saul, when she is taken hostage by an inept bank robber, Jake Simms. Jake takes her south, first on a bus, then in a stolen car. The novel alternates chapters of Charlotte's narration of this trip with her account of her own history, interweaving her present and past. Charlotte's voice is amused and ironic. We must question her reliability as a narrator, though, as Tyler rarely seems to give us a voice in any of her novels that can tell us how to interpret events.

The main example of Charlotte's untrustworthiness as a narrator is her faulty memory of being told that she is not her mother's real daughter, that somehow she had been switched at the hospital with her mother's actual child. This belief seems to be based on the fact that her overweight mother had not realized she was pregnant but thought that she was going through menopause and suffering from a tumor. As a child, Charlotte may have construed her mother's surprise at being handed a baby to take home into surprise at being given the wrong baby. As usual, Tyler does not explain. Further, as Charlotte was not a happy child, convinced that she was ugly and that her morose parents did not love her, she seems to have engaged in that typical childhood fantasy of having other, better parents. She remembers, ''my two main worries when I was a child: one was that I was not their true daughter, and would be sent away. The other was that I *was* their true daughter and would never, ever manage to escape to the outside world.'' Charlotte continues a similar fantasy in her adult life when she thinks that the mother of Jiggs, her adopted son, will someday come to claim him.

Charlotte has contemplated leaving home for years, ever since an event in her childhood that she remembers as a kidnapping but admits she doesn't remember clearly. Since that time she has tried to prepare for leaving, for an existence stripped down to what she can carry herself: ''My life has been a history of casting off encumbrances, paring down to the bare essentials, stripping for the journey. Possessions make me anxious.'' She fights against high odds, though: her husband has moved his mother's furniture into their house, and his brother makes doll furniture, adding to the clutter. Charlotte is surrounded by things and duplicates of things and miniatures of things, all of which she would like to discard.

When she finally finds herself traveling, she hardly recognizes what has happened. She stares out the window of the bus at the passing scenery, glad to have the window seat, in spite of the fact that Jake is pressing a gun into her side. She thinks of screaming to draw attention to herself, but says, ''I would rather die than make any sort of disturbance.'' When Jake finds a traveler's check in her billfold, he asks her why she hasn't mentioned it. She replies, ''Well, I've had it for so long, you see. I mean I had it for just one purpose. I forgot it could be used for anything else.'' But her purpose for the check is for traveling, and Jake reminds her, ''we *are* traveling.'' All she can say is, ''Oh.''

After cashing the traveler's check, Charlotte gives Jake the money and tells him that she is leaving. In spite of his pleas and threats, she walks away, thinking at first that she has escaped without injury, but then realizes, "Come to think of it, I wasn't so unscathed after all." She leaves with Jake not only the money she had kept secret for traveling but a Keep on Truckin' badge that she had found in a cereal box and taken as a sign. Her attitude toward traveling has changed. Back home with Saul, she reassures him that they do not need to take a trip. "I don't see the need, I say. We have been traveling for years, traveled all our lives, we are traveling still. We couldn't stay in one place if we tried."

Morgan's Passing (1980), in spite of its weak plotting and characterization, won a Janet Heidinger Kafka Prize and nominations for a National Book Critics Circle Award and an American Book Award. Once again, Tyler writes about an artist, Morgan Gower, who recreates himself every day through changes in costumes and who imagines the lives of himself and others without much regard for reality. Morgan is clearly an eccentric who makes those around him (including the reader) sometimes impatient.

Once again, the novel covers a period of about a decade, from 1967, when Morgan first meets Emily and Leon Meredith, until 1979, when he finds his obituary in the morning paper—his "passing," in one sense. The book tells the story of Morgan's friendship with the Merediths, a young couple whose baby he delivers while posing as a doctor. The narrative point of view is wider than that which Tyler usually uses, allowing us to see the meeting between Morgan and the Merediths entirely from the outside, not entering any of the characters' minds. Only in the second chapter do we find ourselves back on familiar ground, with Tyler's third-person narration from the point of view of Morgan himself.

Emily and Leon represent for Morgan a life free from the encumbrances of things. They give puppet shows at carnivals and birthday parties,

and Morgan thinks of them as vagabonds, footloose carnies, "stark, pared down." He stares up at the windows of their apartment and imagines what would be inside: "He enjoyed imagining their eat-in kitchen, with just two plates and two sets of silver and an earthenware bowl for the baby. He liked to think that their bathroom contained a bar of Ivory soap and three hotel towels. Well, and Leon's shaving things, of course. But nothing else." Emily is suspicious of him, telling him, "We're not who you believe we are," but when Morgan explains how he finds himself "giving a false impression" when people so easily believe his stories, Emily responds, "I see what he means, in a way. . . . He just . . . has to get out of his life, sometimes."

Morgan turns to the Merediths because he thinks they are unlike the clutter of his own family—his wife Bonny, his mother Brindle, his sister Louisa, and seven daughters. Like Ben Joe Hawkes, he is in a family that does not need him. His wife's family is wealthy: her father gave them a house; her uncle gave Morgan a job as manager of a hardware store. The house is crowded and messy: "The three smaller bedrooms, intended for a tasteful number of children, barely contained Morgan's daughters, and Brindle and Louisa shared an edgy, cramped existence on the third floor. The lawn was littered with rusty bicycles and raveling wicker furniture." Bonny calls repairmen for the house when they are needed; Morgan's assistant at the hardware store does the work. So Morgan makes meaning in his life by imagining it.

Eventually Morgan and Emily fall in love and have an affair. When Emily becomes pregnant, Morgan is determined to take responsibility and leaves his wife, who sends all his clutter, including mother and sister, after him. Morgan moves his costumes, furniture, and relatives into Emily's small apartment. Ironically, Emily likes all the confusion.

At the end of the novel, Morgan and Emily

have joined the Holy Word Entertainment Troupe, a traveling carnival. He and Emily live in a trailer with only the items they consider essential. Yet Morgan's new life may only be a change in role, rather than a change in character. For example, he has given up his name, and in the last scene of the novel, he impersonates a postal worker and takes a woman's letters, intending to steam them open and read them before mailing them. This is the old Morgan, intruding into the lives of others in ways that are simply unacceptable. In the last paragraph of the novel, he feels "light-hearted" as he approaches Emily: "Everything he looked at seemed luminous and beautiful, and rich with possibilities." His joyous welcoming of the future is reassuring, but not a guarantee that he has truly changed.

Dinner at the Homesick Restaurant (1982) won a PEN/Faulkner Award for Fiction, a nomination for a Pulitzer, and Tyler's second nomination for a National Book Critics Circle Award. As one of Tyler's finest novels, it is certainly worthy of the critical and scholarly attention it received.

The novel begins with Pearl Tull on her deathbed, remembering her past life, and ends with the family dinner after her funeral. In between, the family's story is told from the points of view of Pearl, her three children (Cody, Ezra, and Jenny), Luke (Cody's son), and even, in the final scene, by Beck (Pearl's long-absent husband). Each character remembers and interprets the past differently. The central event involves an archery set and takes place during an afternoon in the country; this event is recounted four times in the course of the novel. Pearl is shot in the shoulder in an accident that she blames on Beck, Beck blames on Cody, Cody blames on Ezra, and Ezra blames on himself. Pearl's wound becomes infected, and she has an allergic reaction to the penicillin she is given. As we learn near the end of the book, this series of events precipitated

Beck's leaving. He tells Cody, "it was the grayness; grayness of things; half-right-and-half-wrongness of things. Everything tangled, mingled, not perfect any more. I couldn't take that. Your mother could, but not me."

After Beck leaves, Pearl pretends, in her pride and hurt, that he is away on another business trip. She keeps up this front for years. Even on her deathbed she is proud of what she has done: "Pearl felt a twinge of angry joy. Apparently she had carried this off—made the transition so smoothly that not a single person guessed. It was the greatest triumph of her life. My one true accomplishment, she thought." Of course, no one is convinced, she is indulging in a fantasy that affects not just herself but her children as well. This fantasy arises from her need to control both social opinion and family myth. Pearl's control over both is in her mind alone, but she lives her life convinced that she has brilliantly carried it off.

Life is not easy for Pearl after Beck leaves. He sends her money monthly, but not enough, so she is forced to go to work as a cashier in a nearby grocery store, a job that hurts her pride. The children remember her rages, the horrible meals of leftovers and canned foods, without fully understanding her self-esteem and her fear of not being able to provide for her children. During a peaceful moment preparing dinner with her mother, Jenny is reminded of her mother's volatility:

> Jenny knew that, in reality, her mother was a dangerous person—hot breathed and full of rage and unpredictable. . . . Which of her children had not felt her stinging slap, with the claw-encased pearl in her engagement ring that could bloody a lip at one flick? Jenny had seen her hurl Cody down a flight of stairs. . . . She herself, more than once, had been slammed against a wall, been called "serpent," "cockroach," "hideous little sniveling guttersnipe."

All three children are, of course, negatively affected by their father's abandonment and their mother's angry, frightened, proud ways. Cody, the oldest, is a bully, jealous of his brother, always wanting attention and always assuming that he isn't getting it. Cody feels responsible for his father's absence, afraid that he has done some terrible thing to make his father leave. He becomes an efficiency expert, moving from factory to factory and from rented house to rented house. He takes Ruth and Luke, his wife and son, with him on business trips, determined not to leave them behind as Beck had left his family. But Cody has another motive for keeping his family with him. He is possessed by jealousy that stems from his belief that he stole Ruth's affection away from Ezra, and he is convinced that Ezra would steal Ruth and Luke from him, given an opportunity.

Jenny, determined to be a doctor, falls into her mother's pattern of child abuse when she finds herself in medical residency with a new baby and a ruined marriage. She repeats her mother's actions with her own daughter: "She slammed Becky's face into her Peter Rabbit dinner plate and gave her a bloody nose. She yanked a handful of her hair." When she starts crying uncontrollably over the phone to her mother, though, her family comes to help, rescuing her from this untenable situation that reflects the one her mother had suffered years earlier. She is able to escape this pattern by "learning how to make it through life on a slant." She pads herself with an overweight husband with six children. The activity and noise of their household makes serious conversation impossible and allows Jenny to avoid controversy.

Ezra owns the Homesick Restaurant, where he tries to nurture people by providing them with food to soothe and heal. He himself is hungry for this kind of home, one he has never known. As many critics have pointed out, feeding is central to this novel. Pearl cannot feed her children. Jenny becomes anorexic, as does her daughter; Ezra uses his restaurant to give people the food

he thinks they need rather than what they ask for. Ezra holds a series of family dinners; none of them is ever completed. Someone, usually Pearl, storms out, angry, refusing to stay. Only at the end, when Pearl is dead, is there some hope that a meal can be finished. Even this one is interrupted, by the flight of the long-absent Beck, but he is brought back to finish the meal (though he insists he will leave before dessert).

The novel ends with one last view of the archery scene, this time from the point of view of Cody. Having seen respect for him in his father's eyes and learned that he was not the cause of his father's leaving, Cody is at last able to remember the good times of his childhood: "the drives, the picnics, the autumn hikes, the wildflower walks in the spring." He reconsiders the archery trip, seeing "his mother's upright form along the grasses, her hair lit gold, her small hands smoothing her bouquet while the arrow journeyed on. And high above, he seemed to recall, there had been a little brown airplane, almost motionless, droning through the sunshine like a bumblebee." It is clearly unnecessary to turn this scene into a Christian blessing of Cody, as some critics have tried to do. Rather, Cody's new view of his previous life offers the possibility—no more—that he can now change. Tyler does not give us assurance; just as we do not know whether Beck will stay for the dessert course, we do not know whether Cody will change. The possibility must be enough.

The Accidental Tourist (1985), which won a National Book Critics Circle Award, tells the story of Macon Leary, a writer of travel guides for businessmen who would prefer to stay home. As in most of *Morgan's Passing,* Tyler tells the story from only one point of view, Macon's. Macon is a writer, an artist, who is suspicious of anyone who is not blood kin. As such, he is the perfect person to write travel guides that are designed not to help their readers see foreign cities, but rather to allow them "to pretend they had never left home." He helps his readers find McDonald's in Amsterdam, Sweet'n'Low in Tokyo, "king-sized Beauty-rest mattresses" in Madrid. Rather than local wines, "Macon's readers searched for pasteurized and homogenized milk."

Macon is an ideal writer for these guides not only because he hates to travel but also because of his systematic approach to life. A year after his twelve-year-old son, Ethan, is murdered in a Burger Bonanza, his marriage falls apart, and he begins reorganizing his house, thinking, "The fact was that running a house required some sort of system." He keeps water and bleach in the sink, adding dishes as he uses them and rinsing them all every other day. He washes his clothes by walking on them while he showers. He sews sheets together into what he calls the "Macon Leary Body Bag" to avoid having to make the bed. He does begin to wonder if he has gone too far; proof that he has comes in a hilarious scene in which his systems break down and he breaks his leg.

To recuperate, Macon returns to his family home, where his sister and two brothers live. It becomes clear that Macon's systems, his reluctance to venture beyond the family, are part of his family background. Charles and Porter, his two brothers, have both been married but returned home when their marriages failed. Rose, who has never married, looks after her brothers. She is even more systematic than Macon, for example, she organizes the kitchen cabinets alphabetically. One sign of the family's insularity is Vaccination, "a card game they'd invented as children, which had grown so convoluted over the years that no one else had the patience to learn it."

It is through Edward, the corgi who had been Ethan's dog, that Macon meets Muriel Pritchett, a dog trainer who astonishes him with her fearlessness as she moves through the world. Edward turned vicious due to the many changes in his life, but he falls for Muriel, who finally trains him. In spite of Muriel's difference from Macon in age, class, and outlook on life, once Macon has admitted to her his pain over Ethan's death, he comes to realize that she, too, has been hurt in her life, that he is not the only person ever to feel pain. He moves in with Muriel and finds himself changing. He speculates "that who you are when you're with somebody may matter more than whether you love her." When Macon is with Muriel he is not detached and cold; he gradually comes to see other people in the world not as faceless mobs but as individuals doing the best they can to get through life.

Macon eventually leaves Muriel to return to his wife, Sarah, and the comfort of familiarity. But after Muriel follows him to Paris and he sees her joyous, open way of dealing with a foreign country, he decides to return to Muriel. When he tries to explain his feelings to Sarah, she points out that other people will think them "one of those mismatched couples no one invites to parties." Macon agrees without feeling intimidated: "he saw now how such couples evolved. They were not, as he'd always supposed, the result of some ludicrous lack of perception, but had come together for reasons that the rest of the world would never guess." This willingness to understand others is a sign of just how much Macon has changed. The novel ends with Macon in a taxi, stopping to pick up Muriel, sunlight on the windshield making "spangles" "so bright and festive, for a moment he thought they were confetti." This ending may remind us of the ending of *Morgan's Passing,* when Macon looks to the future with such eagerness. But here, unlike in the earlier novel, there is no reason for us to think that Macon and Muriel will not be happy, that Macon's sense of joy must be somehow qualified.

Breathing Lessons (1988), winner of the Pulitzer Prize for fiction in 1989, elicited many negative responses from critics. The problem with the book is its main character, Maggie Moran. Maggie, somewhat like Morgan Gower, reimagines the world in which she lives. Maggie, though, is more of a meddler, not content to offer variations on herself but insisting to others that her falsified account of events is true and encouraging them to act based on her account. Her insistence borders on the foolish; the reader is embarrassed for her.

The real time of the novel is the day on which Ira and Maggie Moran go to Deer Lick, Pennsylvania, for the funeral of Max Gill, the husband of Maggie's childhood friend Serena. Maggie convinces Ira, much against his will, to visit Cartwheel, Pennsylvania, where their ex-daughter-in-law, Fiona, and their granddaughter, Leroy, live. Once there, Maggie tries, not for the first time, to convince Fiona that divorcing Jesse had not been a good idea. She lures them to Baltimore, only to have her plan end badly. Undaunted, she thinks up a new scheme to have Leroy come live in Baltimore, ostensibly for better schools, which Ira vetoes.

Part of the problem with Maggie's character is that we see most of the book from her point of view. If we remember, though, that in a Tyler novel we cannot depend on any one character's point of view as authorial or dependable, we can understand that Maggie is not the person she sees herself to be. She thinks of herself as fat, even obese, an eternal klutz, unable to do anything competently. Part 2 of the novel offers another perspective, Ira's. He does not think Maggie is fat and does not approve of her dieting: ''Depriving herself meal after meal when in Ira's opinion she was just exactly right as she was— not even what you'd call plump; just a satisfying series of handfuls, soft, silky breasts and a creamy swell of bottom.'' He feels deep love for Maggie, jealously questioning whether all the outsiders she has brought home, even their two children, have been ''interrupting their most pri-

vate moments, wedging between the two of them?'' Ira's overall view of his marriage is that it is ''as steady as a tree; not even he could tell how wide and deep the roots went.''

The energy that Maggie devotes to convincing others, to lies that grow larger and entrap her, is more extreme than usual on the day of Max Gill's funeral because Maggie is facing a difficult moment in her life: the next day she and Ira will take their daughter, Daisy, to college for the first time. She is worried, as many mothers are, about what her life will be like once her children are gone. Maggie cannot articulate her distress until the end of the novel, when she asks Ira, ''what are we two going to live for, all the rest of our lives?'' He puts his arm around her for comfort.

Ultimately, the book is about marriage. The book begins with Maggie's hearing a radio talk show discussion of marriage. Other marriages— those of Serena and Max Gill, Jesse and Fiona, Daniel and Duluth Otis—offer variations on ways marriages succeed and fail. Maggie knows that her dream of a perfect marriage, of the look on Ira's face the first night they were married lasting forever, is not the basis of a long-term relationship. At the end of the novel, she and Ira are still together despite the disappointments of their lives, continuing their relationship despite their disagreements.

Saint Maybe (1991) returns to one of the main themes of *The Clock Winder*: a death that could be due to either accident or suicide and the guilt felt by the person who feels responsible for that death. Ian tells his brother, Danny, who has been drinking, that his new wife, Lucy, is not faithful and that her newborn child is not Danny's. Danny then runs his car into a wall. Everyone else assumes that his death was a result of drinking, an accident, and Ian realizes that to relieve himself of his guilt by telling them otherwise would only hurt them more. Danny's wife then dies, also by accident or design, of an overdose of pills, increasing Ian's sense of guilt. When Ian joins the Church of the Second Chance, the minister tells him that he must make reparations for his sin and that he must tell his family what he has done. He goes on to care for the three children left behind, abandoning his college career and becoming a carpenter. The novel follows Ian's life for the next twenty years.

Ian's struggle to raise the children, his doubts about ever being forgiven, his occasional railing against the restricted life he is forcing himself to live, are all ultimately resolved in his marriage and the birth of his own child. However, doubts remain. We are fairly sure that Daphne was conceived before Lucy met Danny, but we are not sure that Lucy was actually unfaithful to Danny. We know that she, like Mary Tell in *Celestial Navigation,* depends on men for her survival and finds herself fooled by their promises, but we do not know that she actually cheated on Danny. Ian is convinced that she did not, that she was "*only shoplifting,*" a much lesser sin.

This novel also deals with a topic Tyler has included at the edges of many of her novels: ministers. In *Earthly Possessions* Charlotte's husband, Saul, is a minister; in *Searching for Caleb* Justine's daughter, Meg, marries Arthur Milsom, a minister. Tyler has said that she is interested in ministers because she is not sure any of us has a right to change anyone else, but that ministers think that they can and should. Reverend Emmett changes Ian's life by expecting him to make reparation for his sin; he then suggests that Ian enter the ministry, saying when Ian questions the need for a call, "Maybe I'm the call." Ian, though, has vowed never to interfere again, never to assume that he knows more about any situation than other people do. He finally tells Reverend Emmett, "It's not only whether I'd be *able* to give people answers ... It's whether I'd want to. Whether I'd feel right about it."

Ian faces a world in which he is always doing penance, never forgiven, always cut off from any-

one other than his family and from the possibility of love in a marriage. To his own surprise as well as everyone else's, he eventually marries Rita di-Carlo, who earns a living as "the Clutter Counselor" organizing people's households. When she becomes pregnant, Ian, having already raised three children who were not his own, feels "the most bewildering mixture of feelings: worry and excitement and also, underneath, a pervasive sense of tiredness." When the baby is born, though, Ian realizes that as Lucy had changed his brother's life, so Rita has changed his. He imagines Lucy as Danny had first introduced her to the family: "And she tipped her head and smiled. After all, she might have said, this was an ordinary occurrence. People changed other people's lives every day of the year. There was no call to make such a fuss about it." Ian finally can accept his responsibility toward others and their effect on him without succumbing to the numbing guilt he has felt for over twenty years. His life has been changed. This ambiguous ending is one of the happiest in Tyler's novels.

Ladder of Years, Tyler's 1995 novel, received mixed reviews. It is the story of another character who seeks escape, this time walking away from a family beach vacation and into another life. Delia Grinstead's life has been the result of wish fulfillment—but not necessarily hers. The youngest of a doctor's three daughters, she was the one her father's new assistant chose to marry. Sam, her husband, tells the story as a fairy tale: "Like the king's three daughters in a fairy tale, he said, they'd been lined up according to age, the oldest farthest left, and like the woodcutter's honest son, he had chosen the youngest and prettiest, the shy little one on the right who didn't think she stood a chance." Delia, feeling unappreciated, unnoticed, and unloved, does not accept this version as true, and she doubts that Sam married her for love.

Living in the house she grew up in, Delia cultivated a persona that is "kind of baby-doll," wearing pastels, ruffles, and lace. When she must cancel a dinner engagement that she accepted without consulting her husband (one that, it turns out, was for the preceding week anyway), she asks her uncommunicative teenage son, "When did this start happening to me? . . . When did sweet and cute turn into silly and inefficient?" When she finds herself, to her own amazement, on her own in a strange town, she begins a new fantasy of being professional, capable, and adult—everything she was not in her other life— and achieves an independent existence as a secretary, whom she thinks of as "Miss Grinstead." Soon, however, she finds herself looking after Joel Miller and his son, Noah, drawn into their family and away from her independence. Her new identity is not just professional: "She seemed to have changed into someone else—a woman people looked to automatically for sustenance."

After a year and a half, invited to her own daughter's wedding, she returns to Baltimore and must choose between the Millers and her own husband and children. During these years away she has broken out of the childish ways she had cultivated just as she has stopped wearing pink and blue clothes. After Delia decides to remain with her family in Baltimore, she evaluates what has happened as being "a time trip that worked" as she is back home and improved. Then she sees the whole experience in terms of her children's growing up:

> Now she saw that June beach scene differently. Her three children, she saw, had been staring at the horizon with the alert, tensed stillness of explorers at the ocean's edge, poised to begin their journeys. And Delia, shading her eyes in the distance, had been trying to understand why they were leaving.

This ending, though, does not sum up everything that has happened in the novel. It does not explain all that Delia has learned. Perhaps the way to view this ending is as another incomplete statement by a flawed character; Delia has grown a great deal, but she may not yet see the situation clearly.

Tyler's work grew and changed as she improved her skills as a novelist and experienced more of life. As she passed through the stages of marriage and motherhood, her focus and emphasis shifted. It is appropriate that, as Tyler's own daughters approached maturity, her novel *Ladder of Years* should deal, in part, with the departure of grown children from the family home. Anne Tyler portrays family life in funny, compassionate ways that illuminate our own lives, showing us the luminous qualities of the everyday.

Selected Bibliography

WORKS OF ANNE TYLER

NOVELS
If Morning Ever Comes. New York: Knopf, 1964.
The Tin Can Tree. New York: Knopf, 1965.
A Slipping-Down Life. New York: Knopf, 1970.
The Clock Winder. New York: Knopf, 1972.
Celestial Navigation. New York: Knopf, 1974.
Searching for Caleb. New York: Knopf, 1976.
Earthly Possessions. New York: Knopf, 1977.
Morgan's Passing. New York: Knopf, 1980.
Dinner at the Homesick Restaurant. New York: Knopf, 1982.
The Accidental Tourist. New York: Knopf, 1985.
Breathing Lessons. New York: Knopf, 1988.
Saint Maybe. New York: Knopf, 1991.
Ladder of Years. New York: Knopf, 1995.

SELECTED SHORT STORIES
"The Artificial Family." *Southern Review,* 11:615–621 (Summer 1975). Reprinted in *The Pushcart Prize: Best of the Small Presses.* Edited by Bill Henderson. New York: Pushcart Book Press, 1976. Pp. 11–18. Reprinted in *Love Stories for the Time*

Being. Edited by Genie D. Chipps and Bill Henderson. Wainscott: Pushcart Press, 1987. Pp. 137–46. Reprinted in *Selected Stories from the* Southern Review, *1965–85.* Edited by Lewis P. Simpson, et al. Baton Rouge: Louisiana State University Press, 1988. Pp. 355–361.

"The Common Courtesies." *McCall's,* June 1968, pp. 62–63. Reprinted in *Prize Stories 1969: The O. Henry Awards.* Edited by William Abrahams. Garden City: Doubleday, 1969. Pp. 121–130.

"The Geologist's Maid." *New Yorker,* July 28, 1975, pp. 29–33. Reprinted in *Stories of the Modern South.* Edited by Benjamin Forkner and Patrick Samway, S.J. New York: Bantam, 1978. Pp. 343–354.

"Holding Things Together." *New Yorker,* January 24, 1977, pp. 30–35. Reprinted in *We Are the Stories We Tell: The Best Short Stories by North American Women since 1945.* Edited by Wendy Martin. New York: Pantheon Books, 1990. Pp. 150–163.

"Teenage Wasteland." *Seventeen,* November 1983, pp. 144–145. Reprinted in *The Editors' Choice: New American Short Stories.* Vol. 1. Edited by George E. Murphy, Jr. New York: Bantam, 1985. Pp. 256–266. Reprinted in *New Women and New Fiction.* Edited by Susan Cahill. New York: New American Library, 1986. Pp. 133–145.

"With All Flags Flying." *Redbook,* 137 (June 1971), pp. 88–89. Reprinted in *Prize Stories 1972: The O. Henry Awards.* Edited by William Abrahams. Garden City: Doubleday, 1971. Pp. 116–126. Reprinted in *Redbook's Famous Fiction.* New York: Redbook Publishing Co., 1972. Pp. 84–87.

"A Woman Like a Fieldstone House." *Ladies Home Journal,* August 1989, p. 86. Reprinted in *Louder Than Words.* Edited by William Shore. New York: Vintage, 1989. Pp. 1–15.

"Your Place is Empty." *New Yorker,* November 22, 1976, pp. 45–54. Reprinted in *The Best American Short Stories 1977: And the Yearbook of the American Short Story.* Edited by Martha Foley. Boston: Houghton Mifflin, 1977. Pp. 317–337.

CHILDREN'S BOOKS

Tumble Tower. New York: Orchard Press, 1993. Illustrations by Mitra Modarressi.

MANUSCRIPT PAPERS

Anne Tyler Papers, Special Collections Department, Duke University Library, Durham, North Carolina.

BIBLIOGRAPHIES

Croft, Robert W. *Anne Tyler: A Bio-Bibliography.* Westport, Conn.: Greenwood Press, 1995.

Gardiner, Elaine, and Catherine Rainwater. "A Bibliography of Writings by Anne Tyler." In *Contemporary American Women Writers: Narrative Strategies.* Edited by Catherine Rainwater and William J. Scheick. Lexington: University Press of Kentucky, 1985. Pp. 142–152.

Nesanovich, Stella. "An Anne Tyler Checklist, 1959–1980," *Bulletin of Bibliography,* 38:53–64 (April–June 1981).

BIOGRAPHICAL AND CRITICAL STUDIES

Almond, Barbara R. "The Accidental Therapist: Interpsychic Change in a Novel." *Literature and Psychology,* 38, nos. 1–2:84–104 (1992).

Bennet, Barbara A. "Attempting to Connect: Verbal Humor in the Novels of Anne Tyler." *South Atlantic Review,* 60:57–75 (January 1995).

Betts, Doris. "The Fiction of Anne Tyler." In *Women Writers of the Contemporary South.* Edited by Peggy Whitman Prenshaw. Jackson: University Press of Mississippi, 1984. First published in *Southern Quarterly,* 21:23–37 (Summer 1983).

Bloom, Alice. "George Dennison, *Luisa Domic,* Bobbie Ann Mason, *In Country,* Anne Tyler, *The Accidental Tourist.*" *New England Review and Bread Loaf Quarterly*, 8:513–524 (Summer 1986).

Bond, Adrienne. "From Addie Bundren to Pearl Tull: The Secularization of the South." *Southern Quarterly,* 24:64–73 (Spring 1986).

Bowers, Bradley R. "Anne Tyler's Insiders." *Mississippi Quarterly,* 42:47–56 (Winter 1988–1989).

Carson, Barbara Harrell. "Complicate, Complicate: Anne Tyler's Moral Imperative." *Southern Quarterly,* 31:24–34 (Fall 1992).

Cuningham, Henry. "An Accidental Tourist's Best Friend: Edward as Four-Legged Literary Device." *Notes on Contemporary Literature,* 23:10–12 (September 1993).

Davis, Davie Susanne. "An Examination of Fairy-Tale Motifs in Anne Tyler's *Dinner at the Homesick Restaurant.*" *Publications of the Arkansas Philological Association,* 16, no. 2:31–40 (1990).

Dvorak, Angeline Godwin. "Cooking as Mission and

Ministry in Southern Culture: The Nurturers of Clyde Edgerton's *Walking Across Egypt,* Fannie Flagg's *Fried Green Tomatoes at the Whistle Stop Cafe,* and Anne Tyler's *Dinner at the Homesick Restaurant.*'' *Southern Quarterly,* 30:90–98 (Winter–Spring 1992).

Eckard, Paula Gallant. ''Family and Community in Anne Tyler's *Dinner at the Homesick Restaurant.*'' *Southern Literary Journal,* 22, no. 2:33–34 (1990).

Evans, Elizabeth. *Anne Tyler.* New York: Twayne, 1993.

Freiert, William K. ''Anne Tyler's Accidental Ulysses.'' *Classical and Modern Literature,* 10:71–79 (Fall 1989).

Gibson, Mary Ellis. ''Family As Fate: The Novels of Anne Tyler.'' *Southern Literary Journal,* 6:47–58 (Fall 1983). Reprinted in Petry, *Critical Essays on Anne Tyler.*

Gilbert, Susan. ''Anne Tyler.'' In *Southern Women Writers: The New Generation.* Edited and prefaced by Tonette Bond Inge, introduced by Doris Betts. Tuscaloosa: University of Alabama Press, 1990.

Johnston, Sue Ann. ''The Daughter As Escape Artist.'' *Atlantis,* 9:10–22 (Spring 1984).

Jones, Anne G. ''Home at Last, and Homesick Again: The Ten Novels of Anne Tyler.'' *Hollins Critic,* 23:1–14 (April 1986).

Koppel, Gene. ''Maggie Moran, Anne Tyler's Madcap Heroine: A Game-Approach to *Breathing Lessons.*'' *Essays In Literature,* 18:276–287 (Fall 1991).

Linton, Karen. *The Temporal Horizon: A Study of the Theme of Time in Anne Tyler's Major Novels.* Uppsala, Sweden: Acta Universitatis Upsaliensis, 1989.

Madden, Deanna. ''Ties That Bind: Identity and Sibling Relationships in Anne Tyler's Novels.'' In *The Significance of Sibling Relationships in Literature.* Edited by Joanna Stephens Mink and Janet Doubler Ward. Bowling Green, Ohio: Popular, 1992. Pp. 58–69.

Miller, Laura. ''Woman as Hostage: Escape to Freedom or Journey into Bondage?'' In *Proceedings of the Second Annual Conference of EAPSCU.* Edited by Malcolm Hayward. N.P.: English Association of the Pennsylvania State Colleges and Universities, 1983. Pp. 49–52.

Papadimas, Julie Persing. ''America Tyler Style: Surrogate Families and Transiency.'' *Journal of American Culture,* 15:45–51 (Fall 1992).

Petry, Alice Hall. ''Bright Books of Life: The Black

Norm in Anne Tyler's Novels.'' *Southern Quarterly,* 31:7–13 (Fall 1992).

———. *Critical Essays on Anne Tyler.* New York: G. K. Hall, 1992.

———. *Understanding Anne Tyler.* Columbia: University of South Carolina Press, 1990.

Robertson, Mary F. ''Anne Tyler: Medusa Points and Contact Points.'' In *Contemporary American Women Writers: Narrative Strategies.* Edited by Catherine Rainwater and William J. Scheick. Lexington: University Press of Kentucky, 1985. Pp. 118–152. Reprinted in Petry, *Critical Essays on Anne Tyler.*

Ross-Bryant, Lynn. ''Anne Tyler's *Searching for Caleb*: The Sacrality of the Everyday.'' *Soundings,* 73:191–207 (Spring 1990).

Shelton, Frank W. ''The Necessary Balance: Distance and Sympathy in the Novels of Anne Tyler.'' *Southern Review,* 20:851–860 (Autumn 1984).

Salwak, Dale, ed. *Anne Tyler As Novelist.* Iowa City: University of Iowa Press, 1994.

Stephens, C. Ralph, ed. *The Fiction of Anne Tyler.* Jackson: University Press of Mississippi, 1990.

Toles, George. ''The Mystery of Crinkle's Nose.'' *Raritan,* 11:80–97 (Winter 1992).

Town, Caren J. ''Rewriting the Family during *Dinner at the Homesick Restaurant.*'' *Southern Quarterly,* 31:14–23 (Fall 1992).

Voelker, Joseph C. *Art and the Accidental in Anne Tyler.* Columbus: University of Missouri Press, 1989.

Willrich, Patricia Rowe. ''Watching through Windows: A Perspective on Anne Tyler.'' *Virginia Quarterly Review,* 68:497–516 (Summer 1992).

Zahlan, Anne R. ''Anne Tyler.'' In *Fifty Southern Writers after 1900: A Bio-Bibliographical Sourcebook.* Edited by Joseph M. Flora and Robert Bain. Westport, Conn.: Greenwood, 1987. Pp. 491–504.

INTERVIEWS AND PERSONAL STATEMENTS

Brown, Laurie L. ''Interviews with Seven Contemporary Writers.'' In *Women Writers of the Contemporary South.* Edited by Peggy Whitman Prenshaw. Jackson: University Press of Mississippi, 1984. First published in *Southern Quarterly,* 21:3–22 (Summer 1983).

Cook, Bruce. ''A Writer—During School Hours.''

Detroit News, April 6, 1980, sec. E, pp. 1, 3. Reprinted in Petry, *Critical Essays on Anne Tyler.*

Lamb, Wendy. "An Interview with Anne Tyler." *Iowa Journal of Literary Studies,* 3, nos. 1–2:59–64 (1981). Reprinted in Petry, *Critical Essays on Anne Tyler.*

Lueloff, Jorie. "Authoress Explains Why Women Dominate in South." Baton Rouge *Morning Advocate,* February 8, 1965, sec. A, p. 11. Reprinted in Petry, *Critical Essays on Anne Tyler.*

Michaels, Marguerite. "Anne Tyler, Writer 8:05 to 3:30." *New York Times Book Review,* May 8, 1977, p. 13, 42–43. Reprinted in Petry, *Critical Essays on Anne Tyler.*

"Olives out of a Bottle." Duke University *Archive,* 87:70–79 (Spring 1975). Reprinted in Petry, *Critical Essays on Anne Tyler.*

Ridley, Clifford A. "Anne Tyler: A Sense of Reticence Balanced by 'Oh, Well, Why Not?' " *National Observer,* July 22, 1972, p. 23. Reprinted in Petry, *Critical Essays on Anne Tyler.*

Tyler, Anne. "Because I Want More Than One Life." *Washington Post,* August 15, 1976, sec. G, pp. 1, 7. Reprinted in Petry, *Critical Essays on Anne Tyler.*

Tyler, Anne. "Still Just Writing." In *The Writer on Her Work: Contemporary Women Writers Reflect on Their Art and Situation.* Edited by Janet Sternburg. New York: Norton, 1980. Pp. 3–16.

—*MARY MARGARET RICHARDS*

Gore Vidal
1925

GORE VIDAL IS a major contemporary writer whose productivity and inventiveness have brought him a vast audience and considerable acclaim from critics. His career spans five decades, and his oeuvre includes twenty-two novels, several collections of essays on literature and politics, a volume of short stories, six Broadway plays, dozens of television plays, film scripts, and even three mystery novels written under the pseudonym of Edgar Box. Unlike so many of his contemporaries, Vidal has been anything but predictable. The novels and plays focus on subjects ranging from World War II (*Williwaw*, 1946), to the ancient world (*Julian*, 1964; *Creation*, 1981), to the postwar gay scene in America (*The City and the Pillar*, 1948), to the politics of Central America (*Dark Green, Bright Red*, 1950), to apocalyptic religion (*Messiah*, 1954; *Kalki*, 1978), to the sexual revolution (*Myra Breckinridge*, 1968; *Myron*, 1974), to the sweep of American history (*Burr*, 1973; *1876*, 1976; *Lincoln*, 1984; *Empire*, 1987; *Hollywood: A Novel of America in the 1920s*, 1990; and *Washington, D.C.*, 1967). His Swiftian satires, *Duluth* (1983) and *Live from Golgotha* (1992), take on themes from pop culture to Christianity.

It is almost impossible to point to any aspect of Vidal's work as typical, although the voice is always unmistakably Vidal's. Consider, for example, the opening paragraphs of *Empire:*

"The war ended last night, Caroline. Help me with these flowers." Elizabeth Cameron stood in the open French window, holding a large blue-and-white china vase filled with roses, somewhat showily past their prime. Caroline helped her hostess carry the heavy vase into the long cool dim dining room.

At forty, Mrs. Cameron was, to Caroline's youthful eye, very old indeed; nevertheless, she was easily the handsomest of America's great ladies and certainly the most serenely efficient, able to arrange a platoon of flower vases before breakfast with the same ease and briskness that her uncle, General Sherman, had devastated Georgia.

"One must always be up at dawn in August." Mrs. Cameron sounded to Caroline rather like Julius Caesar, reporting home. "Servants—like flowers—tend to wilt. We shall be thirty-seven for lunch. Do you intend to marry Del?"

"I don't think I shall ever marry anyone." Caroline frowned with pleasure at Mrs. Cameron's directness. Although Caroline thought of herself as American, she had actually lived most of her life in Paris and so had little contact with women like Elizabeth Sherman Cameron, the perfect modern American lady—thus, earth's latest, highest product, as Henry James had not too ironically proclaimed.

The reader is not challenged in such a passage, as in a novel by James Joyce or William Faulkner. Vidal is no modernist in that sense; he is more in the realm of Henry James and George Eliot, where little is left for the reader to do but sit back and enjoy the scenery, the exchange of witticisms, the development of characters, the accumulating sense of a many-layered social and political world. Vidal's self-assured, even mandarin tone (which is commonly found in his work) not only relates to the sense of the world as a fait accompli, it also exists in every aspect of the actual content. This is a fictional world where French windows and china vases and people with connections to the likes of General William Tecumseh Sherman or Del Hay (the son of John Hay, who had been President Abraham Lincoln's personal assistant) are taken for granted.

Vidal writes, always, as an insider himself—a man who knows the world and the way it works—and he communicates a sense of knowingness; it is part of his tone. This quality is present in most of the fiction and all the essays; indeed, the tone *is* the essays, giving them their wonderfully acerbic edge and their vitality. Vidal invites his reader to share the ''knowingness'' of it all, to feel as though he or she is somehow privy to a world elsewhere. Nevertheless, Vidal keeps the reader at some distance, too. Especially in the essays, he is a rather formal host, definitely *not* a relative. The reader learns from him and admires his turn of phrase, his illuminations, but the reader is not going to come away from a Vidal essay feeling on intimate terms with the author.

One aspect of Vidal's critical writing that immediately strikes the reader is his ability to describe a text. He does so with an acute eye and attentive ear, as when he writes about John O'Hara's stories (in his collection *United States*):

The Hat on the Bed is a collection of twenty-four short stories. They are much like Mr. O'Hara's other short stories, although admirers seem to prefer them to earlier collections. Right off, one is aware of a passionate interest in social distinctions. Invariably we are told not only what university a character attended but also what prep school. Clothes, houses, luggage (by Vuitton), prestigious restaurants are all carefully noted, as well as brand names. With the zest of an Internal Revenue man examining deductions for entertainment, the author investigates the subtle difference between the spending of old middle-class money and that of new middle-class money. Of course social distinctions have always been an important aspect of the traditional novel, but what disturbs one in reading Mr. O'Hara is that he does so little with these details once he has noted them. If a writer chooses to tell us that someone went to St. Paul's and to Yale and played squash, then surely there is something about St. Paul's and Yale and squash which would make him into a certain kind of person so that, given a few more details, the reader is then able to make up his mind as to just what that triad of experience means, and why it is different from Exeter-Harvard-lacrosse. But Mr. O'Hara is content merely to list schools and sports and makes of cars and the labels on clothes.

This excerpt is typical of Vidal at his best, whether he is describing the theory of the French ''new novel''; introducing the Italian writer Italo Calvino to an American audience; rethinking the importance of Sinclair Lewis, James, or William Dean Howells; or rediscovering a ''lost'' writer like Dawn Powell. But Vidal is not just a superb literary critic. He is also a shrewd social critic, although his attitudes and opinions have won him few friends, except on the extreme left of the political spectrum. Writing in *Esquire* in one of his periodic ''State of the Union'' mock speeches, for instance, Vidal says:

Fascism is probably just a word for most of you. But the reality is very much present in this country. And the fact of it dominates most of the world today. Each year there is less and less freedom for more and more people. Put simply, fascism is the control of the state by a single man or by an oligarchy, supported by the military and the police. This is why I keep emphasizing the dangers of corrupt police forces, of uncontrolled *secret* police, like the FBI and the CIA and the Bureau of Narcotics and the Secret Service and Army counterintelligence and the Treasury men—what a lot of sneaky types we have, spying on us all!

The strong influence of Oscar Wilde is registered boldly in the tendency to formulate an aphorism rather than to argue, in the creation of overly neat parallels for the sake of argument, and in the underlying note of contempt for those who do not agree with him. This rhetorical model has a long and distinguished history, in fact, and Vidal is simply a vivid example of the genre. But he has, for all his generalizing, been largely correct in his descriptions and assessment of what he calls the National Security State. Like Noam Chomsky, whom he has always admired, Vidal has consistently refused to "tone it down." He describes what he sees, and if what he sees looks to him like fascism, he calls it fascism.

Vidal's deadpan approach can be devastating, as in the beginning of his essay on the "Real Two-Party System," from *The Second American Revolution and other Essays* (1982). "In the United States there are two political parties of equal size," he writes. "One is the party that votes in presidential elections. The other is the party that does not vote in presidential elections." Behind all the wit lies Vidal's firm conviction that America is a country run *by* the rich and *for* the rich, that America's pretense of being a great "democracy" is a sham, and that we as a nation have caused a good deal of pain, misery, and danger in the world by continuing the practice of imperialism begun by our forefathers. In particular, Vidal focuses his critical attention on the media (which he has known well from first-hand experience) and their obeisance to those in power. The world he describes is one of folly and arrogance—a world drawn rather sharply in caricature, but one that seems all too true.

Probably no American writer since Ernest Hemingway has lived his life so much in the public eye. While most writers cannot tolerate this kind of attention, Vidal has thrived on it. It began on October 3, 1925, when Eugene Luther Vidal was born in West Point, New York, into a family with high political and social connections. His father, for whom he was named, was a pioneer in the American aviation industry who held a subcabinet-level position in the Franklin D. Roosevelt administration as director of air commerce from 1933 until 1937. His maternal grandfather was Senator Thomas Pryor Gore of Oklahoma, a Democrat who cut a commanding figure in Washington politics for many decades. Vidal grew up in the company of people like Huey Long and Eleanor Roosevelt, and he learned from the inside how life in the upper echelons of society was conducted. His mother, Nina Gore Vidal, divorced his father in 1935, when Vidal was ten, and married the well-known financier Hugh D. Auchincloss, who in turn divorced *her* and married Jacqueline Bouvier Kennedy's mother, thus establishing a connection between Vidal and the Kennedy clan that persisted through the presidency of John F. Kennedy. (Vidal's witty take on the Bouvier sisters occurs in one of his most clever but least-known works, *Two Sisters: A Memoir in the Form of a Novel,* which appeared in 1970.)

Vidal was largely raised by his grandfather, whom he idolized (and about whom he later wrote and narrated a moving television documentary: "The Indestructible Mr. Gore," which appeared on NBC on December 13, 1959). Senator Gore was blind, and he often asked his grandson to read to him; this, in effect, was the beginning of Vidal's education. In the fall of 1940, having newly christened himself Gore Vidal, he entered the Phillips Exeter Academy in New Hampshire, where his career as a writer began with poems and stories in the *Phillips Exeter Review*. (Vidal's life at Exeter has been fictionalized by John Knowles, who apparently based the character of Brinker Hadley in *A Separate Peace* [1960] on him, though it would be foolish to assume that Vidal's life at Exeter was much like that described by Knowles.) According to Vidal, these were happy years. He graduated in June 1943 and entered the Enlisted Reserve Corps of the U.S. Army.

The fall of 1943 was spent at the Virginia Military Institute, where he briefly studied engineering. He joined the Army Transportation Corps as an officer that winter and was immediately sent to the Aleutian Islands. In December 1944 he began his first novel, *Williwaw,* during a run between Chernowski Bay and Dutch Harbor. Suffering a bad case of frostbite, Vidal was sent back to the States, where he finished the novel in less than a year. Published in 1946, *Williwaw* focused on a rivalry between two maritime officers; in style it owed something to Hemingway and Stephen Crane, while its overall movement derives, to some extent, from Joseph Conrad's seafaring novels, such as *Lord Jim* (1900). For a writer barely out of his teens, the book was an extraordinary achievement, and it retains a certain luster. Writing in the *New York Times* (June 17, 1946) about *Williwaw,* Orville Prescott said that the "Aleutian climate and scenery, the Army talk and Army thought are all palpable and real." Prescott, perhaps the most influential reviewer of the day, judged this novel "absolutely authentic" as a whole—an assessment that was commonly shared by reviewers at the time and recapitulated by John W. Aldridge in his famous study of postwar fiction, *After the Lost Generation: A Critical Study of the Writers of Two Wars* (1951).

Vidal worked briefly in New York after the war, for the publishing firm E. P. Dutton, before turning to full-time writing. The critical success of *Williwaw* emboldened him, and he made the brave decision—a crucial one—to live from his pen. Having little money, he moved to Guatemala, where the living was cheap. There he bought an abandoned fortress—the first of his many unusual (and often) grand dwellings. One of his closest friends in Guatemala was Anaïs Nin, who wrote a good deal about Vidal (some of it not very complimentary) in her diaries of that

period. By any standard, the postwar years were amazingly productive for the young Vidal, who published eight novels (besides his mysteries) in quick succession between 1946 and 1954. While some of these novels are slight and only occasionally rise above what one might call workmanlike writing, there are nevertheless three important novels of the period: *The City and the Pillar, The Judgment of Paris* (1952), and *Messiah.*

The City and the Pillar is remarkable for many reasons. It is, to begin with, a compelling story written in elegantly spare prose. Vidal's hero is Jim Willard; as the novel opens he is sitting in a New York bar in the postwar period recalling the years 1937–1943 as his fingers trace islands and rivers in the water spilling on the tabletop from his drink. What he visualizes through the watery haze is the time he first made love to Bob Ford—an American as prototypical as his name. The pursuit of Ford by Willard across the waters of the world gives the novel a mythic shape, though Vidal is ever the satirist, ready to send up any convention that stumbles into his path.

Jim's quest takes many fascinating turns; among them is a tour of the postwar homosexual demimonde of California, which Vidal writes about with reportorial cool. The quest ends, tragically, in a reconciliation that quickly becomes a nightmare. In the 1948 version of the novel, Jim strangles Bob and walks out into the morning air, having taken himself beyond the bounds of morality and the possibility of love. In a later (1965) revision, Vidal eliminates the melodramatic quality of the first ending, transforming the murder to a rape—an altogether more believable ending. But the change of endings goes beyond mere verisimilitude, as Claude J. Summers notes in "*The City and the Pillar* as Gay Fiction," a seminal article on this novel. The "conclusion of the 1965 revision is altogether more satisfying," he writes. "Here, when Jim makes a pass at the sleeping Bob, the latter initiates the violence. A menacing Bob, his fists ready, attacks Jim, and Jim, overwhelmed by an equal mixture of rage and desire, responds by overpowering and, finally, raping his dream lover.''

Summers puts *The City and the Pillar* in the context of postwar gay fiction:

> Prime among the novels that challenge the widespread Anglo-American contempt for homosexuality and homosexuals is Vidal's pioneering work, which is one of the first explicitly gay fictions to reach a large audience. Emphasizing the normality of gay people, *The City and the Pillar* traces the coming out process of a young man as ordinary and American as apple pie. Coming at the beginning of the postwar decade, the novel is an important and exemplary contribution to the emerging popular literature of homosexuality.

While this may be so, Vidal's bold entry into the world of gay fiction did nothing to help his burgeoning career as a novelist. This was, after all, the late forties, a time the general public's attitude toward homosexuality was anything but sympathetic.

The consequences of publishing a gay novel in 1948 were severe, and Vidal's literary career nearly ground to a premature halt. His next five novels were largely dismissed by the mainstream press, and one can feel the hostility to him in the period reviews of those novels. The reaction of Aldridge is typical: ''His writing after *Williwaw* is one long record of stylistic breakdown and spiritual exhaustion. It is confused and fragmentary, pulled in every direction by the shifting winds of impressionism. It is always reaching, always feeling and seeing; but it never signifies because it never believes.'' Aldridge just could not forgive Vidal for failing to blossom into the Hemingway who seemed to be lying dormant in *Williwaw.* Typically, Vidal refused to be anyone but Vidal.

A few of the best critics did find merit in Vidal's work after *The City and the Pillar.* Leafing through Robert J. Stanton's invaluable bibliog-raphy of Vidal criticism, one finds a scattering of intelligent and laudatory reviews. Edward Wagenknecht, for instance, reviewed *A Search for the King: A Twelfth-Century Legend* (1950) with care and insight in the *Chicago Sunday Tribune Magazine of Books* (January 15, 1950), calling Vidal ''just the man to redeem the historical novel from the lushness and bad taste into which it is always in danger of falling.'' This sparsely written novel retells the thirteenth-century story of Blondel de Néel and his search for Richard the Lion-Hearted, and in many ways it points toward Vidal's future, when he would become a major reinventor of the historical novel.

Among the best of Vidal's novels in the postwar decade was *Messiah,* a book that, according to Heather Neilson, ''depicts the period of the 1950s, in which it was composed, as an age of anxiety and superstition, of supernatural phenomena, ripe for a new object of worship.'' This prophetic and inventive novel makes deft use of the modernist technique (pioneered in this century by André Gide in *The Counterfeiters* [1926]) of the journal within the memoir—a form that Vidal would exploit to good effect in later novels. *Messiah*'s memoirist is Eugene Luther, who is writing under the pseudonym Richard Hudson about the 1950s from around the year 2000. He recalls the spread of a strange religious cult based on the figure of John Cave, whose message to the planet is terribly simple, if not simpleminded. Cave preaches the goodness of death and encourages suicide among his followers (those who adhere to ''Cavesway''), but he is not exactly willing to practice what he preaches; thus he is murdered, and his ashes are spread across the country. In a manner that seems eerily and especially American, Cave is merchandized to the hilt; indeed, the selling of Cave can hardly fail to remind a latter-day reader of television preachers like Jim Bakker and others who use evangelical religion as a platform for naked self-promotion. The religion that evolves in Cave's wake is fiercely hierarchical and bound to the literal "Cavesword" created by his Pauline apostles, and it is all brilliantly satirized by Vidal.

In *Messiah*, Vidal for the first time moves away from more conventional narrative forms and addresses larger issues, such as the American obsession with apocalyptic visionaries; in this sense the novel looks forward to his more speculative fiction of later years, such as *Kalki* and *Live from Golgotha*. In an odd turn, *Messiah* was originally published in a line of science fiction books, and for many years it enjoyed a coterie in that genre. It is not, however, a genre novel by any stretch of the imagination; Vidal simply uses the sci-fi novel as a base from which he extrapolates and invents.

After a period of wandering in Europe with his friend Tennessee Williams in 1948 (in Paris he was greeted by Gide as a prophet of the sexual revolution), Vidal settled along the Hudson River valley. There, in 1950, he bought Edgewater, an impressive Greek revival mansion built in 1820 by a former New York governor. Among other projects of this period was the writing of *The Judgment of Paris,* one of his most compelling early novels. The ghost of James hovers over this elegant novel, controlling its theme and the manner of characterization, but it is written in a style that looks forward to the later Vidal: dryly witty, sonorous, crisply ironic—a kind of dry run for the style that makes *Burr* the great book it is. But *The Judgment of Paris* is a lovely novel in its own right, describing the European sojourn of a young man who must choose among three women; each represents a different track for Vidal's hero: a political life, an intellectual life, and a sensual life. (The story is based on a Greek myth in which Paris is forced to choose among Hera, Athena, and Aphrodite.)

Vidal sat happily in his mansion—the great house on the Hudson—in the early fifties, but he needed money badly. His novels were simply not selling. With ferocious single-mindedness, he set about to make himself financially independent as quickly as possible. Under the pseudonym of Edgar Box, he wrote three conventional, but extremely witty mystery novels: *Death in the Fifth Position* (1952), *Death before Bedtime* (1953), and *Death Likes It Hot* (1954). These clever thrillers, which play off the conventions of the genre with typical Vidalian gusto, have never been out of print, although they apparently did not solve their creator's financial problems. Prompted by his agent, he decided to try his hand at writing scripts. The so-called Golden Age of television had begun, and Vidal took naturally to the new medium, producing dozens of scripts in the course of the next decade. Among his large number of adaptations were Faulkner's "Barn Burning" and James's *Turn of the Screw.* His best original teleplay was "Visit to a Small Planet," televised on May 8, 1955.

Not surprisingly, Vidal soon turned to Hollywood and Broadway to expand his outlets for scripts. He wrote a full-length stage version of *Visit to a Small Planet,* which opened in 1957 and ran for an amazing 338 performances. In an essay on the American writer Dawn Powell (included in *At Home*) Vidal recalls the opening night of his first play on Broadway:

> One evening back there in once upon a time (February 7, 1957, to be exact) my first play opened at the Booth Theatre. Traditionally, the playwright was invisible to the audience: One hid out in a nearby bar, listening to the sweet nasalities of Pat Boone's rendering of "Love Letters in the Sand" from a glowing jukebox. But when the curtain fell on this particular night, I went into the crowded lobby to collect someone. Overcoat collar high about my face, I moved invisibly through the crowd, or so I thought. Suddenly, a voice boomed-tolled across the lobby. *"Gore!"* I stopped, everyone stopped. From the cloakroom a small round figure, rather like a Civil War cannon ball, hurtled toward me and collided. As I looked into that familiar round face with its snub nose and shining bloodshot eyes, I heard, the entire crowded lobby heard: *"How could you do this? How could you*

sell out like this? To *Broadway!* To *Commercialism!* How could you give up *The Novel?''*

The plot of *Visit* concerns a visitor from outer space who goes to Virginia with the fond hope of viewing the first Battle of Bull Run, in 1861. Having arrived about a century too late, he establishes himself as the houseguest of a family called Spelding. When the federal government learns that this visitor, called Kreton, wants to start World War III, panic breaks loose. But Kreton is hardly a vicious fellow. In fact, he would like to see a war because he adores the primitive aspects of men and he considers war the greatest achievement of this curious race. Why not let them blow themselves to bits?

Eventually, Kreton is recalled by his fellow planeteers, who explain apologetically that he is not a mature member of their race; indeed, he is a mentally (and morally) retarded child. In its whimsy and satirical edge, this brilliant play recalls the earlier work of Wilde and George Bernard Shaw, though it reverberates with Vidal's own unmistakable style, characterized by cool detachment and wry one-liners. In a laudatory review in the *New York Times* (February 24, 1957), critic Brooks Atkinson said that the play ''makes us look ridiculous in a low-comedy carnival that has its own insane logic and never runs out of ideas.''

What Vidal wrote about himself as a playwright in ''Putting on *Visit to a Small Planet''* (in *Rocking the Boat,* 1962) shortly after the success of the play, seems true of his relationship to the genre of drama in general: ''I am not at heart a playwright. I am a novelist turned temporary adventurer; and I chose to write television, movies, and plays for much the same reason that Henry Morgan selected the Spanish Main for his peculiar—and not dissimilar—sphere of operations.'' In short, Vidal was never completely won over by playwrighting; as a result, he did not develop as a dramatist. He did, however, write

a remarkably good political play, *The Best Man: A Play About Politics* (1960), which outran *Visit to a Small Planet* on Broadway (520 performances); it was also made into a highly successful film in 1964 with script by Vidal. That play, set at a political convention, feels somewhat dated today, but it still works brilliantly on the stage. Two other plays for Broadway, neither of which attracted much in the way of favorable comment, were *Romulus: A New Comedy* (1962), adapted from Friedrich Dürrenmatt's *Romulus der Grosse,* and *An Evening with Richard Nixon* (1972).

Vidal entered into contract with MGM in the mid-1950s, and he remained active as a screenwriter. His numerous early credits include *The Catered Affair* (1956), *I Accuse!* (1958), and *Suddenly, Last Summer* (1959). He also worked on the script of *Ben-Hur* (1959). He wrote a television version of *Dress Gray* (1986; based on a novel by Lucian K. Truscott) that received an Emmy nomination, and adapted his own early teleplay, *The Death of Billy the Kid* (1955), for Turner Network Television in 1989. As ever, Vidal is a thorough professional; his scripts are invariably put together with skill and a firm sense of what must be done to hold the attention of a diverse audience.

Although it seems unbelievable, Vidal was not content just to write novels, short stories, plays and screenplays, essays, and reviews. For a long time he had watched the political world from the sidelines, having been raised in a family where politics and life were inseparable. When he threw his hat into the ring in 1960 and ran for Congress as a Democrat-Liberal in New York's traditionally Republican Twenty-ninth District, it was simply a natural move. Vidal took many wildly controversial stances, including advocating the recognition of the People's Republic of China, limiting the Pentagon's budget, and increasing federal aid to education. Not surprisingly, he lost the election, but he won a significant number of votes for a man running on a liberal platform in a traditionally conservative district, winning more votes than Kennedy, who ran at the top of his ticket. In 1982, he ran in the Democratic primary for the U.S. Senate in California, where he finished just behind Jerry Brown.

How seriously are we to take Vidal's bids for public office? One can hardly imagine a man of his literary energies content to sit, day after day, in the House or Senate. Still, one has to admire the fact that he has engaged the issues of his day with such fervor, that he has ventured farther afield than almost any American writer of this century into nonliterary regions. The experience of running for office can only have helped him when he wrote the series of novels about American politics that begins with *Washington, D.C.,* and continues through *Burr, 1876, Lincoln, Empire,* and *Hollywood.* Reading these political novels, one quickly senses that Vidal knows the world he is writing about. Sitting at dinner with his grandfather, with President Kennedy, with politicos and business people, he acquired an inward sense of how the "real" world operates. That sense of the world, which is Vidal's own supreme fiction, animates the novels in this impressive sequence.

The sixties were, for Vidal, a watershed period. He stepped back, a little, from the bustle, concentrating on his main career as novelist. Most important, he decided to leave the United States and moved, in the early part of the decade, to Italy—which he has often referred to (rather impishly) in interviews as a "pre-Christian country." Italy was doubtless connected in his mind with a highly personal notion of the civilized life; there he resumed his primary vocation as a novelist. In Rome, with the library of the American Academy available to him for research, he worked on *Julian,* a book that Robert F. Kiernan has shrewdly judged the "first novel of his artistic maturity." But in his heart Vidal did not leave the United States. As William Vance notes

in *America's Rome* (1989), his two-volume study of Americans in Rome, Americans continue abroad to "labor as Americans for America." James Tatum expands upon Vance's insight in "The *Romanitas* of Gore Vidal," where he writes:

> By returning to the source of all *Romanitas,* Vidal recovered the original version of what the artists and founding fathers of Washington's Capitol had sought to re-create.

Julian was the magnificent first fruit of Vidal's reinvention of himself as a Roman. Ever a ventriloquist, he enters into the mind of the Emperor Julian with an eerie nonchalance. Vidal tracks Julian as he renounces Christianity and embraces paganism, and follows his transformation from philosopher to soldier, then his elevation to emperor. The well-researched period details of the book are fascinating, enhanced by Vidal's clever embellishments. One little example is when Vidal, writing as Julian, comments on the strange voices of the eunuchs (who were very much a part of the imperial scene). He relates this voice—and its childlike tones—to their position of power over Constantius:

> In actual fact, the voice of a eunuch is like that of a particularly gentle child, and this appeals to the parent in both men and women. Thus subtly do they disarm us, for we tend to indulge them as we would a child, forgetting that their minds are as mature and twisted as their bodies are lacking.

Vidal's authority here, as everywhere in this strong novel, makes the tapestry of history ever more radiant.

Reviewers were apprehensive about *Julian,* which seemed to come out of nowhere. *Newsweek,* for instance, called it a "metaphysical costume drama," while in Britain the anonymous reviewer in the London *Times* felt that the novel lacked coherence, that it needed a wider scope "than the hero's idiosyncratic vision of his times.'' But the best reviewers were sympathetic. Walter Allen, writing in the *New York Review of Books* (July 30, 1964), said that *Julian* ''brings together and dramatizes more effectively and with much greater authority than ever before preoccupations that have been present in his fiction almost from its beginnings.'' Anthony Burgess said in the *Spectator* (October 16, 1964) that Vidal ''handles his huge cast well, achieves a triumph in his portrait of . . . Constantius and makes his hero perhaps more sympathetic than the tradition of bitter aggressiveness would approve.'' My own feeling is that *Julian* ranks high among Vidal's creations, a novel in all ways equal to *Burr, Lincoln, Myra Breckinridge,* and *Duluth.* As a historical novel about the ancient world, it is every bit the equal of anything by Mary Renault or Robert Graves; in fact, Vidal as a writer is generally more sophisticated than Renault and less cranky than Graves.

It has often been noted that Vidal twins his novels. *Messiah* is a prelude to a later apocalyptic novel, *Kalki. Myra Breckinridge* has its sequel, *Myron.* And *Julian,* in its way, beckons *Creation: A Novel* into being. The latter poses as the autobiography of an aged diplomat, Cyrus Spitama, who is half Persian and half Greek. This memoir becomes a panoramic minihistory of the ancient world in the fifth century B.C., taking in the Persian Wars as well as visits to India and China. Spitama, in over thirty years of service to the Persian empire, has been everywhere and seen everything. He was there when Zoroaster was assassinated, met the Buddha as well as Confucius, and he even (almost accidentally) bumped into Socrates, whom he hires to repair a masonry wall. The conceit is startling, of course. Who but Vidal would think of it?

Creation is brilliantly conceived and highly entertaining, but it lacks the aesthetic tightness of *Julian* (a tightness borne of Julian's own idiosyncratic voice, which is pure Vidal). Spitama is just too global, and his voice often seems too much the disembodied voice of History. Spitama is endlessly knowledgeable and a trifle weary of the great world he knows so well, as in the following passage from near the end of his wanderings:

> During the next weeks I dealt with the various merchants and guilds who wanted to do business with Persia. I was by now something of a merchant myself. I knew what could be sold at Susa; and for how much. I quite enjoyed the hours of haggling in the tents that are set up in the central market. Needless to say, whenever I found myself in the company of an important merchant or guild treasurer, the name of the Egibis would be mentioned. In a sense, that firm was a sort of universal monarch. Wherever one goes in the world, its agents have already been there, and done business.

Reading *Creation,* one is struck by the staggering amount of sheer information that Vidal has assimilated and transformed into fiction. Even when Spitama is being somewhat overly didactic, telling us more than we might really want to know about the philosophical theories of Democritus or specific protocol at the court of Darius, there is always the pleasure of the prose. As Kiernan says, ''Vidal's sentences . . . glimmer through any amount of dust and through the most overbearing and unnecessary amplitude. Classically graceful, totally poised, and brimming with quiet intelligence, they are the masterstrokes in all his fictions.''

In 1968, Vidal took satire into new realms of outrageousness and produced what some critics regard as his masterpiece: *Myra Breckinridge.* Again, the memoir form proved the ideal vehicle for Vidal's novelistic talents. This time we hear from Myra, formerly (via a sex change) Myron, nephew of Buck Loner, a retired horse opera star. Myra has returned to Hollywood to reclaim her inheritance, owed by Buck to Myron; he appeases her by making her a teacher at the Academy of Drama and Modeling—an astute appointment, since Myra is, among other things, the prototypical couch potato, a cinema junkie of the first order who celebrates "celluloid, *blessed* celluloid." She is also a protofeminist who repeatedly warns, "No man will ever possess Myra Breckinridge." One of the kinkiest, funniest, and most shocking scenes in any Vidal novel is Myra's subjection, through seduction, of a strapping young student called Rusty Godowsky, who is anally raped with a dildo by the triumphant Myra.

Again, the voice is everything, as *Myra* begins:

> I am Myra Breckinridge whom no man will ever possess. Clad only in garter belt and one dress shield, I held off the entire elite of the Trobriand Islanders, a race who possess no words for "why" or "because." Wielding a stone axe, I broke the arms, the limbs, the balls of their finest warriors, my beauty binding them, as it does all men, unmanning them in the way that King Kong was reduced to a mere simian whimper by beauteous Fay Wray whom I resemble left three-quarter profile if the key light is no more than five feet high during the close shot.

As Catharine R. Stimpson notes, in choosing the form of *Myra Breckenridge,* Vidal

> picks over the various narrative forms available to the twentieth-century writer: the *nouveau roman;* the memoir, written or taped; the client's confession to the therapist/analyst; the Hollywood star biography/autobiography; the Hollywood novel; and the female impersonator's monologue, which both pays lavish tribute to traditional femininity and tosses acid at the world.

Vidal's catalogue of narrative possibilities is seen to be a "tough-minded elegy for literary culture." Stimpson concludes:

> If we are to believe her creator, in a post-Gutenberg age our most popular gods and goddesses will be born and borne from celluloid, not paper. Our new interpreters of signs and symbols will huddle around television or movie screens. For those of us who still read, there yet remains the glow of pleasurable embers that Vidal throws on his pages—the occasional graffiti, the provocations of satire, and the risible comfort of the Myra/Myronic cult figures.

Myron follows *Myra,* as the night the day. Published in 1974, it picks up the story about five years later. In many ways, *Myron* is a novel of restoration, or a parody of restoration. The splintered psyche of Myra/Myron is fused in the narrative. Swinging backward and forward in time, blending celluloid reality with everyday reality, Vidal in *Myron* actually pushes beyond the mock realism of *Myra Breckinridge* into something utterly strange, yet resonant. And Myron's rhetoric, which might be called "American square squared," presents a terribly funny contrast to Myra's decadently baroque ebullience.

In one minor vein of *Myron,* Vidal explores the links between Hollywood-style fantasy and American politics as Richard Nixon appears on the scene in various guises. At one point, for instance, Nixon turns up at Metro-Goldwyn-Mayer on the back lot and wants to know if 1948 has an extradition treaty with the future. This link between the twin capitals of Washington and Hollywood became a dominant theme in the later novels of Vidal's American sequence, *Empire* and *Hollywood,* where these links are explicitly and (as opposed to *Myron*) realistically invoked.

The American chronicle that begins with *Washington, D.C.,* and ends with *Hollywood* may well be regarded by future critics as Vidal's main achievement. The author, however, had nothing like a sequence in mind when he wrote *Washington, D.C.* That fairly conventional novel begins in 1937 at a party where the defeat of President Franklin Roosevelt's bid to enlarge the Supreme Court is being celebrated by a group of political insiders. The two main families whose lives are chronicled over a decade of national events are those of Senator James Burden Day and Blaise Sanford, who owns the *Washington*

GORE VIDAL / 687

Tribune. Clay Overbury is a protégé of Senator Day, and he serves as a link between the two families by marrying Enid Sanford, daughter of the newspaper baron.

The novel turns on a bribe that is ultimately the senator's undoing. While nothing in the plot would surprise anyone familiar with the traditions of political fiction, there is always the Vidalian style to redeem the moment. The language of *Washington, D.C.,* is remarkably imagistic; one quickly senses that Vidal is writing about a world that he has known intimately. The foibles and obsessions of the late 1930s and 1940s are skillfully summoned. As an observer of American political life, Vidal has few peers. He knows how these people talk—or, at least, he is able to make us believe that this is how people in power talk (which, for a novelist, is what actually matters). Vidal also has a firm sense of the way the machinery of power works, as in his description of the Club to which senators either belong or do not:

> No one was ever quite sure who belonged to The Club since members denied its existence but everyone knew who did not belong. The Club was permanently closed to the outside personality, to the firebrand tribune of the people, to the Senator running too crudely for President. Members of The Club preferred to do their work quietly and to get re-elected without fanfare. On principle they detested the President, and despite that magnate's power to loose and to bind, The Club ruled the Senate in its own way and for its own ends, usually contrary to those of the President.

While there is much to admire in *Washington, D.C.,* nobody could have guessed how Vidal's American chronicle would unfold from this modestly unexceptional beginning. *Burr: A Novel,* the next to appear (in 1973), is among the richest of Vidal's works, a mature novel that brings into play virtually all the author's various talents. It was finished about the time Vidal moved from Rome to Ravello, an idyllic town perched on a cliff side overlooking the Mediterranean Sea between Salerno and Naples. (The villa that Vidal and his longtime companion, Howard Austen, moved into is called La Rondinaia, meaning ''Swallow's Nest.'' It has remained Vidal's base of operations since 1972.)

The narrative voice in *Burr* belongs to Charlie Schuyler, a young law clerk and journalist who works for Aaron Burr, the man who killed Alexander Hamilton in a duel in 1804 and who, two years later, initiated a secessionist conspiracy that challenged the assumptions of America's founding fathers, all of whom Burr knew well. Donald E. Pease, in ''America and the Vidal Chronicles,'' connects Vidal's revisionist approach to American history with the New Historicist effort to revitalize literary studies by plunging into the archives: ''When construed as the historical consciousness missing from the counterculture, Vidal's chronicles can be understood to historicize the New Historicists' project.'' Pease argues that Vidal has succeeded in undermining the separation of fact from fiction, using the traditions of the historical narrative to revitalize both history and literature by insisting on their parity and permeability. As a leading voice of the countercultural revolution of the late sixties, Vidal has worked with incredible diligence to rethink the past, to create a new sense of historical consciousness that was simply missing during the sixties.

Vidal's essays have always been published at regular intervals between the novels, and collections such as *Matters of Fact and Fiction: Essays 1973–1976* (1977), *The Second American Revolution and Other Essays (1976–1982)* (1982), and *At Home: Essays, 1982–1988* (1988) attest to the historical and political preoccupations that set the various novels of each period in motion. In 1992, his collected essays appeared in a volume called *United States—Essays, 1951–1991,* and it was given the National Book Award in 1993.

There is an intriguing relationship between the essays and the novels. Vidal's ''Note on Abraham Lincoln'' in *The Second American Revolution,* for instance, might be read as the author's working notes for *Lincoln,* which appeared in 1984. The essay called ''Hollywood!'' in *At Home* is obviously a spin-off of the work that went into the writing of *Hollywood* the novel. Reading back and forth between the essays and the novels, one is inevitably struck by the continuity of voice, the blending of fiction and fact into a kind of meta-narrative in which literal and imaginative truth merge.

The novel *1876* soon followed *Burr,* continuing the story of Charlie Schuyler, who returns to New York on the eve of America's centennial year. It is a brilliant sequel—a form that Vidal has perfected; he sketches a portrait of the Gilded Age with an acid pen, scanning that gaudy and energetic period in American history with an eye for the kind of idiosyncratic detail that marked *Creation.* The reader hears about the building of new churches in Brooklyn, about goats trotting down East Twenty-fourth Street, about the beginnings of Chinatown and the European idea of a city park as the origins of Central Park. Schuyler is the panoptical observer, taking in everything from a discreet distance. He sees but is rarely seen—the ideal Vidalian hero, who might be thought of as a spy—or a fly on the wall of history.

It is nearly axiomatic that good historical novels provide a kind of resonance with contemporary affairs, and *1876* is no exception (indeed, it was published in America's bicentennial year of 1976). Vidal cleverly aligns his echoes, so that Samuel J. Tilden reminds one of the idealistic yet ineffective George McGovern, while Rutherford B. Hayes recalls the stumbling and bumbling Gerald Ford. Mark Twain (in his white suit) comes off as a Tom Wolfe figure, a bright-winged insect buzzing in society's ear. Vietnam and the Civil War are eerily drawn into parallel rows of absurdity and cruelty, while the Lincoln assassination reminds one inevitably of President Kennedy's assassination in 1963. The Babcock break-in might be taken as a dry run for Watergate, and so forth. Violence, low-mindedness, greed, and corruption form the constants of American political life—a view not designed to instill total admiration in Vidal's critics, who remain inclined to view America as the greatest (or at least the most well-intentioned) show on earth.

As usual, Vidal's blend of cynicism with old-fashioned storytelling elicited mixed reviews, with some critics complaining that the novelist often wrote with scorn for his own characters. Edwin Morgan, for instance, suggested in the London *Sunday Times* (March 28, 1976) that ''Vidal's Laodicean ironies, clever and devastating as they are, in the end fail to satisfy on any deeper level.'' The most thoughtful of the reviewers of this volume was Peter Conrad, who wrote a lengthy assessment of the novel in the *Times Literary Supplement.* He regarded Vidal's political novels in general as the ''result of a precarious, dazzling partnership between Gore the researcher and Vidal the frivolous meddler with history.'' Vidal's work was seen not as straightforward history but as a playful version of the same, with Shakespeare's Roman plays as his natural precursor. ''America is Rome reborn,'' said Conrad. ''The decadent comedy of ancient history happens a second time as coarse, uncultivated farce.''

Surveying the reviews of *1876* and virtually every other book by Vidal, it becomes clear that English reviewers have almost always understood him better than his compatriots. This is partly, I suspect, because of the ironic mode that Vidal has cultivated, which has affiliations with the English novel from Henry Fielding to Evelyn Waugh and Kingsley Amis. The English have also been more able to appreciate Vidal's mandarin style, with its controlled ironies, its neatly balanced syntactical parallelisms, and its occasional baroque flurries of eloquence. The American novel has, by contrast, been either seemingly without style in the manner of Theodore Dreiser and Norman Mailer or, like Crane and Hemingway, somehow ''beyond'' style. There have been important exceptions, of course, such as James and F. Scott Fitzgerald, although both of these writers suffered a kind of exile. James could not live comfortably in America, where his style and manner clashed with those of his contemporaries. Fitzgerald found the United States an alien place as well, however much he loved it; he was quickly shut out by the culture that briefly embraced him, and he ended up in one of the most unreal places on earth—Hollywood. While Vidal does not consider himself an ''ex-patriot'' (even though he has lived much of his life abroad in the past few decades), one does find Jamesian echoes in his work (and, indeed, he has written about James with astonishing perspicuity). The Fitzgeraldian side is there too: the lure of Hollywood, the shimmering prose style, the stylish affect and preoccupation with ''style'' in its many guises, the concern with ''success.''

Vidal's readership expanded widely after *Julian;* nevertheless, *Lincoln: A Novel* was a vast best-seller, bringing Vidal his largest audience yet. In some ways, however, *Lincoln* is Vidal's least Vidalian novel. The prose contrasts rather severely with that of *1876,* being much less ornate and flashy. The subject, for once, takes center stage. The very weight of the historical material pushes the author to one side (and it is to Vidal's credit that he knew enough to stay in the background).

Reviewing the novel on the front page of the *New York Times Book Review,* Joyce Carol Oates said that *Lincoln* was

> not so much an imaginative reconstruction of an era as an intelligent, lucid and highly informative transcript of it, never less than workmanlike in its blocking out of scenes and often extremely compelling. No verbal pyrotechnics here, nothing to

challenge a conservative esthetics biased against the house of fiction itself. By subordinating the usual role of the novelist to the role of historian-biographer, Mr. Vidal acknowledges his faith in the high worth of his material.

The most comprehensive and influential discussion of *Lincoln* was definitely Harold Bloom's review in the *New York Review of Books.* In ''The Central Man,'' Bloom describes Vidal as a ''masterly American historical novelist, now wholly matured, who has found his truest subject, which is our national political history during precisely those years when our political and military histories were as one, one thing and one thing only: the unwavering will of Abraham Lincoln to keep the states united.'' Bloom discusses *Lincoln* in the context of Vidal's developing career, turning at the end of his essay to the ''still ambiguous question of Vidal's strength or perhaps competing strengths as a novelist.'' Adamantly, Bloom concludes: *''Lincoln,* together with the curiously assorted trio of *Julian, Myra Breckinridge,* and *Burr,* demonstrates that his narrative achievement is vastly underestimated by American academic criticism, an injustice he has repaid amply in his essayist attacks upon the academy, and in the sordid intensities of *Duluth.''*

Vidal continuously draws a contrast in *Lincoln* between Salmon P. Chase and Lincoln. Chase is presented as the archetypal Republican abolitionist, who is nevertheless endlessly jealous of the President, selfish in almost comical ways, conniving, and crudely pious. Lincoln comes across as bizarrely single-minded, ready to sacrifice anything—including the Constitution and human rights—to preserve a theoretical ideal. Chase, it seems, is genuinely concerned about the slaves, while Lincoln clearly does not care; abolition is merely an issue he can use to defend his notion of union. That Lincoln was willing to go to any end—a dreadful and terrible end, as it were—to perpetuate an idea that appears, in retrospect, curiously abstract, is Vidal's underlying theme. One senses, throughout, Vidal's admiration for Lincoln's Machiavellian aspects; at the same time, Vidal's judgment of Lincoln is severe in its way, and the novel—as a whole—offers a unique and gripping portrait of the man who is clearly the most important figure in the political history of the United States.

The originality of *Lincoln* has not been overly discussed or even noticed. Most critics, in fact, treated the novel as one of Vidal's most conventional. In conventional historical novels, however, such as those by Walter Scott, or later, Paul Scott, history is really nothing more than a backdrop to a fictional melodrama that takes center stage. Vidal, by placing Lincoln at the fictional center of his novel, has, in effect, reversed the traditional method. For many years to come, this may well be the most popular of Vidal's fictions.

The last two novels in the American chronicle, *Empire: A Novel* and *Hollywood,* in many ways constitute one work appearing in two installments. Both novels are written self-consciously in anticipation of *Washington, D.C.,* drawing on the Sanford family as key figures. Vidal is uncanny in the way he links his various heroes and heroines to history and to each other. Caroline Sanford, for instance, is being pushed at the beginning of *Empire*—as we have seen—to marry Del Hay. Another major character who emerges from "real" life is William Randolph Hearst, who takes on Caroline Sanford's half brother, Blaise Sanford (who reappears in *Washington, D.C.*), as a protégé. Other historical figures—Theodore Roosevelt, William McKinley, William Jennings Bryan, James, and Henry Adams—mingle with Vidal's creations. Fact and fiction become, once again, permeable; the world, recast by Vidal, is given the kind of unity that only fiction can generate. One sees history—the chronology of public events—unfold and made sense of in the private lives of "real" and imagined figures. As Richard Poirier notes in "American Emperors," "Vidal

manages inextricably to mix the fictive and the historical, the social and the legendary. These elements are so fused in his style that none can be differentiated from the others. All partake of the same issues of inheritance, legitimacy, rivalry, deception, and ambition.''

The connections between Hollywood and Washington have been of interest to Vidal from the beginning, but it was not until the eighties that history served up on a platter the presidency of Ronald Reagan, thus bringing the two worlds into fantastic juncture. Responding to history's little gift, Vidal began—in essays as well as novels—to explore these connections, finding Woodrow Wilson there at the beginning, fully aware of the infinite propaganda potential represented by Hollywood. With his intimate knowledge of the history of the movies and the history of American politics, Vidal was perfectly situated to explore these links. Against the continuing saga of the Sanford family, the rise and fall of presidents from McKinley to Wilson and Warren G. Harding is heard like the beating of waves on the shore throughout *Empire* and *Hollywood;* the parallels with the present become increasingly shocking and converge like infinite railroad tracks in the not-so-imaginary future, where Reagan stands with arms folded, his smile in place. He was, as Vidal memorably puts it, "our first Acting President."

Reviewing *Hollywood* in the *New York Times Book Review* (January 21, 1990), Joel Connaroe noted that "reviewers have tended to greet each installment of Vidal's saga with hyperbole, suggesting that he regularly manages to outdo even his previous outdoings, as if he were involved in some sort of novelistic Olympics." He continues: "My own sense is that with the exception of *Washington, D.C.,* which lacks both the trenchant wit and the historical players of the other works, the novels are pretty much of a piece, huge chapters in a continuing opus rather than self-contained entities." There is merit to this viewpoint, but while one must sometimes strain to find much narrative connection between, say, *Burr* and *Hollywood,* all the novels have, in fact, the unifying theme of Vidal's approach to certain revisionist aspects of American political history.

There is also, of course, the capital itself: Washington, D.C.—which serves to yoke these novels in a geographical plane that is both social and sociological, if not pathological as well. Writing in the *Times Literary Supplement,* Michael Wood notes that "Washington for Vidal is like some Jacobean court, a city where even the smallest movement is interesting and dangerous, and where strokes and suicide have taken the place of poison." Then again, the novels widen out so dramatically from Washington—especially in *Hollywood,* which (despite its title) is centered in the capital—that one hesitates to place too much emphasis on this point. Perhaps the point is not to look for more unity in the sequence than exists but to let the novels live where they do, in a kind of daisy chain of historical moments and history-based conjurations that interlock in a delicate way.

The action of *Hollywood* spans the years 1917–1923, an era riveted by World War I and the scandal-ridden administration of President Harding. In the course of Vidal's novel, the reader encounters such well-known people as Woodrow Wilson and the Roosevelts, Franklin and Eleanor; Hearst is there, and so are D. W. Griffith, Douglas Fairbanks, Mary Pickford, and Charlie Chaplin. Even Fatty Arbuckle steps forward for a mug shot. Caroline Sanford, owner of the influential *Washington Tribune,* takes center stage, a fictional character amid the "real" people. As she extends her power to Hollywood, the fatal confluence of politics and show business becomes the subtext, then the text, of Vidal's novel. "Reality could now be entirely invented and history revised," she says, realizing the full potential of the Hollywood-Washington connection. "Suddenly, she knew what God must have felt when he gazed upon chaos, with nothing but himself upon his mind." Vidal's anatomy of

American politics is both impressive and chilling; he sits back and watches his characters exercise their godlike powers with icy detachment.

Apart from the American chronicle, Vidal's later satirical novels—*Kalki, Duluth,* and *Live from Golgotha*—reach back to *Messiah* through *Myra Breckinridge* and *Myron.* Written almost as a pause between *1876* and *Lincoln,* they are Vidal's darkest creations. John Simon (in the *Saturday Review,* April 29, 1978) called *Kalki* a "diabolically clever" novel, and he is right. An apocalyptic thriller about a man who would take over the world, and full of satirical jibes at religious gurus who create satanic cults to screen their egotistical and greedy sensibilities, the novel wheels through contemporary culture making fun of everything. As usual, Vidal's interest in the transmogrifications of celluloid are crucial: "This was a commonplace in that era," says Vidal's narrator, a bisexual aviatrix and feminist called Teddy Ottinger. "Events were only real if experienced second hand, preferably through the medium of the camera."

Kalki is not as wildly inventive or entertaining as *Duluth,* Vidal's bleakest (but also, in many ways, his funniest) book. The novel might well be seen as a Swiftian rant against what life in America has become. Angela McRobbie, writing in the *New Statesmen* (May 6, 1983), said:

> Just imagine what Derrida might do with *Dallas.* Consider what might be Gore Vidal's relationship to each of these, dare I say it, signifiers. *Duluth* ('Love It Or Loathe It, You Can Never Leave It Or Lose It') could well be seen as an answer. Both Vidal and Barthes before him have commented on the practice of summarizing a text as a kind of re-writing: not a claim most critics in their modesty would make. In any case, *Duluth* almost denies the possibility of its own summary.

McRobbie went on: "I find this book one of the most brilliant, most radical and most subversive pieces of writing to emerge from America in recent years."

The conceit of the novel is postmodern: it is purportedly the property of one Rosemary Klein Kantor, the Wurlitzer Prize winner who, like the infinite number of monkeys in a room who somehow type out *Hamlet* by accident, creates the novel *Duluth* (as well as the TV series *Duluth*) out of a word processor that contains the plots of ten thousand previously published novels. Full of outrageous wordplay, endless gags, whims of irony, sleights of thought, and baroque fictional whirligigs, *Duluth* is Vidal's most open assault on the excesses of American mass culture. In many ways a novel designed to deconstruct before our very eyes, *Duluth* can be thought of as a cultural maze in which the endless free-floating signifiers of a culture with no definite frame of reference coalesce and swirl in the polluted stream of contemporary life. The novel brings into harsh focus the same obsessions with politics as with the celluloid and video culture that are dealt with more realistically in the American chronicle. One might think of *Duluth* and *Kalki* together as fiendish midnight cackles occasioned by Vidal's prodigious day laborings on *1876* and *Lincoln*.

Live from Golgotha inhabits the same netherworld as *Duluth, Messiah,* and *Kalki,* combining a fierce satirical impulse with the longtime interest in messianic figures. This wild burlesque of the New Testament is set at the end of the second millennium. The novel assumes that science and technology dominate the world, making it possible for holograms, even people, to be shifted back in time with ease. NBC is filming the Crucifixion, and the first bishop of Ephesus, Timothy, has been hired as an anchorman. There is a glitch, however; a computer hacker has sent a virus to corrupt the extant Gospels, so Timothy must get the "true" story. Saint Paul, Shirley MacLaine, Oral Roberts, and Mary Baker Eddy are present at the Crucifixion, making matters worse. In the end, there is no "true" story; there are only fictions, each crazier than the next one. It seems possible that Timothy is himself, like a character from the work of Jorge Luis Borges, merely a dreamer, dreaming the universe.

How does one summarize such a vastly productive and various career? One sees a talented young man who, still in his teens, realizes his vocation. He begins as a follower of Hemingway and Crane, writing realistic fiction; he swings from genre to genre, acquiring the technical abilities to write screenplays and teleplays. His interest in satire emerges, and in historical fiction. He runs for political office, meanwhile, and begins to inject his knowledge of political history into his fiction. Eventually, he creates a huge tapestry of American history. In another mode, he writes witty, even sardonic, essays on politics and culture; he becomes a singularly brilliant essayist, possibly the very best in our nation's history. He writes satires in fiction, too.

One steps back from Gore Vidal's opus–surely one of the largest and most intellectually and artistically substantial of any American writer in our time—with mingled awe and exhaustion. Interpreters of Vidal from Mitchell S. Ross and Joseph Epstein on the right of the political spectrum to Russell Jacoby on the left have tried to put a finger on Vidal, seeing him variously as a "detoured politician" (Ross) or an Edmund Wilson–like "last intellectual" (Jacoby). But no single tag can explain this career. A few things, however, seem clear: Vidal's work is steeped in an intimate acquaintance with American history and culture, with the twin capitals of Washington and Hollywood, and with the ways that Americans have chosen to conduct their lives. A satirist at heart, his writing recalls that of H. L. Mencken as an immediate precursor and Jonathan Swift as a long-distance ancestor. In a country not known for (or kind to) its satirists, Vidal stands out as something of a national treasure in this regard. Although one can easily find connections between Vidal and previous American writers from

Twain and James to Menken and Wilson, Vidal is *sui generis*—an American original. One can never really guess which writers will survive the winnowing process of time, but Vidal has as good a chance as any writer of his generation.

Selected Bibliography

WORKS OF GORE VIDAL

NOVELS

Williwaw. New York: E. P. Dutton, 1946.

In a Yellow Wood. New York: E. P. Dutton, 1947.

The City and the Pillar. New York: E. P. Dutton, 1948. Rev. ed., New York: E. P. Dutton, 1965.

The Season of Comfort. New York: E. P. Dutton, 1949.

Dark Green, Bright Red. New York: E. P. Dutton, 1950. Rev. ed., New York: New American Library, 1968.

A Search for the King: A Twelfth-Century Legend. New York: E. P. Dutton, 1950.

Death in the Fifth Position. Edgar Box, pseud. New York: E. P. Dutton, 1952.

The Judgment of Paris. New York: E. P. Dutton, 1952. Rev. ed., Boston: Little, Brown, 1965.

Death Before Bedtime. Edgar Box, pseud. New York: E. P. Dutton, 1953.

Death Likes It Hot. Edgar Box, pseud. New York: E. P. Dutton, 1954.

Messiah. New York: E. P. Dutton, 1954. Rev. ed., Boston: Little, Brown, 1965.

Julian. Boston: Little, Brown, 1968.

Washington, D.C. Boston: Little, Brown, 1967.

Myra Breckinridge. Boston: Little, Brown, 1968.

Two Sisters: A Memoir in the Form of a Novel. Boston: Little, Brown, 1970.

Burr: A Novel. New York: Random House, 1973.

Myron. New York: Random House, 1974.

1876: A Novel. New York: Random House, 1976.

Kalki: A Novel. New York: Random House, 1978.

Creation: A Novel. New York: Random House, 1981.

Duluth. New York: Random House, 1983.

Lincoln: A Novel. New York: Random House, 1984.

Empire: A Novel. New York: Random House, 1987.

Hollywood: A Novel of America in the 1920s. New York: Random House, 1990.

Live from Golgotha. New York: Random House, 1992.

SHORT STORIES

A Thirsty Evil: Seven Short Stories. New York: Zero Press, 1956.

NONFICTION

Rocking the Boat. Boston: Little, Brown, 1962.

Reflections upon a Sinking Ship. Boston: Little, Brown, 1969.

Homage to Daniel Shays: Collected Essays, 1952–1972. New York: Random House, 1972.

Matters of Fact and Fiction: Essays 1973–1976. New York: Random House, 1977.

The Second American Revolution and Other Essays (1976–1982). New York: Random House, 1982.

Armageddon? Essays, 1983–1987. London: Andre Deutsch, 1987.

At Home: Essays, 1982–1988. New York: Random House, 1988.

A View from the Diners' Club: Essays 1987–1991. London: Andre Deutsch, 1991.

The Decline and Fall of the American Empire. Berkeley, Calif.: Odonian Press, 1992.

Screening History. The William E. Massey Sr. Lectures in the History of American Civilization. Cambridge: Harvard University Press, 1992.

United States—Essays, 1951–1991. New York: Random House, 1992.

Palimpsest: A Memoir. New York: Random House, 1995.

DRAMA

Visit to a Small Planet and Other Television Plays. Boston: Little, Brown, 1956.

Visit to a Small Planet: A Comedy Akin to Vaudeville (Broadway version). Boston: Little, Brown, 1957.

The Best Man: A Play about Politics. Boston: Little, Brown, 1960.

On the March to the Sea: A Southern Comedy. Evergreen Playscript Series. New York: Grove Press, n.d. Based on Vidal's teleplay "Honor."

Romulus: A New Comedy, Adapted from a Play by

Friedrich Dürrenmatt. New York: Dramatists Play Service, 1962.

Three Plays. London: William Heinemann, 1962.

Weekend: A Comedy in Two Acts. New York: Dramatists Play Service, 1968.

An Evening with Richard Nixon. New York: Random House, 1972.

FILMS

The Catered Affair. Metro-Goldwyn-Mayer, 1956. Screenplay by Vidal, adapted from Paddy Chayefsky's teleplay *Wedding Breakfast.*

I Accuse! Metro-Goldwyn-Mayer, 1958. Screenplay by Vidal, based on the book by Nicholas Halasz.

The Scapegoat. Metro-Goldywn-Mayer, 1959. Screenplay by Robert Hamer, based on Vidal's adaptation of the novel by Daphne du Maurier.

Suddenly, Last Summer. Columbia Pictures, 1959. Screenplay by Vidal and Tennessee Williams, adapted from Williams' play.

The Best Man. United Artists, 1964. Screenplay by Vidal, adapted from his play.

Is Paris Burning? Paramount Pictures and Seven Arts, 1966. Screenplay by Vidal, Francis Ford Coppola, et al., adapted from the book by Larry Collins and Dominique LaPierre. Not credited to Vidal on screen.

The Last of the Mobile Hot-Shots. Warner Brothers and Seven Arts, 1970. Screenplay by Vidal, adapted from Tennessee Williams' *The Seven Descents of Myrtle.*

WRITING FOR TELEVISION

"Dark Possession." *Studio One.* CBS, February 15, 1954. Screenplay by Vidal.

"Smoke." *Suspense.* CBS, May 4, 1954. Screenplay by Vidal, adapted from the story by William Faulkner.

"Barn Burning." *Suspense.* CBS, August 17, 1954. Screenplay by Vidal, adapted from the story by William Faulkner.

"A Sense of Justice." *Philco Television Playhouse.* NBC, February 6, 1955. Screenplay by Vidal.

"The Turn of the Screw." *Omnibus.* CBS, February 13, 1955. Screenplay by Vidal, adapted from the novel by Henry James.

"The Blue Hotel." *Danger.* CBS, February 22, 1955. Screenplay by Vidal, adapted from the story by Stephen Crane.

"Stage Door." *The Best of Broadway.* CBS, April 6, 1955. Screenplay by Vidal, adapted from the drama by George S. Kaufman and Edna Ferber.

"Summer Pavilion." *Studio One.* CBS, May 2, 1955. Screenplay by Vidal.

"Visit to a Small Planet." *Goodyear Television Playhouse.* NBC, May 8, 1955. Screenplay by Vidal.

"A Farewell to Arms." *Climax.* CBS, May 26, 1955. Screenplay by Vidal, adapted from the novel by Ernest Hemingway.

"The Death of Billy the Kid." *Philco Television Playhouse.* NBC, July 24, 1955. Screenplay by Vidal.

"Dr. Jekyll and Mr. Hyde. *Climax.* CBS, July 28, 1955. Screenplay by Vidal, adapted from the story by Robert Louis Stevenson.

Portrait of a Ballerina. Screenplay by Vidal, as Edgar Box, adapted from his novel *Death in the Fifth Position.* CBS, January 1, 1956.

"Honor." *Playwrights 56. NBC, June 19, 1956. Screenplay by Vidal.*

"The Indestructible Mr. Gore." *Sunday Showcase.* NBC, December 13, 1959. Screenplay and narration by Vidal.

"Dear Arthur." *Ford Startime.* NBC, March 22, 1960. Screenplay by Vidal, adapted from the drama by Ferenc Molnar.

Dress Gray. NBC, March 9–10, 1986. Screenplay by Vidal, adapted from the novel by Lucian K. Trescott IV.

Vidal in Venice. WNET, June 30, 1986. Text and narration by Vidal.

Gore Vidal's Billy the Kid. TNT, May 10, 1989. Screenplay by Vidal, adapted from his teleplay *The Death of Billy the Kid.*

MANUSCRIPTS

The largest collection of Vidal's papers is held by the State Historical Society of Wisconsin at Madison. The libraries associated with the University of Florida, Yale University, Boston University, Syracuse University, and the University of Texas also have some of his papers.

BIBLIOGRAPHY

Stanton, Robert J. *Gore Vidal: A Primary and Secondary Bibliography.* Boston: G. K. Hall, 1978.

BIOGRAPHICAL AND CRITICAL STUDIES

Aldridge, John W. "Gore Vidal: The Search for a King." In his *After the Lost Generation: A Critical Study of the Writers of Two Wars.* New York: McGraw-Hill, 1951. Pp. 170–183.

Barton, David. "Narrative Patterns in the Novels of Gore Vidal." *Notes on Contemporary American Literature,* 7:3–9 (September 1981).

Bloom, Harold. "The Central Man." *New York Review of Books,* July 19, 1984, pp. 5–8.

Boyette, Purvis E. " 'Myra Breckinridge' and Imitative Form." *Modern Fiction Studies,* 17:229–238 (Summer 1971).

Buckley, William F., Jr. "On Experiencing Gore Vidal." *Esquire,* August 1969, pp. 108–113.

Clemons, Walter. "Gore Vidal's Chronicle of America." *Newsweek,* June 9, 1984, pp. 74–75, 78–79.

Conrad, Peter, "Halls of Mirrors: The Novels of Gore Vidal." London *Sunday Times,* March 27, 1977, p. 35.

———. "Look at Us." *New Review,* 2:63–66 (July 1975).

———. "Reinventing America." *Times Literary Supplement,* March 26, 1976, pp. 347–348.

Dick, Bernard F. *The Apostate Angel: A Critical Study of Gore Vidal.* New York: Random House, 1974.

Edwards, Owen Dudley. "Fiction As History: On an Earlier President." *Encounter,* January 1985, pp. 33–42.

Epstein, Joseph. "What Makes Vidal Run." *Commentary,* June 1977, pp. 72–75.

Fletcher, M. D. "Vidal's *Duluth* as 'Post-Modern' Political Satire." *Thalia: Studies in Literary Humor,* 9:10–21 (Spring-Summer 1986).

Hines, Samuel M., Jr. "Political Change in America: Perspectives from the Popular Historical Novels of Michener and Vidal." In *Political Mythology and Popular Fiction.* Edited by Ernest J. Yanarella and Lee Sigelman. New York: Greenwood, 1988. Pp. 81–99.

Kakutani, Michiko. "Gore Vidal." In her *Poet at the Piano: Portraits of Writers, Filmmakers, Playwrights, and Other Artists at Work.* New York: Times Books, 1988. Pp. 89–92.

Kiernan, Robert F. *Gore Vidal.* New York: Frederick Ungar, 1982.

Krim, Seymour. "Reflections on a Ship That's Not Sinking At All." *London Magazine,* May 1970, pp. 26–43.

LaHood, Marvin J. "Gore Vidal: A Grandfather's Legacy." *World Literature Today,* 64:413–417 (Summer 1990).

Mitzel, John, Steven Abbott, and the Gay Study Group. "Some Notes on Myra B." *Fag Rag,* Fall 1973, pp. 21–25.

Mitzel, John. *Myra & Gore: A New View of Myra Breckinridge and a Candid Interview with Gore Vidal—A Book for Vidalophiles.* Dorchester, Mass.: Manifest Destiny, 1974.

Neilson, Heather. "The Fiction of History in Gore Vidal's *Messiah.*" In *Gore Vidal: Writer against the Grain.* Edited by Jay Parini. New York: Columbia University Press, 1992. Pp. 106–199. Adapted from her Oxford University D.Phil. thesis.

Nin, Anaïs. *The Diary of Anaïs Nin.* Volume 4, 1944–1947. Edited by Gunther Stuhlmann. New York: Harcourt Brace Jovanovich, 1971. Pp. 106, 113, 121.

Parini, Jay, ed. *Gore Vidal: Writer against the Grain.* New York: Columbia University Press, 1992. Contains articles by Claude J. Summers, Heather Neilson, James Tatum, and Donald E. Pease.

Pease, Donald. "America and the Vidal Chronicles." In *Gore Vidal: Writer against the Grain.* Edited by Jay Parini. New York: Columbia University Press, 1992. Pp. 247–277.

Poirier, Richard. "American Emperors." *New York Review of Books,* September 24, 1987, pp. 31 33.

Ross, Mitchell S. "Gore Vidal." In his *Literary Politicians.* Garden City, N.Y.: Doubleday, 1978. Pp. 247–300.

Stimpson, Catherine R.. "My O My O Myra." *New England Review: Middlebury Series,* 14:102–115 (Fall 1991).

Summers, Claude J. " 'The Cabin and the River,' Gore Vidal's *The City and the Pillar.*" In his *Gay Fictions: Wilde to Stonewall: Studies in a Male Homosexual Literary Tradition.* New York: Continuum, 1990. Pp. 112–129. This article appears as *"The City and the Pillar* as Gay Fiction" in Parini.

Tatum, James. "The *Romanitas* of Gore Vidal." In *Gore Vidal: Writer against the Grain.* Edited by Jay Parini. New York: Columbia University Press, 1992. Pp. 199–220.

White, Ray Lewis. *Gore Vidal.* New York: Twayne, 1968.

Wilhelm, John F., and Mary Ann Wilhelm. "Myra

Breckinridge': A Study of Identity.'' *Journal of Popular Culture,* 3:590–599 (Winter 1969).

Ziolkowski, Theodore. *Fictional Transfigurations of Jesus.* Princeton, N.J.: Princeton University Press, 1972. Pp. 250–257.

INTERVIEWS

''*Playboy* Interview: Gore Vidal.'' *Playboy,* June 1969, pp. 77–96, 238.

Auchincloss, Eve, and Nancy Lynch. ''Disturber of the Peace: Gore Vidal.'' *Mademoiselle,* September 1961, pp. 132–133, 176–179.

Clarke, Gerald. ''Petronius Americanus: The Ways of Gore Vidal.'' *Atlantic,* March 1972, pp. 44–51.

———. ''The Art of Fiction.'' *Paris Review,* 15:130–165 (Fall 1974).

Cooper, Arthur. ''Gore Vidal on . . . Gore Vidal.'' *Newsweek,* November 18, 1974, pp. 97–99.

Dreifus, Claudia. ''Gore Vidal: The Writer as Citizen.'' *Progressive,* September 1986, pp. 36–39.

Duffy, Martha. ''A Gadfly in Glorious, Angry Exile.'' *Time,* September 28, 1992, pp. 64–66.

Halpern, Daniel. ''Interview with Gore Vidal.'' *Antaeus,* 1:67–76 (1971).

Hutchings, David. ''Gospel According to Gore.'' *People,* November 2, 1992, pp. 103–106.

Johnson, Diane. ''Gore Vidal, Scorekeeper.'' *New York Times Book Review,* April 17, 1977, p. 47.

Katz, Robert. ''Gore Goes to War.'' *American Film,* 13:43–46 (November 1987).

[Kelly, Ken.] ''*Penthouse* Interview: Gore Vidal.'' *Penthouse,* April 1975, pp. 97–98, 104–106.

Lasky, Michael S. ''The Complete Works on Gore Vidal: His Workings.'' *Writer's Digest,* 55:20–26 (March 1975).

Mallory, Carole. ''Mailer and Vidal: The Big Schmooze.'' *Esquire,* May 1991, pp. 105–112.

Parini, Jay. ''An Interview with Gore Vidal.'' In his *Gore Vidal: Writer against the Grain.* New York: Columbia University Press, 1992. Pp. 278–290.

Ruas, Charles. ''Gore Vidal.'' *Conversations with American Writers.* New York: Knopf, 1985. Pp. 57–74.

Segell, Michael. ''The Highbrow Railings of Gore Vidal.'' *Rolling Stone,* May 15, 1980, pp. 40–43.

Stanton, Robert J., and Gore Vidal. *Views from a Window: Conversations with Gore Vidal.* Secaucus, N.J.: Lyle Stuart, 1980.

Walter, Eugene. ''Conversations with Gore Vidal.'' *Transatlantic Review,* 4 (Summer 1960): 5–17.

—*JAY PARINI*

INDEX

Index

*Arabic numbers printed in bold-face type refer
to extended treatment of a subject.*

Carnegie, Dale, **Supp. I, Part 2,** 608

"Carnegie Hall: Rescued" (Moore), **III,** 215

Carnell, Edward J., **III,** 312

"Carnival with Spectres" (Benét), **Supp. I, Part 2,** 626

Carnovsky, Morris, **III,** 154

"Carol of Occupations" (Whitman), **I,** 486

Caroling Dusk: An Anthology of Verse by Negro Poets (Cullen), **Supp. IV, Part 1,** 166, 169

"Carpe Noctem, if You Can" (Thurber), **Supp. I, Part 2,** 620

Carpenter, Frederic I., **II,** 20, 23; **III,** 243, 407

Carpenter, George Rice, **Supp. I, Part 2,** 706

Carpenter's Gothic (Gaddis), **Supp. IV, Part 1,** 288, 289–291, 293, 294

Carpentered Hen and Other Tame Creatures, The (Updike), **IV,** 214

Carpet-Bag (magazine), **IV,** 193

Carr, Dennis W., **Supp. IV, Part 2,** 560

Carrall, Aaron, **Supp. IV, Part 2,** 499

Carrel, Alexis, **IV,** 240

"Carriage from Sweden, A" (Moore), **III,** 212

Carrier of Ladders (Merwin), **Supp. III, Part 1,** 339, 346, 350–352, 356, 357

"Carriers of the Dream Wheel" (Momaday), **Supp. IV, Part 2,** 481

Carriers of the Dream Wheel: Contemporary Native American Poetry (ed. Niatum), **Supp. IV, Part 2,** 484, 505

Carrington, Carroll, **I,** 199

Carrington, George C., Jr., **II,** 293, 294

"Carrion Spring" (Stegner), **Supp. IV, Part 2,** 604

Carroll, Charles, **Supp. I, Part 2,** 525

Carroll, Lewis, **I,** 432; **II,** 431; **III,** 181; **Supp. I, Part 1,** 44, **Part 2,** 622, 656

Carroll, Paul, **IV,** 47

Carrouges, Michel, **Supp. IV, Part 1,** 104

"Carrousel, The" (Rilke), **III,** 558

Carruth, Hayden, **I,** 189; **III,** 289; **Supp. IV, Part 1,** 66

"Carry" (Hogan), **Supp. IV, Part 1,** 412

Carse, James, **I,** 564

Carson, Edward Russell, **III,** 384

Carson, Johnny, **Supp. IV, Part 2,** 526

Carter, Elliott, **Supp. III, Part 1,** 21

Carter, Everett, **II,** 148, 294

Carter, Jimmy, **Supp. I, Part 2,** 638

Carter, Mary, **Supp. IV, Part 2,** 444

Cartier, Jacques, **Supp. I, Part 2,** 496, 497

"Cartographies of Silence" (Rich), **Supp. I, Part 2,** 571–572

Carver, Raymond, **Supp. III, Part 1, 135–151; Supp. IV, Part 1,** 342

Cary, Richard, **II,** 413

"Casabianca" (Bishop), **Supp. I, Part 1,** 86

Case of the Crushed Petunias, The (Williams), **IV,** 381

Case of the Officers of Excise (Paine), **Supp. I, Part 2,** 503–504

Casements (magazine), **IV,** 286

Cash, Arthur, **Supp. IV, Part 1,** 299

"Cask of Amontillado, The" (Poe), **II,** 475; **III,** 413

Casper, Leonard, **IV,** 258

Cass Timberlane (Lewis), **II,** 455–456

Cassady, Neal, **Supp. II, Part 1,** 309, 311

"Cassandra Southwick" (Whittier), **Supp. I, Part 2,** 693

Cassirer, Ernst, **I,** 265; **IV,** 87, 89

Cast a Cold Eye (McCarthy), **II,** 566

Castaway (Cozzens), **I,** 363, 370, 374, 375, 379

"Caste in America" (Du Bois), **Supp. II, Part 1,** 169

Castiglione, Baldassare, **I,** 279; **III,** 282

"Castilian" (Wylie), **Supp. I, Part 2,** 714

Castle Sinister (Marquand), **III,** 58

"Castles and Distances" (Wilbur), **Supp. III, Part 2,** 550

Castro, Fidel, **II,** 261, 434

"Casual Incident, A" (Hemingway), **II,** 44

Cat Inside, The (Burroughs), **Supp. III, Part 1,** 105

Cat on a Hot Tin Roof (Williams), **II,** 190; **IV,** 380, 382, 383, 386, 387, 389, 390, 391, 394, 395, 397–398

"Catbird Seat, The" (Thurber), **Supp. I, Part 2,** 623

Catcher in the Rye, The (Salinger), **I,** 493; **III,** 551, 552, 553–558, 567, 571; **Supp. I, Part 2,** 535

Catch-22 (Heller), **III,** 558; **Supp. IV, Part 1,** 379, 380, 381–382, 382, 383, 384–386, 386, 387, 390, 391, 392, 393, 394

Cater, Harold Dean, **I,** 24; **II,** 317

Catered Affair, The (film), **Supp. IV, Part 2,** 683

Catharine Beecher: A Study in American Domesticity (Sklar), **Supp. I, Part 2,** 601

Cathay (Pound), **II,** 527

Cathcart, Wallace H., **II,** 245

Cathedral (Carver), **Supp. III, Part 1,** 144–146

"Cathedral" (Carver), **Supp. III, Part 1,** 144–145

Cathedral, The (Lowell), **Supp. I, Part 2,** 407, 416–417

Cather, Charles, **I,** 312, 330

Cather, Mrs. Charles, **I,** 330

Cather, Willa, **I, 312–334,** 405; **II,** 51, 96, 177, 404, 412, 413, 414; **III,** 453; **IV,** 190; **Supp. I, Part 2,** 609, 719; **Supp. IV, Part 1,** 31

Catherine II, **Supp. I, Part 2,** 433

Catherine, Saint, **II,** 211

Catholic Anthology (publication), **III,** 460

Cato, **II,** 114, 117

Cat's Cradle (Vonnegut), **Supp. III, Part 2,** 758, 759, 767–768, 770, 771, 772

"Catterskill Falls" (Bryant), **Supp. I, Part 1,** 160

Catullus (Gai Valeri Catulli Veronensis Liber) (Zukofsky), **Supp. III, Part 2,** 625, 627, 628, 629

Catullus, Gaius Valerius, **I,** 381; **Supp. I, Part 1,** 261, Part 2, 728

Cause for Wonder (Morris), **III,** 232–233

" 'Cause My House Fell Down': The Theme of the Fall in Baldwin's Novels" (Foster), **Supp. I, Part 1,** 70

"Causerie" (Tate), **IV,** 129

"James Thurber: The Comic Prufrock" (De Vries), **Supp. I, Part 2,** 627

"James Thurber: The Primitive, the Innocent, and the Individual" (Elias), **Supp. I, Part 2,** 627

"James Thurber's Compounds" (Baldwin), **Supp. I, Part 2,** 626

"James Thurber's Dream Book" (Cowley), **Supp. I, Part 2,** 627

"James Whitcomb Riley (From a Westerner's Point of View)" (Dunbar), **Supp. II, Part 1,** 198

Jameson, F. R., **Supp. IV, Part 1,** 119

Jameson, Sir Leander Starr, **III,** 327

Jamison, A. Leland, **I,** 566

Jammes, Francis, **II,** 528

"Jan, the Son of Thomas" (Sandburg), **III,** 593–594

Jane Addams: A Biography (Linn), **Supp. I, Part 1,** 27

"Jane Addams: An American Heroine" (Conway), **Supp. I, Part 1,** 27

"Jane Addams and the Future" (MacLeish), **Supp. I, Part 1,** 27

Jane Addams and the Liberal Tradition (Levine), **Supp. I, Part 1,** 27

"Jane Addams and the Radical Impulse" (Lynd), **Supp. I, Part 1,** 27

"Jane Addams on Human Nature" (Curti), **Supp. I, Part 1,** 27

Jane Talbot: A Novel (Brown), **Supp. I, Part 1,** 145–146

Janet, Pierre, **I,** 248, 249, 252

"Janet Waking" (Ransom), **III,** 490, 491

Janeway, Elizabeth, **Supp. I, Part 1,** 46, 198

Jantz, Harold S., **Supp. I, Part 1,** 112, 123

"January" (Barthelme), **Supp. IV, Part 1,** 54

Jara, Victor, **Supp. IV, Part 2,** 549

Jarman, Mark, **Supp. IV, Part 1,** 68

Jarrell, Mrs. Randall (Mary von Schrader), **II,** 368, 385

Jarrell, Randall, **I,** 167, 169, 173, 180, 189; **II, 367–390,** 539–540; **III,** 134, 194, 213, 217, 268, 289, 527; **IV,** 352, 411, 422, 423, 424; **Supp.**

I, Part 1, 89, 96, **Part 2,** 552; **Supp. II, Part 1,** 109, 135; **Supp. III, Part 1,** 64, **Part 2,** 541, 550; **Supp. IV, Part 2,** 440

Jarvis, John Wesley, **Supp. I, Part 2,** 501, 520

Jaskoski, Helen, **Supp. IV, Part 1,** 325

"Jason" (MacLeish), **III,** 4

Jaspers, Karl, **III,** 292; **IV;** 491

Jay, William, **I,** 338

"Jazz Age Clerk, A" (Farrell), **II,** 45

"Jaz Fantasia" (Sandburg), **III,** 585

"Jazzonia" (Hughes), **Supp. I, Part 1,** 324

"Jazztet Muted" (Hughes), **Supp. I, Part 1,** 342

"Jeff Briggs's Love Story" (Harte), **Supp. II, Part 1,** 355

Jeffers, Robinson, **I,** 66; **III,** 134; **Supp. II, Part 2, 413–440**

Jeffers, Una Call Kuster (Mrs. Robinson Jeffers), **Supp. II, Part 2,** 414

Jefferson, Thomas, **I,** 1, 2, 5, 6–8, 14, 485; **II,** 5, 6, 134, 217, 300, 301, 437; **III,** 3, 17, 18, 294–295, 306, 310, 473, 608; **IV,** 133, 243, 249, 334, 348; **Supp. I, Part 1,** 146, 152, 153, 229, 230, 234, 235, **Part 2,** 389, 399, 456, 474, 475, 482, 507, 509, 510, 511, 516, 518–519, 520, 522

"Jefferson Davis as a Representative American" (Du Bois), **Supp. II, Part 1,** 161

Jeffersonian Magazine (publication), **Supp. I, Part 2,** 455

Jelliffe, Robert A., **II,** 75

J-E-L-L-O (Baraka), **Supp. II, Part 1,** 47

"Jelly-Bean, The" (Fitzgerald), **II,** 88

"Jellyfish, A" (Moore), **III,** 215

Jemie, Onwuchekwa, **Supp. I, Part 1,** 343, 348

Jenkins, J. L., **I,** 456

Jenkins, Kathleen, **III,** 403

Jenkins, Susan, **IV,** 123

Jenks, Deneen, **Supp. IV, Part 2,** 550, 554

Jennie Gerhardt (Dreiser), **I,** 497, 499, 500, 501, 504–505, 506, 507, 519

"Jennie M'Grew" (Masters), **Supp. I, Part 2,** 468

Jennifer Lorn (Wylie), **Supp. I, Part 2,** 709, 714–717, 718, 721, 724

"Jenny Garrow's Lover" (Jewett), **II,** 397

"Jerboa, The" (Moore), **III,** 203, 207, 209, 211–212

"Jericho" (Lowell), **II,** 536

Jerome, Judson, **III,** 289

"Jersey City Gendarmerie, Je T'aime" (Lardner), **II,** 433

"Jesse B. Semple: Negro American" (Davis), **Supp. I, Part 1,** 348

"Jesse B. Semple Revisited and Revised" (Carey), **Supp. I, Part 1,** 348

Jesuits in North America in the Seventeenth Century, The (Parkman), **Supp. II, Part 2,** 597, 603–605

Jesus, **I,** 27, 34, 68, 89, 136, 552, 560, **II,** 1, 16, 197, 198, 214, 215, 216, 218, 219, 239, 373, 377, 379, 537, 538, 539, 549, 569, 585, 591, 592; **III,** 39, 173, 179, 270, 291, 296–297, 300, 303, 305, 307, 311, 339, 340, 341, 342, 344, 345, 346, 347, 348, 352, 353, 354, 355, 436, 451, 489, 534, 564, 566, 567, 582; **IV,** 51, 69, 86, 107, 109, 117, 137, 138, 141, 144, 147, 149, 150, 151, 152, 155, 156, 157, 158, 159, 163, 164, 232, 241, 289, 293, 294, 296, 331, 364, 392, 396, 418, 430; **Supp. I, Part 1,** 2, 54, 104, 107, 108, 109, 121, 267, 371, **Part 2,** 379, 386, 458, 515, 580, 582, 583, 587, 588, 683

"Jesus Asleep" (Sexton), **Supp. II, Part 2,** 693

"Jesus Papers, The" (Sexton), **Supp. II, Part 2,** 693

"Jesus Raises Up the Harlot" (Sexton), **Supp. II, Part 2,** 693

Jetée, La (film), **Supp. IV, Part 2,** 436

"Jeune Parque, La" (Valéry), **IV,** 92

"Jewbird, The" (Malamud), **Supp. I, Part 2,** 435

"Jewboy, The" (Roth), **Supp. III, Part 2,** 412

Jewett, Caroline, **II,** 396

Matheson, John Wiliam, **III,** 550

Mathews, Cornelius, **III,** 81; **Supp. I, Part 1,** 317

Mathews, Shailer, **III,** 293

"Matinees" (Merrill), **Supp. III, Part 1,** 319, 327

Matisse, Henri, **III,** 180; **IV,** 24, 90, 407; **Supp. I, Part 2,** 619

Matlock, Lucinda, **Supp. I, Part 2,** 462

Matson, Peter, **Supp. IV, Part 1,** 299

Matters of Fact and Fiction: Essays 1973–1976 (Vidal), **Supp. IV, Part 2,** 687

Matthew (biblical book), **IV,** 164

Matthew Arnold (Trilling), **Supp. III, Part 2,** 500–501

Matthews, T. S., **II,** 430

Matthiessen, F. O., **I,** 254, 259–260, 404, 517, 520, 590; **II,** 23, 4l, 246, 340, 341, 365, 413, 554; **III,** 310, 453; **IV,** 181, 189, 259; **Supp. IV, Part 2,** 422

Matthiessen, Peter, **IV,** 119

Mattingly, Garrett, **Supp. IV, Part 2,** 601

"Maud Island" (Caldwell), **I,** 310

Maud Martha (Brooks), **Supp. III, Part 1,** 74, 78–79, 87

"Maud Muller" (Whittier), **Supp. I, Part 2,** 698

Maude, John Edward, **II,** 364

Maugham, W. Somerset, **III,** 57, 64; **Supp. IV, Part 1,** 209

Maulc, Harry E., **II,** 460

Maule's Curse: Seven Studies in the History of American Obscurantism (Winters), **Supp. II, Part 2,** 807–808, 812

"Mau-mauing the Flak Catchers" (Wolfe), **Supp. III, Part 2,** 577

Maupassant, Guy de, **I,** 309, 421; **II,** 191–192, 291, 325, 591; **IV,** 17; **Supp. I, Part 1,** 207, 217, 223, 320

"Maurice Barrès and the Youth of France" (Bourne), **I,** 228

Maurier, George du, **II,** 338

Mauve Gloves & Madmen, Clutter & Vine (Wolfe), **Supp. III, Part 2,** 581

Maverick in Mauve (Auchincloss), **Supp. IV, Part 1,** 26

"Mavericks, The" (play)

(Auchincloss), **Supp. IV, Part 1,** 34

"Mavericks, The" (story) (Auchincloss), **Supp. IV, Part 1,** 32

"Max" (Miller), **III,** 183

Max and the White Phagocytes (Miller), **III,** 178, 183–184

Maximilian (emperor of Mexico), **Supp. I, Part 2,** 457–458

Maximilian: A Play in Five Acts (Masters), **Supp. I, Part 2,** 456, 457–458

Maximus Poems, The (Olson), **Supp. II, Part 2,** 555, 556, 563, 564–580, 584

Maximus Poems 1–10, The (Olson), **Supp. II, Part 2,** 571

Maximus Poems IV, V, VI (Olson), **Supp. II, Part 2,** 555, 580, 582–584

Maximus Poems Volume Three, The (Olson), **Supp. II, Part 2,** 555, 582, 584–585

"Maximus, to Gloucester" (Olson), **Supp. II, Part 2,** 574

"Maximus to Gloucester, Letter 19 (A Pastoral Letter)" (Olson), **Supp. II, Part 2,** 567

"Maximus to Gloucester, Sunday July 19" (Olson), **Supp. II, Part 2,** 580

"Maximus, to himself" (Olson), **Supp. II, Part 2,** 565, 566, 567, 569, 570, 572

"Maximus to himself June 1964" (Olson), **Supp. II, Part 2,** 584

Maxwell, D. E. S., **I,** 590

Maxwell, Gilbert, **IV,** 401

Maxwell, William, **Supp. I, Part 1,** 175; **Supp. III, Part 1,** 62

May, Abigail (Abba), *see* Alcott, Mrs. Amos Bronson (Abigail May)

May, John R., **Supp. I, Part 1,** 226

May Alcott: A Memoir (Ticknor), **Supp. I, Part 1,** 46

"May Day" (Fitzgerald), **II,** 88–89

"May Day Dancing, The" (Nemerov), **III,** 275

"May Day Sermon to the Women of Gilmer County, Georgia, by a Woman Preacher Leaving the Baptist Church" (Dickey), **Supp. IV, Part 1,** 182

"May Sun Sheds an Amber Light,

The" (Bryant), **Supp. I, Part 1,** 170

"May Swenson: The Art of Perceiving" (Stanford), **Supp. IV, Part 2,** 637

Maybe (Hellman), **Supp. IV, Part 1,** 12

Mayer, Elizabeth, **Supp. II, Part 1,** 16; **Supp. III, Part 1,** 63

Mayfield, Julian, **Supp. I, Part 1,** 70

Mayflower, The (Stowe), **Supp. I, Part 2,** 585, 586

Maynard, Theodore, **I,** 263

Maynard, Tony, **Supp. I, Part 1,** 65

Mayo, Robert, **III,** 478

Mayorga, Margaret, **III,** 167; **IV,** 381

"Maypole of Merrymount, The" (Hawthorne), **II,** 229

"Maze" (Eberhart), **I,** 523, 525–526, 527

Mazzaro, Jerome, **II,** 390, 557

Mazzini, Giuseppe, **Supp. I, Part 1,** 2, 8; **Supp. II, Part 1,** 299

"Me and the Mule" (Hughes), **Supp. I, Part 1,** 334

"Me, Boy Scout" (Lardner), **II,** 433

"Me Decade and the Third Great Awakening, The" (Wolfe), **Supp. III, Part 2,** 581

Me, Vashya! (Williams), **IV,** 381

Mead, Elinor, *see* Howells, Mrs. William Dean (Elinor Mead)

Mead, George Herbert, **II,** 27, 34; **Supp. I, Part 1,** 5, **Part 2,** 641

Mead, Margaret, **Supp. I, Part 1,** 49, 52, 66

Meaders, Margaret Inman, **III,** 360

Mean Spirit (Hogan), **Supp. IV, Part 1,** 397, 404, 407–410, 415, 416–417

"Meaning of a Literary Idea, The" (Trilling), **Supp. III, Part 2,** 498

"Meaning of Death, The, An After Dinner Speech" (Tate), **IV,** 128, 129

"Meaning of Life, The" (Tate), **IV,** 137

"Meaningless Institution, A" (Ginsberg), **Supp. II, Part 1,** 313

Mearns, Hughes, **III,** 220

"Measuring My Blood" (Vizenor), **Supp. IV, Part 1,** 262

"Mechanism in Thought and Morals" (Holmes), **Supp. I, Part 1,** 314

Pan-African movement, **Supp. II, Part 1,** 172, 175
"Pandora" (Adams), **I,** 5
"Pangolin, The" (Moore), **III,** 210
Panic: A Play in Verse (MacLeish), **III,** 2, 20
Panic in Needle Park (film), **Supp. IV, Part 1,** 198
Pantagruel (Rabelais), **II,** 112
"Pantaloon in Black" (Faulkner), **II,** 71
Pantheism, **Supp. I, Part 1,** 163
Panther and the Lash, The (Hughes), **Supp. I, Part 1,** 342–344, 345–346
"Papa and Mama Dance, The" (Sexton), **Supp. II, Part 2,** 688
Paper Boats (Butler), **Supp. I, Part 1,** 275
"Paper House, The" (Mailer), **III,** 42–43
Papers on Literature and Art (Fuller), **Supp. II, Part 1,** 292, 299
Papp, Joseph, **Supp. IV, Part 1,** 234
"Paprika Johnson" (Barnes), **Supp. III, Part 1,** 33
Par le Détroit (cantata) (Bowles), **Supp. IV, Part 1,** 82
"Parade of Painters" (Swenson), **Supp. IV, Part 2,** 645
"Paradigm, The" (Tate), **IV,** 128
Paradise (Barthelme), **Supp. IV, Part 1,** 52
Paradise Lost (Milton), **I,** 137; **II,** 168, 549; **IV,** 126
Paradise Lost (Odets), **Supp. II, Part 2,** 530, 531, 538–539, 550
"Paradise of Bachelors and the Tartarus of Maids, The" (Melville), **III,** 91
Paradox of Progressive Thought, The (Noble), **Supp. I, Part 2,** 650
"Paradoxes and Oxymorons" (Ashbery), **Supp. III, Part 1,** 23–24
"Paraphrase" (Crane), **I,** 391–392, 393
"Pardon, The" (Wilbur), **Supp. III, Part 2,** 544, 550
Pareto, Vilfredo, **II,** 577
Paretsky, Sarah, **Supp. IV, Part 2,** 462
Paris France (Stein), **IV,** 45
Paris Review (publication), **I,** 97, 381, 567, 587; **II,** 563, 574, 579; **III,**

194; **IV,** 102, 217, 218, 221, 246, 250; **Supp. I, Part 2,** 618; **Supp. IV, Part 1,** 199, 201, 202, 203, 289, **Part 2,** 576
"Paris, 7 A.M." (Bishop), **Supp. I, Part 1,** 85, 89
Park, Robert, **IV,** 475
"Park Bench" (Hughes), **Supp. I, Part 1,** 331–332
"Park Street Cemetery, The" (Lowell), **II,** 537, 538
Parker, Charlie, **Supp. I, Part 1,** 59
Parker, Dorothy, **Supp. IV, Part 1,** 353
Parker, Hershel, **III,** 95, 97
Parker, Robert B., **Supp. IV, Part 1,** 135, 136
Parker, Theodore, **Supp. I, Part 1,** 38, **Part 2,** 518
Parker, Thomas, **Supp. I, Part 1,** 102
"Parker's Back" (O'Connor), **III,** 348, 352, 358
Parkes, Henry Bamford, **I,** 287, 564; **II,** 23; **Supp. I, Part 2,** 617
Parkinson, Thomas, **II,** 557
Parkman, Francis, **II,** 278, 310, 312; **IV,** 179, 309; **Supp. I, Part 2,** 420, 479, 481–482, 486, 487, 493, 498; **Supp. II, Part 2,** 589–616
Parkman Reader, The (ed. Morison), **Supp. I, Part 2,** 494
Parks, Edd Winfield, **Supp. I, Part 1,** 373
Parks, Edw., **III,** 432
Parks, Larry, **Supp. I, Part 1,** 295
Parks, Rosa, **Supp. I, Part 1,** 342
Parliament of Fowls, The (Chaucer), **III,** 492
Parmenides (Plato), **II,** 10
Parmenter, Ross, **IV,** 377
Parnassus (Emerson), **II,** 8, 18
Parnassus (publication), **Supp. IV, Part 1,** 68
Parnell, Charles Stewart, **II,** 129, 137
Parrington, Vernon Louis, **I,** 254, 357, 517, 561, 565; **III,** 335, 606; **IV,** 173; **Supp. I, Part 2,** 484, 640
"Parrot, The" (Merrill), **Supp. III, Part 1,** 320
"Parsley" (Dove), **Supp. IV, Part 1,** 245, 246
Parson, Annie, **Supp. I, Part 2,** 655
Parsons, Edward, **I,** 564
Parsons, Elsie Clews, **I,** 231, 235

Parsons, Talcott, **Supp. I, Part 2,** 648
Parsons, Theophilus, **II,** 396, 504; **Supp. I, Part 1,** 155
"Part of a Letter" (Wilbur), **Supp. III, Part 2,** 551
"Parthian Shot, The" (Hammett), **Supp. IV, Part 1,** 343
Partial Portraits (James), **II,** 336
Parties (Van Vechten), **Supp. II, Part 2,** 739, 747–749
"Parting" (Kunitz), **Supp. III, Part 1,** 263
"Parting Gift" (Wylie), **Supp. I, Part 2,** 714
"Parting Glass, The" (Freneau), **Supp. II, Part 1,** 273
"Partings" (Hogan), **Supp. IV, Part 1,** 413
Partington, Blanche, **I,** 199
Partisan Review (publication), **I,** 168, 170, 256; **II,** 562; **III,** 35, 292, 337–338; **IV,** 128; **Supp. I, Part 1,** 58, 89; **Supp. IV, Part 1,** 70, 84, 286
"Partner, The" (Roethke), **III,** 541–542
Partners, The (Auchincloss), **Supp. IV, Part 1,** 31, 34
Partridge, John, **II,** 110, 111
"Parts of a Journal" (Gordon), **Supp. IV, Part 1,** 310
"Party, The" (Dunbar), **Supp. II, Part 1,** 198, 205–206
Party at Jack's, The (Wolfe), **IV,** 451–452, 469
Pascal, Blaise, **II,** 8, 159; **III,** 292, 301, 304, 428
"Passage" (Crane), **I,** 391
"Passage in the Life of Mr. John Oakhurst, A" (Harte), **Supp. II, Part 1,** 353–354
"Passage to India" (Whitman), **IV,** 348
Passage to India, A (Forster), **II,** 600
"Passenger Pigeons" (Jeffers), **Supp. II, Part 2,** 437
"Passing Show, The" (Bierce), **I,** 208
"Passing Through" (Kunitz), **Supp III, Part 1,** 265
"Passion, The" (Barnes), **Supp. III, Part 1,** 36
"Passion, The" (Merwin), **Supp. III, Part 1,** 343